The
CIVIL WAR
In the Words of Its Greatest Commanders

The CIVIL WAR

In the Words of Its Greatest Commanders

Personal Memoirs of U.S. Grant

Memoirs of Robert E. Lee

by Armistead L. Long

ThunderBay
P·R·E·S·S

San Diego, California

PAGE 2: Ulysses S. Grant.

OPPOSITE: Robert E. Lee and Thomas "Stonewall" Jackson.

PAGES 4–5: Battle of the Wilderness.

PAGES 10–11: The Fall of Petersburg.

Thunder Bay Press
An imprint of the Advantage Publishers Group
5880 Oberlin Drive, San Diego, CA 92121-4794
www.thunderbaybooks.com

Personal Memoirs of U.S. Grant copyright © 1995
Memoirs of Robert E. Lee copyright © 1998
Copyright © 2002 World Publications Group, Inc.

All notations of errors or omissions should be addressed to Thunder Bay Press, editorial department, at the above address. All other correspondence (author inquiries, permissions) concerning the content of this book should be addressed to World Publications Group, Inc., 455 Somerset Avenue, North Dighton, MA 02764, www.wrldpub.com

ISBN 1-57145-837-9

Library of Congress Cataloging-in-Publication Data available upon request.

Printed in China.

1 2 3 4 5   06 05 04 03 02

CONTENTS

Introduction

Tom Carhart, Ph.D.

No national experience can really compete with the Unite States Civil War as the central watershed moment in American experience. The American Revolution is, of course, an important historical moment in that it broke our bonds with England and resulted in the launching of a new nation. But the American "Great Experiment" in self-governance was challenged by the secession of southern states that brought on the Civil War. And in terms of scale and politically transformational power, even our creative spasm of 1776 must give ground, for Union victory in the Civil War gave rise to a new birth of freedom that profoundly changed American society for all times.

The actual combat of that war between brothers was, as historians have noted, a very close call: Despite the North's advantages in numbers and equipment, General Robert E. Lee's Army of Northern Virginia long dominated fighting in the main theater of operations close to Washington, D.C. It took several years before President Abraham Lincoln found the man, Ulysses S. Grant, who could lead the Union's Army of the Potomac to victory against that most important Confederate army that constantly threatened our nation's capital. And at the dawn of the 21st century, this Civil War remains one of the most popular topics in American history.

Despite the tens of thousands of books that have appeared on the subject, new treatments pour out every year. Almost all of these books, of course, involve assessments by nonparticipants long after the fact. And while such new appreciations can be valuable, it is difficult for them to compete in impact and poignancy with older books that appeared soon after the Civil War and consist of personal experiences narrated by participants.

Such tracts can be quite compelling, although this often depends on the position of the narrator as well as his narrative skill.

OPPOSITE: A montage of General Grant's military career.

BELOW: General Lee at the Battle of Spottsylvania.

TOP RIGHT: Julia Dent Grant as First Lady during her husband's postwar administration.

BELOW: A formal portrait of the great Union commander.

OPPOSITE: The distinguished Robert E. Lee at his home in the Confederate capital of Richmond, Virginia.

But the book you hold in your hands is a condensation and compilation of what are widely accepted to be the two most important Civil War texts, the memoirs of Ulysses S. Grant and Robert E. Lee. These are two centrally important accounts of the Civil War that, while often complementary, differ dramatically in both their nature and their style.

It is important to note at the outset a most important distinction between these two works: Grant's *Memoirs* were actually written by him, while the so-called Lee's Memoirs were penned by Brigadier General Armistead L. Long, C.S.A. It should be noted that Long was a fellow Virginian; had known Lee before the Civil War; served as Lee's military secretary during key segments of the war; and remained his lifelong confidant and personal friend. In writing these memoirs, Long drew on materials provided by others who served under Lee and he had the complete support

of the Lee family in the preparation of his manuscript. The fact remains, though, that when we read " Memoirs," we are not reading Lee's own words.

Grant's style alone is one of the most important aspects of his work. He wrote the way he lived: straightforward, simple, to the point, with minimal use of adverbs or adjectives. The result is an easily accessible work, understandable to virtually all Americans, with or without personal military experience, and one that is utterly devoid of ego gratification. It is a book praised by individuals as different as Mark Twain in 1885 and Edmund Wilson in 1962 – the latter described it as the best work of its kind since Julius Caesar's *Commentaries*. In 1987, John Keegan, the British military historian, described it as "the most revelatory autobiography of high command to exist in any language."

While Long's prose does not rise to the same level, Lee's Memoirs remain a wonderful compilation of events and experiences that occurred under his immediate command or within the wide span of his control. Seen in this way from the wheelhouse of command, the Army of Northern Virginia emerges in an entirely different light.

Immediately after the Civil War, neither Lee nor Grant felt the need to write his personal memoirs, although both were heavily solicited to do so by various parties. After his second term as president, Grant went on a

RIGHT: Confederate General Armistead Long, biographer of Robert E. Lee.

FAR RIGHT: Future CSA commander Cadmus Wilcox was a member of Grant's wedding in 1848.

BELOW: The Mexican War battle of Resaca de la Palma, in which Grant took part.

worldwide tour. Upon his return, he invested his life savings in a New York brokerage house, then settled into a comfortable retirement. In 1884, the brokerage house lost everything in speculative ventures, leaving Grant with no money and an enormous debt.

Stunned by this reversal of fortune, Grant initially wrote three magazine articles about the Civil War for $500 each, and so discovered his unsuspected skill with a pen. At the same time, he learned that he had cancer in his throat, a cancer he knew would kill him. His last efforts, therefore, would be devoted to removing the debt and establishing a financial cushion for his wife. For the next two years, Grant worked hard virtually every

day at recording his wartime experiences. On July 10 1885, he finished his book, and died a few weeks later, on the 23rd of July. But Grant's *Memoirs* were to be an immediate and overwhelming success, ultimately earning nearly half a million dollars for his widow Julia.

In July 1886, *Memoirs of Robert E. Lee* by General Long was published. General Long acknowledges having had access to Grant's *Memoirs* while writing, but it would seem to have been of only marginal value to him. This compilation of key excerpts from the two manuscripts, however, offers an "insider's view" of the Civil War from the military commander's perspective on each side. As such, it presents a rare and fascinating look at the ways in which the war was conducted, at the key decisions that were made and the factors that led to them.

The text that follows this introduction will consist of segments taken from the two memoirs that deal with key moments in the Civil War. It therefore combines abridgments of

BELOW: Grant with Julia and their four children about 1865.

the most important memoirs from that war under one cover, an arrangement that will allow the reader to make comparisons between the wartime actions of the two generals. This is most important in the later stages of the war, in 1864 and 1865, when the armies commanded by Lee and Grant literally faced each other and the two greatest generals of the Civil War did everything in their power to destroy each other.

In their original editions, however, both memoirs cover quite a bit of ground before the Civil War. In order to give the reader a fuller sense of their contents, therefore, this introduction will briefly synopsize material covered at more length in the two works. Of particular importance will be the Mexican-American War, where Lee, Grant, and many other famous Civil War generals as well, first learned some of the realities of life-and-death combat from a junior offi-

BELOW: Lee's family tree traces six generations in America from 1641.

cer level. But before the memoirs discuss their service in that war, they provide some background on their lives and careers.

Robert Edward Lee was the descendant of a family that probably came as close to American nobility as was possible under our Constitution. The founder of the family, we are told, was Launcelot Lee, who entered England with William the Conqueror, distinguished himself at the Battle of Hastings, and acquired an estate in Essex. A descendant, Richard Lee, came to America in 1641 as colonial secretary under the governorship of Sir William Berkeley. His descendants lived in Virginia, primarily in Westmoreland County, where they played important roles as landowners and members of the House of Burgesses.

When the Revolution came, Henry Lee had just completed his studies at Princeton and was about to embark for England to study law. Instead, he raised a company of cavalry, and his exploits are remembered as those of "Light Horse Harry" Lee. After the war, he served as governor of Virginia for three terms and wrote Washington's eulogy, which includes the famous American words of endearment for our first president: "first in war, first in peace, and first in the hearts of his countrymen."

Henry Lee's first wife died in 1790, and after three years, he married Anne Hill Carter, a descendant of another of the most distinguished families in Virginia. His third son of this marriage was Robert E. Lee, who was born in 1807 in one of the Lee mansions, Stratford Hall. According to family tradition, he was born in the same room in which two signers of the Declaration of Independence had also been born.

By this time, Henry Lee had left governmental service behind and had begun to buy and sell real estate. Always seeking great wealth through what he believed to be his own financial talents, he was prone to taking chances that would have been ignored by a more prudent man. Unfortunately for him and his family, he turned out to be a very poor businessman. He borrowed large sums for his highly speculative endeavors, and he made many bad decisions that cost him dearly. Creditors soon bedeviled him, and he even spent time in 1809 and 1810 in two different debtor's prisons. Thereafter, he desperately sought governmental stations overseas, but to no avail.

Bereft of funds, in 1811 he finally moved his family to a small brick house in Alexandria, where income from his wife's trust paid for room and board and little else. In 1812, while

defending a political ally in Baltimore, he was savagely beaten, suffering injuries from which he would never fully recover. Because of these infirmities, he was unfit for service in the young American army in the war that loomed with England. Instead, having been shamed by his own business failures, Henry Lee left for the

ABOVE: Richard Lee, ancestor of the Lee family, came to the future United States as colonial secretary to Virginia's governor Sir William Berkeley.

LEFT: Robert E. Lee's father, nicknamed "Light-Horse Harry" for his role as a cavalry leader in the Revolutionary War.

RIGHT: Captain Lee with his first son.

BELOW: The fight against abolitionist John Brown's insurgents at the U.S. arsenal at Harper's Ferry, Virginia. Then-Colonel Robert E. Lee led a detachment of Marines that captured Brown.

Caribbean, where he hoped to recover both health and self-respect in Barbados.

When Henry left his family in 1813, Robert was only six, and he was never to see his father again. Although Henry eventually tried to come home in 1818, he stopped on the way at the Georgia home of his old Revolutionary War comrade-in-arms Nathaniel Greene, where he died and was buried. Robert, meanwhile, was educated in a school maintained by his mother's wealthy family, then later in the Alexandria Academy.

Throughout his youth, his mother repeatedly urged him to practice self-denial and self-control, to work to attain the strictest economy in financial matters. She continually emphasized the power of high moral character and the importance of self-reliance. For despite his high name and blood connections, the lack of financial and material assets was the reality that surrounded his youth, and the shame of family scandals was the flame that annealed his soul. It is not altogether surprising, therefore, that an elevated sense of personal integrity became the rock on which he anchored his life. Throughout his life, he was to be a paragon of moral virtue. As he came of age, there was no money to send him to college, but influential relatives were willing to write letters. In 1825, he received an appointment to the U.S. Military Academy at West Point, fifty miles north of New York City.

At the turn of the 21st century, Robert E. Lee's years at West Point resonate still. Academically, he missed graduating first in his class by the narrowest of margins, and was ranked second out of 46 men who graduated in June 1829. But recognized early on as a splendid future officer, he had risen steadily in cadet rank, attaining the highest rank of Adjutant of the Corps of Cadets during his First Class, or senior, year. And during his four years, not a single demerit blemished his cadet record. Upon graduation in June, he was commissioned in the prestigious Corps of Engineers. It was already clear, even at this early date, that if he stayed in the army, he would one day rise to become an important general officer.

One month after his graduation, Robert E. Lee's mother died, and he was at her side. They had been very close, and Lee would later say that he owed everything to her. Initially assigned to help build coastal defenses along the coast of Georgia, he kept his social attention focused on Virginia. It gradually became clear that he was pursuing Mary Anne Randolph Custis, the daughter of George Washington Custis, who was Martha Washington's grandson from an earlier marriage and George Washington's adopted son. As the only surviving child, Mary would inherit Arlington House, where Lafayette had stayed, and two other plantations in southern Virginia. Arlington House was a domain of 15,000 acres worked by 250 slaves, and the immense main house was perched on a bluff overlooking the city of Washington. The view from its veranda, according to Lafayette, was the finest in the world.

Mary was a beautiful, slender blonde, but she could be temperamental and very difficult. After Lee had been reassigned to Fort Monroe, Virginia, they were wed in Arlington House on June 30, 1831. Mary returned there to bear their first child in 1832, and she would eventually bear him seven children, three of them sons who would eventually serve in the Confederate army, two as general officers. In 1834, Lee was assigned to Washington, and while there, he lived with the family in the nearby mansion on the hill.

BELOW: Agnes Lee, the third daughter of Mary and Robert E. Lee.

BELOW: The Custis estate at Arlington, Virginia, future site of Arlington National Cemetery.

THE UNION MUST AND SHALL BE PRESERVED

FREE SPEECH.
FREE HOMES.
FREE TERRITORY.

PROTECTION TO AMERICAN INDUSTRY

FOR PRESIDENT
ABRAHAM LINCOLN
OF ILLINOIS

FOR VICE PRESIDENT
HANNIBAL HAMLIN
OF MAINE

ABOVE: Campaign poster for the 1860 presidential election, in which the victory of Republican Abraham Lincoln sparked secession of the Southern states.

Over the next five years, Lee was sent to Michigan on an engineering mission, then later to St. Louis, but he always returned with a brighter image as a military engineer. In 1840, he was sent to New York, where he did extensive work on the harbor defenses, with only occasional visits to Arlington House. Finally, in August 1846, he received orders to join General Wool in San Antonio, Texas, for the invasion of Mexico.

On April 27, 1822, the child who would later be known as Ulysses S. Grant was born in Mount Pleasant, Ohio, a small town that was little more than a collection of houses along the banks of the Ohio River. His parents named him Hiram Ulysses Grant, and he was generally known as Ulysses, or "Lys" for short. Although he would not share the blueblood lines of Robert E. Lee, the opening lines of his autobiography indicate his proud feelings about his stock: "My family is American, and has been for generations, in all branches, direct and collateral."

Matthew Grant, the founder of the branch in America, arrived in Dorchester, Massachusetts, in 1630, and Ulysses was in the eighth generation of his descendants. His great-grandfather Noah held an English commission, and in 1756, fought and died during the French and Indian War. That man's son and the grandfather of Ulysses, also named Noah, fought with a Connecticut unit during the Revolutionary War, after which he settled in Pennsylvania, then later moved to Ohio. Among his five children was Jesse, who was to be the father of Ulysses. But when Noah's wife died, the family broke up, for Noah could only manage two children, and he farmed the rest out to relatives and friends.

After a few years living with the Tod family, Jesse left and went into business with his brother Peter, who had a tannery in Maysville, Kentucky. For several years, he lived there with a family by the name of Brown. One of the Brown boys he shared residence and youthful friendship with was John Brown, who would become famous as the zealot who led a raid in Harper's Ferry, Virginia, attempting to foment a slave uprising.

Jesse was only able to acquire about six months of formal schooling, but he knew its value. He soon set up his own tannery in Ohio, and in 1821 he married Hannah Simpson. A year later, Ulysses was born, and the family moved to nearby Georgetown, Ohio, where Ulysses lived until he left for West Point in 1839. The schools of the time were not free, and were rather rudimentary. But Jesse thought schooling was important, and he paid for Ulysses to attend classes from the time he was five until he was seventeen.

From his earliest days, Ulysses disliked the tannery, preferring to work in the great outdoors. And one enduring love he developed early on was for horses. He had a special way with them, and was soon a master rider: men would hire him to break their toughest stock, and it was said that Lys could ride anything. His father later told stories of how he could ride a horse bareback and standing up at the age of five, and that he could balance on one foot on the back of a galloping steed by the age of seven. These stories are no doubt exaggerated, but as his horsemanship would later prove, there must have been some truth in them. And then, in a somewhat unusual turn of events, Jesse Grant was able to get an appointment to West Point for Ulysses, despite the fact that he and his congressman had a still-unburied bone of contention between them.

Ulysses wasn't sure he wanted to go to West Point, but his father's wishes quickly changed his mind. In May 1839, he made the long trip by train and boat, finally arriving at West Point. Then, after a few weeks and to his great surprise, he sailed through the arduous admissions tests and joined the Corps of Cadets.

One surprise did await him, however. When he first got to West Point, he found that there was no opening for "Hiram Ulysses Grant," but that a "Ulysses Simpson Grant" had been appointed from Ohio. Realizing that his congressman had sent in the incorrect name, using Ulysses, by which he was known, as his first name and assuming his mother's maiden name of Simpson for his middle name, he tried to have it changed. But this was to be a losing fight against an immovable governmental bureaucracy. When other cadets saw his name posted as "U.S. Grant," they quickly tagged him "Uncle Sam," and then just plain Sam, by which, from that time forward, most close friends knew him.

Not nearly as bright a light at West Point as Lee had been, Grant was ranked generally in the middle of his class in academics. He enjoyed math and drawing, did poorly in French, and felt no attraction whatever to a career in the army. And while he was not particularly gregarious, his skill at horsemanship endured. At commencement, the story goes, he was called out in the riding ring on a magnificent horse named York. The riding instructor held his long whip above his head at the end of his outstretched arm and tilted his hand perpendicularly, so that the tip of the whip

LEFT: Frederick Tracy Dent, Grant's brother-in-law, had been his roommate at West Point.

touched the wall of the riding hall more than eight feet above ground level. Grant spurred his mount into a canter and, in one enormous burst of power, horse and rider sailed over the outstretched whip. It is said that Grant repeated the feat a second time, and that onlookers could not believe their eyes.

At graduation, Grant was ranked 21st in a class of 39. He had hoped for an assignment to the dragoons, as mounted soldiers were then designated, but instead was given his second choice, and assigned to the 4th Infantry Regiment at Jefferson Barracks in St. Louis, Missouri. He reported to his duty station in September 1843, fully intending at the time to leave the army soon and perhaps become a mathematics teacher.

LEFT: President James K. Polk in 1845, when Texas was annexed to the United States.

23

FAR RIGHT: General Zachary Taylor, under whom Grant first served in Mexico.

Grant was far from home in Ohio, but the family of one of his West Point roommates, Frederick Dent, lived at White Haven, only five miles away. Soon enough, he found himself spending most of his leisure time there, and he became very close to one of Dent's younger sisters, Julia. She was just seventeen at the time, but she was a gifted horsewoman, and she and Sam spent many happy hours riding the countryside together. But then the hot wind of war blew up from the south.

Relations between the United States and Mexico had been uneasy since 1836. In that year, the Mexican province of Texas, dominated by English-speaking immigrants from the north, had declared its independence and resisted all Mexican attempts to forcibly reintegrate it. Thereafter, Texas appealed for admission to the United States. But the Van Buren and Tyler administrations resisted these appeals in order to avoid antagonizing Mexico, and also because of the imbalance this new state would cause in a Congress torn by pro- and anti-slavery forces. But passions rose, and Texas was formally annexed in the first year of James K. Polk's administration, in December 1845.

In March of 1844, Grant's regiment had already been posted to the Louisiana border with Texas. He hurriedly formalized his engagement to Julia, and she agreed to wait for him. It would be over four years before they would finally wed. In his autobiography, he noted that the war with Mexico was "one of the most unjust ever waged by a stronger against a weaker nation. It was an instance of a republic following the bad example of European monarchies, in not considering justice in their desire to acquire additional territories." But despite his political condemnation of the war with Mexico, Grant realized that his duty was with his army unit, and he went with them when they were sent to fight.

The war with Mexico was to be the proving ground for a large number of the men who would lead armies on both sides in the Civil War, and Grant and Lee were primary among them. But they were not alone. George McClellan, Pierre Beauregard, James Longstreet, George Meade, Joseph Hooker, even Jefferson Davis – the list goes on and on of major leaders in the American Civil War who cut their teeth in the Mexican War, almost all of them West Point graduates. The American commander, General Winfield Scott, not an academy graduate himself, was quickly won over by the performance of West Pointers under the gun. He later commented on their performance in that war as follows:

"I give it as my fixed opinion that but for our graduated cadets the war between the United States and Mexico might, and probably would have lasted some four or five years, with, in its first half, more defeats than victories falling to our share, whereas in less than two campaigns we conquered a great country and a peace without the loss of a single battle or skirmish."

General Zachary Taylor (another non-West Pointer) landed a force at Corpus Christi, Texas, then marched south to the Rio Grande. On May 8, 1845, at a place called Palo Alto, his 2300 American soldiers were confronted by a Mexican force twice its size. But superior American artillery ploughed through their ranks, causing hundreds of casualties, while Mexican return fire was so weak that 2nd Lieutenant Grant, who was with this force, watched the cannonballs bounce and ricochet so slowly that Americans could easily move aside. The Mexicans fell back, and during the night, they disappeared. On May 9, Taylor's pursuing army found them at Resaca de la Palma, but the demoralized Mexicans put up little fight before fleeing, once again badly battered. Taylor had neither boats nor bridging equipment with which to cross the Rio Grande and continue the pursuit, so he paused.

On May 11–12, Congress finally declared war, and President Polk and General Winfield Scott decided on a three-pronged offensive. Taylor would continue west to Monterrey, while another column under General Wool came south from Texas and took the town of

Chihuahua. A third force, under Colonel Stephen Watts Kearny, would head west, take Santa Fe, and end up in San Diego on the California coast.

These columns were all victorious. As they moved, Taylor's men were repeatedly engaged, but drove Mexican forces before them. Grant, meanwhile, had been made quartermaster of his regiment, but constantly sought to be near the front. During the siege of Monterrey, his brigade was pinned down, and he volunteered to carry this news to higher headquarters. He took the written message and galloped through hostile fire, hanging from the saddle on one side of his horse like the trick rider he was.

Wool's force eventually joined that of Taylor, and on February 23, 1847, Taylor defeated a much larger force at Buena Vista. All that remained was the capture of the national capital, Mexico City. General Winfield Scott led the force that would achieve this purpose, and after it landed at Vera Cruz it fought its way inland.

Lee's actions in the Mexican War had a somewhat higher profile than those of Grant. Although he was only a captain and, as such, a very junior officer, Lee had graduated from West Point fourteen years before Grant, and with his extensive experience in the army,

LEFT: Dennis Hart Mahan, a respected military educator from West Point, whose texts were used by officers on both sides of the Civil War.

he was almost an officer from a different generation. Indeed, in Mexico, his performance of engineering duties was so exemplary that he soon was called to join Scott's staff. In that role, staff officers above him were awed by his intelligence and his abilities, and he was able to directly advise and guide the hand of General Scott.

BELOW: Taylor's forces take Monterrey in a crucial engagement of the Mexican War.

Once the U.S. forces had made their way to the edge of Mexico City, the first major challenge Scott faced was to find a way to take or bypass the seemingly impregnable Mexican defenses at San Augustin and San Antonio, two major fortresses on the road to Mexico City. Lee several times conducted personal, high-risk reconnaissance, both by day and by night, deep into territory held by Mexican forces. He several times hid as Mexican soldiers passed close by, thus risking discovery and death or captivity. And while jeopardizing the crucial eyes, ears, and brain of General Scott's most important adviser might have been criticized had he been killed or taken,

he was not, and he returned with plans to flank Mexican forces with surprise attacks.

Orders for the attacks followed, and Lee was with the troops as they confronted the obstacles he had warned of, such as ravines, canals, and the nearly impassable broken ground of the Pedregal. Lee showed them how to continue their advance, and during the night, while American soldiers rested, he twice crossed the two-mile-wide stretch of the Pedregal on foot. He did this to keep General Scott informed of the progress of his forces, and Lee was back with the infantry when they finally launched their attacks on Mexican positions the following morning.

RIGHT: Grant routs Mexican forces at San Cosme by mounting a howitzer in a church belfry.

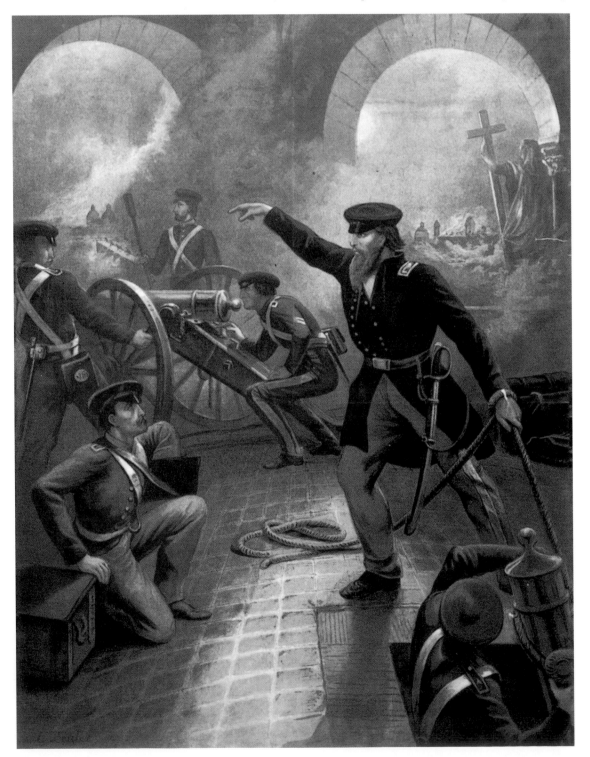

The attacks, of course, were successful.

This operation went on for several days, from around the 11th to the 20th of August, 1847, and Lee was heavily involved in every part of it, from reconnaissance to planning to execution. Every general in the American force had the highest praise for Lee, and when General Scott forwarded to Washington the names of those who deserved commendation, he named "Captain R.E. Lee (as distinguished for felicitous execution as for science and daring)." In later testimony before a court of inquiry, Scott would say that Captain Lee had there rendered "the greatest feat of physical and moral courage performed by any individual, in my knowledge, pending the campaign."

Lee was to receive three brevet promotions for his actions in Mexico, the last to colonel. But when he had just become a major outside of Mexico City, 2nd Lt. Grant was finally able to shake loose the bonds of quartermaster and fight. At San Cosme, a Mexican artillery piece had stopped all movement down a key road. Grant led a column of volunteers around one flank, attacked, and drove them off in confusion. He then had a brilliant, if unusual, idea. Spying a church dominating a city square and a main gate, he had a mountain howitzer carried into the belfry. Once in place, its fire was devastating, and Mexicans forces fled yet again.

This action of Grant and the howitzer in the church belfry was mentioned in the official reports of General Worth, Colonel Garland, and Major Robert E. Lee. Though it is doubtful that Grant and Lee ever met in Mexico, it seems clear that they at least knew of each other. Lee was to distinguish himself once again in taking the heights of Chapultepec, where he was slightly wounded.

Lee and Grant both returned from Mexico in 1848. Grant married Julia on August 22, and they decided he should stay in the army for awhile. The Grants spent the next four years in New York and Michigan, a happy time of marital contentment. Then, in 1852, Grant was assigned to San Francisco, and they decided that Julia, expecting their second child, should wait to follow him west at a later point.

Grant's duties took him north to Vancouver, then to Humboldt Bay, close to San Francisco. And while he loved the West Coast, life in San Francisco was prohibitively expensive, and it was clear that he could not afford to keep his family there. It has often been charged that Grant had begun to drink too much, and that he had perhaps blown up at a superior officer who then threatened to court-martial him

LEFT: Colonel Robert E. Lee as superintendent of the United States Military Academy.

unless he resigned. Whether that is true or not, or whatever role liquor may have played, is long beyond recovery. But in any case, Grant resigned his commission in 1854 and returned to Julia and his two sons near St. Louis.

Grant was eager to enter civilian life at first, and began farming land Julia had inherited. But after four unproductive years, he finally gave in, sold off his livestock and farm implements, and tried his hand in the real estate business. No better luck awaited him there, however, and he fell back on his family for support. In 1860, he was a salaried clerk working behind the counter in a leather goods store owned by his father in Galena, Illinois.

Life after Mexico had been quite different for Lee. When he returned home, his first assignment was to improve the defenses of Baltimore Harbor. Then, in September 1852, he took over as the ninth Superintendent at West Point. And while he had a strong influence on the academy, where he was the driving force behind numerous significant improvements, he was badly needed in the army. In 1855, he was assigned to the 2nd Cavalry in west Texas, which tried to protect civilian settlers from raids by Comanche Indians.

Lee returned to Arlington House periodically. On October 17, 1859, during one such trip, he received a visit from Lieutenant J.E.B. Stuart, who had been his son's classmate and close friend, and a good friend of the family while Lee was Superintendent. Stuart bore a note directing Lee to report to the Secretary of War. Lee was ordered to lead a detachment

RIGHT: Secession Hall in Charleston, South Carolina, birthplace of the Confederate States of America.

BELOW: Former South Carolina slaves at Hilton Head, liberated by the Federal occupation of 1861, sort cotton on a confiscated plantation.

of Marines to Harpers Ferry. And so it was that Lee, with Stuart at his side, commanded the force that captured John Brown, a man whose execution would long reverberate across America. This was the same John Brown who, in his youth, had shared a residence and friendship with Jesse Grant, the father of Ulysses.

After Lincoln's election in November 1860, southern states began to secede. General Winfield Scott told Lincoln that Lee was the finest officer in the US Army, and a week after Fort Sumter fell on April 13, Lincoln offered Lee the command of the Union army. He declined. Two days later, he went to Richmond, where command of the army of Virginia was offered to him. This offer he accepted. Although there are instances of officers going over to the enemy, it is unparalleled in history that a man would be offered the command of the two hostile armies.

After frustrating efforts to save the counties of Virginia that were to become the state of West Virginia, Lee was sent on a tour of the coastal defenses of South Carolina, Georgia, and Florida. As soon as he returned to Richmond, Jefferson Davis, the new President of the Confederate States of America, made him his chief military adviser.

When McClellan led the Union's Army of the Potomac on the Peninsular Campaign in 1862, it was Lee who organized the defenses of Richmond, and it was also Lee who was

behind the brilliant diversion of sending General Thomas "Stonewall" Jackson storming through the Shenandoah Valley. On May 31, word got back to Richmond that General Joseph Johnston, commanding the resistance to McClellan, had been grievously wounded. Davis immediately sent Lee to replace Johnston, and thus fulfill his destiny as commander of the Army of Northern Virginia.

Grant, meanwhile, had been working as a civilian volunteer in the office of the governor of Illinois, helping to enlist regiments of volunteers. In 1861, General Winfield Scott, the commanding general of the US Army, had decided to keep the Regular Army units together and only supplement them with volunteer units drawn from the states. Grant refused service with these Illinois volunteers, and instead wrote to the Adjutant General of the US Army in Washington, offering to command a regiment in the Regular Army. But his offer was ignored.

As the call for more regiments came in, Grant wanted to join the fight. With the help of Congressman Elihu Washburn of Illinois, the governor of Illinois appointed Grant to command the 21st Illinois Volunteer Infantry Regiment, and he prepared to march off to war with his men.

Although Lee and Grant would become the commanders of the two main armies in the Civil War, they would not actually face each other on the battlefield until April 1864, after Grant had been promoted to Lieutenant General by Act of Congress and had become the Commanding General of the US Army. And while both men earned their spurs, so to speak, in the Mexican War, the lessons were quite different. Lee, as a senior captain on the commanding general's staff, filled a position that had a much higher profile, both politically and professionally. Grant, on the other hand, had graduated from West Point fourteen years after Lee, and as a junior officer was unable to avoid being detailed to the lowly position of quartermaster, from which few exploits demonstrating his personal courage or quick insight were expected or even possible. Still, lessons were learned in Mexico that had lasting impact on both men.

The excerpts from both memoirs that follow begin in early 1862. But 1861, the year when southern states seceded and Fort Sumter in Charleston Harbor was bombarded and taken by Confederate forces, was a crucial year. On July 21, 1861, Union forces were driven from the field in disorder at the Battle of Bull Run (Union designation) or First Manassas (Confederate) just south of

BUILT FROM THE RUINS.

the nation's capital in Washington D.C. Although this was the period in the Civil War when both sides were learning how and where and when to fight, both Lee and Grant began to establish a personal reputation of sorts. They became known by their military and political superiors, within the ranks of their respective armies, and, through newspaper accounts of their performance of their duties, in the minds of Americans living in both the North and the South. Before getting into the segments of the memoirs that follow, therefore, it is important for the reader to understand some of the earlier factors in the war that may have helped to shape them as the senior military leaders of each side. While Lee was by far the better-known and more widely respected figure to the public, as well as to military and governmental leaders, their early wartime careers almost seem to defy the differences in their ages and experience.

By July 1861, Grant felt that he had trained the 21st Illinois well enough to take the field, and soon enough, they had orders to attack a Confederate regiment commanded by

ABOVE: An engraving of the banner of South Carolina's convention of secession.

ABOVE: Steamships, armored vessels, and other craft played a key role in warfare on the inland waterways.

a Colonel Thomas Harris, located some twenty-five miles south of their encampment in Missouri. As they marched south through generally deserted countryside, Grant began to reflect on the role he was now filling as a regimental commander. He had certainly faced life-and-death combat in Mexico, but always as a junior officer. Now, he was in command of a thousand men, and their success or failure depended absolutely on his decisions. He reflected that, had he been a lieutenant colonel operating under the command of someone else as colonel, he'd have had no fears. But that was not the case, and as they moved forward, Grant grew anxious.

They believed that Harris and his men were encamped along a certain streambed, and as they began to climb the ridge in front of it, Grant says that his heart began to rise in his chest until he thought it was in his throat. He would have given anything, he said, to have been back in Illinois, but did not have the moral courage to stop his regiment's advance, so they kept going. When they got to the brow of the hill, Grant found that, although the markings of a military encampment were clear in the valley below them, it

was obvious that Harris and his men had left in a hurry. It was only then, Grant recalled, that he realized that the enemy commander had as much reason to fear his forces as he had to fear those of the Confederates. It was a lesson, he reported, that he never forgot during the course of the war.

At the end of July, Grant was promoted to Brigadier General, and one of the first to join his staff was John Rawlins, a lawyer friend from Galena, Illinois, and an adamant enemy of whiskey. He knew Grant's weakness there, and throughout the rest of the war he almost always succeeded in keeping his commander away from alcohol.

Grant was stationed in Cairo, Illinois, and some twenty miles south of him, at Columbus, Kentucky, a sizable Confederate force was forming. When he learned in October that Rebel troops were crossing the Mississippi to Belmont, Missouri, he decided that they must be stopped. On November 7, 1861, he took about 3000 men downriver in a surprise attack, landed, and drove the enemy before him. His troops then began looting the abandoned camp, and he and his staff struggled to get them turned around. But by the time they did, reinforcing Confederate forces had gotten between them and their boats and were moving toward them in an attack. When some tremulous officers began to say that they were surrounded and must surrender, Grant rejected their advice out of hand, telling his men that they had cut their way in and they could cut their way out just as well.

And indeed they did. Grant got his men deployed for the attack, and they tore through the Rebel ranks standing in their way. With the enemy too stunned to pursue, they boarded their steamships and headed north to Cairo and safety, taking 175 captives and two captured cannon with them. Union casualties at Belmont were 485 from an engaged force of 2500 men, while Confederate casualties were 642 out of a force of about 7500. The war was still young, and while this could hardly be called a smashing victory, it both reinforced Grant's confidence and gave him a stage on which to demonstrate his fundamental mastery of the art of war.

For Lee, already an established military champion in the eyes of his superiors, his peers, and the doting Southern public, the early days of the war were not so kind. Some ten days before the battle of Manassas, thirty-four-year-old General George McClellan had made his mark in trans-Allegheny Virginia. With 20,000 men, he planned to encircle and trap a small army of 4500 rebels under General Robert Garnett at Rich Mountain. When the attack was finally launched on July 11, 1861, one brigade under William S. Rosecrans flanked 1300 Confederates, inflicting 130 casualties and routing Garnett's entire force. But McClellan misinterpreted the sounds of battle and, afraid that his force was losing (a tendency he retained throughout the war), he failed to launch the follow-up attack that might have bagged the entire Rebel force. Instead, they got away.

Northwest Virginia, however, was cleared of organized Confederate forces by this action. This allowed a convention to meet in Wheeling and pass a separate statehood ordinance, an act that eventually resulted in the state of West Virginia. And McClellan, already superior at self-promotion, ensured that his victory was reported in the most glowing terms. Soon enough, tales of the battlefield triumph of America's "young Napoleon" at Rich Mountain reverberated throughout the land.

On July 13, pursuing Union forces killed the Rebel commander, General Robert Garnett – the first general officer to be killed in the war – and Confederate morale was dwindling fast. President Jefferson Davis want-

ed not only to stem the emotional tide of Union victory, but also to spread the renown of a Confederate battlefield hero far and wide. Therefore, he sent Robert E. Lee, his best soldier, to the rescue in August. By that time, the Confederates were also able to muster nearly 20,000 troops in the region, though most were poorly trained and armed. Southern newspapers, however, were loudly predicting that he would soon drive Yankee forces back to Ohio.

Lee aggressively led 10,000 men toward 3000 Union soldiers under Rosecrans at Cheat Mountain, not far from the site of the Confederate defeat a few months earlier. Lee's plan called for five different columns to converge on two Union positions, and his soldiers moved out in the rain over mountainous terrain on September 10. But uncontrolled small-arms fire by moving Rebel forces soon gave away all hope of surprise, and the maneuver plan itself proved far too complex for these very green troops. After several days of confused floundering in the mud by inexperienced, sick, and exhausted troops, and

ABOVE: A song sheet inscribed to the popular General George B. McClellan, first commander of the Army of the Potomac.

31

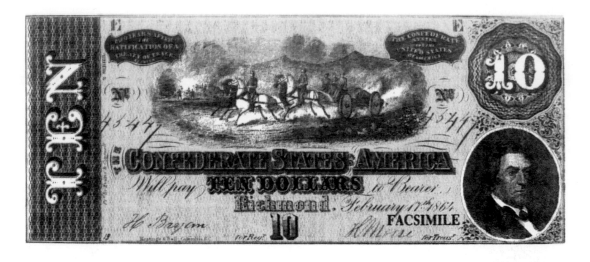

the loss of several hundred men from each side to confused skirmishing, Lee finally saw that the operation was hopeless. He called it off on August 15, leaving Federal forces in control of the Allegheny passes.

Lee then withdrew his men south to the Kanawha Valley, where they joined other Confederates soldiers and once again outnumbered a Union force before them. But on October 6 Lee's effort to trap them was foiled by rain, difficult terrain, and Rosecrans's timely withdrawal of his forces to a more easily defended location. A frustrated Lee returned to Richmond at the end of October, and the southern press was highly critical of his dismal failures against smaller Union forces. He was soon sent to South Carolina to strengthen coastal defenses, but the military reputation he left behind was not good.

In November 1861, Lee arrived in Savannah, Georgia, as the commander of the south Atlantic coastal defenses. With limited resources and mobility, he saw immediately that Union naval forces, simply because they were afloat, were able them to attack when and where they wished. He therefore conceded access to most of the coastline to Union forces, concentrating his defenses only at certain strategic points along the Confederate coast.

This dismal occupation was interrupted in March 1862, when President Davis called Lee back to Richmond as his military adviser, a sort of assistant commander-in-chief. As McClellan landed his huge army at Fort Monroe and started moving them up the peninsula toward Richmond, General Joseph Johnston was the field commander of Confederate forces posed before them and trying to hinder their advance. Lee, meanwhile, was bolstering Richmond's defenses, and he sent Stonewall Jackson up into the Shenandoah Valley to harass the three Union

armies there and so threaten Washington. This movement had its desired effect, as President Lincoln held back some 50,000 troops to defend Washington D.C. – 50,000 of the 150,000 McClellan expected to have with him on the Peninsula. But this reduction did little to retard Union forces in the face of far inferior Confederate forces. And even though McClellan was excessive in his hesitation to attack, he still regularly and ponderously drove back the forces led by an uninspired Joe Johnston. Finally, on May 31, 1862, Johnston was grievously wounded, and with no hesitation, Jefferson Davis appointed Lee as his replacement. The result is what has become known as the Seven Days' Campaign.

In the account of this campaign in the memoirs, you will see the aggression for which Lee was to become renowned. And even though by most traditional measures Lee lost heavily in all the battles he started during these seven days, it was his fury and unrelenting pressure that really unnerved McClellan and caused him to retreat back down the Peninsula. And if the end result of an attack is the adversary's retreat from the field of battle, that is generally the most important result, for it means victory.

Grant, meanwhile, was attempting to unleash his own aggression at Fort Henry and Fort Donelson. Despite the hesitation, reluctance, or downright opposition of his superior officers, Grant was able to field his army in concert with Union gunboats and take both Confederate strong points. Fort Henry was all but conceded by the Rebels with little more than token resistance, but they intended to make a stand at Fort Donelson. Grant's superior initiative, however, and his gritty determination when things looked bad after an apparently successful Confederate breakout, were the skills that won the day and a most impressive set of Union victories.

Those victories won Grant another star. A new Major General, he was encamped in northern Mississippi near Pittsburg Landing on the Tennessee River in early April 1862. The Union plan called for General Henry Halleck, the commander of all Union forces west of the Appalachians, to join him there with 35,000 troops to be added to Grant's 40,000 for a Union offensive. But before Halleck arrived, Grant's troops were attacked by 42,000 shrieking Confederates near a small church known as Shiloh. This is a very important chapter, for it shows Grant as a pillar of strength while many commanders around him were collapsing from the pressure. Despite calls to cross the Tennessee River and flee or surrender, Grant would have none of it. He told his subordinates that they would stay, counterattack in the morning, and whip the enemy. And reinforced by fresh troops during the night, that's just what they did. Grant is very self-effacing in his retelling of this story,

LEFT: Cool under fire, General Grant makes campaign plans while his officers react to an artillery barrage at Fort Harrison.

but it should be noted that, among Union commanders, he was the only oak in a field of reeds.

Although Halleck was his commander, he was bitterly envious of Grant's victories, first at Fort Donelson and now at Shiloh. And indeed, Grant's opponents within the army were legion. Halleck tried first to obscure Grant, but when word still got out about his battlefield prowess, he and others tried to destroy him with *ad hominem* attacks. Lincoln was told that Grant's first major error was to have been surprised at Shiloh. A greater blunder, however, was that after victory he had failed to follow up with a pursuit that might have destroyed the Confederate army. And worst of all, the rumor was that these and other failings were attributable to the fact that Grant drank too much. But President Lincoln would not listen. "I can't spare this man" he said, "he fights!" – a quality all too absent among senior Union army commanders in the early years of the war. In Grant, Lee had finally found the man who could lead the Union army to victory.

After Shiloh, Halleck arrived on the scene at Pittsburg Landing and asserted his authority. He personally took command of the army, but then he led it in a slow and cautious advance against a Confederate army supposed to be in Corinth. When they finally got there, of course, this town proved to be empty. For this operation, Halleck had made Grant his "second in command" – a useless function that had Grant ready to resign.

Fortunately for the Union forces, Halleck was eventually moved east to Washington, and Grant took over command in the west. His biggest problem was the Confederate fortress atop the cliffs along the Mississippi at the town of Vicksburg. Because of the enormous artillery fire that could be delivered here and at other sites farther south, a stretch of the Mississippi was kept open for free passage of agricultural products, general commerce, and Rebel soldiers between the states of Arkansas, Louisiana, and Texas and the rest of the Confederacy. Cutting off the piece west of the Mississippi was a key

part of ultimate Union victory, but the problem was much easier to state than it was to solve. Grant decided that he would take Vicksburg, but it was to be a long, hard fight.

But this was also to be Grant's brightest moment. Although he was dismissed after the war by his enemies as a man of no daring or maneuver warfare capability, an unimaginative commander capable of winning only when he led superior numbers and met an enemy who would stay in place and fight, this is a false image that is simply unfair. This is no doubt because of the last year of the war, when Grant met Lee and was forced to adopt conservative tactics and simply slug it out. But one has only to look at the Vicksburg campaign to recognize Grant's true military genius, for there, Grant showed himself to be the true master of maneuver warfare and a leader of the highest daring.

He started the campaign with conventional overland infantry attacks against Vicksburg from the north, but these quickly bogged down. Next, he tried to dig canals that would divert the Mississippi, but again met failure. It was his final effort that was the most daring, and which all his subordinate generals, including William T. Sherman, hotly opposed. He proposed to run a fleet of gunboats past Vicksburg, then cross the Mississippi with his army and march south on the Louisiana side; once well below Vicksburg, his forces would be ferried back across the mighty river and then they would strike inland. In so doing, of course, he would cut off his line of supply, which was widely condemned as madness. But Grant was confident that he could live off the land, and that his weapon and ammunition stores would be replenished from the supplies of Rebel forces he would defeat. The fact that he would be maneuvering against two enemy armies, that of General John Pemberton at Vicksburg and General Joseph Johnston at Jackson which, if joined, would heavily outnumber his own force, was of little concern to him, for he was confident he could divide them and defeat them in detail. And that is precisely what he did: Pemberton surrendered Vicksburg to him on July 3.

In Virginia, meanwhile, Lee had driven McClellan back down the Peninsula, and was increasingly confident he would not renew his advance toward Richmond. Accordingly, he began to move his forces north to take on the new Army of Virginia that Lincoln had formed under General John Pope. And at the Battle of Second Manassas, the armies clashed. On August 28 and 29, the commanders felt each other out. On the 30th, Pope was induced to attack Jackson's corps in a strong defensive position strengthened by railroad cuts. And as they pressed their attack,

BELOW: Former slaves follow General Pope's troops in their retreat from Cedar Mountain, Virginia.

RIGHT: Robert E. Lee as general-in-chief of Confederate armies, surrounded by his principal generals.

the Union left flank was hit by Longstreet's corps, a stunning surprise that resulted in the utter rout of Pope's entire army. This was not the blind aggression Lee had shown in the Seven Days', but rather a careful baiting of a trap, followed by the hammer slamming down on the mouse nibbling at the cheese. It was a military master stroke, demonstrated by a commander from whom it should have been expected.

In late summer, the political decision had been made for Lee to move north and try to win a victory outside the Confederacy. Accordingly, he began to move his army down the Shenandoah Valley and crossed the Potomac into Maryland in early September. McClellan was pursuing in his cautious way with 90,000 men when his troops found a copy of Lee's orders to all his 40,000 troops for this campaign. Inspired by this, McClellan accelerated his movement and trapped Lee's forces in front of the town of Sharpsburg, behind the Antietam Creek with the Potomac flowing at their rear. McClellan attacked on the 17th of September – still regarded as the bloodiest day in American history – but was unable to defeat Lee. On the 18th, both forces stayed in place, and McClellan did not renew his attacks. That night, Lee and his forces slipped back across the Potomac and down the Shenandoah Valley.

This was too much for Lincoln, who replaced McClellan with Ambrose Burnside. This new commander of the Army of the Potomac decided to advance against Lee's forces and crossed the Rappahannock River

at Fredericksburg. On December 13, after a contested crossing, Burnside launched repeated and useless attacks against Lee's army dug in at the foot and on the top of Marye's Heights, a ridge west of town. After Union attacks had been thoroughly repulsed at great cost, Lee remarked that "It is well that war is so terrible, else men would learn to love it too much." When early spring rains soaked the countryside, Burnside tried to flank Lee with the infamous and unsuccessful "Mud March" along the wet banks of the Rappahannock that made him the laughingstock of both armies.

General Joseph Hooker was the next commander of the Army of the Potomac, and in the spring of 1863 he decided to conduct a major ruse. He left some 40,000 troops under

John Sedgwick in Fredericksburg, but took 80,000 more far to the north and west, where they crossed the Rappahannock at fords and began to descend on Lee's rear. But Lee had been alerted, and left only 10,000 men at Fredericksburg while he moved his main force to the west to await Hooker's attack. On May 3, despite his superior numbers, Hooker pulled into a defensive position. Lee saw his opportunity and sent Jackson with 30,000 men on a great circuitous march around the Union right, keeping only 15,000 men in Hooker's front. Jackson attacked the Union rear late that afternoon and completely routed all Union soldiers before them. This was to be the greatest Confederate victory, although the great Stonewall Jackson was badly wounded here and would die within days. This bat-

ABOVE: Union recruits arrive to reinforce Grant's troops at Peebles' Farm during the campaign of September 1864.

tle was Lee's maneuver-warfare mastery demonstrated at its greatest.

After Union troops withdrew toward Washington, Lee once again headed down the Shenandoah Valley and then north, this time into Pennsylvania. The Army of the Potomac, commanded by George Meade, followed carefully, and they met on July 1–3 at the battle of Gettysburg. Pickett's Charge on July 3 failed to break through Union resistance, and the two armies stayed in place on July 4th. That night, Lee headed home, and Union army pursuit was hesitant. But less than a year after the fall of Vicksburg, Lee would face a new Union commander in the east, the man who was finally to be his match.

That fall of 1863, Grant moved eastward to rescue Union forces besieged at Chattanooga. On the 24th of November, Grant launched his attack against Confederates on the surrounding heights, and his forces broke through the following day. As the Confederates retreated toward Atlanta far to the southeast, Grant assumed his next duty would be to pursue them in the spring through Atlanta and thus cut the Confederacy in two. Instead, Lincoln – impressed by Grant's aggressive actions – called Grant to Washington, where he was promoted, by Act of Congress, to Lieutenant General and named General-in-Chief of all Union armies. For the first time in this war, Grant and Lee were now to confront one another, and each knew that his main objective would be to defeat the other's forces. Grant kept Meade in technical command of the Army of the Potomac, but he took the field with that army and commenced the relentless pursuit of Lee that would not end for another 11 months.

On May 5, 1864, Grant plunged right into

the Wilderness and tore at Lee's forces. But the senior officers in the Army of the Potomac had seen this effort many times before, and he was constantly reminded, in fearful tones, of Lee's tactical skill by officers in his own command. On the second day, a particularly distraught brigadier general told him that all was lost and Lee would soon destroy them. In a rare outburst, Grant said he was tired of hearing what Lee was going to do. "Some of you always think he is going to turn a double somersault and land on our rear and on both flanks at the same time!" he snapped at the brigadier. "Go back to your command and try to think what we are going to do ourselves instead of what Lee is going to do!"

But in the thick undergrowth, the Union superiority in artillery was to be of little use, and both sides were heavily bled in a basic standoff. On the evening of the 7th, Grant marched his troops out of the Wilderness. But instead of turning north and retreating toward Washington, as virtually all previous Union army commanders had done after their first defeat by Lee, Grant turned south and headed for Spotsylvania. This brought cheers from his men, who now knew they were led by a man who was both a fighter and a winner.

Once again, Union forces were stymied by Confederate defenses. And so again, Grant turned south, this time attacking Lee's lines at Cold Harbor. But the defenses were stout, and the attack he ordered on June 3 was to be the only order he ever regretted after the war, for it meant a ferocious Union bloodletting to virtually no avail. By this time, Grant had lost 50,000 casualties, some 40 percent of his total strength. But with a smaller army and the lower casualty figures coming from his defensive posture, Lee had still suffered more, having lost over 45 percent of his army. And Grant gave him no peace.

After Cold Harbor, Grant edged steadily south until mid-June, when he lunged for Petersburg, a dozen miles south of Richmond and a key rail intersection whose capture would strangle the Confederacy. But his commanders failed to rush the town when they got there, and within a few days, Lee's forces had arrived and were soon manning massive defenses. Grant tried all through the fall and winter to reach around these defenses to their south and cut the last rail lines on which Richmond depended. It wasn't until April 3, 1865, that he was successful, and on that night Lee finally pulled his 35,000 starving men out of Petersburg. He hoped to entrain them at Amelia Courthouse and carry them south to join other Confederate forces in North Carolina and continue the war. But Grant's pursuit was both masterful and relentless, and he never let him break contact as he pursued; he also pushed other Federal forces ahead to surround Lee. Finally, Union cavalry and infantry corps blocked his movement west, and Lee ran out of options. On April 9, he surrendered the Army of Northern Virginia

to Grant at Appomattox Court House, thus effectively ending the Civil War.

The meeting of these two commanders at the surrender ceremony in the house of Wilmer McClean is one of the great "set pieces" of American history, and in this volume the reader will be able to experience it in the words of Grant and the reported version of Lee's biographer. In general, both accounts are in agreement. Grant's is much the more detailed, however, and it is his observations about the difference of the uniforms they wore on the occasion that are so often cited: how Lee "was dressed in a full uniform which was entirely new" and Grant was "in my rough traveling suit, the uniform of a private with the straps of a lieutenant-general." It is customary to use this contrast in their clothing that day as a metaphor for the difference between the two men's lives and characters, and up to a point it seems fair enough. Lee *was* a man of punctilious formality, Grant *was* a man of homespun informality. But just how far this contrast can be extended when it comes to their conduct in fighting the battles of the Civil War is something that readers of these two memoirs should be able to consider for themselves.

BELOW: A postwar studio portrait of veterans of Pittsburg Landing and the Siege of Corinth.

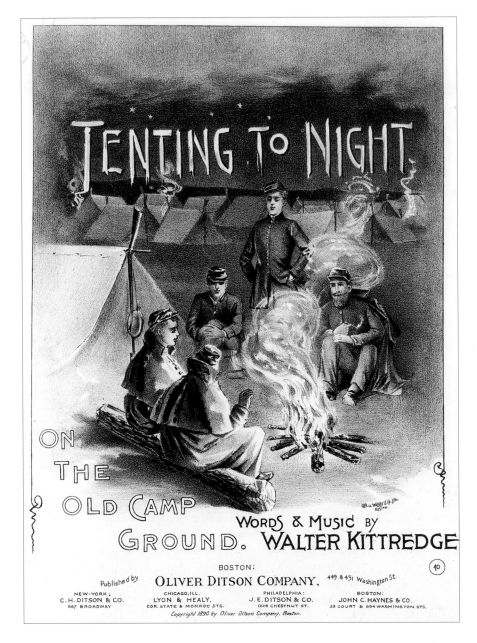

ABOVE: Sheet music for one of the most popular Union songs of the war.

mand, not to some "old army buddy." Indeed, when at the surrender Lee claims "that he remembered me very well in the old army," Grant writes that he suspects that "I had not attracted his attention sufficiently to be remembered by him after such a long interval." Certainly nowhere in his account of his service in the Mexican War does Grant ever refer to meeting Lee.

That issue aside, what did they think of each other as adversarial commanders? Here we are at some disadvantage, because we do not have Lee's own words but are dependent on Long's versions of events. And usually Long portrays Lee in an entirely idealized manner, never showing him as anything except a wise and brave commander, while Grant is portrayed – well, not negatively, but subtly not quite the leader that Lee was. Consider how Long describes the siege of Petersburg, commencing with Grant's "deciding to accomplish by patient siege what he had failed to achieve by reckless application of force. With this decision began a new chapter in the history of war, and one of the most remarkable sieges known to history was inaugurated – that in which the Confederate commander behind the breastworks of Petersburg for a full year baffled every effort by his powerful foe." Grant, in Lee's memoirs, is portrayed as a general who is fortunate to have more men he can afford to lose. Again, though, it must be stressed: Lee's memoirs are Long's words.

Grant, meanwhile, does express his feelings about Lee on several occasions. He is always aware of Lee's reputation as a Knight in Shining Armor and on occasion, it is clear that Grant gets a bit annoyed at Lee's reputation as some ingeniously clever commander. We have mentioned above how at the Battle of the Wilderness he upbraids his officers for talking as though Lee can perform superhuman feats. On another occasion he complains that he hears that even Union officers say, "Well, Grant has never met Bobby Lee yet" – the implication being that Grant would lose in such a contest. That said, Grant always respects Lee's generalship: often he will decide to do something or not do it on the basis of what he knows the intelligent commander Lee will be doing.

In the end, it is the many battles and campaigns these two men fought, separately or together, that speak to the respective strengths of each as army officers. Not all of these battles and campaigns can be included in the selections that follow. This compilation of key excerpts from the two manuscripts, however, offers an "insider's view" of the Civil War

One question that these memoirs might well raise in the minds of readers is what each of these generals had to say about the other – and related to that, how well did they know one another. As to the latter, it is sometimes suggested that when they met at the surrender at Appomattox Court House, they greeted each other like two old army veterans, or at least two colleagues from the Mexican War. In fact, it was not quite that way. It is true that both had gone to West Point and both had served in the war in Mexico, but Lee was effectively a whole generation older than Grant. Beyond that, in Mexico – the only time they served in the same locales during their years in the army – Lee was a highly visible officer on the staff of General Winfield Scott while Grant was an obscure quartermaster. It is true that Grant in his memoirs will say that "I knew Lee personally," but from the context it seems quite clear that he is referring to his knowledge of Lee's manner of com-

from the military commander's perspective on each side. As such, it presents a rare and fascinating look at the ways in which the war was conducted, at the key decisions that were made, and the factors that led to them. And it provides the reader with a view of Lee and Grant that no historian, however eloquent, can match.

One last note about the text. Bridging passages that occur occasionally are condensations by the editor of passages in the original texts; ellipses mark the omission of words or sentences; three asterisks between lines denote the omission of paragraphs. The editor has in some cases also supplied first names or initials where these were not supplied by the authors. The captioned illustrations and maps, of course, were not in the original editions, but it is assumed that contemporary readers will find they add immeasurably to an understanding and appreciation of the events described.

LEFT: A memorable portrait of General Lee in full dress uniform, from the Anne S.K. Brown Military Collection, Brown University.

Ulysses S. Grant

Chapter I

Fort Henry and Fort Donelson

Fort Henry occupies a bend in the river which gave the guns in the water battery a direct fire down the stream. The camp outside the fort was intrenched, with rifle pits and outworks two miles back on the road to Donelson and Dover. The garrison of the fort and camp was about 2,800, with strong reinforcements from Donelson halted some miles out. There were seventeen heavy guns in the fort. The river was very high, the banks being overflowed except where the bluffs come to the water's edge. A portion of the ground on which Fort Henry stood was two feet deep in water. Below, the water extended into the woods several hundred yards back from the bank on the east side. On the west bank Fort Heiman stood on high ground, completely commanding Fort Henry. The distance from Fort Henry to Donelson is but eleven miles. The two positions were so important to the enemy, *as he saw his interest*, that it was natural to suppose that reinforcements would come from every quarter from which they could be got. Prompt action on our part was imperative.

The plan was for the troops and gunboats to start at the same moment. The troops were to invest the garrison and the gunboats to attack the fort at close quarters. General [Charles F.] Smith was to land a brigade of his division on the west bank during the night of the 5th and get it in rear of Heiman.

At the hour designated the troops and gunboats started. General Smith found Fort Heiman had been evacuated before his men

Grant as a Lieutenant general in 1864. His elevation to the highest military rank his country could confer was all but unimaginable two years earlier. It was the capture of forts Henry and Donelson that began his meteoric rise.

arrived. The gunboats soon engaged the water batteries at very close quarters, but the troops which were to invest Fort Henry were delayed for want of roads, as well as by the dense forest and the high water in what would in dry weather have been unimportant beds of streams. This delay made no difference in the result. On our first appearance [Confederate General Lloyd] Tilghman had sent his entire command, with the exception of about one hundred men left to man the guns in the fort, to the outworks on the road to Dover and Donelson, so as to have them out of range of the guns of our navy; and before any attack on the 6th he had ordered them to retreat on Donelson. He stated in his subsequent report that the defence was intended solely to give his troops time to make their escape.

Tilghman was captured with his staff and ninety men, as well as the armament of the fort, the ammunition and whatever stores were there. Our cavalry pursued the retreating column towards Donelson and picked up two guns and a few stragglers; but the enemy had so much the start, that the pursuing force did not get in sight of any except the stragglers.

All the gunboats engaged were hit many times. The damage, however, beyond what could be repaired by a small expenditure of money, was slight, except to the *Essex*. A shell penetrated the boiler of that vessel and exploded it, killing and wounding forty-eight men, nineteen of whom were soldiers who had been detailed to act with the navy. On several occasions during the war such details were made when the complement of men with the navy was insufficient for the duty before them. After the fall of Fort Henry Captain [S.L.] Phelps, commanding the iron-clad *Carondelet*, at my request ascended the Tennessee River and thoroughly destroyed the bridge of the Memphis and Ohio Railroad. . . .

On the 7th, the day after the fall of Fort Henry, I took my staff and the cavalry – a part of one regiment – and made a reconnoissance to within about a mile of the outer line of works at Donelson. I had known General [Gideon] Pillow in Mexico, and judged that with any force, no matter how small, I could march up to within gunshot of any intrenchments he was given to hold. I said this to the officers of my staff at the time. I knew that [John B.] Floyd was in command, but he was no soldier, and I judged that he would yield to Pillow's pretensions. I met, as I ex-

LEFT: Charles Ferguson Smith was probably Grant's ablest lieutenant in the assault on forts Henry and Donelson. He would die soon thereafter of an injury received at Shiloh.

BELOW: Confederate General Gideon Pillow was second in command at Fort Donelson. He amply confirmed Grant's low opinion of his abilities when Grant attacked the fort.

pected, no opposition in making the reconnoissance and, besides learning the topography of the country on the way and around Fort Donelson, found that there were two roads available for marching; one leading to the village of Dover, the other to Donelson.

Fort Donelson is two miles north, or down the river, from Dover. The fort, as it stood in 1861, embraced about one hundred acres of land. On the east it fronted the Cumberland; to the north it faced Hickman's creek, a small stream which at the time was deep and wide because of the back-water from the river; on the south was another small

stream, or rather a ravine, opening into the Cumberland. This also was filled with backwater from the river. The fort stood on high ground, some of it as much as a hundred feet above the Cumberland. Strong protection to the heavy guns in the water batteries had been obtained by cutting away places for them in the bluff. To the west there was a line of rifle-pits some two miles back from the river at the farthest point. This line ran generally along the crest of high ground, but in one place crossed a ravine which opens into the river between the village and the fort. The ground inside and outside of this in-

LEFT: The U.S.S. *St. Louis* was the first of a series of ironclad river gunboats built for the Union navy by the engineer James Buchanan Eads. She was part of the squadron led by Andrew Hull Foote against Fort Donelson while Grant was attacking the place on land. Grant's respect for the Navy and readiness to work with it in combined operations was highly unusual among U.S. Army officers, and it would stand Grant in good stead in the Vicksburg Campaign.

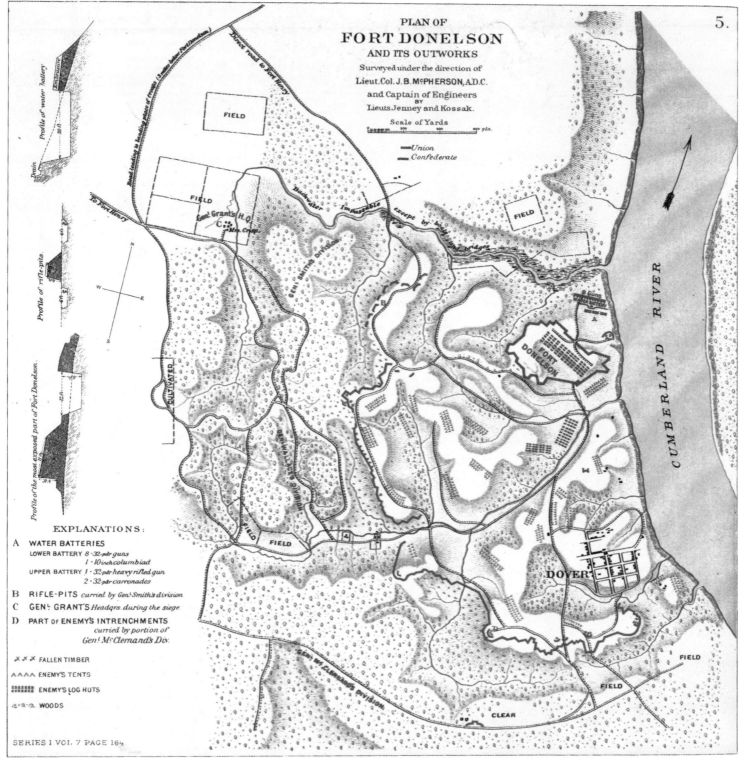

PLAN OF
FORT DONELSON
AND ITS OUTWORKS

Surveyed under the direction of
Lieut. Col. J. B. McPHERSON, A.D.C.
and Captain of Engineers
BY
Lieuts. Jenney and Kossak.

Scale of Yards

— Union
— Confederate

EXPLANATIONS:

A WATER BATTERIES
   LOWER BATTERY 8 · 32-pdr guns
                  1 · 10 inch columbiad
   UPPER BATTERY 1 · 32-pdr heavy rifled gun
                  2 · 32-pdr carronades
B RIFLE-PITS carried by Gen! Smith's division
C GEN! GRANT'S Headqrs. during the siege
D PART OF ENEMY'S INTRENCHMENTS
   carried by portion of
   Gen! McClernand's Div.

✗ ✗ ✗ FALLEN TIMBER
∧∧∧∧ ENEMY'S TENTS
▦▦▦ ENEMY'S LOG HUTS
⬟⬟⬟ WOODS

SERIES 1 VOL. 7 PAGE 164

trenched line was very broken and generally wooded. The trees outside of the rifle-pits had been cut down for a considerable way out, and had been felled so that their tops lay outwards from the intrenchments. The limbs had been trimmed and pointed, and thus formed an abatis in front of the greater part of the line. Outside of this intrenched line, and extending about half the entire length of it, is a ravine running north and south and opening into Hickman creek at a point north of the fort. The entire side of this ravine next to the works was one long abatis. . . .

I was very impatient to get to Fort Donelson because I knew the importance of the place to the enemy and supposed he would reinforce it rapidly. I felt that 15,000 men on the 8th would be more effective than 50,000 a month later. I asked Flag-officer [Andrew] Foote, therefore, to order his gunboats still about Cairo to proceed up the Cumberland River and not to wait for those gone to Eastport and Florence; but the others got back in time and we started on the 12th. I had moved [General John A.] McClernand out a few miles the night before so as to leave the road as free as possible. . . .

ABOVE: A contemporary U.S. Army map shows the position of opposing forces during the investment of Fort Donelson.

OPPOSITE: John B. Floyd, the confederate commander of Fort Donelson. Grant's contempt for Pillow, Floyd's second in command, was mild compared to his feelings about Floyd.

along the crest of the ridges. The artillery was protected by being sunk in the ground. The men who were not serving the guns were perfectly covered from fire on taking position a little back from the crest. The greatest suffering was from want of shelter. It was midwinter and during the siege we had rain and snow, thawing and freezing alternately. It would not do to allow camp-fires except far down the hill out of sight of the enemy, and it would not do to allow many of the troops to remain there at the same time. In the march over from Fort Henry numbers of the men had thrown away their blankets and overcoats. There was . . . much discomfort and . . . suffering.

During the 12th and 13th, and until the arrival of [General Lewis] Wallace and [Colonel] Thayer on the 14th, the National forces, composed of but 15,000 men, without intrenchments, confronted an intrenched army of 21,000, without conflict further than what was brought on by ourselves. Only one gunboat had arrived. There was a little skirmishing each day, brought on by the movement of our troops in securing commanding positions; but there was no actual fighting during this time except once, on the 13th, in front of McClernand's command. That general had undertaken to capture a battery of the enemy which was annoying his men. Without orders or

ABOVE: Flag Officer Andrew Hull Foote, commander of the Navy's riverine flotilla and a staunch admirer and ally of General Grant.

RIGHT: General Lewis (Lew) Wallace, one of Grant's abler lieutenants at Donelson, later became famous as the author of the novel *Ben Hur*.

I started from Fort Henry with 15,000 men, including eight batteries and part of a regiment of cavalry, and, meeting with no obstruction to detain us, the advance arrived in front of the enemy by noon. That afternoon and the next day were spent in taking up ground to make the investment as complete as possible. . . . The troops were not intrenched, but the nature of the ground was such that they were just as well protected from the fire of the enemy as if rifle-pits had been thrown up. Our line was generally

authority he sent three regiments to make the assault. The battery was in the main line of the enemy, which was defended by his whole army present. Of course the assault was a failure, and of course the loss on our side was great for the number of men engaged. . . .

During the night of the 13th Flag-officer Foote arrived with the iron-clads *St. Louis, Louisville* and *Pittsburg* and the wooden gunboats *Tyler* and *Conestoga*, convoying Thayer's brigade. On the morning of the 14th Thayer was landed. Wallace, whom I had ordered over from Fort Henry, also arrived about the same time. . . .

The plan was for the troops to hold the enemy within his lines, while the gunboats should attack the water batteries at close quarters and silence his guns if possible. Some of the gunboats were to run the batteries, get above the fort and above the village of Dover. . . .

By three in the afternoon of the 14th Flag-officer Foote was ready, and advanced upon the water batteries with his entire fleet. After coming in range of the batteries of the enemy the advance was slow, but a constant fire was delivered from every gun that could be brought to bear upon the fort. I occupied a position on shore from which I could see the advancing navy. The leading boat got within a very short distance of the water battery, not further off I think than two hundred yards, and I soon saw one and then another of them dropping down the river, visibly disabled. Then the whole fleet followed and the engagement closed for the day. The gunboat which Flag-officer Foote was on, besides having been hit about sixty times, several of the shots passing through near the waterline, had a shot enter the pilot-house which killed the pilot, carried away the wheel and wounded the flag-officer himself. The tiller-

ropes of another vessel were carried away and she, too, dropped helplessly back. Two others had their pilot-houses so injured that they scarcely formed a protection to the men at the wheel.

The enemy had evidently been much demoralized by the assault, but they were jubilant when they saw the disabled vessels

TOP: The naval attack on Fort Donelson, led by *St. Louis*.

ABOVE: Mortimer Leggett, who led a regiment of green Ohio volunteers against Donelson, later became a distinguished Union General.

THE ASSAULT ON FORT DONELSON

dropping down the river entirely out of control of the men on board. Of course I only witnessed the falling back of our gunboats and felt sad enough at the time over the repulse. Subsequent reports, now published, show that the enemy telegraphed a great victory to Richmond. The sun went down on the night of the 14th of February, 1862, leaving the army confronting Fort Donelson anything but comforted over the prospects. The weather had turned intensely cold; the men were without tents and could not keep up fires where most of them had to stay, and, as previously stated, many had thrown away their overcoats and blankets. Two of the strongest of our gunboats had been disabled, presumably beyond the possibility of rendering any present assistance. I retired this night not knowing but that I would have to intrench my position, and bring up tents for the men or build huts under the cover of the hills.

On the morning of the 15th, before it was yet broad day, a messenger from Flag-officer Foote handed me a note, expressing a desire to see me on the flag-ship and saying that he had been injured the day before so much that he could not come himself to me. I at once made my preparations for starting. . . .

When I reached the fleet I found the flag-ship was anchored out in the stream. A small boat, however, awaited my arrival and I was soon on board with the flag-officer. He explained to me in short the condition in which he was left by the engagement of the evening before, and suggested that I should intrench while he returned to Mound City with his disabled boats, expressing at the time the belief that he could have the necessary repairs made and be back in ten days. I saw the absolute necessity of his gunboats going into hospital and did not know but I should be forced to the alternative of going

through a siege. But the enemy relieved me from this necessity. . . .

Just as I landed I met Captain Hillyer of my staff, white with fear, not for his personal safety, but for the safety of the National troops. He said the enemy had come out of his lines in full force and attacked and scattered McClernand's division, which was in full retreat. The roads, as I have said, were unfit for making fast time, but I got to my command as soon as possible. . . .

I saw everything favorable for us along the line of our left and centre. When I came to the right appearances were different. The enemy had come out in full force to cut his way out and make his escape. McClernand's division had to bear the brunt of the attack from this combined force. His men had stood up gallantly until the ammunition in their cartridge-boxes gave out. There was abundance of ammunition near by lying on the ground in boxes, but at that stage of the war it was not all of our commanders of regiments, brigades, or even divisions, who had been educated up to the point of seeing that their men were constantly supplied with ammunition during an engagement. When the men found themselves without ammunition they could not stand up against troops who seemed to have plenty of it. The division broke and a portion fled, but most of the men, as they were pursued, only fell back out of range of the fire of the enemy. It must have been about this time that Thayer pushed his brigade in between the enemy and those of our troops that were without ammunition. At all events the enemy fell back within his intrenchments and was there when I got on the field.

I saw the men standing in knots talking in the most excited manner. No officer seemed to be giving any directions. The soldiers had their muskets, but no ammunition, while

OPPOSITE TOP: Grant watches the progress of C. F. Smith's charge against enemy forces before Fort Donelson on the afternoon of February 15.

OPPOSITE BOTTOM: The same charge as imagined by another artist (with a somewhat more developed taste for scenes of heroic drama).

BELOW: Two of the eight well-protected batteries Grant was able to deploy against the defenders of Fort Donelson.

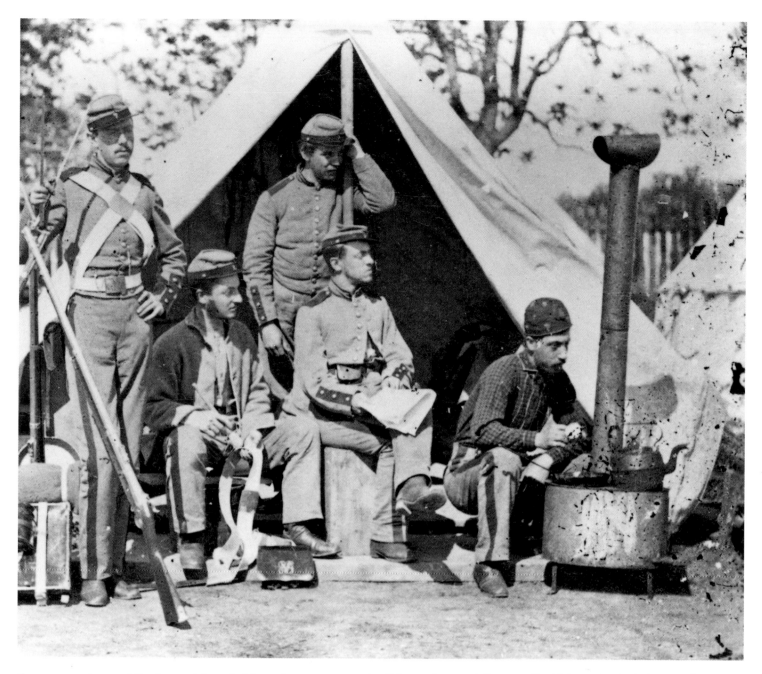

there were tons of it close at hand. I heard some of the men say that the enemy had come out with knapsacks, and haversacks filled with rations. They seemed to think this indicated a determination on his part to stay out and fight just as long as the provisions held out. I turned to Colonel J. D. Webster, of my staff, who was with me, and said: "Some of our men are pretty badly demoralized, but the enemy must be more so, for he has attempted to force his way out, but has fallen back: the one who attacks first now will be victorious and the enemy will have to be in a hurry if he gets ahead of me." . . . I directed Colonel Webster to ride with me and call out to the men as we passed: "Fill your cartridge-boxes, quick, and get into line; the enemy is trying to escape and he must not be permitted to do so." This acted like a charm. The men only wanted some one to give them a

command. We rode rapidly to Smith's quarters, when I explained the situation to him and directed him to charge the enemy's works in his front with his whole division, saying at the same time that he would find nothing but a very thin line to contend with. The general was off in an incredibly short time, going in advance himself to keep his men from firing while they were working their way through the abatis intervening between them and the enemy. The outer line of rifle-pits was passed, and the night of the 15th General Smith, with much of his division, bivouacked within the lines of the enemy. There was now no doubt but that the Confederates must surrender or be captured the next day.

There seems from subsequent accounts to have been much consternation, particularly among the officers of high rank, in

ABOVE: A vignette of typical Union army camp life in 1862. The men shown here belong to the 7th New York militia.

OPPOSITE: Grant's campaign against the Cumberland River forts established his name as a "fighting general." This modern portrait by N. C. Wyeth well conveys that facet of Grant's complex personality.

Dover during the night of the 15th. General Floyd, the commanding officer, who was a man of talent enough for any civil position, was no soldier and, possibly, did not possess the elements of one. He was further unfitted for command, for the reason that his conscience must have troubled him and made him afraid. As Secretary of War he had taken a solemn oath to maintain the Constitution of the United States and to uphold the same against all its enemies. He had betrayed that trust. As Secretary of War he was reported through the northern press to have scattered the little army the country had so that the most of it could be picked up in detail when secession occurred. About a year before leaving the Cabinet he had removed arms from northern to southern arsenals. He continued in the Cabinet of President Buchanan until about the 1st of January, 1861, while he was working vigilantly for the establishment of a confederacy made out of United States territory. Well may he have been afraid to fall into the hands of National troops. He would no doubt have been tried for misappropriating public property, if not for treason, had he been captured. General Pillow, next in command, was conceited, and prided himself much on his services in the Mexican war. He telegraphed to General [Albert S.] Johnston, at Nashville, after our men were within the rebel rifle-pits, and almost on the eve of his making his escape, that the Southern troops had had great success all day. Johnston forwarded the dispatch to Richmond. While the authorities at the capital were reading it Floyd and Pillow were fugitives.

A council of war was held by the enemy at which all agreed that it would be impossible

OPPOSITE: This view of the 94th Pennsylvania at drill gives a good idea of the size of a typical regiment of the Union army's infantry.

BELOW: The final assault on Fort Donelson as imagined by the printmakers Kurz & Allison.

to hold out longer. General [Simon Bolivar] Buckner, who was third in rank in the garrison but much the most capable soldier, seems to have regarded it a duty to hold the fort until the general commanding the department, A. S. Johnston, should get back to his headquarters at Nashville. Buckner's report shows, however, that he considered Donelson lost and that any attempt to hold the place longer would be at the sacrifice of the command. Being assured that Johnston was already in Nashville, Buckner too agreed that surrender was the proper thing. Floyd turned over the command to Pillow, who declined it. It then devolved upon Buckner, who accepted the responsibility of the position. Floyd and Pillow took possession of all the river transports at Dover and before morning both were on their way to Nashville, with the brigade formerly commanded by Floyd and some other troops, in all about 3,000. Some marched up the east bank of the Cumberland; others went on the steamers. During the night (N.B.) Forrest

also, with his cavalry and some other troops, about a thousand in all, made their way out, passing between our right and the river. They had to ford or swim over the backwater in the little creek just south of Dover.

Before daylight General Smith brought to me the following letter from General Buckner:

SIR:- In consideration of all the circumstances governing the present situation of affairs at this station, I propose to the Commanding Officer of the Federal forces the appointment of Commissioners to agree upon terms of capitulation of the forces and fort under my command, and in that view suggest an armistice until 12 o'clock to-day.

I am, sir, very respectfully,
Your ob't se'v't,
S. B. BUCKNER

To this I responded as follows:

SIR:- Yours of this date, proposing armistice and appointment of Commissioners to settle terms of capitulation, is just received. No terms except an unconditional and immediate surrender can be accepted. I propose to move immediately upon your works.

I am, sir, very respectfully,
Your ob't se'v't,
U. S. GRANT

To this I received the following reply:

SIR:- The distribution of the forces under my command, incident to an unexpected change of commanders, and the overwhelming force under your command, compel me, notwithstanding the brilliant success of the Confederate arms yesterday, to accept the ungenerous and unchivalrous terms which you propose.

I am, sir,
Your ob't se'v't,
S. B. BUCKNER

I had been at West Point three years with Buckner and afterwards served with him in the army, so that we were quite well acquainted. In the course of our conversation, which was very friendly, he said to me that if he had been in command I would not have got up to Donelson as easily as I did. I told him that if he had been in command I should not have tried in the way I did: I had invested their lines with a smaller force than they had to defend them, and at the same time had sent a brigade full 5,000 strong, around by water; I had relied very much upon their commander to allow me to come safely up to the outside of their works. . . .

BELOW: Confederate General Simon Bolivar Buckner succeeded to the command of Fort Donelson after his two superiors fled. An old friend of Grant, he expected that Grant would offer him lenient surrender terms. Instead, Grant's terms were flatly unconditional.

ABOVE: The railway station at Corinth, Mississippi. Because Grant's superiors failed to follow up his victory over the river forts, the enemy was able to regroup in Corinth and mount the counterstroke that resulted in the Battle of Shiloh in early April.

LEFT: Bushrod R. Johnson was among the senior Confederate officers who escaped from Fort Donelson. He would clash with Grant again less than two months later at Shiloh.

59

Chapter II

Shiloh

The news of the fall of forts Henry and Donelson was received with delight in the victory-starved North and served to focus national attention for the first time on "Unconditional Surrender" Grant, who was promptly promoted to the grade of major-general. Grant was convinced – then, and to the end of his days – that if the capture of the two strategically-located river forts had quickly been followed up with a series of coordinated Federal strikes at Chattanooga, Corinth, Memphis, and Vicksburg, virtually all of the Confederacy west of the Alleghenies might have fallen to the Union in 1862. But such daring thinking was beyond the grasp of the plodding, ungracious Halleck. Instead, Halleck took no coherent action, set up a great clamor for reinforcements, and even found occasion to *pick a petty quarrel with Grant and to remove him – fortunately, only temporarily – from his command. In the meantime, the enemy was granted precious time to regroup his armies and to fortify new positions. By mid-March, when Grant was restored to his command of the District of Cairo, the Confederates had assembled a considerable army in Corinth, in northern Mississippi, under the command of the redoubtable Albert Sidney Johnston and his celebrated lieutenant P. G. T. Beauregard. It was against this force that Grant, whose troops were then centered on Savannah, in southern Tennessee, was now belatedly ordered to move. But Johnston moved even Faster: the result would be the bloodiest battle yet fought in the Western Hemisphere.*

RIGHT: Don Carlos Buell, the commander of the Department of the Ohio, whose troops were to join with those of Grant for the assault on the enemy forces in Corinth.

OPPOSITE: Henry W. Halleck, overall, commander of Union armies in the West, was a constant thorn in Grant's side, failing to follow up on Grant's victories and forever picking quarrels with him.

When I reassumed command on the 17th of March I found the army divided, about half being on the east bank of the Tennessee at Savannah, while one division was at Crump's landing on the west bank about four miles higher up, and the remainder at Pittsburg landing, five miles above Crump's. The enemy was in force at Corinth, the junction of the two most important railroads in the Mississippi valley – one connecting Memphis and the Mississippi River with the East, and the other leading south to all the cotton states. Still another railroad connects Corinth with Jackson, in west Tennessee. If we obtained possession of Corinth the enemy would have no railroad for the transportation of armies or supplies until that running east from Vicksburg was reached. It was the great strategic position at the West between the Tennessee and the Mississippi rivers and between Nashville and Vicksburg.

I at once put all the troops at Savannah in motion for Pittsburg landing, knowing that the enemy was fortifying at Corinth and

collecting an army there under Johnston. It was my expectation to march against that army as soon as [General Don Carlos] Buell, who had been ordered to reinforce me with the Army of the Ohio, should arrive; and the west bank of the river was the place to start from. . . .

On the 17th of March the army on the Tennessee River consisted of five divisions, commanded respectively by Generals C. F. Smith, [J. A.] McClernand, L. Wallace, [S.] Hurlbut, and [W. T.] Sherman. General W. H. L. Wallace was temporarily in command of Smith's division, General Smith, as I have said, being confined to his bed. Reinforcements were arriving daily and as they came up they were organized, first into brigades, then into a division, and the command given to General [Benjamin] Prentiss, who had been ordered to report to me. General Buell was on his way from Nashville with 40,000 veterans. . . .

At this time I generally spent the day at Pittsburg and returned to Savannah in the evening. I was intending to remove my headquarters to Pittsburg, but Buell was expected daily and would come in at Savannah. I remained at this point, therefore, a few

days longer than I otherwise should have done, in order to meet him on his arrival. The skirmishing in our front, however, had been so continuous from about the 3d of April that I did not leave Pittsburg each night until an hour when I felt there would be no further danger before the morning. . . .

On the 5th General [William] Nelson, with a division of Buell's army, arrived at Savannah and I ordered him to move up the east bank of the river, to be in a position where he could be ferried over to Crump's landing or Pittsburg as occasion required. I had learned that General Buell himself would be at Savannah the next day, and desired to meet me on his arrival. . . . While I was at breakfast, however, heavy firing was heard in the direction of Pittsburg landing, and I hastened there, sending a hurried note to Buell informing him of the reason why I could not meet him at Savannah.

Up to that time I had felt by no means certain that Crump's landing might not be the point of attack. On reaching the front, however, about eight A.M., I found that the attack on Pittsburg was unmistakable. . . .

Some two of three miles from Pittsburg landing was a log meeting-house called

OPPOSITE: William Tecumseh Sherman. During the siege of Fort Donelson, Sherman, even though Grant's superior in rank, had offered to place himself under Grant's orders. At Shiloh he proved to be, by far, Grant's most effective lieutenant. From this early association was born what was to become one of the greatest partnerships in the history of warfare.

BELOW: Union troops foraging for food. The troops in this scene happened to belong to the division commanded by Benjamin Prentiss, soon to be the hero of the "Hornet's Nest" at Shiloh.

ABOVE: Grant's headquarters at Savannah, Tennessee, the center of his command before he began shifting his forces to Pittsburg Landing, where the Battle of Shiloh would erupt on April 6, 1862.

RIGHT: Union General William Nelson brought the first of Buell's troops (a division) that were to reinforce Grant at Pittsburg Landing.

OPPOSITE: The battlefield of Shiloh. This map is useful primarily as a geographic reference, since it depicts (somewhat self-servingly) only Buell's troop positions.

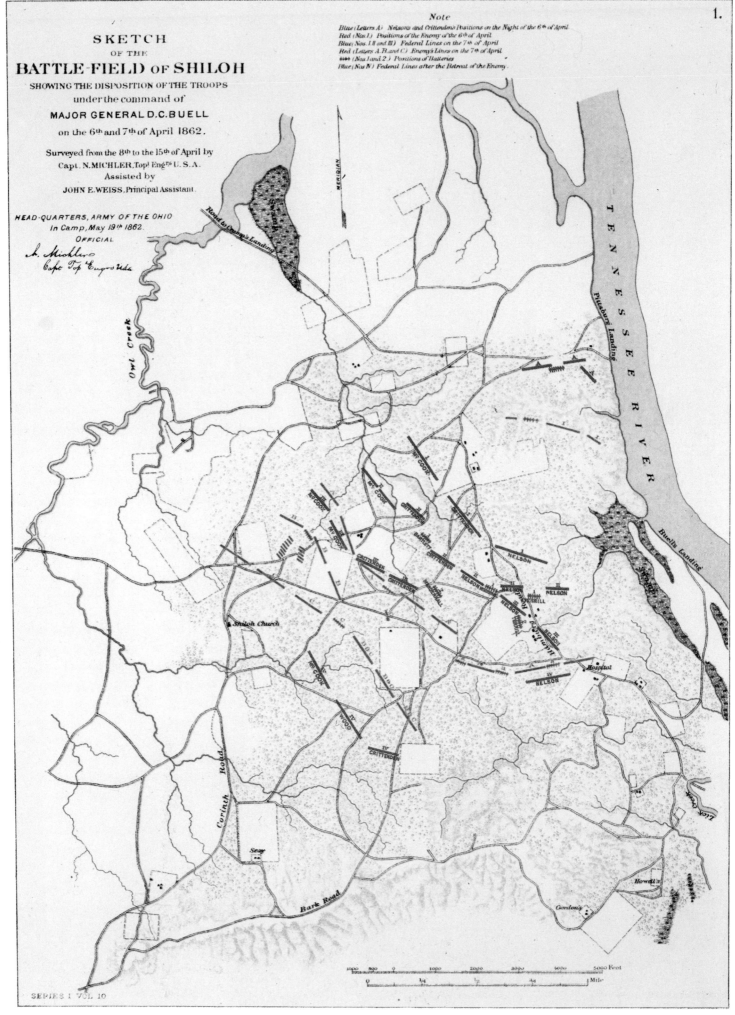

1.

SKETCH
OF THE
BATTLE-FIELD OF SHILOH
SHOWING THE DISPOSITION OF THE TROOPS
under the command of
MAJOR GENERAL D.C. BUELL
on the 6th and 7th of April 1862.

Surveyed from the 8th to the 15th of April by
Capt. N. MICHLER, Topl Engrs U.S.A.
Assisted by
JOHN E. WEISS, Principal Assistant.

HEAD-QUARTERS, ARMY OF THE OHIO
In Camp, May 19th 1862.
OFFICIAL

N. Michler
Capt Topl Engrs Uda.

Note

Blue (Letters A) Nelsons and Crittendens Positions on the Night of the 6th of April.
Red (Nos.1.) Positions of the Enemy of the 6th of April
Blue: Nos. I, II and III) Federal Lines on the 7th of April
Red (Letters A, B, and C) Enemy's Lines on the 7th of April
┼┼┼ (Nos.1 and 2.) Positions of Batteries
Blue (Nos IV) Federal Lines after the Retreat of the Enemy.

TENNESSEE RIVER

Pittsburg Landing

Buells Landing

Owl Creek

Corinth Road

Bark Road

Shiloh Church

Road to Crump's Landing

MERIDIAN

Hospital

Seay's

Gordon's

Howell's

Lick Creek

1000 500 0 1000 2000 3000 5000 Feet
0 1/4 1/2 3/4 1 Mile

Shiloh. It stood on the ridge which divides the waters of Snake and Lick creeks, the former emptying into the Tennessee just north of Pittsburg landing, and the latter south. This point was the key to our position and was held by Sherman. His division was at that time wholly raw, no part of it ever having been in an engagement; but I thought this deficiency was more than made up by the superiority of the commander. McClernand was on Sherman's left, with troops that had been engaged at forts Henry and Donelson and were therefore veterans so far as western troops had become such at that stage of the war. Next to McClernand came Prentiss with a raw division, and on the extreme left, [Col. David] Stuart with one brigade of Sherman's division. Hurlbut was in rear of Prentiss, massed, and in reserve at the time of the onset. The division of General C. F. Smith was on the right, also in reserve. General Smith was still sick in bed at Savannah, but within hearing of our guns. His services would no doubt have been of inestimable value had his health permitted his presence. The command of his division devolved upon Brigadier General W. H. L. Wallace, a most estimable and able officer;

a veteran too, for he had served a year in the Mexican war and had been with his command at Henry and Donelson. Wallace was mortally wounded in the the first day's engagement, and with the change of commanders . . . in the heat of battle the efficiency of his division was much weakened.

The position of our troops made a continuous line from Lick Creek on the left to Owl Creek, a branch of Snake Creek, on the right, facing nearly south and possibly a little west. The water in all these streams was very high at the time and contributed to protect our flanks. The enemy was compelled, therefore, to attack directly in front. This he did with great vigor, inflicting heavy losses on the National side, but suffering much heavier on his own.

The Confederate assaults were made with such a disregard of losses on their own side that our line of tents soon fell into their hands. The ground on which the battle was fought was undulating, heavily timbered with scattered clearings, the woods giving some protection to the troops on both sides. There was also considerable underbrush. A number of attempts were made by the enemy to turn our right flank, where Sher-

ABOVE: The Confederates begin their attack at Shiloh. In the party of officers on the right A. S. Johnston is shown in the center, with P.G.T. Beauregard on his right.

OPPOSITE: The home of Union General W.H.L. Wallace in Ottawa, Illinois, with his portrait and horse. Wallace, who had temporary command of the division of the ailing C.F. Smith, was killed on the first day of Shiloh.

RIGHT: "Bloody Shiloh." The scene here, of the second day of battle, shows a Wisconsin volunteer regiment charging a New Orleans battery.

man was posted, but every effort was repulsed with heavy loss. But the front attack was kept up so vigorously that, to prevent the success of these attempts to get on our flanks, the National troops were compelled, several times, to take position to the rear nearer Pittsburg landing. When the firing ceased at night the National line was all of a mile in rear of the position it had occupied in the morning.

In one of the backward moves, on the 6th, the division commanded by General Prentiss did not fall back with the others. This left his flanks exposed and enabled the enemy to capture him with about 2,200 of his officers and men. General [Adam] Badeau gives four o'clock of the 6th as about the time this capture took place. He may be right as to the time, but my recollection is that the hour was later. General Prentiss himself gave the hour as half-past five. I was with him, as I was with each of the division commanders that day, several times, and my recollection is that the last time I was with him was about half-past four, when his division was standing up firmly and the General was as cool as if expecting victory. But no matter whether it was four or later, the story that he and his command were surprised and captured in their camps is without any foundation whatever. If it had been true, as currently reported at the time and yet believed by thousands of people, that Prentiss and his division had been captured in their beds, there would not have been an all-day struggle, with the loss of thousands killed and wounded on the Confederate side.

BELOW: The "Hornet's Nest," a wooded area in the center of the Union line, became a focal point of resistance to the devastating Confederate surprise attack that struck Grant's army on the morning of April 6, the first day of the Battle of Shiloh.

With the single exception of a few minutes after the capture of Prentiss, a continuous and unbroken line was maintained all day from Snake Creek or its tributaries on the right to Lick Creek or the Tennessee on the left above Pittsburg. There was no hour during the day when there was not heavy firing and generally hard fighting at some

point on the line, but seldom at all points at the same time. . . .

During the whole of Sunday I was continuously engaged in passing from one part of the field to another, giving directions to division commanders. In thus moving along the line, however, I never deemed it important to stay long with Sherman. Although his troops were then under fire for the first time, their commander, by his constant presence with them, inspired a confidence in officers and men that enabled them to render services on that bloody battle-field worthy of the best of veterans. McClernand was next to Sherman, and the hardest fighting was in front of these two divisions. McClernand told me on that day, the 6th, that he profited much by having so able a commander supporting him. A casualty to Sherman that would have taken him from the field that day would have been a sad one for the troops engaged at Shiloh. And how near we came to this! On the 6th Sherman was shot twice, once in the hand, once in the shoulder, the ball cutting his coat and making a slight wound, and a third ball passed through his hat. In addition to this he had several horses shot during the day. . . .

The situation at the close of Sunday was as follows: along the top of the bluff just south of the log-house which stood at Pittsburg landing, Colonel J. D. Webster, of my staff, had arranged twenty of more pieces of artillery facing south or up the river. This line of artillery was on the crest of a hill overlooking a deep ravine opening into the Tennessee. Hurlbut with his division intact was on the right of this artillery, extending west and possibly a little north. McClernand came next in the general line, looking more to the west. His division was complete in its

RIGHT: Daniel Weisiger Adams was among the junior Southern officers who won distinction at Shiloh, where he led the 1st Louisiana Regulars. Adams would subsequently fight at Perryville, Murfreesboro, and Chickamauga.

BELOW: A noteworthy junior officer in the Union army at Shiloh was future President James Abram Garfield, then a brigadier general.

This is a portrait of Shiloh veteran James W. Denver, then a Union brigadier general. Denver, Colorado, is named for him.

organization and ready for any duty. Sherman came next, his right extending to Snake Creek. His command, like the other two, was complete in its organization and ready, like its chief, for any service it might be called upon to render. All three divisions were, as a matter of course, more or less shattered and depleted in number from the terrible battle of the day. The division of W. H. L. Wallace, as much from the disorder arising from changes of division and brigade commanders, under heavy fire, as from any other cause, had lost its organization and did not occupy a place in the line as a division. Prentiss' command was gone as a division, many of its members having been killed, wounded or captured; but it had rendered valiant services before its final dispersal, and had contributed a good share to the defence of Shiloh. . . .

During the night of the 6th the remainder of Nelson's division, Buell's army, crossed the river and were ready to advance in the morning, forming the left wing. Two other divisions [J. L.] Crittenden's and [A. M.]

LEFT: Not yet a Confederate general officer at the time of the Battle of Shiloh was Basil Duke of the "Lexington Rifles." He would eventually become a brigadier general and a noted cavalry leader.

BELOW: An engraving of the Battle of Shiloh, Tennessee, on April 6, 1862.

McCook's, came up the river from Savannah in the transports and were on the west bank early on the 7th. Buell commanded them in person. My command was thus nearly doubled in numbers and efficiency.

During the night rain fell in torrents and our troops were exposed to the storm without shelter. I made my headquarters under a tree a few hundred yards back from the river bank. My ankle was so much swollen from the fall of my horse the Friday night preceding, and the bruise was so painful, that I could get no rest. The drenching rain would have precluded the possibility of sleep without this additional cause. Some time after midnight, growing restive under the storm and the continuous pain, I moved back to

the log-house under the bank. This had been taken as a hospital, and all night wounded men were being brought in, their wounds dressed, a leg or an arm amputated as the case might require, and everything being done to save life or alleviate suffering. The sight was more unendurable than encountering the enemy's fire, and I returned to my tree in the rain.

The advance on the morning of the 7th developed the enemy in the camps occupied by our troops before the battle began, more than a mile back from the most advanced position of the Confederates on the day before. It is known now that they had not yet learned of the arrival of Buell's command. Possibly they fell back so far to get the shel-

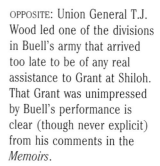

OPPOSITE: Union General T.J. Wood led one of the divisions in Buell's army that arrived too late to be of any real assistance to Grant at Shiloh. That Grant was unimpressed by Buell's performance is clear (though never explicit) from his comments in the *Memoirs*.

BELOW: Alexander McCook led one of the three divisions of Buell's reinforcing army that did arrive in time to play a useful role on the second day of the Battle of Shiloh.

ABOVE: General William Hardee led the corps that mounted the Confederate attack on the Union right wing (Sherman) on the first day of the battle.

ter of our tents during the rain, and also to get away from the shells that were dropped upon them by the gunboats every fifteen minutes during the night.

The position of the Union troops on the morning of the 7th was as follows: General Lew. Wallace on the right; Sherman on his left; then McClernand and then Hurlbut. Nelson, of Buell's army, was on our extreme left, next to the river. Crittenden was next in

line after Nelson and on his right; McCook followed and formed the extreme right of Buell's command. My old command thus formed the right wing, while the troops directly under Buell constituted the left wing of the army. These relative positions were retained during the entire day, or until the enemy was driven from the field.

In a very short time the battle became general all along the line. This day everything was favorable to the Union side. We had now become the attacking party. The enemy was driven back all day, as we had been the day before, until finally he beat a precipitate retreat. The last point held by him was near the road leading from the landing to Corinth, on the left of Sherman and right of McClernand. About three o'clock, being near that point and seeing that the enemy was giving way everywhere else, I gathered up a couple of regiments, or parts of regiments, from troops near by, formed them in line of battle and marched them forward, going in front myself to prevent premature or long-range firing. At this point there was a clearing between us and the enemy favorable for charging, although exposed. I knew the enemy were ready to break and only wanted a little encouragement from us to go quickly and join their friends who had started earlier. After marching to within musket-range I stopped and let the troops pass. The command, *Charge*, was given, and was executed with loud cheers and with a run; when the last of the enemy broke.

* * *

Shiloh was the severest battle fought at the West during the war, and but few in the East equalled it for hard, determined fight-

ing. I saw an open field, in our possession on the second day, over which the Confederates had made repeated charges the day before, so covered with dead that it would have been possible to walk across the clearing, in any direction, stepping on dead bodies, without a foot touching the ground. On our side National and Confederate troops were mingled together in about equal proportions; but on the remainder of the field nearly all were Confederates. On one

ABOVE: Union troops under General Rousseau's command recapture artillery that the Confederates had taken from them earlier in the battle.

LEFT: Kentucky-bred Unionist Lovell H. Rousseau fought with distinction at Shiloh and elsewhere. He stayed in the army after the war and rose to the permanent rank of brigadier general.

part, which had evidently not been ploughed for several years, probably because the land was poor, bushes had grown up, some to the height of eight or ten feet. There was not one of these left standing unpierced by bullets. The smaller ones were all cut down.

Contrary to all my experience up to that time, and to the experience of the army I was then commanding, we were on the defensive. We were without intrenchments or defensive advantages of any sort, and more than half the army engaged the first day was without experience or even drill as soldiers. The officers with them, except the division commanders and possibly two or three of the brigade commanders, were equally inexperienced in war. The result was a Union victory that gave the men who achieved it great confidence in themselves ever after.

The enemy fought bravely, but they had started out to defeat and destroy an army and capture a position. They failed in both, with very heavy loss in killed and wounded, and must have gone back discouraged and convinced that the "Yankee" was not an enemy to be despised. . . .

General Albert Sidney Johnston, who commanded the Confederate forces at the beginning of the battle, was disabled by a wound on the afternoon of the first day. This wound, as I understood afterwards, was not necessarily fatal, or even dangerous. But he was a man who would not abandon what he deemed an important trust in the face of danger and consequently continued in the saddle, commanding, until so exhausted by the loss of blood that he had to be taken from his horse, and soon after died. The

ABOVE: A patriotic engraving shows Grant leading an heroic charge at Shiloh. It does not much matter that the officer in question looks little like Grant, since there was never any such charge.

LEFT: Confederate dead await burial. Shiloh, with combined casualties of around 24,000, was easily the most bloody battle so far fought in the Western Hemisphere.

RIGHT: When Albert Sidney Johnston received a mortal wound at Shiloh many in the South believed that the CSA had lost its greatest general. Grant, however, was never much impressed by the tactics that Johnston used at Shiloh.

news was not long in reaching our side and I suppose was quite an encouragement to the National soldiers.

I had known Johnston slightly in the Mexican war and later as an officer in the regular army. He was a man of high character and ability. His contemporaries at West Point, and officers generally who came to know him personally later and who remained on our side, expected him to prove the most formidable man to meet that the Confederacy would produce.

I once wrote that nothing occurred in his brief command of an army to prove or disprove the high estimate that had been placed upon his military ability; but after studying the orders and dispatches of Johnston I am compelled to materially modify my views of that officer's qualifications as a soldier. My judgment is now that he was vacillating and undecided in his actions. . . .

He knew the National troops were preparing to attack him in his chosen position. But he had evidently become so disturbed at the results of his operations that he resolved to strike out in an offensive campaign which would restore all that was lost, and if successful accomplish still more. . . . The design was a bold one; but . . . in the execution Johnston showed vacillation and indecision. He left Corinth on the 2d of April and was not ready to attack until the 6th. The distance his army had to march was less than twenty miles. [General P. G. T.] Beauregard, his second in command, was opposed to the attack for two reasons: first, he thought, if let alone the National troops would attack the Confederates in their intrenchments; second, we were in ground of our own choosing and would necessarily be intrenched. Johnston not only listened to the objection of Beauregard to an attack, but held a council of war on the subject on the morning of the 5th. On the evening of the same day he was in consultation with some of his generals on the same subject, and still again on the morning of the 6th. During this last consultation, and before a decision had been reached, the battle began by the National troops opening fire on the enemy. This seemed to settle the question as to whether there was to be any battle of Shiloh. It also seems to me to settle the question as to whether there was a surprise.

I do not question the personal courage of General Johnston, or his ability. But he did not win the distinction predicted for him by many of his friends. He did prove that as a general he was over-estimated.

General Beauregard was next in rank to Johnston and succeeded to the command, which he retained to the close of the battle and during the subsequent retreat on Corinth, as well as in the siege of that place. His tactics have been severely criticised by Confederate writers, but I do not believe his fallen chief could have done any better under the circumstances. Some of these critics claim that Shiloh was won when Johnston fell, and that if he had not fallen the army under me would have been annihilated or captured. *Ifs* defeated the Confederates at Shiloh. There is little doubt that we would have been disgracefully beaten *if* all the shells and bullets fired by us had passed harmlessly over the enemy and *if* all of theirs had taken effect. Commanding generals are liable to be killed during engagements; and the fact that when he was shot Johnston was leading a brigade to induce it to make a charge which had been repeatedly ordered, is evidence that there was neither the universal demoralization on our side nor the unbounded confidence on theirs which has been claimed. . . .

The endeavor of the enemy on the first day was simply to hurl their men against ours – first at one point, then at another, some-times at several points at once. This they did with daring and energy, until at night the rebel troops were worn out. Our effort during the same time was to be prepared to resist assaults wherever made. The object of the Confederates on the second day was to get away with as much of their army and material as possible. Ours then was to drive them from our front, and to capture or destroy as great a part as possible of their men and material. We were successful in driving them back, but not so successful in captures as if farther pursuit could have been made. As it was, we captured or recaptured on the second day about as much artillery as we lost on the first; and, leaving out the one great capture of Prentiss, we took more prisoners on Monday than the enemy gained from us on Sunday. . . .

Our loss in the two days' fight was 1,754 killed, 8,408 wounded and 2,885 missing. Of these, 2,103 were in the Army of the Ohio. Beauregard reported a total loss of 10,699, of whom 1,728 were killed, 8,012 wounded and 957 missing. This estimate must be incorrect. We buried, by actual count, more of the

BELOW: William Bate was still serving as an enlisted man in a Tennessee regiment when he was wounded at Shiloh. By the war's end he would be a Confederate major general.

RIGHT: Army Picture Gallery (undated) from the Mathew Brady Collection.

BELOW: John C. Breckinridge commanded the Confederate corps that would cover the Southern retreat at the end of the second day's fighting at the Battle of Shiloh.

enemy's dead in front of the divisions of McClernand and Sherman alone than here reported, and 4,000 was the estimate of the burial parties for the whole field. Beauregard reports the Confederate force on the 6th at over 40,000, and their total loss during the two days at 10,699; and at the same time declares that he could put only 20,000 men in battle on the morning of the 7th. . . .

Up to the battle of Shiloh I, as well as thousands of other citizens, believed that the rebellion against the Government would collapse suddenly and soon, if a decisive victory could be gained over any of its armies. Donelson and Henry were such victories. . . . But when Confederate armies were collected which not only attempted to hold a line farther south, from Memphis to Chattanooga, Knoxville and on to the Atlantic, but assumed the offensive and made such a gallant effort to regain what had been lost, then, indeed, I gave up all idea of saving the Union except by complete conquest. . . .

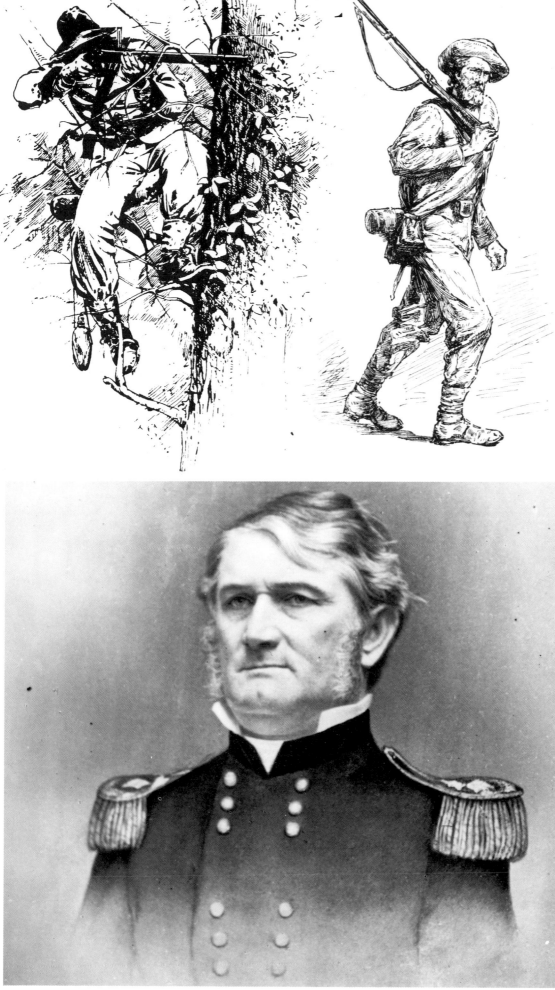

FAR LEFT: From his vantage point on the limb of a tree a Confederate sharpshooter takes aim at an enemy.

LEFT: A typically-equipped Confederate infantryman.

LEFT: Leonidas Polk, who led one of the four Confederate corps that fought at Shiloh, was an Episcopalian bishop. Though a West Point graduate, he had never served in the field before Jefferson Davis gave him a major generalcy in 1861. In practice, he proved to be a mediocre commander.

81

Chapter III

Vicksburg

Shiloh was unquestionably a Union victory, but because Grant's exhausted forces failed to pursue the retreating enemy aggressively enough Shiloh remained an unexploited victory. Those among Grant's equals and superiors who were inclined to be critical of him (Henry Halleck among them) harped on this and on the fact that Grant had allowed himself to be surprised by the enemy. But Abraham Lincoln had been impressed by how hard – and ultimately successfully – Grant had fought, and could not help contrasting this to the ponderous, excessively cautious conduct of the campaign that Union General George McClellan was then mounting on the Virginia peninsula. "I can't spare this man," said Lincoln of Grant. "He fights." And certainly the fact that McClellan's Peninsular Campaign soon turned into a debacle (to be followed by a whole string of Eastern disasters at Second Manassas, Fredericksburg, and Chancellorsville) did nothing to change Lincoln's opinion of this rising star in his Western armies.

Lincoln's support no doubt helped Grant, but it did not altogether save him from his critics. After Shiloh, Halleck assumed direct field command of the Western armies, in effect kicking Grant upstairs by giving him a more-or-less ceremonial posting as second-in-command. By April 29, 1862, Halleck was ready to move on Corinth. Incredibly, it took him until May 25 to get there, and then, instead of attacking the city, he besieged it. Of this period

BELOW: President Lincoln with his cabinet. Though Halleck and some other senior Union army officers were inclined to belittle Grant's victory at Shiloh, the President was impressed, a fact that did much for Grant's career.

ABOVE: The Battle of Corinth, fought on October 3-4, 1862. Grant's successful defense of Corinth was a considerable strategic victory, but Grant was nevertheless critical of his principal commander in the field, William Rosecrans, for not pursuing the fleeing enemy more aggressively.

LEFT: An encampment of the Union army outside Corinth during Halleck's siege of the city in May 1862. Grant was disgusted by Halleck's lack of enterprise in choosing to besiege rather than attack.

OPPOSITE RIGHT: David Glasgow Farragut, greatest Federal naval commander of the Civil War, played a crucial role in opening the Mississippi to Union control when, in April 1862, he daringly ran past powerful Confederate river forts to capture the key port city of New Orleans.

OPPOSITE LEFT: Earl Van Dorn was one of the more luckless Confederate generals. Though he had some minor successes as a raider, he lost both of the major battles – Pea Ridge and Corinth – in which he was in command. He was killed by a jealous husband in 1863.

BELOW: Union batteries repel the attacking Confederate forces of Earl Van Dorn at Corinth on October 4, 1862.

Grant wrote: "For myself I was little more than an observer. . . . My position was so embarrassing in fact that I made several applications during the siege to be relieved."

P. G. T. Beauregard, who commanded the Confederate forces in Corinth, could see no point in allowing himself to be starved into submission, and on the night of May 29-30 he evacuated the city. Halleck did not pursue him. "The possession of Corinth by the National troops was of strategic importance," wrote Grant, "but the victory was barren in every other particular." Nevertheless, on July 11 a grateful Washington recalled Halleck to the capital to make him general-in-chief of all the Union armies. His departure ended Grant's purgatory, leaving him de facto command of District of Tennessee (he would be formally named to that post only in October).

The Union armies that Halleck had concentrated around Corinth began to disperse soon after his departure for Washington, and Confederate forces accordingly began to gather for the reconquest of Corinth and southern Tennessee. The assault on Corinth, led by Confederate General Earl Van Dorn, began on October 3. A fierce two-day battle followed, but Grant's troops eventually routed the attackers. "The

battle," said Grant, "relieved me of any further anxiety for the safety of the territory within my jurisdiction, and soon after receiving reinforcements I suggested to the general-in-chief a forward movement against Vicksburg." Halleck approved the proposal.

The Confederate fortress-city of Vicksburg, Mississippi, was indeed now the key to Union victory in the West – and perhaps in the East as well. Union grand strategy was heavily predicated on gaining control of the entire Mississippi River, thus bisecting the greater South along a north-south axis. If this could be done, the Union could then concentrate on trying to bisect the Old South along an east-west axis, most likely via a drive east through Georgia to the sea. By the autumn of 1862 eventual Federal conquest of the Mississippi had become a real possibility. Ever since April, when U.S. Admiral David Farragut had captured New Orleans, Union land and naval forces along the river had gradually extended the area under their control until Confederate holdings were effectively reduced to that (considerable) stretch of the left bank that lay between Port Hudson, Louisiana, and Vicksburg. Yet Vicksburg would prove to be a singularly tough nut to crack, as Grant's Memoirs make all too clear.

Vicksburg was important to the enemy because it occupied the first high ground coming close to the river below Memphis. From there a railroad runs east, connecting with other roads leading to all points of the Southern States. A railroad also starts from the opposite side of the river, extending west as far as Shreveport, Louisiana. Vicksburg was the only channel, at the time of the events of which this chapter treats, connecting the parts of the Confederacy divided by the Mississippi. So long as it was held by the enemy, the free navigation of the river was prevented. Hence its importance. Points on the river between Vicksburg and Port Hudson were held as dependencies; but their fall was sure to follow the capture of the former place.

The campaign against Vicksburg commenced on the 2d of November as indicated in a dispatch to the general-in-chief in the following words: "I have commenced a movement on Grand Junction, with three divisions from Corinth and two from Bolivar. Will leave here [Jackson, Tennessee] to-morrow, and take command in person. If found practicable, I will go to Holly Springs, and, may be, Grenada, completing railroad and telegraph as I go."

At this time my command was holding the Mobile and Ohio railroad from about twenty-five miles south of Corinth, north to Columbus, Kentucky; the Mississippi Central from Bolivar north to its junction with the Mobile

and Ohio; the Memphis and Charleston from Corinth east to Bear Creek, and the Mississippi River from Cairo to Memphis. My entire command was no more than was necessary to hold these lines, and hardly that if kept on the defensive. By moving against the enemy and into his unsubdued, or not yet captured, territory, driving their army before us, these lines would nearly hold themselves; thus affording a large force for field operations. My moving force at that time was about 30,000 men, and I estimated the enemy confronting me, under [General John C.] Pemberton, at about the same number. General [James] McPherson commanded my left wing and General C. S. Hamilton the centre, while [General William T.] Sherman was at Memphis with the right

wing. Pemberton was fortified at the Talla-hatchie, but occupied Holly Springs and Grand Junction on the Mississippi Central railroad. On the 8th we occupied Grand Junction and La Grange, throwing a considerable force seven or eight miles south, along the line of the railroad. The road from Bolivar forward was repaired and put in running order as the troops advanced. . . .

Grant had hoped that the lure of frustrating the deliberate Union advance on Vicksburg might induce Pemberton to move his forces far enough north of the city so that Sherman could get in behind them and cut them off. But it was not to be: by mid-December Pemberton had safely withdrawn behind Vicksburg's formidable defenses

LEFT: The most famous of the very powerful defenses that made Vicksburg impregnable from any attack from the west was "Whistling Dick," a big 18-pounder that was so-named because the rifling in its barrel imparted a peculiar spin to cannonballs, causing them to emit an eerie high-pitched noise when in flight. "Whistling Dick" would send the Union gunboat *Cincinnati* to the bottom while Grant was besieging Vicksburg in 1863.

before Sherman could engage him. Grant suffered another, smaller vexation when John A. McClernand, one of his "political generals," persuaded his political sponsors in Washington to let him undertake a brief detached (and, as it happened, successful) campaign against Confederate Fort Hindman on the Arkansas River, thus weakening Grant's army at just the time it was assembling before Vicksburg. But by the end of January 1863 Grant had gotten Halleck to order the insubordinate McClernand to place himself completely under Grant's authority, and the real work on the Vicksburg campaign could begin. From his new headquarters at Young's Point, Louisiana, a little upriver from Vicksburg, Grant pondered the difficulties that lay before him.

ABOVE RIGHT: In command of the big Vicksburg garrison was Confederate General John C. Pemberton, yet another of Grant's former comrades-in-arms from pre-Civil War days. Grant's personal knowledge of Pemberton's character and abilities would serve Grant well in the coming campaign.

RIGHT: Union General John A. McClernand was easily the most troublesome of Grant's lieutenants in 1862-63. A "political general," he was ambitious, often insubordinate, and not overly effective in the field. Grant's dislike of him is made all too clear in the *Memoirs*.

It was in January the troops took their position opposite Vicksburg. The water was very high and the rains were incessant. There seemed no possibility of a land movement before the end of March or later, and it would not do to lie idle all this time. The effect would be demoralizing to the troops and injurious to their health. Friends in the North would have grown more and more discouraged, and enemies in the same section more and more insolent in their gibes and denunciation of the cause and those engaged in it. . . .

Vicksburg, as stated before, is on the first high land coming to the river's edge, below that on which Memphis stands. The bluff, or high land, follows the left bank of the Yazoo for some distance and continues in a southerly direction to the Mississippi River, thence it runs along the Mississippi to Warrenton, six miles below. The Yazoo River leaves the high land a short distance below Haines' Bluff and empties into the Mississippi nine miles above Vicksburg. Vicksburg is built on this high land where the Mississippi washes the base of the hill. Haines' Bluff, eleven miles from Vicksburg, on the

Yazoo River, was strongly fortified. The whole distance from there to Vicksburg and thence to Warrenton was also intrenched, with batteries at suitable distances and rifle-pits connecting them.

From Young's Point the Mississippi turns in a north-easterly direction to a point just above the city, when it again turns and runs south-westerly, leaving vessels, which might attempt to run the blockade, exposed to the fire of batteries six miles below the city before they were in range of the upper batteries. Since then the river has made a cut-off, leaving what was the peninsula in front of the city, an island. North of the Yazoo was all a marsh, heavily timbered, cut up with bayous, and much overflowed. A front attack was therefore impossible, and was never contemplated; certainly not by me. The problem then became, how to secure a landing on high ground east of the Mississippi without an apparent retreat. Then commenced a series of experiments to consume time, and to divert the attention of the enemy, of my troops and of the public generally. I, myself, never felt great confidence that any of the experiments resorted

BELOW: A view of Vicksburg from the Mississippi River. The bluff rising behind the riverfront was dotted with batteries, making attack from the river almost unthinkable. The land to the north of the city was swampy and nearly impassable, and that to the south not much better and heavily defended. Thus the only good military avenue to Vicksburg was from the east, *ie.*, from *inside* territory held by the enemy.

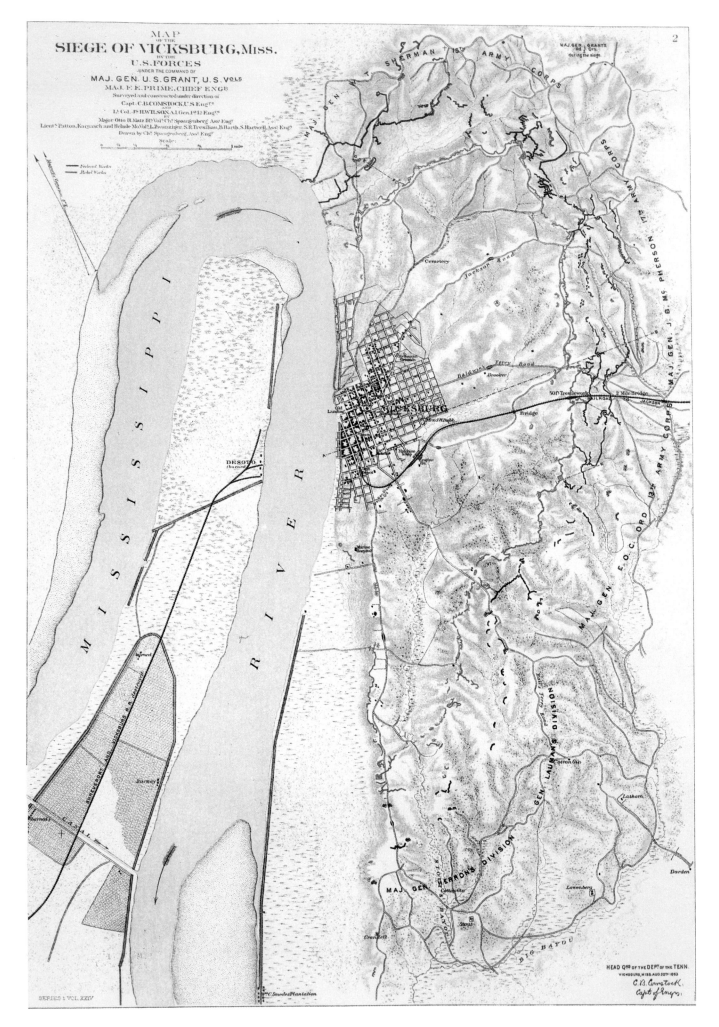

MAP
OF THE
SIEGE OF VICKSBURG, Miss.
BY THE
U.S. FORCES
UNDER THE COMMAND OF
MAJ. GEN. U.S. GRANT, U.S. VOLS
MAJ. F. E. PRIME, CHIEF ENGR

to would prove successful. Nevertheless I was always prepared to take advantage of them in case they did.

In 1862 General Thomas Williams had come up from New Orleans and cut a ditch ten or twelve feet wide and about as deep, straight across from Young's Point to the river below. The distance across was a little over a mile. It was Williams' expectation that when the river rose it would cut a navigable channel through; but the canal started in an eddy from both ends, and, of course, it only filled up with water on the rise without doing any execution in the way of cutting. Mr. Lincoln had navigated the Mississippi in his younger days and understood well its tendency to change its channel, in places, from time to time. He set much store accordingly by this canal. General McClernand had been, therefore, directed before I went to Young's Point to push the work of widening and deepening this canal. After my arrival the work was diligently pushed with about 4,000 men – as many as could be used to advantage – until interrupted by a sudden rise in the river that broke a dam at the upper end, which had been put there to keep the water out until the excavation was completed. This was on the 8th of March.

Even if the canal had proven a success, so far as to be navigable for steamers, it could not have been of much advantage to us. It runs in a direction almost perpendicular to the line of bluffs on the opposite side, or east bank, of the river. As soon as the enemy discovered what we were doing he established a battery commanding the canal throughout its length. This battery soon drove out our dredges, two in number, which were doing the work of thousands of men. Had the canal been completed it might have proven of some use in running transports through, under the cover of night, to use below; but they would yet have to run batteries, though for a much shorter distance.

While this work was progressing we were busy in other directions, trying to find an available landing on high ground on the east bank of the river, or to make water-ways to get below the city, avoiding the batteries. . . .

Another expedient that was tried that winter involved trying to open a canal to Lake Providence, from which Federal gunboats might, by following a somewhat tortuous route through rivers and bayous, re-enter the Mississippi south of Vicksburg. It was eventually abandoned in favor of two efforts to cut across the Yazoo delta, first via

OPPOSITE: A Union army map showing Vicksburg and its environs at the time of the siege. Virtually the whole outer ring of Confederate defenses was sited high on commanding bluffs.

BELOW: A view from Vicksburg looking northwest toward the hairpin bend of the river.

ABOVE: Central Vicksburg. The town was fairly large and prosperous, but it still had something of a frontier look about it in 1862.

OPPOSITE TOP: Union General Francis Blair (center) with his staff. One of Sherman's better division commanders, he would have the misfortune to be temporarily attached to McClernand's do-nothing corps in the critical Battle of Champion's Hill.

OPPOSITE BOTTOM: General G.W. Morgan led a division in the failed Union effort to take the Chickasaw Bluffs on the Yazoo, north of Vicksburg, in December 1862. Such early setbacks convinced Grant that there could be no easy solution to the problem of how to capture Vicksburg.

the so-called Yazoo Pass Route and then via the Steel's Bayou Route. Both projects failed. By March, when the fairweather campaigning season was at hand, it seemed clear that the only way Admiral David Dixon Porter's riverine squadron would ever get south of Vicksburg would be sailing directly under the guns of the city's massive batteries. The risks were appalling, but they had to be faced, for Grant had concluded that his only hope now lay in ferrying his army across the river and attacking Vicksburg from the east, from inside *enemy territory.*

I had had in contemplation the whole winter the movement by land to a point below Vicksburg from which to operate, subject only to the possible but not expected success of some one of the expedients resorted to for the purpose of giving us a different base. This could not be undertaken until the waters receded. I did not therefore communicate this plan, even to an officer of my staff, until it was necessary to make preparations for the start. My recollection is that

Admiral Porter was the first one to whom I mentioned it. The co-operation of the navy was absolutely essential to the success (even to the contemplation) of such an enterprise. I had no more authority to command Porter than he had to command me. It was necessary to have part of his fleet below Vicksburg if the troops went there. Steamers to use as ferries were also essential. The navy was the only escort and protection for these steamers, all of which in getting below had to run about fourteen miles of batteries. Porter fell into the plan at once, and suggested that he had better superintend the preparation of the steamers selected to run the batteries, as sailors would probably understand the work better than soldiers. I was glad to accept his proposition, not only because I admitted his argument, but because it would enable me to keep from the enemy a little longer our designs. Porter's fleet was on the east side of the river above the mouth of the Yazoo, entirely concealed from the enemy by the dense forests that intervened. Even spies could not get near him, on account of the undergrowth and overflowed lands. Suspicions of some

mysterious movements were aroused. Our river guards discovered one day a small skiff moving quietly and mysteriously up the river near the east shore, from the direction of Vicksburg, towards the fleet. On overhauling the boat they found a small white flag, not much larger than a handkerchief, set up in the stern, no doubt intended as a flag of truce in case of discovery. The boat, crew and passengers were brought ashore to me. The chief personage aboard proved to be Jacob Thompson, Secretary of the Interior under the administration of President Buchanan. After a pleasant conversation of half an hour or more I allowed the boat and crew, passengers and all, to return to Vicksburg, without creating a suspicion that there was a doubt in my mind as to the good faith of Mr. Thompson and his flag.

Admiral Porter proceeded with the preparation of the steamers for their hazardous passage of the enemy's batteries. The great essential was to protect the boilers from the enemy's shot, and to conceal the fires under the boilers from view. This he accomplished by loading the steamers, between the guards and boilers on the boiler deck up to the deck

ABOVE: Flag Officer David Dixon Porter's Mississippi Squadron makes its daring run past the big guns of the Vicksburg batteries on the night of April 16, 1863. The ships were under heavy fire for over two hours, but only one, a transport, was lost.

RIGHT: David Dixon Porter. For his contribution to the success of Grant's Vicksburg Campaign, Porter was rewarded by a promotion that jumped him two grades in permanent rank to a rear admiralcy.

above, with bales of hay and cotton, and the deck in front of the boilers in the same way, adding sacks of grain. The hay and grain would be wanted below, and could not be transported in sufficient quantity by the muddy roads over which we expected to march.

Before this I had been collecting, from St. Louis and Chicago, yawls and barges to be used as ferries when we got below. By the 16th of April Porter was ready to start on his perilous trip. The advance, flagship *Benton*, Porter commanding, started at ten o'clock at night, followed at intervals of a few minutes by the *Lafayette* with a captured steamer, the *Price*, lashed to her side, the *Louisville*, *Mound City, Pittsburgh* and *Carondelet* – all of these being naval vessels. Next came the transports – *Forest Queen, Silver Wave* and *Henry Clay*, each towing barges loaded with coal to be used as fuel by the naval and transport steamers when below the batteries. The gunboat *Tuscumbia* brought up the rear. Soon after the start a battery between Vicksburg and Warrenton opened fire across the intervening peninsula, followed by the upper batteries, and then by batteries all along the line. The gunboats ran up close under the bluffs, delivering their fire in return at short distances, probably without much effect. They were under fire for more than two hours and every vessel was struck many times, but with little damage to the gunboats. The transports did not fare so well. The *Henry Clay* was disabled and deserted by her crew. Soon after a shell burst in the cotton packed about the boilers, set the vessel on fire and burned her to the water's edge. The burning mass, however, floated down to Carthage before grounding, as did also one of the barges in tow.

The enemy were evidently expecting our fleet, for they were ready to light up the river by means of bonfires on the east side and by firing houses on the point of land opposite the city on the Louisiana side. The sight was magnificent, but terrible. I witnessed it from the deck of a river transport, run out into the middle of the river and as low down as it was prudent to go. My mind was much relieved when I learned that no one on the transports had been killed and but few, if any, wounded. During the running of the batteries men were stationed in the holds of the transports to partially stop with cotton shot-holes that might be made in the hulls. All damage was afterwards soon repaired under the direction of Admiral Porter. . . .

Once Porter's squadron was below Vicksburg, Grant set his army in motion. While Sherman made a demonstration north of Vicksburg, McClernand's and McPherson's corps moved south along the Louisiana shore, sometimes marching and sometimes ferried in Porter's transports, until they reached a point a little south of the Confederate stronghold Grand Gulf.

When the troops debarked, the evening of the 29th, it was expected that we would have to go to Rodney, about nine miles below, to find a landing; but that night a colored man came in who informed me that a good landing would be found at Bruinsburg, a few miles above Rodney, from which point there was a good road leading to Port Gibson some twelve miles in the interior. The information was found correct, and our landing was effected without opposition.

Sherman had not left his position above Vicksburg yet. On the morning of the 27th I ordered him to create a diversion by moving his corps up the Yazoo and threatening an attack on Haines' Bluff.

My object was to compel Pemberton to keep as much force about Vicksburg as I could, until I could secure a good footing on high land east of the river. The move was eminently successful and, as we afterwards learned, created great confusion about Vicksburg and doubts about our real design. Sherman moved the day of our attack on Grand Gulf, the 29th, with ten regiments of his command and eight gunboats which Porter had left above Vicksburg.

He debarked his troops and apparently

BELOW: River steamers unload supplies at Young's Point, Grant's headquarters above Vicksburg, in March 1863.

ABOVE: The Confederates had no monopoly on artillery in the Vicksburg Campaign. Here, a Union battery composed of mixed siege and field guns.

OPPOSITE TOP: Some of the larger houses in Vicksburg. The house in the foreground would be taken over by the U.S. Army Signal Corps after the city's capture.

OPPOSITE BOTTOM: General John A. Logan (fifth from right) was an excellent divisional commander in McPherson's corps. He was given a corps command of his own at the end of the Vicksburg Campaign.

made every preparation to attack the enemy while the navy bombarded the main forts at Haines' Bluff. This move was made without a single casualty in either branch of the service. On the first of May Sherman received orders from me (sent from Hard Times the evening of the 29th of April) to withdraw from the front of Haines' Bluff and follow McPherson with two divisions as fast as he could.

I had established a depot of supplies at Perkins' plantation. Now that all our gunboats were below Grand Gulf it was possible that the enemy might fit out boats in the Big Black with improvised armament and attempt to destroy these supplies. McPherson was at Hard Times with a portion of his corps, and the depot was protected by a part of his command. The night of the 29th I directed him to arm one of the transports with artillery and send it up to Perkins' plantation as a guard; and also to have the siege guns we had brought along moved there and put in position.

The embarkation below Grand Gulf took place at De Shroon's, Louisiana, six miles above Bruinsburg, Mississippi. Early on the morning of 30th of April McClernand's corps

and one division of McPherson's corps were speedily landed.

When this was effected I felt a degree of relief scarcely ever equalled since. Vicksburg was not yet taken it is true, nor were its defenders demoralized by any of our previous moves. I was now in the enemy's country, with a vast river and the stronghold of Vicksburg between me and my base of supplies. But I was on dry ground on the same side of the river with the enemy. All the campaigns, labors, hardships and exposures from the month of December previous to this time that had been made and endured, were for . . . this one object.

I had with me the 13th corps, General McClernand commanding, and two brigades of [John A.] Logan's division of the 17th corps, General McPherson commanding – in all not more than twenty thousand men to commence the campaign with. These were soon reinforced by the remaining brigade of Logan's division and [M.M.] Crocker's division of the 17th corps. On the 7th of May I was further reinforced by Sherman with two divisions of his, the 15th corps. My total force was then about thirty-three thousand men.

OPPOSITE TOP: A U.S. Army map of the theater of Grant's brilliant Vicksburg Campaign. In 18 days after crossing the Mississippi he would march 200 miles, win every battle, and divide and outwit Rebel forces larger than his own – all behind enemy lines.

OPPOSITE BOTTOM: John Logan as a major general. After the war he would represent the state of Illinois in the U.S. House of Representatives and the Senate for two decades.

BELOW: A famous Mathew Brady photograph of Ulysses S. Grant in the field.

The enemy occupied Grand Gulf, Haines' Bluff and Jackson with a force of nearly sixty thousand men. Jackson is fifty miles east of Vicksburg and is connected with it by a railroad. My first problem was to capture Grand Gulf to use as a base. . . .

The key to the taking of Grand Gulf was the capture of strategically-located Port Gibson, 12 miles inland. Both the Grand Gulf garrison and Grant's troops raced toward Port Gibson, clashed there, and the Union prevailed. During the night of May 2 the Confederates evacuated Grand Gulf.

When I reached Grand Gulf May 3rd I had not been with my baggage since the 27th of April and consequently had had no change of underclothing, no meal except such as I could pick up sometimes at other headquarters, and no tent to cover me. The first thing I did was to get a bath, borrow some fresh underclothing from one of the naval officers and get a good meal on the flagship. Then I wrote letters to the general-in-chief informing him of our present position, dispatches to be telegraphed from Cairo, orders to General [J. C.] Sullivan commanding above Vicksburg, and gave orders to all my corps commanders. About twelve o'clock at night I was through my work and

started for Hankinson's ferry, arriving there before daylight. While at Grand Gulf I heard from [Nathaniel] Banks, who was on the Red River, and who said that he could not be at Port Hudson before the 10th of May and then with only 15,000 men. Up to this time my intention had been to secure Grand Gulf, as a base of supplies, detach McClernand's corps to Banks and co-operate with him in the reduction of Port Hudson.

The news from Banks forced upon me a different plan of campaign from the one intended. To wait for his co-operation would have detained me at least a month. The reinforcements would not have reached ten thousand men after deducting casualties and necessary river guards at all high points close to the river for over three hundred miles. The enemy would have strengthened his position and been reinforced by more men than Banks could have brought. I therefore determined to move independently of Banks, cut loose from my base, destroy the rebel force in rear of Vicksburg and invest or capture the city.

Grand Gulf was accordingly given up as a base and the authorities at Washington were notified. I knew well that Halleck's caution would lead him to disapprove of this course; but it was the only one that gave any chance of success. The time it would take to communicate with Washington and get a reply would be so great that I could not be interfered with until it was demonstrated whether my plan was practicable. Even Sherman, who afterwards ignored bases of supplies other than what were afforded by the country while marching through four States of the Confederacy with an army more than twice as large as mine at this time, wrote me from Hankinson's ferry, advising me of the impossibility of supplying our army over a single road. He urged me to "stop all troops till your army is partially supplied with wagons, and then act as quick as possible; for this road will be jammed, as sure as life." To this I replied: "I do not calculate upon the possibility of supplying the army with full rations from Grand Gulf. I know it will be impossible without constructing additional roads. What I do expect is to get up what rations of hard bread, coffee and salt we can, and make the country furnish the balance." . . .

Up to this point our movements had been made without serious opposition. My line was now nearly parallel with the Jackson and Vicksburg railroad and about seven

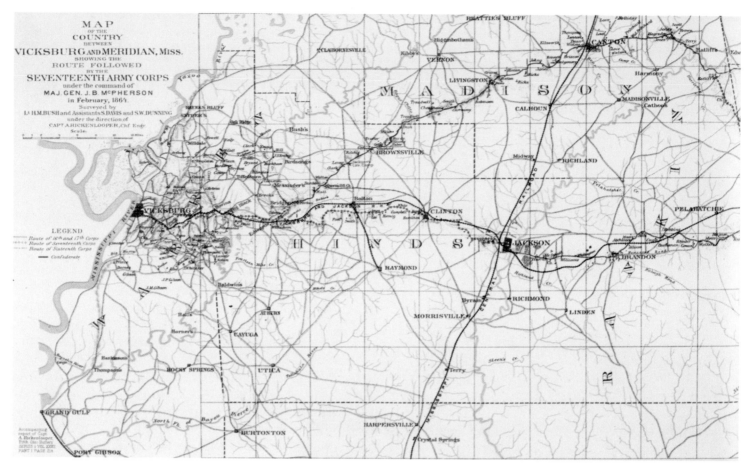

MAP
OF THE
COUNTRY
BETWEEN
VICKSBURG AND MERIDIAN, MISS.
SHOWING THE
ROUTE FOLLOWED
BY THE
SEVENTEENTH ARMY CORPS
under the command of
MAJ. GEN. J. B. McPHERSON
in February, 1864.
Surveyed by
Lt. H.M.BUSH and Assistants S.DAVIS and S.W.DUNNING
under the direction of
CAPT. A.HICKENLOOPER, Chf. Engr.
Scale.

LEGEND
Route of 16th and 17th Corps
Route of Seventeenth Corps
Route of Sixteenth Corps
Confederate

miles south of it. The right was at Raymond eighteen miles from Jackson, McPherson commanding; Sherman was in the centre on Fourteen Mile Creek, his advance thrown across; McClernand to the left, also on Fourteen Mile Creek, advance across, and his pickets within two miles of Edward's station, where the enemy had concentrated a considerable force and where they undoubtedly expected us to attack. McClernand's left was on the Big Black. In all our moves, up to this time, the left had hugged the Big Black closely, and all the ferries had been guarded to prevent the enemy throwing a force on our rear.

McPherson encountered the enemy, five thousand strong with two batteries under General [J.] Gregg, about two miles out of Raymond. This was about two P.M. Logan was in advance with one of his brigades. He deployed and moved up to engage the enemy. McPherson ordered the road in rear to be cleared of wagons, and the balance of Logan's division, and Crocker's, which was still farther in rear, to come forward with all dispatch. The order was obeyed with alacrity. Logan got his division in position for assault before Crocker could get up, and attacked with vigor, carrying the enemy's position easily, sending Gregg flying from the field not to appear against our front

again until we met at Jackson.

In this battle McPherson lost 66 killed, 339 wounded, and 37 missing – nearly or not quite all from Logan's division. The enemy's loss was 100 killed, 305 wounded, besides 415 taken prisoners. . . .

When the news reached me of McPherson's victory at Raymond about sundown my position was with Sherman. I decided at once to turn the whole column towards Jackson and capture that place without delay.

Pemberton was now on my left, with, as I supposed, about 18,000 men; in fact, as I learned afterwards, with nearly 50,000. A force was also collecting on my right, at Jackson, the point where all the railroads communicating with Vicksburg connect. All the enemy's supplies of men and stores would come by that point. As I hoped in the end to besiege Vicksburg, I must first destroy all possibility of aid. I therefore determined to move swiftly towards Jackson, destroy or drive any force in that direction and then turn upon Pemberton. But by moving against Jackson, I uncovered my own communication. So I finally decided to have none – to cut loose altogether from my base and move my whole force eastward. I then had no fears for my communications, and if I moved quickly enough could turn upon Pemberton before he could attack me in the rear. . . .

General Joseph E. Johnston arrived at Jackson in the night of the 13th from Tennessee, and immediately assumed command of all the Confederate troops in Mississippi. I knew he was expecting reinforcements from the south and east. . . .

I notified General Halleck that I should attack the State capital on the 14th. A courier carried the dispatch to Grand Gulf through an unprotected country.

Sherman and McPherson communicated with each other during the night and arranged to reach Jackson at about the same hour. It rained in torrents during the night of the 13th and the fore part of the day of the 14th. The roads were intolerable, and in some places on Sherman's line, where the land was low, they were covered more than a foot deep with water. But the troops never murmured. By nine o'clock Crocker, of McPherson's corps, who was now in advance, came upon the enemy's pickets and speedily drove them in upon the main body. They were outside of the intrenchments in a strong position, and proved to be

the troops that had been driven out of Raymond. Johnston had been reinforced during the night by Georgia and South Carolina regiments, so that his force amounted to eleven thousand men, and he was expecting still more.

Sherman also came upon the rebel pickets some distance out from the town, but speedily drove them in. He was now on the south and south-west of Jackson confronting the Confederates behind their breastworks, while McPherson's right was nearly two miles north, occupying a line running north and south across the Vicksburg railroad. Artillery was brought up and reconnoissances made preparatory to an assault. McPherson brought up Logan's division while he deployed Crocker's for the assault. Sherman made similar dispositions on the right. By eleven A.M. both were ready to attack. . . .

I slept that night in the room that Johnston occupied the night before. . . .

On the night of the 13th Johnston had sent the following dispatch to Pemberton at Edward's station: "I have lately arrived, and learn that Major-General Sherman is between us with four divisions at Clinton. It is important to establish communication, that you may be reinforced. If practicable, come up in his rear at once. To beat such a detachment would be of immense value. All the troops you can quickly assemble should be brought. Time is all-important." This dispatch was sent in triplicate, by different messengers. One of the messengers happened to be a loyal man who had been expelled from Memphis some months before by Hurlbut for uttering disloyal and threatening sentiments. There was a good deal of parade about his expulsion, ostensibly as a warning to those who entertained the sentiments he expressed; but Hurlbut and the expelled man understood each other. He delivered his copy of Johnston's dispatch to McPherson who forwarded it to me.

ABOVE: Sherman with some of the generals who accompanied him on the historic Georgia and Carolinas campaigns of 1864-65. Long before anyone else, Grant recognized in his premier lieutenant the spark of true military genius.

OPPOSITE TOP: Grant's foes in the Vicksburg Campaign were not to be taken lightly. The Confederacy could offer few generals more talented than Joseph E. Johnston.

OPPOSITE BOTTOM: One of the many minor players in the Vicksburg drama, W.T. Clark was adjutant general on James McPherson's staff. He later became a hated carpetbagger.

101

RIGHT: General William T.
Sherman. This great general
is as controversial today as
he was in his own time. His
admirers have always hailed
him as a genius who had an
uncanny grasp of how warfare
was changing in the modern
era. His critics have always
thought him an unchivalrous
and callous brute. Grant's
admiration for Sherman as a
commander was unqualified,
surpassed only by Sherman's
admiration for Grant.

Receiving this dispatch on the 14th I ordered McPherson to move promptly in the morning back to Bolton, the nearest point where Johnston could reach the road. Bolton is about twenty miles west of Jackson. I also informed McClernand of the capture of Jackson and sent him the following order: "It is evidently the design of the enemy to get north of us and cross the Big Black, and beat us into Vicksburg. We must not allow them to do this. Turn all your forces towards Bolton station, and make all dispatch in getting there. Move troops by the most direct road from wherever they may be on the receipt of this order." . . .

Johnston stopped on the Canton road only six miles north of Jackson, the night of the 14th. He sent from there to Pemberton dispatches announcing the loss of Jackson, and the following order:

"As soon as the reinforcements are all up, they must be united to the rest of the army. I am anxious to see a force assembled that may be able to inflict a heavy blow upon the enemy. Can Grant supply himself from the Mississippi? Can you not cut him off from it, and above all, should he be compelled to fall back for want of supplies, beat him."

The concentration of my troops was easy, considering the character of the country. McPherson moved along the road parallel with and near the railroad. McClernand's command was, one division ([Alvin] Hovey's) on the road McPherson had to take, but with a start of four miles. One ([Peter] Osterhaus) was at Raymond, on a converging road that intersected the other near Champion's Hill' one ([Eugene] Carr's) had to pass over the same road with Osterhaus, but being back at Mississippi Springs, would not be detained by it; the fourth ([A. J.] Smith's) with [Francis] Blair's division, was near Auburn with a different road to pass over. McClernand faced about and moved promptly. His cavalry from Raymond seized Bolton by half-past nine in the morning, driving out the enemy's pickets and capturing several men.

The night of the 15th Hovey was at Bolton; Carr and Osterhaus were about three miles south, but abreast, facing west; Smith was north of Raymond with Blair in his rear.

McPherson's command, with Logan in front, had marched at seven o'clock, and by four reached Hovey and went into camp; Crocker bivouacked just in Hovey's rear on the Clinton road. Sherman with two divisions, was in Jackson, completing the destruction of roads, bridges and military factories. I rode in person out to Clinton. On my arrival I ordered McClernand to move early in the morning on Edward's station, cautioning him to watch for the enemy and not bring on an engagement unless he felt very certain of success.

I naturally expected that Pemberton would endeavor to obey the orders of his superior, which I have shown were to attack us at Clinton. This, indeed, I knew he could not do; but I felt sure he would make the attempt to reach that point. It turned out, however, that he had decided his superior's plans were impracticable, and consequently determined to move south from Edward's station and get between me and my base. I, however, had no base, having abandoned it more than a week before. On the 15th Pemberton had actually marched south from Edward's station, but the rains had swollen Baker's Creek, which he had to cross, so much that he could not ford it, and the bridges were washed away. This brought him back to the Jackson road, on which there was a good bridge over Baker's Creek.

BELOW: The defensive tactic known as the hollow square is practiced by a Pennsylvania regiment. In the Civil War rising levels of battlefield firepower were making such traditional tactics obsolete, something only a handful of commanders in both armies readily understood.

ABOVE: A Union army battery crosses a stream via a crude ferry. Increasingly during the war, both sides called on their engineer services to devise faster ways to move large formations and heavy matériel over long distances and natural barriers.

RIGHT: Frederick Steele led a division in Sherman's corps during the Vicksburg Campaign. He would later conduct the 1864 Arkansas Campaign.

Some of his troops were marching until midnight to get there. Receiving here early on the 16th a repetition of his order to join Johnston at Clinton, he concluded to obey, and sent a dispatch to his chief, informing him of the route by which he might be expected.

About five o'clock in the morning (16th) two men, who had been employed on the Jackson and Vicksburg railroad, were brought to me. They reported that they had passed through Pemberton's army in the night, and that it was still marching east. They reported him to have eighty regiments of infantry and ten batteries; in all, about twenty-five thousand men.

I had expected to leave Sherman at Jackson another day in order to complete his work; but getting the above information I sent him orders to move with all dispatch to Bolton, and to put one division with an ammunition train on the road at once, with directions to its commander to march with all possible speed until he came up to our

rear. Within an hour after receiving this order [Frederick] Steele's division was on the road. At the same time I dispatched to Blair, who was near Auburn, to move with all speed to Edward's station. McClernand was directed to embrace Blair in his command for the present. Blair's division was a part of the 15th army corps (Sherman's); but as it was on its way to join its corps, it naturally struck our left first, now that we had faced about and were moving west. The 15th corps, when it got up, would be on our extreme right. McPherson was directed to get his trains out of the way of the troops, and to follow Hovey's division as closely as possible. McClernand had two roads about three miles apart, converging at Edward's station, over which to march his troops. Hovey's division of his corps had the advance on a third road (the Clinton) still farther north. McClernand was directed to move Blair's and A. J. Smith's divisions by the southernmost of these roads, and Osterhaus and Carr by the middle road. Orders were to move cautiously. . . .

Smith's division on the most southern road was the first to encounter the enemy's pickets, who were speedily driven in. Osterhaus, on the middle road, hearing the firing, pushed his skirmishers forward, found the enemy's pickets and forced them back to the main line. About the same time Hovey encountered the enemy on the northern or direct wagon road from Jackson to Vicksburg. McPherson was hastening up to join Hovey, but was embarrassed by Hovey's trains occupying the road. I was still back at Clinton. McPherson sent me word of the situation, and expressed the wish that I was up. By half-past seven I was on the road and proceeded rapidly to the front, ordering all trains that were in front of troops off the road. When I arrived Hovey's skirmishing amounted almost to a battle.

McClernand was in person on the middle road and had a shorter distance to march to reach the enemy's position than McPherson. I sent him word by a staff officer to push forward and attack. These orders were repeated several times without apparently expediting McClernand's advance.

Champion's Hill, where Pemberton had chosen his position to receive us, whether taken by accident or design, was well selected. It is one of the highest points in that section, and commanded all the ground in range. On the east side of the ridge, which is quite precipitous, is a ravine running first

ABOVE: Union General Edward Otho Cresap Ord and family. Ord, who had fought beside Grant at Corinth, commanded a corps in the final stages of the Vicksburg Campaign.

LEFT: Thomas E.G. Ransom led a brigade in McPherson's corps during the campaign. Grant later called him "the best man I ever had to send on expeditions."

north, then westerly, terminating at Baker's Creek. It was grown up thickly with large trees and undergrowth, making it difficult to penetrate with troops, even when not defended. The ridge occupied by the enemy terminated abruptly where the ravine turns westerly. The left of the enemy occupied the north end of this ridge. The Bolton and Edward's station wagon-road turns almost due south at this point and ascends the ridge, which it follows for about a mile; then turning west, descends by a gentle declivity to Baker's Creek, nearly a mile away. On the west side the slope of the ridge is gradual and is cultivated from near the summit to the creek. There was, when we were there, a narrow belt of timber near the summit west of the road.

From Raymond there is a direct road to Edward's station some three miles west of Champion's Hill. There is one also to Bolton. From this latter road there is still another, leaving it about three and a half miles before reaching Bolton and leads directly to the same station. It was among these two roads that three divisions of McClernand's corps, and Blair of Sherman's, temporarily under McClernand, were moving. Hovey of McClernand's command was with McPherson, farther north on the road from Bolton direct to Edward's station. The middle road comes into the northern road at the point where the latter turns to the west and descends to Baker's Creek; the southern road is still several miles south and does not intersect the others until it reaches Edward's station. Pemberton's lines covered all these

roads, and faced east. Hovey's line, when it first drove in the enemy's pickets, was formed parallel to that of the enemy and confronted his left.

By eleven o'clock the skirmishing had grown into a hard-contested battle. Hovey alone, before other troops could be got to assist him, had captured a battery of the enemy. But he was not able to hold his position and had to abandon the artillery. McPherson brought up his troops as fast as possible, Logan in front, and posted them on the right of Hovey and across the flank of the enemy. Logan reinforced Hovey with one brigade from his division; with his other two he moved farther west to make room for Crocker, who was coming up as rapidly as the roads would admit. Hovey was still being heavily pressed, and was calling on me for more reinforcements. I ordered Crocker, who was now coming up, to send one brigade from his division. McPherson ordered two batteries to be stationed where they nearly enfiladed the enemy's line, and they did good execution.

From Logan's position now a direct forward movement carried him over open fields, in rear of the enemy and in a line parallel with them. He did make exactly this move, attacking, however, the enemy through the belt of woods covering the west slope of the hill for a short distance. Up to this time I had kept my position near Hovey where we were the most heavily pressed; but about noon I moved with a part of my staff by our right around, until I came up with Logan himself. I found him near the road leading

RIGHT: The division led by M.M. Crocker (of McPherson's corps) in action at Jackson on May 14, 1863.

FAR LEFT TOP: Confederate General Carter L. Stevenson fought Grant at Vicksburg and would fight him again at Lookout Mountain.

FAR LEFT BOTTOM: Alfred Cumming led one of the Rebel brigades that tried vainly to lift the Vicksburg siege.

LEFT: Robert K. Scott fought under Grant throughout the Vicksburg Campaign. Not yet a general officer at that time, he would attain a permanent major generalcy by 1865.

down to Baker's Creek. He was actually in command of the only road over which the enemy could retreat; Hovey, reinforced by two brigades from McPherson's command, confronted the enemy's left; Crocker, with two brigades, covered their left flank; McClernand two hours before, had been within two miles and a half of the centre with two divisions, and the two divisions, Blair's and A. J. Smith's, were confronting the rebel right; [T.E.G.] Ransom, with a brigade of [John] McArthur's division of the 17th corps (McPherson's), had crossed the river at Grand Gulf a few days before, and was coming up on their right flank. Neither Logan nor I knew that we had cut off the retreat of the enemy. Just at this juncture a messenger came from Hovey, asking for more reinforcements. There were none to spare. I then gave an order to move McPherson's command by the left flank around to Hovey. This uncovered the rebel line of retreat, which was soon taken advantage of. . . .

During all this time, Hovey, reinforced as he was by a brigade from Logan and another from Crocker, and by Crocker gallantly coming up with two other brigades on his right, had made several assaults, the last one about the time the road was opened to the rear. The enemy fled precipitately. This was between three and four o'clock. I rode forward, or rather back, to where the middle road intersects the north road, and found the skirmishers of Carr's division just coming in. Osterhaus was farther south and soon after came up with skirmishers advanced in like manner. Hovey's division, and McPherson's two divisions with him, had marched and fought from early dawn, and were not in the best condition to follow the retreating foe. I sent orders to Osterhaus to pursue the enemy, and to Carr, whom I saw personally, I explained the situation and directed him to pursue vigorously as far as the Big Black, and to cross it if he could; Osterhaus to follow him. The pursuit was continued until after dark.

The battle of Champion's Hill lasted about four hours, hard fighting, preceded by two or three hours of skirmishing, some of which almost rose to the dignity of battle. Every man of Hovey's division and of McPherson's two divisions was engaged during the battle. No other part of my command was engaged at all, except that as described before. Osterhaus's and A. J. Smith's divisions had encountered the rebel advanced pickets as early as half-past seven. Their positions were admirable for advancing upon the

RIGHT: One of the South's most brilliant cavalry leaders, Nathan Bedford Forrest had first clashed with Grant at Fort Donelson, then again at Shiloh. During the Vicksburg Campaign he vexed Grant by raiding his rear supply lines.

BELOW: After Vickburg's fall men of the 8th Wisconsin pose with the regimental mascot, an eagle named "Old Abe."

enemy's line. McClernand, with two divisions, was within a few miles of the battlefield long before noon, and in easy hearing. I sent him repeated orders by staff officers fully competent to explain to him the situation. These traversed the wood separating us, without escort, and directed him to push forward; but he did not come. It is true, in front of McClernand there was a small force of the enemy and posted in a good position behind a ravine obstructing his advance; but if he had moved to the right by the road my staff officers had followed the enemy must either have fallen back or been cut off. Instead of this he sent orders to Hovey who belonged to his corps, to join on to his right flank. Hovey was bearing the brunt of the battle at the time. To obey the order he would have had to pull out from the front of the enemy and march back as far as McClernand had to advance to get into battle, and substantially over the same ground. Of course I did not permit Hovey to obey the order of his intermediate superior.

We had in this battle about 15,000 men absolutely engaged. This excludes those that did not get up, all of McClernand's command except Hovey. Our loss was 410 killed, 1,844 wounded and 187 missing. Hovey alone lost 1,200 killed, wounded and missing – more than one-third of his division.

Had McClernand come up with reasonable promptness, or had I known the ground as I did afterwards, I cannot see how Pemberton could have escaped with any organized force. As it was he lost over three thousand killed and wounded and about three thousand captured in battle and in pursuit. [William W.] Loring's division, which was the right of Pemberton's line, was cut off from the retreating army and never got back into Vicksburg. Pemberton himself fell back that night to the Big Black River. His troops did not stop before midnight and many of them left before the general retreat commenced, and no doubt a good part of them returned to their homes. . . .

Though Grant pursued the retreating Pemberton closely, the Confederate General narrowly succeeded in getting his troops back inside the formidable Vicksburg defenses before Grant could catch them. On arriving at Vicksburg, Grant almost immediately (May 22) ordered a general assault on the Confederate lines. It was so bloodily re- pulsed that Grant was obliged to settle in for what looked like a long and – Johnston was still somewhere at his back – potentially dangerous siege.

My line was more than fifteen miles long, extending from Haines' Bluff to Vicksburg, thence to Warrenton. The line of the enemy was about seven. In addition to this, having an enemy at Canton and Jackson, in our rear, who was being constantly reinforced, we required a second line of defence facing the other way. I had not troops enough under my command to man these. General Halleck appreciated the situation and, without being asked, forwarded reinforcements with all possible dispatch.

The ground about Vicksburg is admirable for defence. On the north it is about two hundred feet above the Mississippi River at the highest point and very much cut up by the washing rains; the ravines were grown up with cane and underbush, while the sides and tops were covered with a dense forest. Farther south the ground flattens out somewhat, and was in cultivation. But here, too, it was cut up by ravines and small streams. The enemy's line of defence followed the crest of a ridge from the river north of the city eastward, then southerly around to the Jackson road, full three miles back of the city; thence in a southwesterly direction to the river. Deep ravines of the description given

ABOVE: Union army barracks set up in Vicksburg after the city's surrender.

lay in front of these defences. As there is a succession of gullies, cut out by rains along the side of the ridge, the line was necessarily very irregular. To follow each of these spurs with intrenchments, so as to command the slopes on either side, would have lengthened their line very much. Generally therefore, or in many places, their line would run from near the head of one gully nearly straight to the head of another, and an outer work triangular in shape, generally open in the rear, was thrown up on the point; with a few men in this outer work they commanded the approaches to the main line completely.

The work to be done, to make our position as strong against the enemy as his was against us, was very great. The problem was also complicated by our wanting our line as near that of the enemy as possible. . . .

We had no siege guns except six thirty-two-pounders, and there were none at the West to draw from. Admiral Porter, however, supplied us with a battery of navy-guns of large calibre, and with these, and the field artillery used in the campaign, the siege began. . . .

In no place were our lines more than six hundred yards from the enemy. It was necessary, therefore, to cover our men by something more than the ordinary parapet. To give additional protection sand bags, bullet-proof, were placed along the tops of the parapets far enough apart to make loopholes for musketry. On top of these, logs were put. By these means the men were enabled to walk about erect when off duty, without fear of annoyance from sharpshooters. The enemy used in their defence

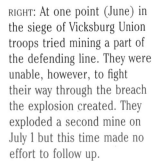

RIGHT: At one point (June) in the siege of Vicksburg Union troops tried mining a part of the defending line. They were unable, however, to fight their way through the breach the explosion created. They exploded a second mine on July 1 but this time made no effort to follow up.

explosive musket-balls, no doubt thinking that, bursting over our men in the trenches, they would do some execution; but I do not remember a single case where a man was injured by a piece of one of these shells. When they were hit and the ball exploded, the wound was terrible. In these cases a solid ball would have hit as well. Their use is barbarous, because they produce increased suffering without any corresponding advantage to those using them. . . .

The siege dragged on through the remainder of May and then through June. Slowly the besiegers compressed the defenders' lines, but by July 1 Vicksburg's defenses had still not been breached. Meantime, evidence was growing that Johnston's long-threatened attack from the east would probably be launched sometime in early July, and Grant ordered that a major assault on the city would be made on July 6, hoping thereby to eliminate the danger of having to fight simultaneously on two fronts before Johnston struck. In the event, neither Johnston's nor Grant's attacks materialized, for on July 3, the same day that Robert E. Lee met defeat at Gettysburg, Pemberton opened negotiations for Vicksburg's surrender. Grant offered generous terms, which Pemberton quickly accepted, and the surrender became a fact on July 4, 1863.

I rode into Vicksburg with the troops, and went to the river to exchange congratulations with the navy upon our joint victory. At that time I found that many of the citizens had been living under ground. The ridges upon which Vicksburg is built, and those back in the Big Black, are composed of a deep yellow clay of great tenacity. Where roads and streets are cut through, perpendicular banks are left and stand as well as if composed of stone. The magazines of the enemy were made by running passage-ways into this clay at places where there were deep cuts. Many citizens secured places of safety for their families by carving out rooms in these embankments. A door-way in these cases would be cut in a high bank, starting from the level of the road or street, and after running in a few feet a room of the size required was carved out of the clay, the dirt being removed by the door-way. In some instances I saw where the two rooms were cut

out, for a single family, with a door-way in the clay wall separating them. Some of these were carpeted and furnished with considerable elaboration. In these the occupants were fully secure from the shells of the navy, which were dropped into the city night and day without intermission.

I returned to my old headquarters outside in the afternoon, and did not move into the town until the sixth. On the afternoon of the fourth I sent Captain Wm. M. Dunn of my staff to Cairo, the nearest point where the telegraph could be reached, with a dispatch to the general-in-chief. It was as follows:

"The enemy surrendered this morning. The only terms allowed is their parole as prisoners of war. This I regard as a great advantage to us at this moment. It saves, probably, several days in the capture, and leaves troops and transports ready for immediate service. Sherman, with a large force, moves immediately on Johnston, to drive him from the State. I will send troops to the relief of Banks, and return the 9th army corps to Burnside."

This news, with the victory of Gettysburg won the same day, lifted a great load of anxiety from the minds of the President, his Cabinet and the loyal people all over the North. The fate of the Confederacy was sealed when Vicksburg fell. Much hard fighting was to be done afterwards and many precious lives were to be sacrificed; but the *morale* was with the supporters of the Union ever after. . . .

ABOVE: During the siege many Vicksburg citizens, in order to escape the effects of the Union bombardment, took to living in artificial caves dug into the sides of bluffs. Life in these caves probably was not quite as hard as this sentimental Southern sketch implies. Grant was impressed with how well furnished some such dwellings were when he viewed them after the city's capitulation on July 4, 1863.

Chapter IV

The Battle of Chattanooga

Soon after the surrender of Vicksburg, Port Hudson (as expected) fell to Federal troops. The entire Mississippi was now in Union hands. It all amounted to an immense strategic victory, but of course it still had to be exploited. A potentially very promising avenue for such exploitation lay in a campaign that Federal General William S. Rosecrans was conducting against Confederate forces under General Braxton Bragg in central Tennessee. Since early summer Rosecrans had steadily (if somewhat slowly) been driving Bragg southeast towards the vital Confederate rail center of Chattanooga. The

alarmed C.S.A. government in Richmond detached General James Longstreet's corps from Lee's army in Virginia and hurried it by rail to reinforce Bragg, but before Longstreet could arrive, Rosecrans, by adroit maneuvering, had, in early September, forced Bragg to evacuate Chattanooga. When Rosecrans attempted to pursue Bragg, however, he permitted his troops to become strung out in unfavorable terrain, and on September 19-20 Bragg, now reinforced by Longstreet, dealt Rosecrans a shattering blow in the Battle of Chickamauga. Rosecrans retreated to Chattanooga, where Bragg surrounded him and held him in a state of siege.

Now it was Washington's turn to be alarmed, and Lincoln and his advisers turned to Grant to retrieve the situation. Grant was given command of a newly-formed Division of the Mississippi (which included everything from that river to the Appalachians) and was dispatched to Chattanooga. Grant arrived in the city on October 24, relieved Rosecrans, and gave executive control of his army to the able George H. Thomas, now famous as the "Rock of Chickamauga." Within a month Grant had re-opened supply lines into Chattanooga, had strongly reinforced the Federal army in the city, and was ready to resume the offensive. Seeking to forestall Grant, Confederate President Jefferson Davis detached Longstreet and 15,000 troops from Bragg's force to move northeast and attack Union General Ambrose Burnside in Knoxville. As Davis had hoped, this move worried Washington and resulted in considerable pressure on Grant to send reinforcements to Burnside. But Grant resisted all efforts to weaken his army, and in the end it was Bragg's army, not Grant's, that Davis's too-clever maneuver weakened.

BELOW: Since the beginning of 1863 General William S. Rosecrans, a good tactician, had steadily been forcing the Confederate army of Braxton Bragg back through Tennessee toward Chattanooga. All his hard-won gains were nearly undone, however, when Bragg beat him at the Battle of Chickamauga in September.

ABOVE: Fought on September 19-20, 1863, the Battle of Chickamauga was one of the last clear-cut Confederate victories. A confusion in the execution of his orders opened a hole in Rosecrans's line, which Longstreet, who had just reinforced Bragg, devastatingly exploited. The beaten Federals retreated to Chattanooga, where Bragg's army besieged them.

LEFT: Union General Ambrose Burnside (center) in an 1861 photograph. In the fall of 1863 he was in Knoxville. By attacking him there, Southern strategists hoped to divert Grant from mounting a new offensive from Chattanooga.

Grant began his offensive on November 24, Sherman making some headway against the main enemy force on Missionary Ridge, to the east of the city, and General Joseph Hooker capturing a secondary Rebel position a little to the south on Lookout Mountain. Now Grant was ready to concentrate all his forces for a major assault on Bragg's well-entrenched army on steep-sloped Missionary Ridge.

The morning of the 25th opened clear and bright, and the whole field was in full view from the top of Orchard Knob. It remained so all day. Bragg's head-quarters were in full view, and officers – presumably staff officers – could be seen coming and going constantly.

The point of ground which Sherman had carried on the 24th was almost discon-nected from the main ridge occupied by the enemy. A low pass, over which there is a wagon road crossing the hill, and near

BELOW: Union General Joseph Hooker, who had been badly beaten at Chancellorsville earlier in 1863, was one of Grant's weaker lieutenants at Chattanooga.

which there is a railroad tunnel, intervenes between the two hills. The problem now was to get to the main ridge. The enemy was fortified on the point; and back farther, where the ground was still higher, was a second fortification commanding the first. Sherman was out as soon as it was light enough to see, and by sunrise his command was in motion. Three brigades held the hill already gained. Morgan L. Smith moved along the east base of Missionary Ridge; [G.] Loomis along the west base, supported by two brigades of John E. Smith's division; and [J.M.] Corse with his brigade was between the two, moving directly towards the hill to be captured. The ridge is steep and heavily wooded on the east side, where M. L. Smith's troops were advancing, but cleared and with a more gentle slope on the west side. The troops advanced rapidly and carried the extreme end of the rebel works. Morgan L. Smith advanced to a point which cut the enemy off from the railroad bridge and the means of bringing up supplies by rail from Chickamauga Station, where the main depot was located. The enemy made brave and strenuous efforts to drive our troops from the position we had gained, but without suc-

cess. The contest lasted for two hours. Corse, a brave and efficient commander, was badly wounded in this assault. Sherman now threatened both Bragg's flanks and his stores, and made it necessary for him to weaken other points of his line to strengthen his right. From the position I occupied I could see column after column of Bragg's forces moving against Sherman. Every Confederate gun that could be brought to bear upon the Union forces was concentrated upon him. . . . This was what I wanted. But it had now got to be late in the afternoon, and I had expected before this to see Hooker crossing the ridge in the neighborhood of Rossville and compelling Bragg to mass in that direction also.

The enemy had evacuated Lookout Mountain during the night, as I expected he would. In crossing the valley he burned the bridge over Chattanooga Creek, and did all he could to obstruct the roads behind him. Hooker was off bright and early, with no obstructions in his front but distance and the destruction above named. He was detained four hours crossing Chattanooga Creek, and thus was lost the immediate advantage I expected from his forces. His reaching Bragg's

ABOVE: Lookout Mountain, as viewed from the Tennessee. It was Hooker's assignment to take the mountain on November 24. He did so but was then dilatory in repositioning his troops to join in the main attack on Missionary Ridge the next day.

RIGHT: A view of Chattanooga looking southwest toward Lookout Mountain.

OPPOSITE: The Union charge up Missionary Ridge.

OPPOSITE BOTTOM: The landing from which the Union forces in Chattanooga received most of their supplies.

BELOW: A Union map of the Chattanooga battle area.

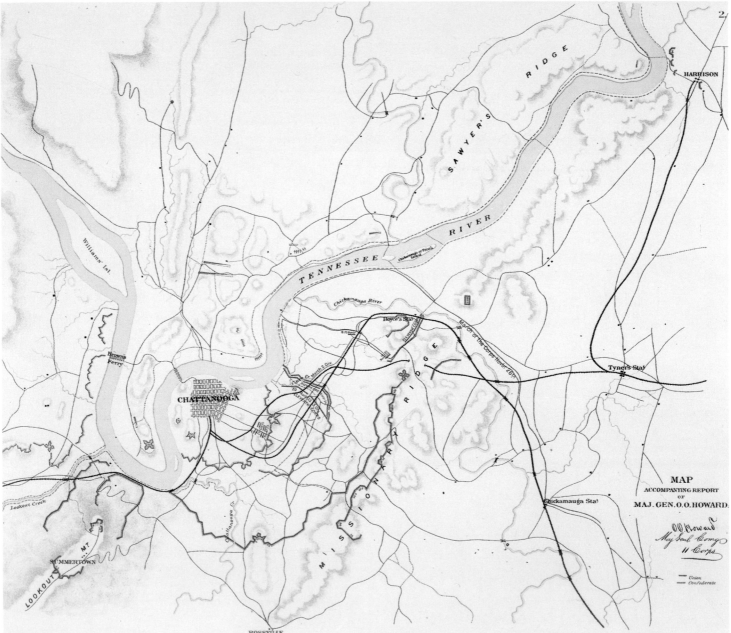

ABOVE: A photograph taken after the battle shows well the terrain the Union army had to cross in attacking Missionary Ridge.

RIGHT: Among the Confederate victors at Chickamauga was Montgomery Dent Corse, who led the brigade that George Pickett had once commanded.

OPPOSITE TOP: After Rebel forces were expelled from the Chattanooga area Union engineers built this bridge over the Tennessee.

flank and extending across it was to be the signal for Thomas's assault of the ridge. But Sherman's condition was getting so critical that the assault for his relief could not be delayed any longer.

[Philip] Sheridan's and [Thomas] Wood's divisions had been lying under arms from early morning, ready to move the instant the signal was given. I now directed Thomas to order the charge at once. a.. [I]n an incredibly short time loud cheering was heard, and [Wood] and Sheridan were driving the enemy's advance before them towards Missionary Ridge. The Confederates were strongly intrenched on the crest of the ridge in front of us, and had a second line half-way down and another at the base. Our men drove the troops in front of the lower line of rifle-pits so rapidly, and followed them so closely, that rebel and Union troops went over the first line of works almost at the same time. Many rebels were captured and sent to the rear under the fire of their own friends higher up the hill. Those that were not captured retreated, and were pursued. The retreating hordes being between friends and pursuers caused the enemy to fire high to avoid killing their own men. In fact, on

that occasion the Union soldier nearest the enemy was in the safest position. Without awaiting further orders or stopping to re-form, on our troops went to the second line of works; over that and on for the crest – thus effectually carrying out my orders of the 18th for the battle and of the 24th for his charge.

I watched their progress with intense interest. The fire along the rebel line was terrific. Cannon and musket balls filled the air: but the damage done was in small proportion to the ammunition expended. The pursuit continued until the crest was reached, and soon our men were seen climbing over the Confederate barriers at different points in front of both Sheridan's and Wood's divisions. The retreat of the enemy along most of his line was precipitate and the panic so great that Bragg and his officers lost all control over their men. Many were captured, and thousands threw away their arms in their flight. . . .

The victory at Chattanooga was won against great odds, considering the advantage the enemy had of position, and was accomplished more easily than was expected by reason of Bragg's making several grave mistakes: first, in sending away his

ablest corps commander with over twenty thousand troops; second, in sending away a division of troops on the eve of battle; third, in placing so much of a force on the plain in front of his impregnable position.

It was known that Mr. Jefferson Davis had visited Bragg on Missionary Ridge a short time before my reaching Chattanooga. It was reported and believed that he had come out to reconcile a serious difference be-

ABOVE: The small frame house in Chattanooga where Sherman made his headquarters during the siege of the city.

RIGHT: Grant (left) surveys
the scene of Joseph Hooker's
victory on Lookout Mountain.

BELOW: The troops of General
George Thomas begin their
charge at Missionary Ridge.

tween Bragg and Longstreet, and finding this difficult to do, planned the campaign against Knoxville, to be conducted by the latter general. I had known both Bragg and Longstreet before the war, the latter very well. We had been three years at West Point together, and, after my graduation, for a time in the same regiment. Then we served together in the Mexican War. I had known Bragg in Mexico, and met him occasionally subsequently. I could well understand how there might be an irreconcilable difference between them.

Bragg was a remarkably intelligent and well-informed man, professionally and otherwise. He was also thoroughly upright. But he was possessed of an irascible temper, and was naturally disputatious. A man of the highest moral character and the most correct habits, yet in the old army he was in frequent trouble. As a subordinate he was always on the lookout to catch his commanding officer infringing his prerogatives; as a post commander he was equally vigilant to detect the slightest neglect, even of the most trivial order. . . .

Longstreet was an entirely different man. He was brave, honest, intelligent, a very capable soldier, subordinate to his superiors, just and kind to his subordinates, but jealous of his own rights, which he had the courage to maintain. He was never on the lookout to detect a slight, but saw one as soon as anybody when intentionally given.

It may be that Longstreet was not sent to Knoxville for the reason stated, but because Mr. Davis had an exalted opinion of his own military genius, and thought he saw a chance of "killing two birds with one stone." On several occasions during the war he came to the relief of the Union army by means of his *superior military genius*. . . .

BELOW: The Battle of Lookout Mountain, as portrayed by the print-makers Kurz and Allison.

Chapter V

The Advance on Richmond

Grant's triumph at Chattanooga hurled Bragg's disorganized forces back into Georgia and made it possible for Grant to send massive reinforcements (two full corps under Sherman) to Burnside, thus dispelling the threat to Knoxville. Though some mopping up remained to be done, the Union was now effectively in control of Tennessee and poised to deliver, when the spring campaigning season began, the long-awaited thrust from the west to east that would cut the Old South in half.

Grant had assumed that this was to be his next assignment, but Washington had other plans for him. In March 1864 he was summoned to Washington, made a lieutenant-general (the highest rank the government had the power to confer), and placed in supreme command of all the armies of the Union. Now he was responsible not only for planning the eastward thrust out of Tennessee but all actions taken by Union armies everywhere.

Grant soon concluded that Union strategy for 1864 should consist of two coordinated major offensives directed at the two biggest Confederate armies then in the field: Robert E. Lee's Army of Northern Virginia and the Army of Tennessee (Bragg's old command, now under the formidable Joseph E. Johnston), currently in the vicinity of Dalton, Georgia. A third, smaller, and essentially diversionary offensive under Nathaniel Banks was to be launched from New Orleans against Mobile and Montgomery. (In the event, it failed.) Grant somewhat reluctantly

BELOW: When he was planning Union army operations for 1864, newly-created Lieutenant General Grant worked in this headquarters on 17th Street in Washington, D.C.

ABOVE: Fort Stevens, part of the outer defense perimeter of Washington, D.C., would bear the brunt of Early's diversionary attack on the city in July 1864.

LEFT: Grant with his eight-man personal staff in the field in 1864.

RIGHT: A curious European print of (l. to r.) Sheridan, Sherman, and Grant, wherein not one of the three is the least bit recognizable.

OPPOSITE TOP: Simultaneous with Grant's 1864 advance on Richmond was Sherman's march towards Atlanta. Shown here is one of the few mistakes Sherman made in the campaign: a frontal attack on strong defenses at Kenesaw Mountain.

OPPOSITE: Downtown Atlanta in 1864. News of Sherman's capture of the city was a political godsend to Lincoln and may have saved him from defeat in the 1864 election.

decided that the Georgia offensive, aimed at Atlanta and Savannah, could safely be left to his favorite lieutenant, William Tecumseh Sherman, and that he, Grant, would be needed to supervise the more dangerous effort by George Meade's Army of the Potomac to get past Lee and capture the Confederate capital of Richmond, Virginia.

Both big offensives began on May 4. Sherman, in a hard-fought war of maneuver, slowly forced Johnston back, but it was not until after Jefferson Davis had replaced Johnston with the less competent John B. Hood that Sherman was able to reach Atlanta and not until September 1 that the Georgia capital finally fell. It was nevertheless a very important victory, especially because 1864 was a presidential election year. As Grant put it: "The news of Sherman's success . . . set the country all aglow. . . . It was followed later by [Philip] Sheridan's campaign in the Shenandoah Valley; and these two campaigns probably had more effect in settling the election of the following November than all the speeches, all the bonfires, and all the parading with banners and bands of music in the North."

The two military successes may finally have guaranteed Lincoln's re-election, but they came precariously late in a year that had brought Washington all-too-little cheering news from the battlefronts, and especially from the Eastern battlefront. Grant had never before faced an opponent of Lee's caliber, and from their very first encounter he must have realized that he was in for a long, difficult, and bloody campaign.

Soon after midnight, May 3rd-4th, the Army of the Potomac moved out from its position north of the Rapidan, to start upon that memorable campaign, destined to result in the capture of the Confederate capital and the army defending it. This was not to be accomplished, however, without as desperate fighting as the world has ever witnessed; not to be consummated in a day, a week, a month, or a single season. The losses inflicted, and endured, were destined to be severe; but the armies now confronting each other had already been in deadly conflict for a period of three years, with immense losses in killed, by death from sickness, captured and wounded; and neither had made any real progress toward accomplishing the final end. It is true the Confederates had, so far, held their capital, and they claimed this to be their sole object. But previously they had boldly proclaimed their intention to capture Philadelphia, New York, and the National Capital, and had

made several attempts to do so, and once or twice had come fearfully near making their boast good – too near for complacent contemplation by the loyal North. They had also come near losing their own capital on at least one occasion. So here was a stand-off. The campaign now begun was destined to result in heavier losses, to both armies, in a given time, than any previously suffered; but the carnage was to be limited to a single year, and to accomplish all that had been anticipated or desired at the beginning in that time. We had to have hard fighting to achieve this. . . .

The Army of the Potomac was composed of three infantry and one cavalry corps, commanded respectively by Generals W. S. Hancock, G. K. Warren, John Sedgwick and P. H. Sheridan. The artillery was commanded by General Henry J. Hunt. . . .

The 5th corps, General Warren commanding, was in advance on the right, and marched directly for Germania Ford, preceded by one division of cavalry, under General J. H. Wilson. General Sedgwick followed Warren with the 6th corps. Germania Ford was nine or ten miles below the right of Lee's line. Hancock, with the 2d corps, moved by another road, farther east, directly upon Ely's Ford, six miles below Germania, preceded by [D. M.] Gregg's division of cavalry, and followed by the artillery. [A. T. A.] Torbert's division of cavalry was left north of the Rapidan, for the time, to picket the river and prevent the enemy from crossing and getting into our rear. The cavalry seized the two crossings before daylight, drove the enemy's pickets guarding them away, and by six o'clock A.M. had the pon-

toons laid ready for the crossing of the infantry and artillery. This was undoubtedly a surprise to Lee. The fact that the movement was unopposed proves this.

[General Ambrose] Burnside, with the 9th corps, was left back at Warrenton, guarding the railroad from Bull Run forward to preserve control of it in case our crossing the Rapidan should be long delayed. He was instructed, however, to advance at once on receiving notice that the army had crossed; and a dispatch was sent to him a little after one P.M. giving the information that our crossing had been successful. . . .

As soon as the crossing of the infantry was assured, the cavalry pushed forward, Wilson's division by Wilderness Tavern to Parker's store, on the Orange Plank Road; Gregg to the left towards Chancellorsville. Warren followed Wilson and reached the Wilderness Tavern by noon, took position there and intrenched. Sedgwick followed Warren. He was across the river and in camp on the south bank, on the right of Warren, by sundown. Hancock, with the 2d corps, moved parallel with Warren and camped about six miles east of him. Before night all the troops, and by the evening of the 5th the trains of more than four thousand wagons, were safely on the south side of the river. . . .

On discovering the advance of the Army of the Potomac, Lee ordered [A. P.] Hill, [Richard] Ewell and [James] Longstreet, each commanding corps, to move to the right to attack us, Hill on the Orange Plank Road, Longstreet to follow on the same road. Longstreet was at this time – middle of the afternoon – at Gordonsville, twenty or more miles away. Ewell was ordered by the

ABOVE: In Washington, D.C., a New York cavalry regiment musters for inspection.

OPPOSITE TOP: James Wilson (sprawling on the steps) led a division in Sheridan's cavalry corps when Grant's 1864 campaign started. He would command his own corps before the year's end.

OPPOSITE: Another divisional commander in Sheridan's corps was David McM. Gregg (seated, right), a veteran of Gettysburg.

Orange Pike. He was near by and arrived some four miles east of Mine Run before bivouacking for the night.

My orders were given through General Meade for an early advance on the morning of the 5th. Warren was to move to Parker's store, and Wilson's cavalry – then at Parker's store – to move on to Craig's meeting-house. Sedgwick followed Warren, closing in on his right. The Army of the Potomac was facing to the west, though our advance was made to the south, except when facing the enemy. Hancock was to move south-westward to join on the left of Warren, his left to reach to Shady Grove Church.

At six o'clock before reaching Parker's store, Warren discovered the enemy. He sent word back to this effect, and was ordered to halt and prepare to meet and attack him. [H. G.] Wright, with his division of Sedgwick's corps, was ordered, by any road he could find to join on to Warren's right, and [George] Getty with his division, also of Sedgwick's corps, was ordered to move rapidly by Warren's rear and get on his left. . . .

It was my plan then, as it was on all other occasions, to take the initiative whenever the enemy could be drawn from his intrenchments if we were not intrenched ourselves. . . . Warren was, therefore, ordered to attack as soon as he could prepare for it. At nine o'clock Hancock was ordered to come up to the support of Getty. He himself arrived

RIGHT: Union General George Washington Getty, a division commander in John Sedgwick's corps, was in the thick of the fighting in the Battle of the Wilderness, where he was severely wounded.

at Getty's front about noon, but his troops were yet far in the rear. Getty was directed to hold his position at all hazards until relieved. About this hour Warren was ready, and attacked with favorable though not decisive results. ... At two o'clock Hancock's troops began to arrive, and immediately he was ordered to join Getty and attack the enemy. ...

Fighting between Hancock and Hill continued until night put a close to it. Neither side made any special progress.

After the close of the battle on the 5th of May my orders were given for the following morning. We knew Longstreet with 12,000 men was on his way to join Hill's right, near the Brock Road, and might arrive during the night. I was anxious that the rebels should not take the initiative in the morning, and therefore ordered Hancock to make an assault at 4:30 o'clock. Meade asked to have the hour changed to six. Deferring to his wishes as far as I was willing, the order was modified and five was fixed as the hour to move.

Hancock had now fully one-half of the Army of the Potomac. [James] Wadsworth with his division, which had arrived the night before, lay in a line perpendicular to that held by Hill, and to the right of Hancock. He was directed to move at the same time, and to attack Hill's left.

Burnside, who was coming up with two divisions, was directed to get in between Warren and Wadsworth, and attack as soon as he could get in position to do so. Sedgwick and Warren were to make attacks in their front, to detain as many of the enemy as they could and to take advantage of any attempt to reinforce Hill from that quarter. Burnside was ordered if he should succeed in breaking the enemy's centre, to swing around to the left and envelop the right of Lee's army. ...

Hancock was ready to advance by the hour named, but learning in time that Longstreet was moving a part of his corps by the Catharpin Road, thus threatening his left flank, sent a division of infantry, commanded by General [Francis] Barlow, with all his artillery, to cover the approaches by which Longstreet was expected. This disposition was made in time to attack as ordered. Hancock moved by the left of the Orange Plank Road, and Wadsworth by the right of it. The fighting was desperate for about an hour, when the army began to break up in great confusion.

ABOVE: A battlefield sketch by artist Edwin Forbes shows Union troops on the Brock Road on May 11. Five days earlier this had been the scene of intensely bloody fighting in the Battle of the Wilderness.

RIGHT: Harvard man Francis Barlow, who led a division in Winfield Scott Hancock's II Corps, fought fiercely to stem the tide of Longstreet's advance on May 6. After the war Barlow, as New York's attorney general, prosecuted Tammany Hall's famous William "Boss" Tweed.

I believed then, and see no reason to change that opinion now, that if the country had been such that Hancock and his command could have seen the confusion and panic in the lines of the enemy, it would have been taken advantage of so effectually that Lee would not have made another stand outside of his Richmond defences. . . .

Hancock followed Hill's retreating forces, in the morning, a mile or more. He maintained this position until, along in the afternoon, Longstreet came upon him. The retreating column of Hill meeting reinforcements that had not yet been engaged, became encouraged and returned with them. They were enabled, from the density of the forest, to approach within a few hundred yards of our advance before being discovered. Falling upon a brigade of Hancock's corps thrown to the advance, they swept it away almost instantly. The enemy followed up his advantage and soon came upon [Gershom] Mott's division, which fell back in great confusion. Hancock made dispositions to hold his advanced position, but after holding it for a time, fell back into the position that he had held in the morning, which was strongly intrenched. In this engagement the intrepid Wadsworth while trying to rally his men was mortally

BELOW: Union General Horatio Gouverneur Wright led VI Corps from the Wilderness through to Appomattox.

131

ABOVE: A pause in the fighting to celebrate St. Patrick's Day, March 17, 1863, in the Army of the Potomac with horse racing by General Thomas Meagher's Irish Brigade.

OPPOSITE TOP: Union cavalry General George A. Custer (right foreground) in 1861, when he was a lieutenant.

OPPOSITE: An Alfred R. Waud sketch of Grant writing out a telegraph message during the 1864 campaign.

wounded and fell into the hands of the enemy. The enemy followed up, but made no immediate attack.

The Confederate General [Micah] Jenkins was killed and Longstreet seriously wounded in this engagement. Longstreet had to leave the field, not to resume command for many weeks. His loss was a severe one to Lee, and compensated in a great measure for the mishap, or misapprehensions, which had fallen to our lot during the day. . . .

At 4:15 in the afternoon Lee attacked our left. His line moved up to within a hundred yards of ours and opened a heavy fire. This status was maintained for about half an hour. Then a part of Mott's division and [J. H. H.] Ward's brigade of [David] Birney's division gave way and retired in disorder. The enemy under R. H. Anderson took advan-

tage of this and pushed through our line, planting their flags on a part of the intrenchments not on fire. But owing to the efforts of Hancock, their success was but temporary. [Samuel] Carroll, of [John] Gibbon's division, moved at a double quick with his brigade and drove back the enemy, inflicting great loss. Fighting had continued from five in the morning sometimes along the whole line, at other times only in places. The ground fought over had varied in width, but averaged three-quarters of a mile. The killed, and many of the severely wounded, of both armies, lay within this belt where it was impossible to reach them. The woods were set on fire by the bursting shells, and the conflagration raged. The wounded who had not strength to move themselves were either suffocated or burned to death. Finally the fire communicated with our breastworks, in

places. Being constructed of wood, they burned with great fury. But the battle still raged, our men firing through the flames until it became too hot to remain longer. . . .

During the night all of Lee's army withdrew within their intrenchments. On the morning of the 7th General [George A.] Custer drove the enemy's cavalry from Catharpin Furnace to Todd's Tavern. Pickets and skirmishers were sent along our entire front to find the position of the enemy. Some went as far as a mile and a half before finding him. But Lee showed no disposition to come out of his works. There was no battle during the day, and but little firing except in Warren's front; he being directed about noon to make reconnoissance in force. This drew some sharp firing, but there was no attempt on the part of Lee to drive him back. This ended the Battle of the Wilderness. . . .

ABOVE: An artist's somewhat romantic version of Grant leading his troops in the fruitless and costly Battle of Spottsylvania Court House, which took place soon after the Battle of the Wilderness.

More desperate fighting has not been witnessed on this continent than that of the 5th and 6th of May. Our victory consisted in having successfully crossed a formidable stream, almost in the face of an enemy, and in getting the army together as a unit. We gained an advantage on the morning of the 6th, which, if it had been followed up, must have proven very decisive. In the evening the enemy gained an advantage; but was speedily repulsed. As we stood at the close, the two armies were relatively in about the same condition to meet each other as when the river divided them. But the fact of having safely crossed was a victory.

Our losses in the Wilderness were very severe. Those of the Confederates must have been even more so; but I have no means of speaking with accuracy upon this point. The Germania Ford bridge was transferred to Ely's Ford to facilitate the transportation of the wounded to Washington. . . .

The Battle of the Wilderness set the pattern for the nightmarish campaign that was to follow. In two days of inconclusive fighting the North had lost

2,246 killed and 12,073 wounded, but Grant was determined not to let up the pressure on the enemy and quickly ordered a flanking movement around Lee's right wing to bring the Union army to Spottsylvania Court House. Lee anticipated the tactic, moved his forces accordingly, and was entrenched in Spottsylvania when Grant arrived. Grant attacked on May 12, made only token headway, and suffered 6800 more casualties. Again Grant wheeled his army to the left around Lee's flank, and again Lee countermaneuvered so as to block Grant's advance on the North Anna River. There followed another stalemated battle, another Union slide to the left, and now the two armies faced one another again at Cold Harbor.

The night of [May] 30th Lee's position was substantially from Atlee's Station on the Virginia Central Railroad south and east to the vicinity of Cold Harbor. Ours was: The left of Warren's corps was on the Shady Grove Road, extending to the Mechanicsville Road and about three miles south of the Totopoto-

LEFT: A rather misleading idea of the kind of terrain on which most of the Battle of the Wilderness was fought is projected in this popular Currier & Ives print.

BELOW: A U.S. Army map shows the general positions of the two armies in the Battle of the Wilderness and gives as well a good impression of how densely wooded the area was.

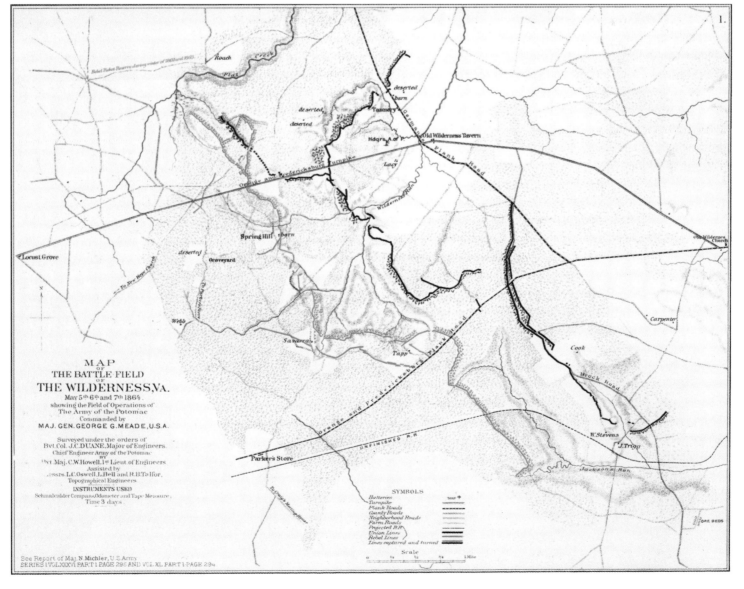

RIGHT: By 1864 railroads had become crucial instruments of war, not only for the rapid movement of men and supplies but also as platforms for mobile artillery. This big 32-lb Confederate rail gun, complete with a protective mantlet, is typical of the new forms of artillery that appeared during the last two years of the Civil War. This particular gun was used at Petersburg and perhaps even earlier in the 1864 campaign.

moy. Burnside to his right, then Hancock, and [H. G.] Wright on the extreme right, extending towards Hanover Court House, six miles south-east of it. Sheridan with two divisions of cavalry was watching our left front towards Cold Harbor. Wilson with his division on our right was sent to get on the Virginia Central Railroad and destroy it as far back as possible. He got possession of Hanover Court House the next day after a skirmish with [P. M. B.] Young's cavalry brigade. The enemy attacked Sheridan's pickets, but reinforcements were sent up and the attack was speedily repulsed and the enemy followed some distance towards Cold Harbor. . . .

On the 31st Sheridan advanced to near Old Cold Harbor. He found it intrenched and occupied by cavalry and infantry. A hard fight ensued but the place was carried. The enemy well knew the importance of Cold Harbor to us, and seemed determined that we should not hold it. He returned with such a large force that Sheridan was about withdrawing without making any effort to hold it against such odds; but about the time he commenced the evacuation he received orders to hold the place at all hazards, until reinforcements could be sent to him. He speedily turned the rebel works to face against them and placed his men in position for defence. Night came on before the enemy was ready for assault.

Wright's corps was ordered early in the evening to march directly to Cold Harbor passing by the rear of the army. It was expected to arrive by daylight or before; but the night was dark and the distance great, so that it was nine o'clock the 1st of June before it reached its destination. Before the arrival of Wright the enemy had made two assaults on Sheridan, both of which were repulsed with heavy loss to the enemy. Wright's corps coming up, there was no further assault on Cold Harbor.

[Corps Commander General William F.] Smith, who was coming up from White House, was also directed to march directly to Cold Harbor, and was expected early on the morning of the 1st of June; but by some blunder the order which reached Smith directed him to Newcastle instead of Cold Harbor. Through this blunder Smith did not reach his destination until three o'clock in the afternoon, and then with tired and worn-out men from their long and dusty march. He landed twelve thousand five hundred men from [Benjamin] Butler's command,

BELOW: At a conference held outside Bethesda Church on June 2 Grant leans over the shoulder of General George Meade to consult his map. The disastrous climax of the Battle of Cold Harbor would take place on the following day.

OPPOSITE TOP: The Battle of Cold Harbor according to Kurz & Allison. Grant regretted for the rest of his life the charge he ordered on June 3 against Lee's well-fortified position, for the charge proved to be an extremely costly failure.

OPPOSITE BOTTOM: Grant made up for his mistake at Cold Harbor in his next maneuver, a brilliant end-run that put him well to the south of Lee. The lower picture shows Grant's men crossing the Pamunkey River en route to the James.

but a division was left at White House temporarily and many men had fallen out of ranks in their long march.

Before the removal of Wright's corps from our right, after dark on the 31st, the two lines, Federal and Confederate, were so close together at that point that either side could detect directly any movement made by the other. Finding at daylight that Wright had left his front, Lee evidently divined that he had gone to our left. At all events, soon after light on the 1st of June [R. H.] Anderson, who commanded the corps on Lee's left, was seen moving along Warren's front. Warren was ordered to attack him vigorously in

GRANT'S GREAT CAMPAIGN—GENERAL BARLOW IN FRONT OF THE REBEL WORKS, TWELVE MILES FROM RICHMOND.—From a Sketch by A. R. Waud.—[See Page 119.]

flank, while Wright was directed to move out and get on his front. Warren fired his artillery at the enemy; but lost so much time in making ready that the enemy got by, and at three o'clock he reported the enemy was strongly intrenched in his front, and besides his lines were so long that he had no mass of troops to move with. He seemed to have forgotten that lines in rear of an army hold themselves while their defenders are fighting in their front. Wright reconnoitered some distance to his front: but the enemy finding Old Cold Harbor already taken had halted and fortified some distance west.

By six o'clock in the afternoon Wright and Smith were ready to make an assault. In front of both the ground was clear for several hundred yards, and then became wooded. Both charged across this open space and into the wood, capturing and holding the first line of rifle-pits of the enemy, and also capturing seven or eight hundred prisoners.

While this was going on, the enemy charged Warren three separate times with vigor, but were repulsed each time with loss. There was no officer more capable, nor one more prompt in acting, than Warren when the enemy forced him to it. There was also an attack upon Hancock's and Burnside's corps at the same time; but it was feeble and probably only intended to relieve Anderson who was being pressed by Wright and Smith.

During the night the enemy made frequent attacks with the view of dispossessing us of the important position we had gained, but without effecting their object.

Hancock was moved from his place in line during the night and ordered to the left of Wright. I expected to take the offensive on the morning of the 2d, but the night was so

BELOW: At his headquarters at City Point, on the James, Grant is visited by his wife and youngest son.

dark, the heat and dust so excessive and the roads so intricate and hard to keep, that the head of column only reached Old Cold Harbor at six o'clock, but was in position at 7:30 A.M. Preparations were made for an attack in the afternoon, but did not take place until the next morning. Warren's corps was moved to the left to connect with Smith: Hancock's corps was got into position to the left of Wright's, and Burnside was moved to Bethesda Church in reserve. While Warren and Burnside were making these changes the enemy came out several times and attacked them, capturing several hundred prisoners. The attacks were repulsed, but not followed up as they should have been. I was so annoyed at this that I directed Meade to instruct his corps commanders that they should seize all such opportunities when they occurred, and not wait for orders, all of our manoeuvres being made for the very purpose of getting the enemy out of his cover.

On this day [J. H.] Wilson returned from his raid upon the Virginia Central Railroad, having damaged it considerably. But, like ourselves, the rebels had become experts in repairing such damage. Sherman, in his memoirs, relates an anecdote of his campaign to Atlanta that well illustrates this point. The rebel cavalry lurking in his rear to burn bridges and obstruct his communications had become so disgusted at hearing trains go whistling by within a few hours after a bridge had been burned, that they proposed to try blowing up some of the tunnels. One of them said, "No use, boys, Old Sherman carries duplicate tunnels with him, and will replace them as fast as you can blow them up; better savé your powder."

BELOW: An almost certainly forged picture purporting to be of Grant at City Point.

ABOVE: City Point, on the south bank of the James, was to be Grant's headquarters for the remainder of the war. With its access to rail and river traffic, City Point became the main supply base of the Army of the Potomac.

Sheridan was engaged reconnoitering the banks of the Chickahominy, to find crossings and the condition of the roads. He reported favorably.

During the night Lee moved his left up to make his line correspond to ours. His lines extended now from the Totopotomoy to New Cold Harbor. Mine from Bethesda Church by Old Cold Harbor to the Chickahominy, with a division of cavalry guarding our right. An assault was ordered for the 3d, to be made mainly by the corps of Hancock, Wright and Smith; but Warren and Burnside were to support it by threatening Lee's left, and to attack with great earnestness if he should either reinforce more threatened points by drawing from that quarter or if a favorable opportunity should present itself.

The corps commanders were to select the points in their respective fronts where they would make their assaults. The move was to commence at half-past four in the morning. Hancock sent [Francis] Barlow and [John]

Gibbon forward at the appointed hour, with [David] Birney as a reserve. Barlow pushed forward with great vigor, under a heavy fire of both artillery and musketry, through thickets and swamps. Notwithstanding all the resistance of the enemy and the natural obstructions to overcome, he carried a position occupied by the enemy outside their main line where the road makes a deep cut through a bank affording as good a shelter for troops as if it had been made for that purpose. Three pieces of artillery had been captured here, and several hundred prisoners. The guns were immediately turned against the men who had just been using them. No assistance coming to him, he (Barlow) intrenched under fire and continued to hold his place. Gibbon was not so fortunate in his front. He found the ground over which he had to pass cut up with deep ravines, and a morass difficult to cross. But his men struggled on until some of them got up to the very parapet covering the enemy. Gibbon gained ground much nearer the enemy than that which he left, and here he intrenched and held fast.

Wright's corps moving in two lines captured the outer rifle-pits in their front, but accomplished nothing more. Smith's corps also gained the outer rifle-pits in its front. The ground over which this corps (18th) had to move was the most exposed of any over which charges were made. An open plain intervened between the contending forces at this point, which was exposed both to a direct and a cross fire. Smith, however, finding a ravine running towards his front, sufficiently deep to protect men in it from cross fire, and somewhat from a direct fire, put [John] Martindale's division in it, and with [W.T.H.] Brooks supporting him on the left and [Charles] Devens on the right succeeded in gaining the outer – probably picket – rifle-pits. Warren and Burnside also advanced and gained ground – which brought the whole army on one line.

This assault cost us heavily and probably without benefit to compensate: but the enemy was not cheered by the occurrence sufficiently to induce him to take the offensive. In fact, nowhere after the battle of the Wilderness did Lee show any disposition to leave his defences far behind him.

Fighting was substantially over by half-past seven in the morning. At eleven o'clock I started to visit all the corps commanders to see for myself the different positions gained and to get their opinion of the practicability of doing anything more in their respective fronts. . . . I concluded . . . to make no more assaults and . . . directed that all offensive action should cease.

I have always regretted that the last assault at Cold Harbor was ever made. . . . At Cold Harbor no advantage whatever was gained to compensate for the heavy loss we sustained. Indeed, the advantages other than those of relative losses, were on the Confederate side. Before that, the Army of Northern Virginia seemed to have acquired a wholesome regard for the courage, endurance, and soldierly qualities generally of the Army of the Potomac. They no longer wanted to fight them "one Confederate to five Yanks." Indeed, they seemed to have given up any idea of gaining any advantage of their antagonist in the open field. They had come to much prefer breastworks in their front to the Army of the Potomac. This charge seemed to revive their hopes temporarily; but it was of short duration. The effect upon the Army of the Potomac was the reverse. When we reached the James River, however, all effects of the battle of Cold Harbor seemed to have disappeared. . . .

BELOW: An Alfred Waud sketch of a Union battery in action at Cold Harbor.

GRANT'S GREAT CAMPAIGN—STEVENS'S BATTERY AT COLD HARBOR.—From a Sketch by A. R. Waud.

[See Page 410.]

The campaign thus far had been appalling. Between the Battle of the Wilderness and the end of the Battle of Cold Harbor on June 3 the Army of the Potomac had suffered approximately 50,000 casualties, 41 percent of its original strength. Lee's losses had been numerically lower, but they represented an even higher percentage of his strength, 46 percent. Equally important, whereas Grant could count on large reinforcements to make good his losses, Lee could not. In theory, therefore, Grant could have continued this brutal war of attrition with reasonable prospects of ultimate success, but instead he chose to change his strategy.

Once again he slid around Lee's right flank, but this time, rather than immediately pausing to re-engage Lee, he kept going, for his new objective lay well to the south. It was Petersburg, a town close to Richmond, that protected the rail lines on which the Confederate capital depended for its links to the rest of the Confederacy. If Grant could capture Petersburg, Richmond's fate would be sealed.

Lee could easily have thwarted this daring move, for he had the advantage of good interior lines of communications, whereas Grant's men would be obliged to march 50 miles over swampy ground and to cross two unbridged rivers, the Chickahominy and the James, before joining forces with Union General Benjamin Butler's isolated and immobilized command at Bermuda Hundred and swinging west to attack Petersburg. But Grant counted on Lee's not understanding until too late what he, Grant, really had in mind, and in this he was correct: the Southern commander was taken completely by surprise and would lose several vital days in trying to divine his enemy's intentions.

Nevertheless, it was bound to be a near-run thing, wholly dependent on speed, secrecy, deception where possible, and heroic efforts by Grant's corps of engineers. Miraculously, it worked. By mid-June, Grant had crossed the James, linked with Butler, and gained a brief window of opportunity to attack Petersburg before the enemy could respond. Everything now depended on the efficiency and enterprise of Grant's commanders in the field.

OPPOSITE: Engravings made from Waud sketches of Cold Harbor. Inevitably, they lack the spontaneous power of the original drawings.

BELOW: General Benjamin F. Butler (center left), led the small Army of the James in 1864. He was one of the most inept and intemperate of the "political generals" who burdened the Union army.

The advance of the Army of the Potomac reached the James on the 14th June. Preparations were at once commenced for laying the pontoon bridges and crossing the river. As already stated, I had previously ordered General Butler to have two vessels loaded with stone and carried up the river to a point above that occupied by our gunboats, where the channel was narrow, and sunk there so as to obstruct the passage and prevent Confederate gunboats boats from coming down the river. . . .

I then, on the 14th, took a steamer and ran up to Bermuda Hundred to see General Butler for the purpose of directing a movement against Petersburg, while our troops of the Army of the Potomac were crossing.

I had sent General W. F. Smith back from Cold Harbor by the way of White House, thence on steamers to City Point for the purpose of giving General Butler more troops with which to accomplish this result. General Butler was ordered to send Smith with his troops reinforced, as far as that could be conveniently done, from other parts of the Army of the James. He gave Smith about six thousand reinforcements, including some twenty-five hundred cavalry under [August] Kautz, and about thirty-five

hundred colored infantry under [Edward] Hinks.

The distance which Smith had to move to reach the enemy's lines was about six miles, and the Confederate advance line of works was but two miles outside of Petersburg. Smith was to move under cover of night, up close to the enemy's works, and assault as soon as he could after daylight. I believed then, and still believe, that Petersburg could have been easily captured at that time. It only had about 2,500 men in the defences besides some irregular troops, consisting of citizens and employees in the city who took up arms in case of emergency. Smith started as proposed, but his advance encountered a rebel force intrenched between City Point and their lines outside of Petersburg. This position he carried, with some loss to the enemy; but there was so much delay that it was daylight before his troops really got off from there. While there I informed General Butler that Hancock's corps would cross the river and move to Petersburg to support Smith in case the latter was successful, and that I could reinforce there more rapidly than Lee could reinforce from his position.

I returned down the river to where the troops of the Army of the Potomac now were, communicated to General Meade, in writing, the directions I had given to General Butler and directed him (Meade) to cross Hancock's corps over under cover of night, and push them forward in the morning to Petersburg; halting them, however, at a designated point until they could hear from Smith. I also informed General Meade that I had ordered rations from Bermuda Hundred for Hancock's corps, and desired him to issue them speedily, and to lose no more time than was absolutely necessary. The rations did not reach him, however, and Hancock, while he got all his corps over during the night, remained until half-past ten in the hope of receiving them. He then moved without them, and on the road received a note from General W. F. Smith, asking him to come on. This seems to be the first information that General Hancock had received of the fact that he was to go to Petersburg, or that anything particular was expected of him. Otherwise he would have been there by four o'clock in the afternoon.

Smith arrived in front of the enemy's lines early in the forenoon of the 15th, and spent the day until after seven o'clock in the even-

ABOVE: River steamers land supplies at extended wharves built by Union engineers at City Point.

OPPOSITE TOP: Union cavalry stables at City Point.

OPPOSITE BOTTOM: Grant's army crosses the James using the extraordinary 2100-foot-long pontoon bridge that Union engineers built specially for the operation.

147

RIGHT: The 1st U.S. Colored Infantry Regiment. Black troops formed a significant part of Grant's army in 1864.

ABOVE: When Grant's advance units failed in their first effort to take Petersburg in June the element of surprise created by Grant's strategy was lost, and a long siege became inevitable. Here, Union snipers fire at the Petersburg defenses.

ing in reconnoitering what appeared to be empty works. The enemy's line consisted of redans occupying commanding positions, with rifle-pits connecting them. To the east side of Petersburg, from the Appomattox back, there were thirteen of these redans extending a distance of several miles, probably three. If they had been properly manned they could have held out against any force that could have attacked them, at least until reinforcements could have got up from the north of Richmond.

Smith assaulted with the colored troops, and with success. By nine o'clock at night he was in possession of five of these redans and, of course, of the connecting lines of rifle-pits. All of them contained artillery, which fell into our hands. Hancock came up and proposed to take any part assigned to him; and Smith asked him to relieve his men who were in the trenches.

Next morning, the 16th, Hancock himself was in command, and captured another redan. Meade came up in the afternoon and succeeded Hancock, who had to be relieved, temporarily, from the command of his corps on account of the breaking out afresh of the wound he had received at Gettysburg. During the day Meade assaulted and carried one more redan to his right and two to his left. In all this we lost very heavily. The works were not strongly manned, but they all had guns in them which fell into our hands, together with the men who were handling them in the effort to repel these assaults.

Up to this time Beauregard, who had commanded south of Richmond, had received no reinforcements, except [Robert] Hoke's division from Drury's Bluff, which had arrived on the morning of the 16th; though he had urged the authorities very strongly to send them, believing, as he did, that Petersburg would be a valuable prize which we might seek.

During the 17th the fighting was very severe and the losses heavy; and at night our troops occupied about the same position they had occupied in the morning, except that they held a redan which had been captured . . . during the day. During the night, however, Beauregard fell back to the line which had been already selected, and commenced fortifying it. . . .

Colonel [Joshua Lawrence] Chamber-

148

lain, of the 20th Maine, was wounded on the 18th. He was gallantly leading his brigade at the time, as he had been in the habit of doing in all the engagements in which he had previously been engaged. He had several times been recommended for a brigadier-generalcy for gallant and meritorious conduct. On this occasion, however, I promoted him on the spot, and forwarded a copy of my order to the War Department, asking that my act might be confirmed and Chamberlain's name sent to the Senate for confirmation without any delay. This was done, and at last a gallant and meritorious officer received partial justice at the hands of his government, which he had served so faithfully and so well.

If General Hancock's orders of the 15th had been communicated to him, that officer, with his usual promptness, would undoubtedly have been upon the ground around Petersburg as early as four o'clock in the afternoon of the 15th. The days were long and it would have given him considerable time before night. I do not think there is any doubt that Petersburg itself could have been carried without must loss; or, at least, if protected by inner detached works, that a line could have been established very much in the rear of the one then occupied by the enemy. This would have given us control of both the Weldon and South Side railroads. This would also have saved an immense amount of hard fighting which had to be done from the 15th to the 18th, and would have given us greatly the advantage in the long siege which ensued. . . .

ABOVE: Union Colonel Joshua Lawrence Chamberlain, of the 20th Maine, was wounded in the fighting at Petersburg on June 17. Grant seized the occasion to award this hero of the Battle of Gettysburg an overdue generalcy.

BELOW: A Union battery at Petersburg in June 1864.

Chapter VI

Petersburg and the Shenandoah Valley

Thus the golden opportunity created by Grant's brilliant strategy slipped away. The Army of Northern Virginia soon pulled in behind the Petersburg defenses and fortified them virtually to the point of impregnability. Both sides dug in for a long siege. But at least some Union officers still held hopes of finding a way to break the stalemate quickly.

OPPOSITE TOP: The now-famous James River pontoon bridge that brought Grant and his army to Petersburg.

OPPOSITE BOTTOM: Engineers' drawings of the typical Rebel defenses at Petersburg.

BELOW: A pencil drawing by A.R. Waud of the explosion at the Union stronghold of City Point, Virginia on August 9, 1864.

On the 25th of June General Burnside had commenced running a mine from about the centre of his front under the Confederate works confronting him. He was induced to do this by Colonel [Henry] Pleasants, of the Pennsylvania Volunteers, whose regiment was mostly composed of miners, and who was himself a practical miner. Burnside had submitted the scheme to Meade and myself, and we both approved of it, as a means of keeping the men occupied. His position was very favorable for carrying on this work, but not so favorable for the operations to follow its

completion. The position of the two lines at that point were only about a hundred yards apart with a comparatively deep ravine intervening. In the bottom of this ravine the work commenced. The position was unfavorable in this particular: that the enemy's line at that point was re-entering, so that its front was commanded by their own lines both to the right and left. Then, too, the ground was sloping upward back of the Confederate line for a considerable distance, and it was presumable that the enemy had, at least, a detached work on this highest point. The work progressed, and on the 23rd of July the mine was finished ready for charging; but I had this work of charging deferred until we were ready for it.

On the 17th of July several deserters came in and said that there was great consternation in Richmond, and that Lee was coming out to make an attack upon us – the object being to put us on the defensive so that he might detach troops to go to Georgia where the army Sherman was operating against was said to be in great trouble. I put the army

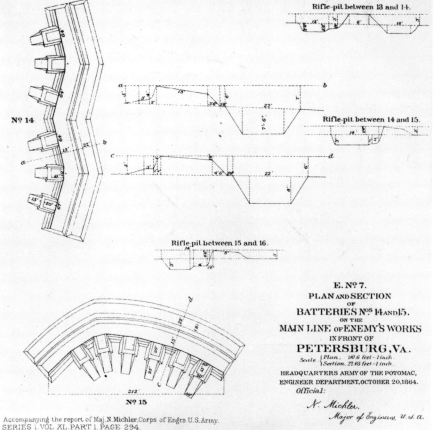

Rifle-pit between 13 and 14.

No 14

Rifle-pit between 14 and 15.

Rifle-pit between 15 and 16.

E. No 7.
PLAN AND SECTION
OF
BATTERIES Nos 14 AND 15.
ON THE
MAIN LINE OF ENEMY'S WORKS
IN FRONT OF
PETERSBURG, VA.
Scale { Plan, 90.6 feet–1 inch.
{ Section, 22.65 feet–1 inch.
HEADQUARTERS ARMY OF THE POTOMAC,
ENGINEER DEPARTMENT, OCTOBER 20,1864.
Official:
N. Michler.
Major of Engineers, U. S. A.

No 15

Accompanying the report of Maj. N. Michler, Corps of Engrs. U. S. Army.
SERIES 1. VOL XL. PART 1. PAGE 294.

ABOVE: General George Meade. As commander of the Army of the Potomac he was Grant's immediate subordinate during the Virginia campaigns of 1864-65, a trying position for a man as temperamental as Meade. Yet he seems to have handled the assignment capably and, on the whole, rather gracefully.

commanders, Meade and Butler, on the lookout, but the attack was not made.

I concluded, then, a few days later, to do something in the way of offensive movement myself, having in view something of the same object that Lee had had. [Horatio] Wright's and [William] Emory's corps were in Washington, and with this reduction of my force Lee might very readily have spared some troops from the defences to send West. I had other objects in view, however, besides keeping Lee where he was. The mine was constructed and ready to be exploded, and I wanted to take that occasion to carry Petersburg if I could. It was the object, therefore, to get as many of Lee's troops away from the south side of the James River as possible. Accordingly, on the 26th, we commenced a movement with Hancock's corps and Sheridan's cavalry to the north side by the way of Deep Bottom, where Butler had a pontoon bridge laid. The plan, in the main, was to let the cavalry cut loose and, joining with Kautz's cavalry of the Army of the James, get by Lee's lines and destroy as much as they could of the Virginia Central Railroad, while, in the mean time, the infantry was to move out so as to protect their rear and cover their retreat back when they should have got through with their work. We were successful in drawing the enemy's troops to the north side of the

James as I expected. The mine was ordered to be charged, and the morning of the 30th of July was the time fixed for its explosion. I gave Meade minute orders on the 24th directing how I wanted the assault conducted, which orders he amplified into general instructions for the guidance of the troops that were to be engaged.

Meade's instructions, which I, of course, approved most heartily, were all that I can see now was necessary. The only further precaution which he could have taken, and

which he could not foresee, would have been to have different men to execute them.

The gallery to the mine was over five hundred feet long from where it entered the ground to the point where it was under the enemy's works, and with a cross gallery of something over eighty feet running under their lines. Eight chambers had been left, requiring a ton of powder each to charge them. All was ready by the time I had prescribed; and on the 29th Hancock and Sheridan were brought back near the James River

with their troops. Under cover of night they started to recross the bridge at Deep Bottom, and to march directly for that part of our lines in front of the mine.

[Gouverneur] Warren was to hold his line of intrenchments with a sufficient number of men and concentrate the balance on the right next to Burnside's corps, while [Edward] Ord, now commanding the 18th corps, temporarily under Meade, was to form in the rear of Burnside to support him when he went in. All were to clear off the

ABOVE: "The Dictator," a huge 13-inch rail-mounted mortar, was one of the most famous siege guns used by the Union at Petersburg.

153

ABOVE: The gabions, trenches, and earthworks used in the construction of the Union's Fort Sedgwick were typical of the passive defenses used by both armies during the siege of Petersburg.

parapets and the *abatis* in their front so as to leave the space as open as possible, and be able to charge the moment the mine had been sprung and Burnside had taken possession. Burnside's corps was not to stop in the crater at all but push on to the top of the hill, supported on the right and left by Ord's and Warren's corps.

Warren and Ord fulfilled their instructions perfectly so far as making ready was concerned. Burnside seemed to have paid no attention whatever to the instructions, and left all the obstruction in his own front for his troops to get over in the best way they could. The four divisions of his corps were commanded by Generals [Robert] Potter, [Orlando] Willcox, [James]· Ledlie and [Edward] Ferrero. The last was a colored division; and Burnside selected it to make

the assault. Meade interfered with this. Burnside then took Ledlie's division – a worse selection than the first could have been. In fact, Potter and Willcox were the only division commanders Burnside had who were equal to the occasion. Ledlie besides being otherwise inefficient, proved also to possess disqualification less common among soldiers.

There was some delay about the explosion of the mine so that it did not go off until about five o'clock in the morning. When it did explode it was very successful, making a crater twenty feet deep and something like a hundred feet in length. Instantly one hundred and ten cannon and fifty mortars, which had been placed in the most commanding positions covering the ground to the right and left of where the troops were to

enter the enemy's lines, commenced playing. Ledlie's division marched into the crater immediately on the explosion, but most of the men stopped there in the absence of any one to give directions; their commander having found some safe retreat to get into before they started. There was some delay on the left and right in advancing, but some of the troops did get in and turn to the right and left, carrying the rifle-pits as I expected they would do.

There had been great consternation in Petersburg, as we were well aware, about a rumored mine that we were going to explode. They knew we were mining, and they had failed to cut our mine off by countermining, though Beauregard had taken the precaution to run up a line of intrenchments to the rear of that part of their line fronting

ABOVE: Ambrose E. Burnside, commander of the Union's IX Corps, had to bear ultimate responsibility for the great "mine disaster" of July 30.

LEFT: Edward Ferrero led the (black) division originally assigned to exploit the mine explosion, but for political reasons another division was given the task at the last minute – one of the many errors that produced a fiasco.

155

where they could see that our men were at work. We had learned through deserters who had come in that the people had very wild rumors about what was going on on our side. They said that we had undermined the whole of Petersburg; that they were resting upon a slumbering volcano and did not know at what moment they might expect an eruption. I somewhat based my calculations upon this state of feeling, and expected that when the mine was exploded the troops to the right and left would flee in all directions, and that our troops, if they moved promptly, could get in and strengthen themselves before the enemy had come to a realization of the true situation. It was just as I expected it would be. We could see the men running without any apparent object except to get away. It was half an hour before musketry

firing, to amount to anything, was opened upon our men in the crater. It was an hour before the enemy got artillery up to play upon them; and it was nine o'clock before Lee got up reinforcements from his right to join in expelling our troops.

The effort was a stupendous failure. It cost us about four thousand men, mostly, however, captured; and all due to inefficiency on the part of the corps commander and the incompetency of the division commander who was sent to lead the assault. . . .

By mid-summer it was clear to everyone that the deadlock before Petersburg would not be broken either easily or soon. With their main armies thus frozen into near immobility, both Grant and Lee searched for ways to

BELOW: Reinforced quarters such as this were referred to as "bomb-proof" by the Petersburg besiegers. But it is doubtful that they could have withstood a direct hit by a large-calibre gun.

regain the initiative via maneuver in adjacent areas. Grant had been probing in the Shenandoah Valley since early June, and Lee had countered by sending a 17,000-man corps under Jubal Early into the Valley at midmonth. Early soon brushed aside the feeble Union opposition there, and, since the Valley was now essentially unguarded, Lee ordered Early to move north and make a demonstration against Washington itself. Early was over the Potomac by July 5, and, as Lee had hoped, Washington was in a state of panic and clamoring for Grant to detach forces from Petersburg to come to the city's rescue. Grant, who perfectly understood Early's "raid" for what it was, resisted; and, indeed, by

ABOVE: A U.S. Army blacksmith shapes a shoe for a cavalry mount before Petersburg in August 1864.

LEFT: Confederate General Jubal Early. In June-August Lee, in an effort to divert Grant from Petersburg, had Early make a demonstration against Washington, but Grant was not to be drawn.

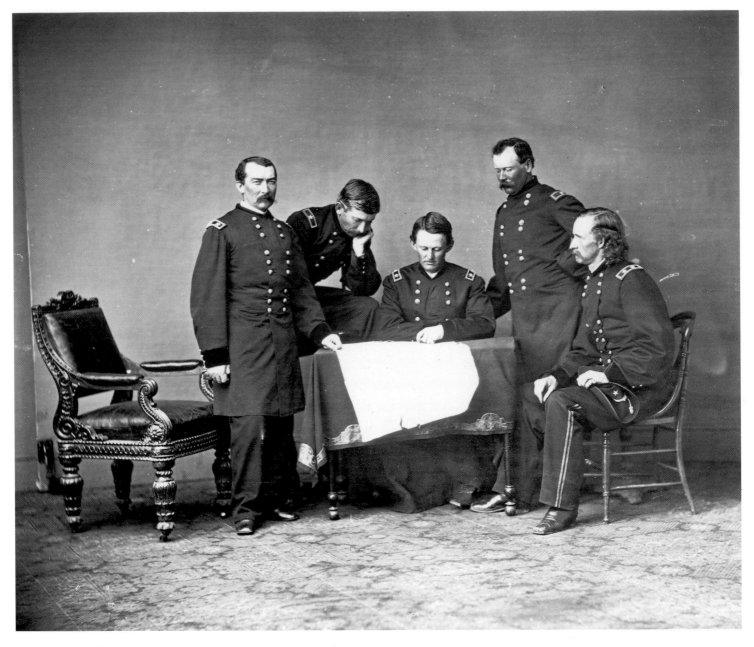

ABOVE: Union cavalry General Philip Sheridan (left) and some of his officers: Wesley Merritt is in the center and George Custer is on the far right. Under Sheridan U.S. cavalry operations for the first time began to surpass those of the Confederates in large-scale effectiveness.

the 12th Early had turned about and was heading back into the Valley.

Grant was not content to let him stay there unmolested. Accordingly, at the beginning of August, Grant created an Army of the Shenandoah and placed it under the command of his premier cavalry general, Philip Sheridan, with orders to clear the Valley once and for all of every vestige of Confederate military presence.

On the 10th of August Sheridan had advanced on Early up the Shenandoah Valley, Early falling back to Strasburg. On the 12th I learned that Lee had sent twenty pieces of artillery, two divisions of infantry and a considerable cavalry force to strengthen Early. It was important that Sheridan should be informed of this, so I sent the information to Washington by telegraph, and directed a courier to be sent from there to get the message to Sheridan at all hazards, giving him the information. The messenger, an officer of the army, pushed through with great energy and reached Sheridan just in time. The officer went through by way of Snicker's Gap, escorted by some cavalry. He found Sheridan just making his preparations to attack Early in his chosen position. Now, however, he was thrown back on the defensive.

On the 15th of September I started to visit General Sheridan in the Shenandoah Valley. My purpose was to have him attack Early, or drive him out of the valley and destroy that source of supplies for Lee's army. I knew it was impossible for me to get orders through Washington to Sheridan to make a move, because they would be stopped there and such orders as Halleck's caution (and that of the Secretary of War) would suggest would

be given instead, and would, no doubt, be contradictory to mine. I therefore, without stopping at Washington, went directly through to Charlestown, some ten miles above Harper's Ferry, and waited there to see General Sheridan, having sent a courier in advance to inform him where to meet me.

When Sheridan arrived I asked him if he had a map showing the positions of his army and that of the enemy. He at once drew one out of his side pocket, showing all roads and streams, and the camps of the two armies. He said that if he had permission he would move so and so (pointing out how) against the Confederates, and that he could "whip them." Before starting I had drawn up a plan of campaign for Sheridan, which I had brought with me; but, seeing that he was so clear and so positive in his views and so confident of success, I said nothing about this and did not take it out of my pocket. . . .

Sheridan moved at the time he had fixed upon. He met Early at the crossing of Opequon Creek, and won a most decisive victory - one which electrified the country. Early had invited this attack himself by his bad generalship and made the victory easy. He had sent G. T. Anderson's division east of the Blue Ridge before I went to Harper's Ferry; and about the time I arrived there he started

ABOVE: A dramatic example of the growing potency of the Union cavalry would be given in September when Sheridan smashed Early's army at the Battle of Winchester.

LEFT: Edwin McM.Stanton, Lincoln's abrasive but able secretary of war, annoyed Grant by going over Grant's head and interfering with Sheridan's operations in the Shenandoah Valley.

with two other divisions (leaving but two in their camps) to march to Martinsburg for the purpose of destroying the Baltimore and Ohio Railroad at that point. Early here learned that I had been with Sheridan and, supposing there was some movement on foot, started back as soon as he got the information. But his forces were separated and, as I have said, he was very badly defeated. He fell back to Fisher's Hill, Sheridan following.

159

The valley is narrow at that point, and Early made another stand there, behind works which extended across. But Sheridan turned both his flanks and again sent him speeding up the valley, following in hot pursuit. The pursuit was continued up the valley to Mount Jackson and New Market. Sheridan captured about eleven hundred prisoners and sixteen guns. The houses which he passed all along the route were found to be filled with Early's wounded, and the country swarmed with his deserters. Finally, on the 25th, Early turned from the valley eastward, leaving Sheridan at Harrisonburg in undisputed possession.

Now one of the main objects of the expedition began to be accomplished. Sheridan went to work with his command, gathering in the crops, cattle, and everything in the upper part of the valley required by our troops; and especially taking what might be of use to the enemy. What he could not take away he destroyed, so that the enemy would not be invited to come back there. I congratulated Sheridan upon his recent great victory and had a salute of a hundred guns fired in honor of it, the guns being aimed at the enemy around Petersburg. I also notified the other commanders throughout the country, who also fired salutes in honor of his victory.

I had reason to believe that the administration was a little afraid to have a decisive battle fought at that time, for fear it might go against us and have a bad effect on the November elections. The convention which had met and made its nomination of the Democratic candidate for the presidency had declared the war a failure. Treason was talked as boldly in Chicago at that convention as ever it had been in Charleston. It was a question whether the government would then have had the power to make arrests and punish those who thus talked treason. But this decisive victory was the most effective campaign argument made in the canvass.

Sheridan, in his pursuit, got beyond where they could hear from him in Washington, and the President became very much frightened about him. He was afraid that the hot pursuit had been a little like that of General Cass was said to have been, in one of our Indian wars, when he was an officer of that army. Cass was pursuing the Indians so closely that the first thing he knew he found himself in their front, and the Indians pursuing him. The President was afraid that Sheridan had got on the other side of Early and

LEFT: Philip Sheridan was in many ways typical of the new kind of leadership that emerged in the Union army in the final years of the war. Tough, ruthless, and aggressive, he had an innate sense of command and a keen grasp of tactics. And like Grant and Sherman, he had the flexibility to adapt to the changing nature of war.

ABOVE: Confederate General William Carter Wickham led a brigade in Early's army in the Shenandoah. He resigned in November 1864 to take a seat in the C.S.A. congress.

more use. I approved of his suggestion, and ordered him to send [Horatio] Wright's corps back to the James River. I further directed him to repair the railroad up the Shenandoah Valley towards the advanced position which we would hold with a small force. The troops were to be sent to Washington by the way of Culpeper, in order to watch the east side of the Blue Ridge, and prevent the enemy from getting into the rear of Sheridan while he was still doing his work of destruction.

The valley was so very important, however, to the Confederate army that, contrary to our expectations, they determined to make one more strike, and save it if possible before the supplies should be all destroyed. Reinforcements were sent therefore to Early, and this before any of our troops had been withdrawn. Early prepared to strike Sheridan at Harrisonburg; but the latter had not remained there.

On the 6th of October Sheridan commenced retiring down the valley, taking or destroying all the food and forage and driving the cattle before him, Early following. At Fisher's Hill Sheridan turned his cavalry back on that of Early, which, under the lead of [Thomas] Rosser, was pursuing closely, and routed it most completely, capturing eleven guns and a large number of prisoners. Sheridan lost only about sixty men. His cavalry pursued the enemy back some twenty-five miles. On the 10th of October the march down the valley was again resumed, Early again following.

I now ordered Sheridan to halt, and to improve the opportunity if afforded by the enemy's having been sufficiently weakened, to move back again and cut the James River Canal and Virginia Central Railroad. But this order had to go through Washington where it was intercepted; and when Sheridan received what purported to be a statement of what I wanted him to do it was something entirely different. Halleck informed Sheridan that it was my wish for him to hold a forward position as a base from which to act against Charlottesville and Gordonsville; that he should fortify this position and provision it.

Sheridan objected to this. . . .

Sheridan having been summoned to Washington City, started on the 15th leaving Wright in command. His army was then at Cedar Creek, some twenty miles south of Winchester. The next morning while at Front Royal, Sheridan received a dispatch from

that Early was in behind him. He was afraid that Sheridan was getting so far away that reinforcements would be sent out from Richmond to enable Early to beat him. I replied to the President that I had taken steps to prevent Lee from sending reinforcements to Early, by attacking the former where he was.

On the 28th of September, to retain Lee in his position, I sent Ord with the 18th corps and Birney with the 10th corps to make an advance on Richmond, to threaten it. Ord moved with the left wing up to Chaffin's Bluff; Birney with the 10th corps took a road farther north; while Kautz with the cavalry took the Darby road, still farther to the north. They got across the river by the next morning, and made an effort to surprise the enemy. In that, however, they were unsuccessful. . . .

Sheridan having driven the enemy out of the valley, and taken the productions of the valley so that instead of going there for supplies the enemy would have to bring his provisions with him if he again entered it, recommended a reduction of his own force, the surplus to be sent where it could be of

Wright, saying that a dispatch from Longstreet to Early had been intercepted. It directed the latter to be ready to move and to crush Sheridan as soon as he, Longstreet, arrived. On the receipt of this news Sheridan ordered the cavalry up the valley to join Wright.

On the 18th of October Early was ready to move, and during the night succeeded in getting his troops in the rear of our left flank, which fled precipitately and in great confusion down the valley, losing eighteen pieces of artillery and a thousand or more prisoners. The right under General [George] Getty maintained a firm and steady front, falling back to Middletown where it took a position and made a stand. The cavalry went to the rear, seized the roads leading to Winchester and held them for the use of our troops in falling back, General Wright having ordered a retreat back to that place.

Sheridan having left Washington on the 18th, reached Winchester that night. The following morning he started to join his command. He had scarcely got out of town, when he met his men returning in panic from the front and also heard heavy firing to the south. He immediately ordered the cavalry at Winchester to be deployed across

ABOVE: Like Wickham, James Connor also commanded one of Early's brigades in the Shenandoah. He lost his leg in the fighting there.

LEFT: General John R. Meigs, an engineer on Sheridan's staff, was killed by one of Wickham's scouts. Sheridan, in retaliation, burned all the houses in a five-mile radius of Dayton, Virginia.

163

the valley to stop the stragglers. Leaving members of his staff to take care of Winchester and the public property there, he set out with a small escort directly for the scene of battle. As he met the fugitives he ordered them to turn back, reminding them that they were going the wrong way. His presence soon restored confidence. Finding themselves worse frightened that hurt the men did halt and turn back. Many of those who had run ten miles got back in time to redeem their reputation as gallant soldiers before night.

When Sheridan got to the front he found Getty and [George Armstrong] Custer still holding their ground firmly between the Confederates and our retreating troops. Everything in the rear was now ordered up. Sheridan at once proceeded to intrench his position; and he awaited an assault from the enemy. This was made with vigor, and was directed principally against Emory's corps, which had sustained the principal loss in the first attack. By one o'clock the attack was repulsed. Early was so badly damaged that he seemed disinclined to make another attack, but went to work to intrench himself with a view to holding the position he had already gained. He thought, no doubt, that Sheridan would be glad enough to leave him unmolested; but in this he was mistaken.

About the middle of the afternoon Sheridan advanced. He sent his cavalry by both flanks, and they penetrated to the enemy's rear. The contest was close for a time, but at length the left of the enemy broke, and disintegration along the whole line soon followed. Early tried to rally his men, but they were followed so closely that they had to give way very quickly every time they attempted to make a stand. Our cavalry, having pushed on and got in the rear of the Confederates, captured twenty-four pieces of artillery, besides retaking what had been lost in the morning. This victory pretty much closed the campaigning in the Valley of Virginia. All the Confederate troops were sent back to Richmond with the exception of one division of infantry and a little cavalry. Wright's corps was ordered back to the Army of the Potomac, and two other divisions were withdrawn from the valley. Early had lost more men in killed, wounded and captured in the valley than Sheridan had commanded from first to last. . . .

OPPOSITE: William W. Averell (seated) was relieved of his brigade command in Sheridan's Shenandoah army for lack of aggressiveness. Such harsh dealing with subordinates was typical of Sheridan.

BELOW: Alfred Waud's sketch of Sheridan's legendary ride at the Battle of Winchester.

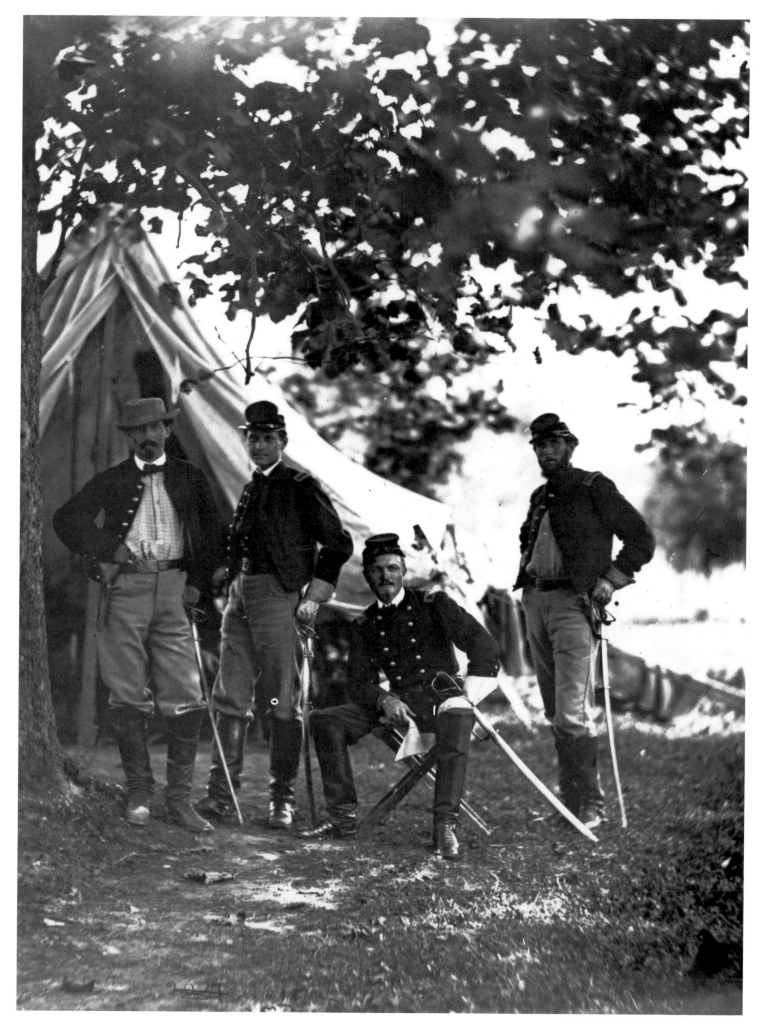

Chapter VII

The Union Victorious

OPPOSITE: Fort McAllister, on the Ogeechee River, was the key to Savannah's outer defenses. Sherman took it on his first try on December 13.

RIGHT: "The Sons of Columbia," a patriotic Union song issued for Independence Day during the war.

BELOW: Sherman's men invade South Carolina, February 1865.

After Sheridan's triumph in the Valley serious campaigning in Virginia halted for the winter, but this was not the case in Georgia. On November 16 Sherman pulled the bulk of his army out of Atlanta and set out on his famous (or, to Southerners, infamous) march through Georgia to Savannah and the sea. The Confederate commander, John B. Hood, had hoped to forestall this move by mounting a diversionary offensive behind Sherman in Tennessee, but Sherman was far too good a strategist to be drawn by such a gambit; instead, he merely detached George Thomas to deal with Hood, while he went on about the more important business of cutting the heart of the South in half.

ABOVE: Sherman's men destroy a Confederate railroad. Even before the March from Atlanta to the Sea it was Sherman's deliberate policy to destroy everything that could be of military value to the enemy.

Thomas proceeded on his assignment with such maddening deliberation that the impatient Grant nearly cashiered him. (As we shall see, later on in his Memoirs *Grant tried to make amends for some of the harsh things he had said about Thomas at the time.) But when Thomas finally did strike Hood, on December 15 in the Battle of Nashville, the effect was devastating: thereafter, for all practical purposes Hood's Army of Tennessee no longer existed.*

Sherman occupied Savannah on December 21, and on February 1, 1865, he embarked on what many historians regard the most brilliant enterprise of his stellar military career, the invasion of the Carolinas. Meanwhile, to the north, Grant was hatching plans for a stroke that he hoped would at last bring the dismal siege of Petersburg to an end. Sheridan, who was essential to the execution of the plan, was temporarily absent, having ridden back into the Shenandoah Valley to mop up what remained of Early's forces, and Grant fretfully awaited his return.

LEFT: The December 15, 1864, Battle of Nashville, in which Union General George Thomas utterly destroyed Hood's Army of Tennessee.

BELOW: Union troops outside Nashville in early December, just before the battle.

ABOVE: A view of Nashville from the roof of the Military College, looking northwest.

Sheridan reached City Point on the 26th day of March. His horses, of course, were jaded and many of them had lost their shoes. A few days of rest were necessary to recuperate the animals and also to have them shod and put in condition for moving. Immediately on General Sheridan's arrival at City Point I prepared his instructions for the move which I had decided upon. The movement was to commence on the 29th of the month.

After reading the instructions I had given him, Sheridan walked out of my tent, and I followed to have some conversation with him by himself – not in the presence of anybody else, even of a member of my staff. In preparing his instructions I contemplated just what took place; that is to say, capturing Five Forks, driving the enemy from Petersburg and Richmond and terminating the contest before separating from the enemy. But the Nation had already become restless and discouraged at the prolongation of the war, and many believed that it would never terminate except by compromise. Knowing that unless my plan proved an entire success it would be interpreted as a disastrous defeat, I provided in these instructions that in a certain event he was to cut loose from the Army of the Potomac and his base of supplies, and living upon the country proceed south by the way of the Danville Rail-

ABOVE: Santa Claus Sherman gives the North a Christmas present in a *Frank Leslie's Illustrated Newspaper* cartoon.

BELOW: Savannah in 1864.

RIGHT: The burden of command is all too evident in this famous informal portrait of an exhausted and careworn Grant at the height of the 1864 campaign.

OPPOSITE: Grant's plan for ending the Petersburg siege in the spring of 1865 was almost wholly dependent on whether Sheridan could turn Lee's flank. "Little Phil" would not let Grant down.

LEFT: Mantled Union guns before Petersburg.

BELOW: "Bomb-proof" quarters at Union Fort Sedgwick (a.k.a. "Fort Hell") in 1865.

road, or near it, across the Roanoke, get in the rear of Johnston, who was guarding that road, and co-operate with Sherman in destroying Johnston; then with these combined forces to help carry out the instructions which Sherman already had received, to act in co-operation with the armies around Petersburg and Richmond.

I saw that after Sheridan had read his instructions he seemed somewhat disappointed at the idea, possibly, of having to cut loose again from the Army of the Potomac, and place himself between the two main armies of the enemy. I said to him: "General, this portion of your instructions I have put in merely as a blind;" and gave him the reason for doing so. . . . I told him that, as a matter of fact, I intended to close the war right here, with this movement, and that he should go no farther. His face at once brightened up, and slapping his hand on his leg he said: "I am glad to hear it, and we can do it." . . .

Finally the 29th of March came, and fortunately there having been a few days free from rain, the surface of the ground was dry, giving indications that the time had come when we could move. On that date I moved out with all the army available after leaving sufficient force to hold the line about Petersburg. . . . The next day, March 30th, we had

made sufficient progress to the south-west to warrant me in starting Sheridan with his cavalry over by Dinwiddie with instructions to then come up by the road leading northwest to Five Forks, thus menacing the right of Lee's line. . . .

My hope was that Sheridan would be able to carry Five Forks, get on the enemy's right flank and rear, and force them to weaken their centre to protect their right so that an assault in the centre might be successfully made. General Wright's corps had been designated to make this assault, which I intended to order as soon as information reached me of Sheridan's success. He was to move under cover as close to the enemy as he could get. . . .

Sheridan succeeded by the middle of the afternoon [of April 1st] or a little later, in advancing up to the point from which to make his designed assault upon Five Forks itself. He was very impatient to make the assault and have it all over before night, because the ground he occupied would be untenable for him in bivouac during the night. Unless the assault was made and was successful, he would be obliged to return to Dinwiddie Court-House, or even further than that for the night. . . .

It was dusk when our troops under Sheri-

dan went over the parapets of the enemy. The two armies were mingled together there for a time in such manner that it was almost a question which one was going to demand the surrender of the other. Soon, however, the enemy broke and ran in every direction; some six thousand prisoners, beside artillery and small-arms in large quantities, falling into our hands. The flying troops were pursued in different directions, the cavalry and 5th corps under Sheridan pursuing the larger body which moved north-west.

This pursuit continued until about nine o'clock at night, when Sheridan halted his troops, and knowing the importance to him of the part of the enemy's line which had been captured, returned, sending the 5th corps across Hatcher's Run to just southwest of Petersburg, and facing them toward it. [Wesley] Merritt, with the cavalry, stopped and bivouacked west of Five Forks.

This was the condition which affairs were in on the night of the 1st of April. I then issued orders for an assault by Wright and [John] Parke at four o'clock on the morning of the 2d. I also ordered the 2d corps, General [Andrew] Humphreys, and General Ord with the Army of the James, on the left, to hold themselves in readiness to take any advantage that could be taken from weakening in their front. . . .

I was afraid that Lee would regard the possession of Five Forks as of so much importance that he would make a last desperate effort to retake it, risking everything upon the cast of a single die. It was for this reason that I had ordered the assault to take place at once, as soon as I had received the news of the capture of Five Forks. The corps commanders, however, reported that it was so dark that the men could not see to move, and it would be impossible to make the assault then. But we kept up a continuous artillery fire upon the enemy around the whole line including that north of the James River, until it was light enough to move, which was about a quarter to five in the morning.

BELOW: Victorious Federals pursue fleeing Rebel troops at Five Forks on April 1.

ABOVE: The Kurz & Allison version of the Union victory at Five Forks.

RIGHT: Engineering expert Andrew A. Humphreys served as Meade's chief-of-staff.

FAR RIGHT: Confederate General George Pickett, famous for his charge at Gettysburg, was the loser at the Battle of Five Forks.

At that hour Parke's and Wright's corps moved out as directed, brushed the *abatis* from their front as they advanced under a heavy fire of musketry and artillery, and went without flinching directly on till they mounted the parapets and threw themselves inside of the enemy's line. Parke, who was on the right, swept down to the right and captured a very considerable length of line in that direction, but at that point the outer was so near the inner line which closely enveloped the city of Petersburg that he could make no advance forward and, in fact, had a very serious task to turn the lines which he had captured to the defence of his own troops and to hold them; but he succeeded in this.

Wright swung around to his left and moved to Hatcher's Run, sweeping everything before him. . . .

In the meantime Ord and Humphreys, in obedience to the instructions they had received, had succeeded by daylight, or very early in the morning, in capturing the intrenched picket-lines in their front; and

LEFT: Confederate General John Pegram, who had fought throughout the 1864 campaign, met his death early in 1865 at Hatcher's Run.

BELOW: This segment of the Confederate defensive line at Petersburg is typical of what confronted Union troops when they made their final assault on April 2, 1865.

LEFT: Grant's army had been stalemated behind defensive works such as these outside Petersburg for the best part of a year, yet when Grant finally hit upon a plan to break the siege, it took him only two days to do it.

ABOVE: Union soldiers storm across the parapets of the Petersburg defenses on April 2, 1865. The Confederates withdrew from the city in the night, and Richmond fell the following day.

RIGHT: When they abandoned Richmond, Confederate troops tried to burn their military facilities in the city. The fires got out of hand, and much of the capital of the Confederacy was destroyed.

before Wright got up to that point, Ord had also succeeded in getting inside of the enemy's intrenchments. The second corps soon followed; and the outer works of Petersburg were in the hands of the National troops, never to be wrenched from them again. When Wright reached Hatcher's Run, he sent a regiment to destroy the South Side Railroad just outside of the city. . . .

Lee made frantic efforts to recover at least part of the lost ground. Parke on our right was repeatedly assaulted, but repulsed every effort. Before noon Longstreet was ordered up from the north side of the James River, thus bringing the bulk of Lee's army around to the support of his extreme right. As soon as I learned this I notified [Godfrey] Weitzel and directed him to keep up close to the enemy and to have [G.L.] Hartsuff, commanding the Bermuda Hundred front, to do the same thing, and if they found any break to go in; Hartsuff especially should do so, for this would separate Richmond and Petersburg.

Sheridan, after he had returned to Five Forks, swept down to Petersburg, coming in on our left. This gave us a continuous line from the Appomattox River below the city to the same river above. . . .

The enemy had in addition to their intrenched line close up to Petersburg, two enclosed works outside of it, Fort Gregg and Fort Whitworth. We thought it had now become necessary to carry them by assault. About one o'clock in the day, Fort Gregg was assaulted by [R.S.] Foster's division of the 24th corps (Gibbon's), supported by two brigades from Ord's command. The battle was desperate and the National troops were repulsed several times; but it was finally carried, and immediately the troops in Fort Whitworth evacuated the place. The guns of Fort Gregg were turned upon the retreating enemy, and the commanding officer with some sixty of the men of Fort Whitworth surrendered.

I cannot explain the situation here better than by giving my dispatch to City Point that evening:

BOYDTON ROAD, NEAR PETERSBURG,
April 2, 1865.-4.40 P.M.
COLONEL T. S. BOWERS,
    City Point

We are now up and have a continuous lines of troops, and in a few hours will be intrenched from the Appomattox below Petersburg to the river above. Heth's and Wilcox's divisions, such part of them as were not captured, were cut off from town, either designedly on their part or because they could not help it. Sheridan with the cavalry and 5th corps is above them. Miles's division, 2d corps, was sent from the White Oak Road to Sutherland Station on the South Side Railroad, where he met

BELOW: An Alfred Waud sketch of a train of railroad cars and a workshop that had been destroyed by Confederates fleeing from Petersburg. The locale is a bridge over the Appomattox River.

ABOVE: Burning of the Fredericksburg and Richmond Railroad Bridge over the North Anna River, May 1864: An A.R. Waud sketch published in *Harper's Weekly*.

RIGHT: A dismal scene of gutted Richmond after the Confederate evacuation.

them, and at last accounts was engaged with them. Not knowing whether Sheridan would get up in time, General Humphreys was sent with another division from here. The whole captures since the army started out gunning will amount to not less than twelve thousand men, and probably fifty pieces of artillery. I do not know the number of men and guns accurately. . . .

I think the President might come out and pay us a visit tomorrow.

U. S. GRANT,
Lieutenant-General.

During the night of April 2d our line was intrenched from the river above to the river below. I ordered a bombardment to be commenced the next morning at five A.M., to be followed by an assault at six o'clock; but the enemy evacuated Petersburg early in the morning. . . .

The fall of Petersburg doomed Richmond, which was occupied by Union troops the following day. Lee's army, now down to about 35,000 starving men and beginning to disintegrate, fled westward toward Amelia Court House, where Lee hoped to entrain his troops on the Danville Railroad and take them to South Carolina to join forces with Joseph Johnston in his fight against Sherman. But Sheridan cut the Danville line on April 5, and Lee's last hope of escape was gone. What was left of the Army of Northern Virginia struggled on for a few more days, but on April 9, at Appomattox Court House, Lee was finally brought to bay and surrounded by overwhelmingly superior Union forces. It was the end. "There is nothing left for me to do but go and see General Grant," said Lee, "and I would rather die a thousand deaths." A few moments later a Southern rider bearing a white flag galloped towards the Union lines.

BELOW: Union cavalry horses stand tethered to an iron fence amid Richmond's ruins.

When the white flag was put out by Lee, as already described, I was [en route] moving towards Appomattox Court House, and consequently could not be communicated with immediately, and be informed of what Lee had done. Lee, therefore, sent a flag to the rear to advise Meade and one to the front to Sheridan, saying that he had sent a message to me for the purpose of having a meeting to consult about the surrender of his army, and asked for a suspension of hostilities until I could be communicated with. As they had heard nothing of this until the fighting had got to be severe and all going against Lee, both of these commanders hesitated very considerably about suspending hostilities at all. They were afraid it was not in good faith, and we had the Army of Northern Virginia where it could not escape except by some deception. They, however, finally consented to a suspension of hostilities for two hours to give an opportunity of communicating with me in that time, if possible. It was found that, from the route I had taken, they would probably not be able to communicate with me and get an answer back within the time fixed unless the messenger should pass through the rebel lines.

Rebel officers coming into Richmond by the Pontoon bridge to give themselves up.

Lee, therefore, sent an escort with the officer bearing this message through his lines to me.

April 9, 1865

GENERAL:– I received your note of this morning on the picket-line whither I had come to meet you and ascertain definitely what terms were embraced in your proposal of yesterday, with reference to the surrender of this army. I now request an interview in accordance with the offer contained in your letter of yesterday for that purpose.

R. E. LEE, General
LIEUTENANT-GENERAL U. S. GRANT

When the officer reached me I was still suffering with [a] sick headache; but the instant I saw the contents of the note I was cured. I wrote the following note in reply and hastened on:

April 9, 1865.

GENERAL R. E. LEE,

Commanding C. S. Armies

Your note of this date is but this moment (11.50 A.M.) received, in consequence of my having passed from the Richmond and Lynchburg road to the Farmville and Lynchburg road. I am at this writing about four miles west of Walker's Church and will push forward to the front for the purpose of meeting you. Notice sent to me on this road where you wish the interview to take place will meet me.

U. S. GRANT,
Lieutenant-General.

I was conducted at once to where Sheridan was located with his troops drawn up in line of battle facing the Confederate army near by. They were very much excited, and expressed their view that this was all a ruse employed to enable the Confederates to get away. They said they believed that Johnston was marching up from North Carolina now, and Lee was moving to join him; and they would whip the rebels where they now were in five minutes if I would only let them go in. But I had no doubt about the good faith of Lee, and pretty soon was conducted to where he was. I found him at the house of a Mr. McLean, at Appomattox Court House, with Colonel Marshall, one of his staff officers, awaiting my arrival. The head of his column was occupying a hill, on a portion of which was an apple orchard, beyond a little valley which separated it from that on the crest of which Sheridan's forces were drawn up in line of battle to the south. . . .

OPPOSITE TOP: The last C.S.A. general in Richmond, Martin W. Gary, escorted Jefferson Davis to (temporary) safety in South Carolina.

OPPOSITE BOTTOM: Not all the Rebel troops in Richmond fled the city. Some, as shown in this Waud sketch, took the city's fall as an occasion to surrender.

BELOW: The house of Wilmer McLean in Appomattox Court House, Virginia. McLean's former house had been ruined in the Civil War's first big battle, First Bull Run. In this house the war would effectively end.

I had known General Lee in the old army, and had served with him in the Mexican War; but did not suppose, owing to the difference in our age and rank, that he would remember me; while I would more naturally remember him distinctly, because he was the chief of staff of General Scott in the Mexican War.

When I had left camp that morning I had not expected so soon the result that was then taking place, and consequently was in rough garb. I was without a sword, as I usually was when on horseback on the field, and wore a soldier's blouse for a coat, with the shoulder straps of my rank to indicate to the army who I was. When I went into the house I found General Lee. We greeted each other, and after shaking hands took our seats. I had my staff with me, a good portion of whom were in the room during the whole of the interview.

What General Lee's feelings were I do not know. As he was a man of much dignity, with an impassible face, it was impossible to say whether he felt inwardly glad that the end had finally come, or felt sad over the result, and was too manly to show it. Whatever his feelings, they were entirely concealed

BELOW: Union General Orville Babcock (right) was Grant's aide-de-camp. It was he who was sent to escort General Lee to the surrender talks at the McLean house.

from my observation; but my own feelings, which had been quite jubilant on the receipt of his letter, were sad and depressed. I felt like anything rather than rejoicing at the downfall of a foe who had fought so long and valiantly, and had suffered so much for a cause, though that cause was, I believe, one of the worst for which a people ever fought, and one for which there was the least excuse. I do not question, however, the sincerity of the great mass of those who were opposed to us.

General Lee was dressed in a full uniform which was entirely new, and was wearing a sword of considerable value, very likely the sword which had been presented by the State of Virginia; at all events, it was an entirely different sword from the one that would ordinarily be worn in the field. In my rough traveling suit, the uniform of a private with the straps of a lieutenant-general, I must have contrasted very strangely with a man so handsomely dressed, six feet high and of faultless form. But this was not a matter that I thought of until afterwards.

We soon fell into a conversation about old army times. He remarked that he remembered me very well in the old army; and I told him that as a matter of course I remembered him perfectly, but from the difference in our rank and years (there being about sixteen

years' difference in our ages), I had thought it very likely that I had not attracted his attention sufficiently to be remembered by him after such a long interval. Our conversation grew so pleasant that I almost forgot the object of our meeting. After the conversation had run on in this style for some time, General Lee called my attention to the object of our meeting, and said that he had asked for this interview for the purpose of getting from me the terms I proposed to give his

ABOVE: General Robert Edward Lee, the greatest commander of the Confederacy.

LEFT: A portion of a note from Lee to Grant, part of the historic correspondence between the two commanders regarding Lee's surrender.

SUNDAY

THE SURRENDER OF GEN. LEE AND HIS ARMY TO LIEUT. GEN. GRANT

Th. Nast.

THE ARMIES OF THE REPUBLIC HAVE, BY THE

BLESSING OF GOD TRIUMPHED OVER THE FOES OF THE UNION

THE CONSTITUTION AND THE LAWS

HONOR THE ILLUSTRIOUS DEAD, AND HEARTILY SYMPATHIZE WITH THE SUFFERINGS OF OUR GALLANT HEROES AND THEIR FAMILIES.

UNION

army. I said that I meant merely that his army should lay down their arms, not to take them up again during the continuance of the war unless duly and properly exchanged. He said that he had so understood my letter.

Then we gradually fell off again into conversation about matters foreign to the subject which had brought us together. This continued for some little time, when General Lee again interrupted the course of the conversation by suggesting that the terms I proposed to give his army ought to be written out. I called to General [Ely] Parker, secretary on my staff, for writing materials, and commenced writing out the following terms:

APPOMATTOX C. H., Va.,
    Apl 9th, 1865.
GEN. R. E. LEE,
    Comd'g C. S. A.
GEN: In accordance with the substance of my letter to you of the 8th inst., I propose to receive the surrender of the Army of N. Va. on the following terms, to wit: Rolls of all the officers and men to be made in duplicate. One copy to be given to an officer designated by me, the other to be retained by such officer or officers as you may designate. The officers to give their individual paroles not to take up arms against the Government of the United States until properly exchanged, and each company or regimental commander sign a like parole for the men of their commands. The arms, artillery and public property to be parked and stacked, and turned over to the officer appointed by me to receive them. This will not embrace the side-arms of the officers, nor their private horses or baggage. This done, each officer and man will be allowed to return to their homes, not to be disturbed by United States authority so long as they observe their paroles and the laws in force where they may reside.
    Very respectfully,
    U. S. GRANT,
    Lt. Gen.

When I put my pen to the paper I did not know the first word that I should make use of in writing the terms. I only knew what was in my mind, and I wished to express it clearly, so that there could be no mistaking it. As I wrote on, the thought occurred to me that the officers had their own private horses and effects, which were important to them, but of no value to us; also that it would be an unnecessary humiliation to call upon them to deliver their side arms.

No conversation, not one word, passed between General Lee and myself, either

ABOVE: The April 9 meeting between Lee and Grant in the McLean house, where the terms upon which Lee surrendered were formally concluded.

OPPOSITE: None of the many artists' versions of Lee's surrender to Grant is fully authentic or even terribly convincing. This one is the work of *Harper's Weekly's* famous Thomas Nast.

RIGHT AND OPPOSITE: Victor and vanquished – Grant and Lee as they looked in 1865. Arguments about who was the better general probably can never be resolved. Both men accomplished things the other did not. Grant never won a battle as dazzling as Lee's famous victory at Chancellorsville; Lee never fought a campaign as brilliant as the one Grant waged against Vicksburg. It is enough to say that both were truly great commanders.

about private property, side arms, or kindred subjects. He appeared to have no objections to the terms first proposed; or if he had a point to make against them he wished to wait until they were in writing to make it. When he read over that part of the terms about side arms, horses and private property of the officers, he remarked, with some feeling, I thought, that this would have a happy effect upon his army.

Then, after a little further conversation,

General Lee remarked to me again that their army was organized a little differently from the army of the United States (still maintaining by implication that we were two countries); that in their army the cavalrymen and artillerists owned their own horses; and he asked if he was to understand that the men who so owned their horses were to be permitted to retain them. I told him that as the terms were written they would not; that only the officers were permitted to take their

private property. He then, after reading over the terms a second time, remarked that that was clear.

I then said to him that I thought this would be about the last battle of the war – I sincerely hoped so; and I said further I took it that most of the men in the ranks were small farmers. The whole country had been so raided by the two armies that it was doubtful whether they would be able to put in a crop to carry themselves and their families through the next winter without the aid of the horses they were then riding. The United States did not want them and I would, therefore, instruct the officers I left behind to receive the paroles of his troops to let every man of the Confederate army who claimed to own a horse or mule take the animal to his home. Lee remarked again that this would have a happy effect.

He then sat down and wrote out the following letter:

LEFT: A postwar photograph of leading generals of the Union armies includes: Sheridan (third from left), Grant (eighth from left), Sherman (center, coat over arm).

HEADQUARTERS ARMY OF NORTHERN VIRGINIA,

April 9, 1865.

GENERAL:– I received your letter of this date containing the terms of the surrender of the Army of Northern Virginia as proposed by you. As they are substantially the same as those expressed in your letter of the 8th inst., they are accepted. I will proceed to designate the proper officers to carry the stipulations into effect.

R. E. LEE, General

LIEUT.-GENERAL U.S. GRANT

While duplicates of the two letters were being made, the Union generals present were severally presented to General Lee.

The much talked of surrendering of Lee's sword and my handing it back, this and much more that has been said about it is the purest romance. The word sword or side arms was not mentioned by either of us until I wrote it in the terms. There was no premeditation, and it did not occur to me until the moment I wrote it down. If I had happened to omit it, and General Lee had called my attention to it, I should have put it in the terms. . . .

General Lee, after all was completed and before taking his leave, remarked that his army was in a very bad condition for want of food, and that they were without forage; that his men had been living for some days on parched corn exclusively, and that he would have to ask me for rations and forage. I told him "certainly," and asked for how many men he wanted rations. His answer was "about twenty-five thousand:" and I

authorized him to send his own commissary and quartermaster to Appomattox Station, two or three miles away, where he could have, out of the trains we had stopped, all the provisions wanted. As for forage, we had ourselves depended almost entirely upon the country for that.

Generals Gibbon, [Charles] Griffin and Merritt were designated by me to carry into effect the paroling of Lee's troops before they should start for their homes – General Lee leaving Generals Longstreet, [John] Gordon and [William] Pendleton for them to confer with in order to facilitate this work. Lee and I then separated as cordially as we had met, he returning to his own lines, and all went into bivouac . . . at Appomattox.

Soon after Lee's departure I telegraphed to Washington as follows:

HEADQUARTERS APPOMATTOX C. H., Va.,

April 9th, 1865, 4.30 P.M.

HON. E. M. STANTON, Secretary of War, Washington.

General Lee surrendered the Army of Northern Virginia this afternoon on terms proposed by myself. The accompanying additional correspondence will show the conditions fully.

U. S. GRANT,

Lieut.-General.

When news of the surrender first reached our lines our men commenced firing a salute of a hundred guns in honor of the victory. I at once sent word, however, to have it stopped. The Confederates were now our prisoners, and we did not want to exult over their downfall. . . .

GEN. GRANT

LOOKOUT MOUNTAIN

RIGHT: Union soldiers pose
for a photograph in front of
the court house building in
Appomattox Court House.

Chapter VIII

Triumph and Tragedy

Lee's surrender effectively ended the Civil War. Five days later the only other important Confederate command left in the field – that of Joseph Johnston, now in North Carolina – asked Sherman for surrender terms, and these were finalized within a week's time.

On April 14, the same day as Johnston's capitulation, Abraham Lincoln asked General and Mrs. Grant to join the President and his wife in attending a play that was to be given that evening at Ford's Theatre in Washington. The Grants regretfully declined on the grounds that they had planned to leave the capital that day to visit their children in New Jersey. The Grants had gotten only as far as Philadelphia when they learned of the President's assassination.

The murder of Lincoln cast a pall over the North's rejoicing, but after a month of mourning the nation's grief was sufficiently purged to permit the observance of at least one solemn tribute to the Union's victorious fighting men. In these closing excerpts from the Memoirs *Grant both describes that impressive ceremony and offers personal impressions of some of the men with whom he served during the war. (It should be noted that the passage relating to General Thomas appears here to be slightly out of sequence.) The final excerpt represents the concluding paragraphs of the* Memoirs.

On the 18th of May orders were issued by the adjutant-general for a grand review by the President and his cabinet of Sherman's and Meade's armies. The review commenced on the 23rd and lasted two days. Meade's army occupied over six hours of the first day in passing the grand stand which had been erected in front of the President's house. Sherman witnessed this review from the grand stand which was occupied by the President and his cabinet. Here he showed his resentment for the cruel and harsh treatment that had unnecessarily been inflicted upon him by the Secretary of War, by refusing to take his extended hand.

Sherman's troops had been in camp on

RIGHT: Lee's surrender on April 9 made that of Johnston inevitable. He began parleys with Sherman on April 17 and surrendered on the 26th. In this picture, unlike most of his photographs, he wears a full white beard, which is historically correct for this particular occasion.

ABOVE: John Wilkes Booth
assassinates Abraham Lincoln
in Ford's Theatre on the
night of April 14, 1865.

LEFT: Booth leaps from the
murdered president's box on
to the theater's stage. He
broke his leg in the leap but
was able to escape from the
scene of the crime. He was
caught on April 26 and killed
in the ensuing shootout.

LEFT: In July 1965 four of the people who were convicted of conspiring with Booth in the assassination plot were hanged. They were Lewis Paine, David Herold, George Atzerodt, and Mary Surratt. The last, Booth's landlady, may well have been innocent.

ABOVE: Lincoln's funeral cortège winds past City Hall in New York City on April 26, 1865. Because Lincoln was a controversial president, the intensity with which the nation grieved his death is all the more extraordinary.

OPPOSITE: On April 21, troops restrain a crowd of grieving Washingtonians from coming too near to the catafalque of the slain president.

the south side of the Potomac. During the night of the 23rd he crossed over and bivouacked not far from the Capitol. Promptly at ten o'clock on the morning of the 24th, his troops commenced to pass in review. Sherman's army made a different appearance from that of the Army of the Potomac. The latter had been operating where they received directly from the North full supplies of food and clothing regularly: the review of this army therefore was the review of a body of 65,000 well-drilled, well-disciplined and orderly soldiers inured to hardship and fit for any duty, but without the experience of gathering their own food and supplies in an enemy's country, and of being ever on the watch. Sherman's army was not so well-dressed as the Army of the Potomac, but their marching could not be excelled; they gave the appearance of men who had been thoroughly drilled to endure hardships, either by long and continuous marches or through exposure to any climate, without the ordinary shelter of a camp. They exhibited also some of the order of march through Georgia where the "sweet potatoes sprung up from the ground" as Sherman's army went marching through. In the rear of a company there would be a cap-

tured horse or mule loaded with small cooking utensils, captured chickens and other food picked up for the use of the men. Negro families who had followed the army would sometimes come along in the rear of the company, with three or four children packed upon a single mule, and the mother leading it.

The sight was varied and grand: nearly all day for two successive days, from the Capitol to the Treasury Building, could be seen a mass of orderly soldiers marching in columns of companies. The National flag was flying from almost every house and store; the windows were filled with spectators; the door-steps and side-walks were crowded with colored people and poor whites who did not succeed in securing better quarters from which to get a view of the grand armies. The city was about as full of strangers who had come to see the sights as it usually is on inauguration day when a new President takes his seat.

It may not be out of place to again allude to President Lincoln and the Secretary of War, Mr. Stanton, who were the great conspicuous figures in the executive branch of the government. There is no great difference of opinion now, in the public mind, as to the

OPPOSITE: One of the most beloved of American icons: Mathew Brady's famed January 8, 1864, portrait of Abraham Lincoln.

characteristics of the President. With Mr. Stanton the case is different. They were the very opposite of each other in almost every particular, except that each possessed great ability. Mr. Lincoln gained influence over men by making them feel that it was a pleasure to serve him. He preferred yielding his own wish to gratify others, rather than to insist upon having his own way. It distressed him to disappoint others. In matters of public duty, however, he had what he wished, but in the least offensive way. Mr. Stanton never questioned his own authority to command, unless resisted. He cared nothing for the feeling of others. In fact it seemed to be pleasanter to him to disappoint than to gratify. He felt no hesitation in assuming the functions of the executive, or in acting without advising with him. If his act was not sustained, he would change it – if he saw the matter would be followed up until he did so.

It was generally supposed that these two officials formed the complement of each other. The Secretary was required to prevent the President's being imposed upon. The President was required in the more responsible place of seeing that injustice was not

BELOW: Lincoln's cabinet in 1863. In the foreground, facing Lincoln, is Secretary of State William Seward, who was badly wounded by Lewis Paine in the execution of the Booth assassination plot.

done to others. I do not know that this view of these two men is still entertained by the majority of the people. It is not a correct view, however, in my estimation. Mr. Lincoln did not require a guardian to aid him in the fulfilment of a public trust.

Mr. Lincoln was not timid, and he was willing to trust his generals in making and executing their plans. The Secretary was very timid, and it was impossible for him to avoid interfering with the armies covering the capital when it was sought to defend it by an offensive movement against the army guarding the Confederate capital. He could see our weakness, but he could not see that the enemy was in danger. The enemy would not have been in danger if Mr. Stanton had been in the field. These characteristics of the two officials were clearly shown shortly after Early came so near getting into the capital.

Among the army and corps commanders who served with me during the war between the States, and who attracted much public attention, but of whose ability as soldiers I have not yet given any estimate, are Meade, Hancock, Sedgwick, Burnside, Terry and Hooker. . . . Of those first named, Burnside at one time had command of the Army of the

RIGHT: Union General Ambrose Burnside receives command of the Army of the Potomac in 1862. Burnside had insisted that he was not up to the post, and soon Washington wished it had listened to him.

BELOW: The Union victory at the Battle of the Gettysburg in 1863 made the reputation of George Meade, who took the command of the Army of the Potomac on June 28, three days before the battle.

Potomac, and later of the Army of the Ohio. Hooker also commanded the Army of the Potomac for a short time.

General [George] Meade was an officer of great merit, with drawbacks to his usefulness that were beyond his control. He had been an officer of the engineer corps before the war, and consequently had never served with troops until he was over forty-six years of age. He never had, I believe, a command of less than a brigade. He saw clearly and distinctly the position of the enemy, and the topography of the country in front of his own position. His first idea was to take advantage of the lay of the ground, sometimes without reference to the direction we wanted to move afterwards. He was subordinate to his superiors in rank to the extent that he could execute an order which changed his own plans with the same zeal he would have displayed if the plan had been his own. He was brave and conscientious, and commanded the respect of all who knew him. He was unfortunately of a temper that would get beyond his control, at times, and make him speak to officers of high rank in the most offensive manner. No one saw this fault more plainly than he himself, and no one regretted it more. This made it unpleasant at times, even in battle, for those around him to approach him even with information. In spite of this defect he was a most valuable officer and deserves a high place in the annals of his country.

General [Ambrose] Burnside was an officer who was generally liked and respected. He was not, however, fitted to command an army. No one knew this better than himself. He always admitted his blunders, and extenuated those of officers under him beyond what they were entitled to. It was hardly his fault that he was ever assigned to a separate command.

Of [Joseph] Hooker I saw but little during the war. I had known him very well before, however. Where I did see him, at Chattanooga, his achievement in bringing his command around the point of Lookout Mountain

BELOW: Meade with his staff in 1863. Regarding Meade's notoriously bad temper, one member of his staff wrote, "I don't know any thin old gentleman . . . who, when he is wrathy, exercises less of Christian charity than my well-beloved chief."

and into Chattanooga Valley was brilliant. I nevertheless regarded him as a dangerous man. He was not subordinate to his superiors. He was ambitious to the extent of caring nothing for the rights of others. His disposition was, when engaged in battle, to get detached from the main body of the army and exercise a separate command, gathering to his standard all he could of his juniors.

[Winfield Scott] Hancock stands the most conspicuous figure of all the general officers who did not exercise a separate command. He commanded a corps longer than any other one, and his name was never mentioned as having committed in battle a blunder for which he was responsible. He was a man of very conspicuous personal appearance. Tall, well-formed and, at the time of which I now write, young and fresh-looking, he presented an appearance that would attract the attention of an army as he passed. His genial disposition made him friends, and his personal courage and his presence with his command in the thickest of the fight won for him the confidence of troops serving under him. No matter how

hard the fight, the 2d corps always felt that their commander was looking after them.

[John] Sedgwick was killed at Spottyslvania before I had an opportunity of forming an estimate of his qualifications as a soldier from personal observation. I had known him in Mexico when both of us were lieutenants, and when our service gave no indication that either of us would ever be equal to the command of a brigade. He stood very high in the army, however, as an officer and a man. He was brave and conscientious. His ambition was not great, and he seemed to dread responsibility. He was willing to do any amount of battling, but always wanted some one else to direct. He declined the command of the Army of the Potomac once, if not oftener.

General Alfred H. Terry came into the army as a volunteer without a military education. His way was won without political influence up to an important separate command – the expedition against Fort Fisher, in January, 1865. His success there was most brilliant, and won for him the rank of brigadier-general in the regular army and of

LEFT: Joseph Hooker (front, second from right) was to some extent in Coventry when he served under Grant in the Battle of Lookout Mountain. Earlier that year Hooker had led the Army of the Potomac to disaster at the Battle of Chancellorsville, and he had subsequently been eased out of his command of the Army of the Potomac and been given more modest responsibilities. Grant thought Hooker fairly competent militarily, but he disliked and distrusted him. "I . . . regarded him," wrote Grant, "as a dangerous man."

major-general of volunteers. He is a man who makes friends of those under him by his consideration of their wants and their dues. As a commander, he won their confidence by his coolness in action and by his clearness of perception in taking in the situation under which he was placed at any given time. . . .

As my official letters on file in the War Department, as well as my remarks in this book, reflect upon General [George H.] Thomas by dwelling somewhat upon his tardiness, it is due to myself, as well as to him, that I give my estimate of him as a soldier. . . . I had been at West Point with Thomas one year, and had known him later in the old army. He was a man of commanding appearance; slow and deliberate in speech and action, sensible, honest and brave. He

possessed valuable soldierly qualities in an eminent degree. He gained the confidence of all who served under him, and almost their love. This implies a very valuable quality. It is a quality which calls out the most efficient services of the troops serving under the commander possessing it.

Thomas's dispositions were deliberately made, and always good. He could not be driven from a point he was given to hold. He was not as good, however, in pursuit as he was in action. I do not believe that he could ever have conducted Sherman's army from Chattanooga to Atlanta against the defences and the commander guarding that line in 1864. On the other hand, if it had been given him to hold the line which Johnston tried to hold, neither that general nor Sherman, nor any other officer could have done it better.

LEFT: Grant's inauguration in 1869. As president, Grant would display once again the shortcomings that had always before blighted his forays into civilian life. The best that can be said of his two terms in office is that they were honorable failures, in which he was constantly being misled or betrayed by men in whom he had naively put his trust and whom he then defended in a spirit of misplaced loyalty.

Thomas was a valuable officer, who richly deserved, as he has received, the plaudits of his countrymen for the part he played in the great tragedy of 1861-5.

*   *   *

I feel that we are on the eve of a new era, when there is to be great harmony between the Federal and Confederate. I cannot stay to be a living witness to the correctness of this prophecy; but I feel it within me that it is to be so. The universally kind feeling expressed for me at a time when it was supposed that each day would prove my last, seemed to me the beginning of the answer to "Let us have peace."

The expressions of these kindly feelings were not restricted to a section of the country, nor to a division of the people. They came from individual citizens of all nationalities; from all denominations – the Protestant, the Catholic, and the Jew; and from the various societies of the land – scientific, educational, religious, or otherwise. Politics did not enter into the matter at all.

I am not egotist enough to suppose all this significance should be given because I was the object of it. But the war between the States was a very bloody and a very costly war. One side or the other had to yield principles they deemed dearer than life before it could be brought to an end. I commanded the whole of the mighty host engaged on the victorious side. I was, no matter whether deservedly so or not, a representative of that side of the controversy. It is a significant and gratifying fact that Confederates should have joined heartily in this spontaneous move. I hope the good feeling inaugurated may continue to the end.

BELOW: Grant with his first cabinet. Among those involved in scandals during Grant's administration were Schuyler Colfax, his vice president during his first term, and W.W. Belknap, his second secretary of war.

LEFT: Ulysses Simpson Grant, 18th president of the United States and one of history's greatest generals.

Robert E. Lee

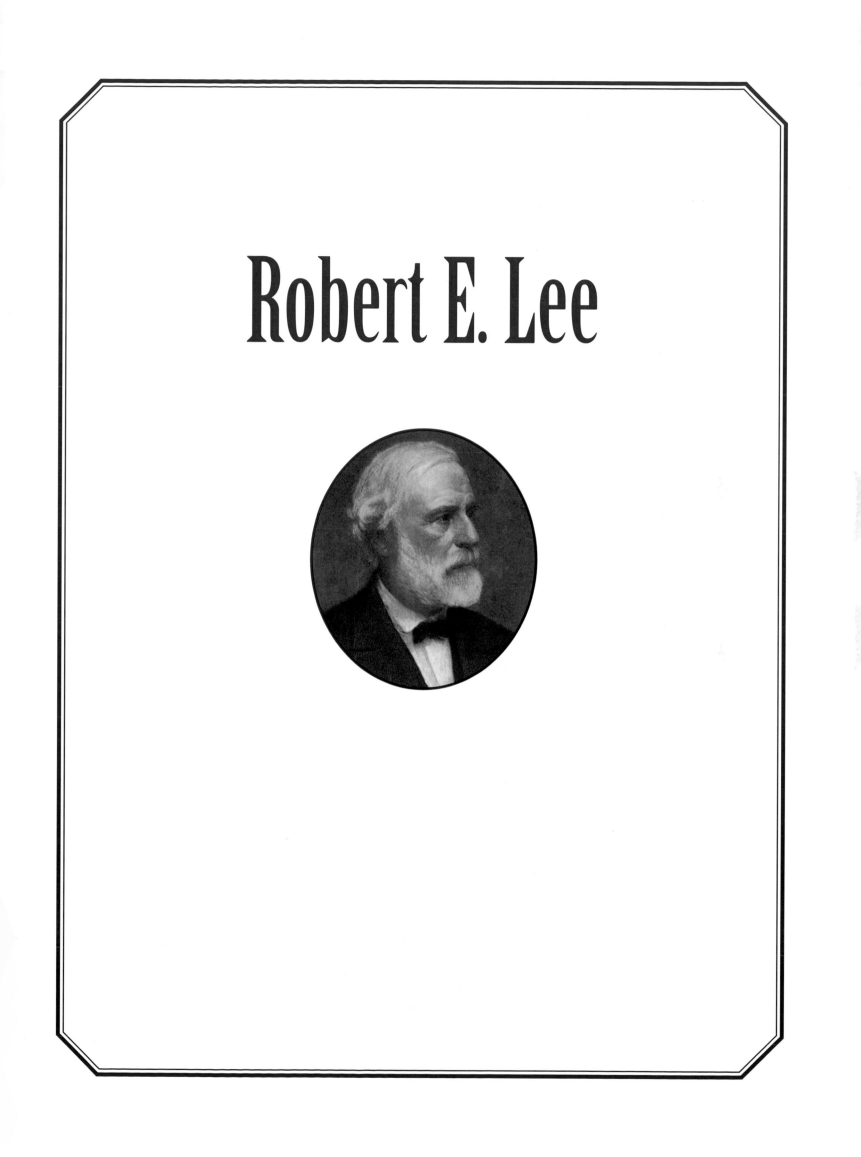

Chapter I

The Seven Days' Campaign

BELOW: Lee, as military adviser to Jefferson Davis, addresses the Confederate president and his cabinet in Richmond.

OPPOSITE: Map showing battle-grounds around Richmond. Lee's defenses at Drewry's Bluff (Drury Bluff on the map) on the James River south of the Confederate capital effectively protected the city against the Union fleet.

In the winter of 1862 the Confederate Congress created the office of "military adviser to the President," with the view of lightening the arduous duties which devolved upon him as commander-in-chief of the Confederate forces. Lee was selected to fill this position, and about the 13th of March, 1862, he entered upon his duties. The staff allowed him consisted of a military secretary with the rank of colonel and four aides with the rank of major. General Lee offered to Major A. L. Long the position of military secretary, and selected for his aides-de-camp Majors Randolph Talcott, Walter H. Taylor, Charles S. Venable, and Charles Marshall. When the writer reported for duty, about the middle of May, he found the general actively engaged in superintending the erection of defences on the James River near Richmond. The battery and obstruc-

tions at Drewry's Bluff were so advanced that the great alarm that had been felt for the safety of the city upon the evacuation of Norfolk began to subside, as there was no longer the fear of an immediate attack. The Federal gunboats had entered the James, and on the 15th the battery at Drewry's Bluff was attacked by the enemy's fleet, consisting of the iron-clads Galena and Naugatuck, a monitor, and two gunboats. These vessels were skilfully handled and gallantly fought. The Galena approached within four hundred yards of the battery, and then opened a spirited fire with her powerful guns; the Naugatuck and monitor closely supported her, while the gunboats delivered their fire at a longer range. After a hotly-contested conflict the fleet was repulsed with heavy loss. The Galena was so severely damaged as to be rendered unfit for future

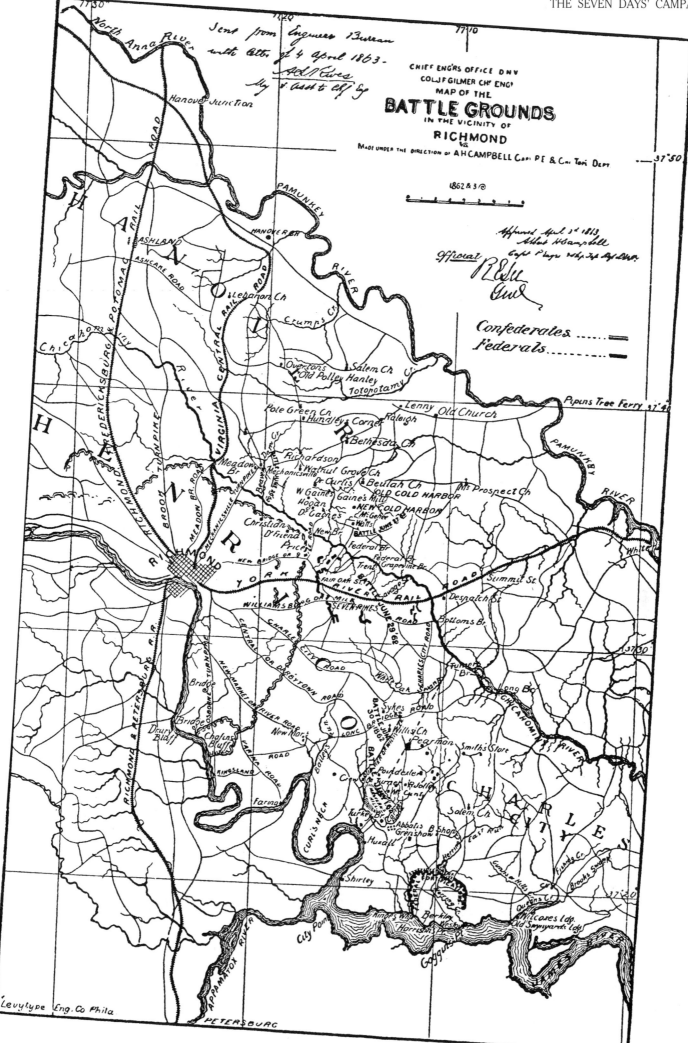

RIGHT: Confederate General Joseph E. Johnston was wounded at the Battle of Seven Pines. President Davis named Lee to replace him as commander of the Army of Northern Virginia.

BELOW: Confederate soldiers wounded in the Battle of Seven Pines are attended by civilians in the streets of Richmond.

service, while the other vessels were more or less injured; the battery sustained but slight damage. This defeat of the gunboats by an incomplete earthwork of only five guns for the first time caused a just value to be placed on defences of that character, which thenceforth became a conspicuous element in defensive operations.

At this time the safety of Richmond was entirely due to the skill and energy of General Lee, for upon the evacuation of Norfolk the James was left enirely open from its mouth to Richmond, and the hastily-constructed defence at Drewry's Bluff was the only barrier interposed between that city and a hostile fleet. After crossing the Chickahominy, about the 20th, General J. E. Johnston assumed the defence of Richmond. He attacked the enemy at Seven Pines on the 31st of May, and was severely wounded, as we have seen, near the close of the action. That event was immediately followed by the appointment of Lee to the command of the Army of Northern Virginia. Though regretting the cause that led to his assignment to the command of the army, he was pleased to be released from the duties of the office for

those of the field, which were far better suited to his active and energetic disposition. He carried with him to the field the same personal staff that had been allowed him in Richmond.

On the afternoon of the 1st of June, General G. W. Smith, on whom the command of the army had devolved when General Johnston was wounded, resigned his command to General Lee, and shortly after retired on account of bad health. It soon appeared that there was considerable depression in the army, the natural consequence of the incidents of war. As some of the officers were apprehensive that the army would not be able to maintain its position should it be attacked, Lee thought it advisable to assemble his principal officers for deliberation on its condition at an early period.

In reference to this point, Mr. Davis, in his *Rise and Fall of the Confederacy*, chap. xxiii., vol. ii., says: "The day after General Lee assumed command I was riding out to the army, when I saw at a house on my left a number of horses, and among them one I recognized as belonging to him. I dismounted and entered the house, where I found him in consultation with a number of his general officers. The tone of the conversation was quite despondent, and one especially pointed out the inevitable consequence of the enemy's advance by throwing out bayoux and constructing successive parallels." Farther on he refers to a want of co-operation that existed among the different divisions during the battle of Fair Oaks and Seven Pines, which was productive of natural distrust that might have resulted in serious demoralization had it not been

ABOVE: Federal reconnaissance balloon *Intrepid* at the Battle of Seven Pines on June 1, 1862.

221

ABOVE: As the Confederates moved to defend Richmond, they were engaged by Federal troops at Williamsburg on the James.

RIGHT: Union charge at Seven Pines. The Confederate defense, in which General Johnston was wounded, caused the Federals to withdraw temporarily, although they continued to threaten the Southern capital.

speedily corrected. The council met, as had been previously ordered, on the Nine Mile road, near the house which had been occupied by Smith as his headquarters.

The principal officers of the army were present, and were almost unanimous in the opinion that the line then occupied should be abandoned for one nearer Richmond which was considered more defensible.

The line in question was that which had been adopted by Johnston prior to the occupation in force of the south bank of the Chickahominy by the enemy, and was the strongest the country presented; but now the dispirited condition of our troops and the occupation in force by the enemy of the south side of the river caused the most prominent Confederate officers to doubt their ability to hold it, and consequently they urged its evacuation and withdrawal to a position nearer Richmond. Lee thus found himself in a situation of great embarrassment. He did not then possess the fame he was destined soon to acquire. He was also unknown to that army, and lacked its confidence. Under these disadvantages he was obliged to assume the responsibility of maintaining a position pronounced untenable by his principal officers, or of hazarding the safety of Richmond by a withdrawal of his forces that would inevitably result in a forced occupation of the outer defences of the capital and its complete investiture by the enemy, which would have ensured the speedy capture of the city. Lee, who had long been accustomed to rely upon himself, quickly decided on the course to be adopted. It was evident that the present position of the army must be maintained or that Richmond must be abandoned to the enemy, and the loss of Richmond at this time would have been of incalculable injury to the Confederate cause. He therefore, in opposition to the opinion of his subordinates, determined to hold the position in which he found the army; but before making known his determination he made a careful reconnoissance of the whole position, and then declared his intention of holding it, ordering it to be immediately fortified in the most effective manner.

General Lee then reorganized his forces and established a strong defensive line. He selected, with slight alterations, the position then occupied by his troops. This line extended from Chaffin's Bluff, on the James River, crossing the river road about four miles, and the Darby Town, Charles City,

Williamsburg, and Nine Mile roads, about five miles from Richmond to a point on the Chickahominy a little above New Bridge, and then continued up that stream to Meadow Bridge. The army consisted of six divisions. Longstreet's division formed the right, while those of Huger, D. H. Hill, Magruder, Whiting, and A. P. Hill, in the order named, extended to the left. The division of A. P. Hill constituted the left of the Confederate position. The greater part of Stuart's cavalry was on the left, picketing on the Rappahannock and having a small force in observation at Fredericksburg. The duty of constructing a fortified line was apportioned among the divisions, each commander being responsible for the defence in his own front. Very soon a continuous line of breastworks appeared, and as these arose the spirits of the men revived and the sullen silence with which their labor began gave place to jokes and laughter. Those who had entered upon the work with reluctance now felt recompensed by the sense of safety it gave them. The defences daily increased until they were sufficiently strong to resist any attack that was likely to be made upon them. In the mean time the stragglers and convalescents began to return, and the army gradually increased. Lee daily appeared upon the lines, and after a few days his presence inspired the troops with confidence and enthusiasm. McClellan established his headquarters on the south side of the

ABOVE: Union General James B. McClellan's Army of the Potomac faced six entrenched divisions of Lee's Army of Northern Virginia as it crossed the Chickahominy in its advance toward Richmond.

Chickahominy about the same time that Lee assumed the command of the Army of Northern Virginia. The Federal army, after deducting the casualties of the late battle, amounted to about 100,000 men for duty; 75,000 of this force were on the south side of the Chickahominy, the remainder on the north of that stream, extending as high up as Mechanicsville. From this position a junction would be easily formed with McDowell's corps of 40,000 men, which, although a part of McClellan's forces, was persistently held in the neighborhood of Fredericksburg as a covering force for Washington.

*   *   *

Lee's headquarters at this time were on the Nine Mile road, a position which gave him a good oversight of the army and brought all portions of the lines within easy reach. Yet the batteries, rifle-pits, and earthworks which had been erected with so much labor under his personal supervision were destined to have no further utility than that already adverted to – the infusion of confidence into the previously dispirited army. It was not the purpose of the commanding general to remain upon the defensive and

BELOW: In an engraving made from a field sketch, Federal pickets are shown defending against a Confederate attack as reinforcements arrive.

await the slow but sure advances of the enemy. He, on the contrary, formed the bolder decision of hurling the force under his command against the serried battalions of the foe, as indicated in the last-quoted extract from the notebook (*Deleted – Ed.*).

When McClellan crossed the Chickahominy it was thought he would advance immediately upon Richmond. This expectation was disappointed, however, for instead of advancing he began to fortify his position. The right wing rested on the Chickahominy a little below New Bridge, and the left extended to the White Oak Swamp, embracing a front of about four miles, nearly parallel with that of the Confederates. The opposing lines were separated by an interval but little exceeding a mile, but each was obscured from the other's view by the intervening forest. The picket-lines were often within close musket-range of each other. At first there was a good deal of picket-skirmishing, but this was soon discontinued by mutual consent, and a lively exchange of newspapers, coffee, and tobacco succeeded it. The strength of the Confederate force was always greatly over-estimated by McClellan, and his frequent and urgent calls for re-

inforcements exposed his want of confidence in his own strength. General Lee knowing this uneasy, insecure feeling of his antagonist, and McDowell's force, which had always been a thorn in his side, being about this time withdrawn from Fredericksburg for the support of Banks and Shields in the Valley, prepared, as we have said, to assume the offensive. He conceived the bold plan of crossing the Chickahominy, and, attacking the Federal right wing, to force it back and seize McClellan's line of communication with his base of operations. This plan being successfully executed, the Federal general would be compelled to save his army as best he could by retreat. Preparatory to the execution of this plan General J. E. B. Stuart was ordered to make a reconnoissance in the rear of the Federal position. This officer, with a force of about 1000 cavalry, executed his instructions with great boldness and success. He made the entire circuit of the Federal army and gained much important information.

This movement, indeed, was so skilful and brilliant that it has been classed among the most daring cavalry raids ever made. In addition to the information gained he captured many prisoners and destroyed Federal stores to the value of seven million dollars; and all this with the loss of but a single man, the lamented Captain Latane, who fell while leading a successful charge against a superior force of the enemy. He finally recrossed the Chickahominy, almost in the face of the enemy, with the same intrepidity he had shown at every step of his progress, and with a prestige of daring and success that for years clung to his banner and gained him the reputation of being the most dashing and brilliant cavalry leader of the war.

His design being confirmed by Stuart's successful reconnoissance, Lee proceeded to organize a force requisite for the accomplishment of his proposed enterprise. The troops that could be conveniently spared from North Carolina, South Carolina, and Georgia were ordered to Richmond. By the 20th of June, Major-general T. H. Holmes, with 6000 men from North Carolina; Brigadier-general Ripley, with 6000 from South Carolina; and Brigadier-general Lawton, with 5000 from Georgia, had arrived in Richmond. At the same time General Jackson was ordered to withdraw secretly from the Valley and proceed with such expedition as

BELOW: After the Battle of Gaines' Mill, Virginia, Confederates advance to capture disabled guns— A.R. Waud sketch, June 27, 1862.

ABOVE: Union General Fitz John Porter, commanding troops north of the Chickahominy, was forced by Lee to abandon his position at Gaines's Mill and rejoin McClellan's main army on the south side of the river.

would enable him to reach Hanover Junction by the afternoon of the 25th of June. In order to mask his designs from the Federals, Lee directed Whiting's division and Lawton's brigade to proceed to Staunton, apparently with the view of reinforcing Jackson, but really under orders to return immediately and join that general on the 25th at Hanover Junction. This movement further strengthened McClellan in his opinion of Lee's vastly superior force, and completely blinded him in regard to the real intentions of that general.

General Lee determined to attack the Federal right wing on the morning of the 26th of June. Jackson was directed to move to Atlee's Station on the Central Railroad. A. P. Hill was directed to cross the Chickahominy at Meadow Bridge as soon as Jackson arrived in supporting distance, attack the Federals at Mechanicsville, and drive them from that place, so that the bridge on the Richmond and Mechanicsville road might be open for the advance of the other troops; Longstreet and D. H. Hill were ordered to move their divisions as near as practicable to the Mechanicsville bridge without discovering themselves to the observation of the Federals; while Magruder, Huger, and Holmes held the lines that were now completed, with instructions to watch closely the

movements of the enemy in their front and act as circumstances might suggest. The effective force of the Army of Northern Virginia, including that brought by Jackson from the Valley, as shown by the field returns of June 24th or 25th, amounted to a little more than 81,000 men: 30,000 of these were left in observation under Magruder, while Lee led 50,000 to the attack of the Federal force north of the Chickahominy, which amounted to about 25,000 men, commanded by Fitz John Porter. One division of this force, about 6000 or 7000 strong, under the command of General J. F. Reynolds, occupied Mechanicsville at the extreme right of the Federal position. The main body, under the immediate command of Porter, was posted near Cold Harbor or Gaines's Mill, about six miles below Mechanicsville, and connected by bridges with the main body of the Federal army south of the Chickahominy.

Jackson, having bivouacked at Ashton on the night of the 25th, and his men being fatigued by previous long marches, did not reach his designated position in line of battle until the afternoon of the 26th. This delay was very embarrassing to Lee, and greatly increased the difficulty of executing his plan of operations, as it exposed his design to the enemy and allowed him time to prepare for the approaching storm. General A. P. Hill, on the arrival of Jackson – about four o'clock – crossed the Chickahominy and made a spirited attack on the Federal force at Mechanicsville and compelled it to retire to a position which had been previously prepared beyond the Beaver Dam, a small stream about one mile south-east of the village. The way being now open, the divisions of Longstreet and D. H. Hill began to cross the Chickahominy. Ripley's brigade, which was the first to cross, was ordered to support A. P. Hill in his attempt to dislodge the Federals from their new position. Failing in their first attempt to dislodge them, the approach of night prevented any other being made to carry their position. Reynolds, finding his position would be turned, retired during the night to Gaines's Mill. On the morning of the 27th, Lee formed his army into three columns. The division of A. P. Hill, forming the centre, moved by the main road from Mechanicsville to Gaines's Mill; Longstreet moved by a road between this and the Chickahominy; while Jackson and D. H. Hill moved by a road to the left which intersected the Mechanicsville road a mile and a half beyond Gaines's Mill or Cold Harbor. Stuart with his cavalry covered the left flank of the army as it advanced. The guide, having received indefinite instructions from Jackson, led his column by a road that intersected with the Mechanicsville road before reaching Gaines's Mill. This brought the head of Jackson's column against Hill's troops. Jackson, being obliged to countermarch in order to gain the right road, caused a delay of several hours in the operations of General Lee and materially affected his plan of attack. It was his intention that when Jackson reached the Mechanicsville road he should form his troops in order of battle and attack the Federal right, while A. P. Hill attacked the centre and Longstreet the left.

The Federal position near Gaines's Mill was a plateau bounded on the north-west side by a bluff eighty or ninety feet in elevation, which, curving to the north and east, gradually diminished into a gentle slope. The plateau was bounded on its north side by a stream flowing along its base, whose banks gradually widened and deepened until, when reaching the bluff, they had gained the width of eight or ten and the depth of five or six feet, thus forming a natural ditch. Three lines of breastworks, rising one above the other, had been constructed upon the base of the bluff, and its crest was crowned with artillery. Three lines of Federal infantry occupied the bluff, and one line extended along the north-east crest for more than a mile, and batteries of artillery were in position in rear of the infantry. The Federal position was very strong, and to carry it required the greatest bravery and resolution on the part of the assailants. McClellan, being now aware of Lee's real design, reinforced Porter, increasing his force to about 40,000 men. When the columns of Hill and Longstreet had arrived in easy attacking-distance, General Lee caused them to halt in order to give Jackson time to gain his position. Waiting until one o'clock, Lee ordered Longstreet and A. P. Hill to commence the attack. The Confederate skirmishers advanced and drove in the Federal pickets. While the column of Longstreet advanced by the road to Dr. Gaines's house, and that of Hill by the main Mechanicsville

ABOVE: General Ambrose P. Hill, a Virginian, was one of Lee's most dependable lieutenants.

BELOW: General Robert E. Lee's headquarters during the battles at Gaines's Mill.

road, the Federal position was hidden from Hill by the intervening woods. Deploying several regiments to support his skirmishers, he pushed them through the woods. Very soon the Federal line was developed by a heavy fire of musketry. Hill's column then deployed and advanced to the attack on the Federal centre.

When Longstreet arrived at Gaines's house he was in full view of the Federal left. Taking advantage of an intervening ridge, the crest of which was parallel with and about three hundred yards from the Federal lines, he deployed his troops under its cover. Hearing Hill's attack, Longstreet approached to gain the Federal left. His first line on reaching the crest of the ridge was met by a storm of shot and shell; without faltering it swept down the slope toward the Federal position in the face of a terrible fire of artillery and musketry until arrested by the wide and steep banks of the stream at the foot. Being unable to cross it, this line was obliged to fall back. These troops, although much cut up, re-formed for a second attack. Several Confederate batteries were served with considerable effect in covering the advance of the infantry. D. H. Hill, on reaching the scene of action, took position on the left of A. P. Hill and engaged the enemy. The battle having become general, General Lee sent several staff officers to bring up Jackson's troops to the support of Hill and Longstreet. Whiting's division and Lawton's brigade were the first to arrive. Whiting was directed to fill the interval between Longstreet and A. P. Hill, and Lawton was sent to the left of D. H. Hill to engage the Federal right. Generals Ewell, Elzey, and Winder, as they arrived, were sent to the support of the Hills, and one brigade was sent to the support of Longstreet. Jackson led in person the remainder of his troops against the Federal right. The battle had raged with great fury for more than two hours, and the Federal lines seemed as unshaken as when it first began. The Confederates had been repulsed in several attempts to force them. The day was now drawing to a close, and Lee decided to end the conflict by a charge of the whole line. The word "Charge!" as it passed along the line, was responded to by a wild shout and an irresistible rush on the Federal position. The Texas brigade, led by the gallant Hood, was the first to penetrate the Federal works. It was immediately followed by other regiments, and in a few minutes the whole position was carried and the plateau was covered with a mass of fugitives. The Federals were in full flight, pursued by the Confederates, who delivered deadly volleys at every step.

While General Lee was attacking Porter's position at Gaines's Mill, Magruder made a

BELOW: The earliest known use of railway artillery was that by a battery under Confederate General John B. Magruder during the battles around Richmond. The idea is believed to have been first outlined in a letter from General Lee to the chief of the Ordnance Department on June 5, 1862.

spirited demonstration against that of McClellan on the south side of the Chickahominy. This double attack served to bewilder McClellan, and caused him to withhold reinforcements that would otherwise have been sent to Porter. This battle is considered by many as the most stubbornly-contested battle of the war. It is true that the troops on both sides displayed great valor and determination, and proved themselves worthy of the nation to which they belonged. Porter deserves much credit for the skilful selection of his position and the gallant manner in which he defended it. The victory was complete. When night closed the Confederates were in undisputed possession of the field. The next morning Lee directed Stuart with his cavalry, supported by Ewell's division of infantry, to seize the York River Railroad. McClellan was thus cut off from his base of supplies, and reduced to the necessity of retreating by one of two routes – the one by the Peninsula, the other by the James River, under the cover of the gunboats. He chose the latter as the shortest and easiest.

General Lee remained on the 28th on the north side of the Chickahominy in observation of McClellan's movements. Instructions were sent at the same time to Magruder to keep a vigilant watch on the Federals and without delay report any movement that might be discovered. These instructions were not as faithfully executed as they should have been, for the retreat of the Federals had commenced on the morning of the 28th, and was not discovered until the morning of the 29th, when the Federal lines were found by two engineer officers, Captains Meade and Johnston, to be abandoned, although the Confederate pickets were in many places less than half a mile from the Federal lines.

The safe retreat of McClellan to the James is mainly due to the advantage thus gained. When General Lee on the morning of the 29th found that the Federal army was in retreat he ordered an immediate pursuit. All of the troops on the north of the Chickahominy, with the exception of the divisions of Ewell and Jackson, and Stuart's cavalry, which were to remain in observation lest the Federals might change their line of retreat, were ordered to recross that stream with the view of overtaking the retreating columns. General Lee on recrossing the Chickahominy found Magruder, Huger, and Holmes preparing to pursue the retreating Federal army. At twelve o'clock the pursuit

was commenced, and about three Magruder came upon Sumner's corps, which was in position near Savage's Station. General Heintzelman having retired, Sumner's and Franklin's corps had to receive Magruder's attack unsupported. Sumner held his position with great obstinacy until night ended the conflict. This determined stand enabled the Federal army to make a safe passage of the White Oak Swamp. In the afternoon of the 29th, Jackson was directed to cross the Chickahominy and relieve Magruder in the pursuit. Lee directed the other divisions of his army to march by several roads leading in the direction of McClellan's line of retreat, with the view of striking his column in the flank while Jackson pressed him in the rear. About three o'clock on the 30th, Lee, with the divisions of Longstreet and A. P. Hill, struck the Federal column at Frazier's Farm, and a fierce combat ensued which was

ABOVE: Confederate soldiers charge a Union battery in the Battle of Frazier's Farm on June 30.

BELOW: Union General Philip Kearney's division at White Oak Swamp on June 30 supported McClellan's withdrawal to a safe position on Malvern Hill.

closely contested until night. Contrary to his expectations, he was not supported in this attack by Generals Jackson and Huger, consequently McClellan again escaped and continued his retreat during the night to Malvern Hill.

The delay on the part of General Jackson was very unusual. The explanation of his delay on this occasion was that, being greatly exhaused by long marches and battles for more than a week, he sought a short repose. His staff, out of mistaken regard for their general, permitted him to sleep far beyond the time he had allowed himself. When he awoke he was greatly chagrined at the loss of time that had occurred, the damage of which he was unable to repair. Though General Lee accomplished all that was at first proposed, yet had the parts assigned to some of his subordinates been performed with the exactness that was naturally expected, the results of his operations would have been far greater than those shown in the sequel.

On the morning of the 1st of July it was discovered that McClellan had occupied in force the strong position of Malvern Hill, while his powerful artillery swept every approach, and the shot of the gunboats fell beyond the Confederate lines. After a careful reconnoissance of McClellan's position, Lee determined to attack his left. His first line, composed of the divisions of Magruder, D. H. Hill, and Jackson, was advanced under cover of the wood near the base of the hill. Magruder was ordered to attack the Federal left, while Hill and Jackson threatened their centre and right. The attack was delayed until near sundown, when Magruder made a most gallant assault. By dint of hard fighting his troops gained the crest of the hill and

forced back the Federal left, but were in turn driven back. The firing continued along the line until ten o'clock. The Confederates lay upon their arms where the battle closed, ready to resume the fight as soon as the daylight should appear.

Under the cover of the night McClellan secretly retired, his retreat being facilitated by a heavy fall of rain, which deadened the sound of his withdrawal. The Confederates the next morning, groping through the dense fog, came upon the abandoned lines. This was the first information they had of the retreat. McClellan had now gained the protection of the Federal gunboats; therefore Lee did not immediately pursue, but ordered a day's rest, which the troops greatly needed. McClellan continued his retreat to Harrison's Landing on the James River, where he took up a position. Lee advanced the next day to that neighborhood and after a careful reconnoissance of the Federal lines deemed it inadvisable to attack, and, as there was no probability of the Army of the Potomac speedily resuming operations, he returned to his former camp near Richmond to rest, recruit, and reorganize his army.

While in the vicinity of Harrison's Landing the attack of Colonel J. Thompson Brown's artillery upon the Federal gunboats afforded a brilliant episode to the last scene of the military drama that had just been acted.

The loss sustained by both armies during the recent operations was considerable; that, however, caused by exhaustion and illness probably equalled the casualties of actual battle. The number of Confederate killed and wounded amounted to about 10,000, whilst the Federal loss exceeded this. Reviewing the operations that have just been described, we cannot fail to observe

BELOW: Union artillery under General Henry W. Slocum engages Confederates on the Charles City Road as General McClellan retreats to Harrison's Landing on the James River.

ABOVE: Soldiers of the Third Georgia Infantry. The two at right, half brothers, died at Malvern Hill.

the important results achieved by the skill and energy of an able commander. On the 1st of June, General Lee assumed the command of an army that did not exceed 50,000 men. With this force he erected defences to withstand any attack that might be made against them, and besides in less than a month increased his army to 80,000 men, without giving up one foot of territory and without endangering either public or private property. He also raised its discipline and spirit to such a height that he was enabled to take the offensive and force his adversary, notwithstanding his superiority of numbers and the finely-appointed state of his army, to abandon a base of operations that had occupied almost the exclusive attention of his Government for more than a year, incurring in doing so a heavy loss of material.

McClellan, after establishing himself at Harrison's Landing, called for large reinforcements to enable him to resume active operations. It was decided to order Burnside from North Carolina to reinforce the Army of the Potomac. When Lee re-

gained his former camp near Richmond he immediately set about reorganizing his army. His victory over McClellan had filled the Confederacy with joy, and the men who had left the army a short time before broken down and depressed returned full of spirit and energy.

Before the end of July the Army of Northern Virginia, with the addition of one or two brigades from South Carolina and Georgia, numbered about 70,000 effective men. This army, having to a great extent supplied itself by captures from the Federal army, was better armed and equipped than it had previously been.

Lee had formed it into two corps, giving one to Longstreet and the other to Jackson, officers who had proved themselves fully worthy of the important commands conferred upon them.

As . . . we progress with our narrative it will be seen to what distinction each rose in defence of the Southern Confederacy.

*   *   *

Chapter II

Second Bull Run

Great ... must have been the disappointment at Washington, after such glorious prospects, on witnessing the precipitate retreat of the Federal army on which such high hopes had been centred ... As there was no probability of McClellan's immediately resuming active operations against Richmond, Lee determined, by assuming the offensive and threatening the Federal capital, to force him to make an entire change in his plan of campaign. With that view he despatched Jackson with three divisions of infantry and a proportionate amount of artillery to the neighborhood of Gordonsville, while remaining himself at Richmond with Longstreet's corps, D. H. Hill's and Anderson's divisions of infantry, and Stuart's cavalry in observation of McClellan, who was now slowly recovering from the stuning effect of his defeat.

* * *

About the 1st of August, the advance of the Federal army having reached Culpeper Court-house, Jackson moved to the Rapidan

RIGHT: General Thomas J. Jackson earned the nickname "Stonewall" for his units' stout defense at the Battle of First Manassas (First Bull Run) in July 1861.

BELOW: A cavalryman awaiting orders at Culpeper Court-house.

and took a position in the vicinity of Orange Court-house ... The forces under Banks, Fremont, and McDowell, ... were formed into an army, the command of which was given to General Pope.

* * *

About the time that Jackson reached the Rapidan, Pope arrived at Culpeper Court-house, and extended his advance corps toward the Rapidan. The Federal cavalry finding the Rapidan occupied by the Confederates, the leading corps took up a position along a range of low hills near Cedar Mountain, about four miles west of Culpeper Court-house. Having learned that a part of the Federal force had not arrived there, Jackson determined to attack Pope before his army could be united. He therefore secretly recrossed the Rapidan, and by a rapid movement on the 9th of August gained the position near Cedar Mountain before the

Federals were aware of his design. The battle was hotly contested for several hours, when the Federals were defeated and driven back to Culpeper Court-house. Jackson . . . then recrossed the Rapidan.

* * *

The advance of Jackson to Gordonsville, above mentioned, and his subsequent advance upon the position of General Pope near Culpeper Court-house, caused the Federal authorities to determine upon the immediate withdrawal of the Army of the Potomac from the James . . . General Lee . . . divined, with the intuition of genius, that his presence and that of his army could be spared from the immediate vicinity of Richmond, and might be able to teach General Pope that the road to New Orleans was "a hard road to travel." Preliminary to future operations he sent forward Longstreet's corps to join Jackson in the vicinity of Gordonsville, and about the middle of August proceeded in person to assume the direction of affairs in that quarter.

On reaching the locality of the projected movements he found Jackson occupying the line of the Rapidan, while Longstreet's force was encamped in the neighborhood of Gordonsville. The army, including Stuart's cavalry, at this time amounted to 65,000 effective men, while the opposing army of Pope numbered 50,000, and occupied a position between Culpeper Court-house and the Rapidan.

Lee at once determined to assume the offensive, and with that purpose in view he moved his whole army below Orange Court-house to a position south of Clark's Mountain, where he could avail himself of the fords of the Rapidan on the flanks of the Federal army. He reached this position on August 17th, the movement having been effected, under cover of the forest, without the knowledge of General Pope.

The absence of Stuart's cavalry delayed the army in this position till the morning of the 20th, and enabled Pope – who, through an unlucky accident, became aware of the movement of his shrewd adversary – to beat a hasty retreat . . . On the 18th, Lee and his staff ascended Clark's Mountain, and reconnoitered the Federal position. In plain view before them lay Pope's army, stretched out in fancied security, and to all appearance in utter ignorance of the vicinity of a powerful foe . . . On the afternoon of the 19th the signal-station on the top of the mountain not-

ABOVE: Federals at the Battle of Cedar Mountain, the start of the Second Manassas (Second Bull Run) campaign, on August 9, 1862.

ified the Confederate commander that a change had occurred in the situation of affairs. The enemy had evidently taken the alarm . . . As it afterward appeared, Pope had learned of Lee's vicinity through the capture of Lieutenant Fitzhugh of Stuart's staff, on whom had been found a letter revealing the fact of the movement of the Confederate army. On gaining this important and somewhat startling information, he had immediately given orders to break camp and retreat in all haste to the line of the Rappahannock . . . .

The retreating Federal army was followed by Lee in rapid pursuit, but it had crossed the Rappahannock by the time he reached the vicinity of that stream. Pope on crossing the river took up a position on the left bank, his left covering Rappahannock Station, his right extending in the direction of Warrenton Springs. Lee confronted him on the right bank of the river . . . .

When it became known at Washington that Pope had been compelled to retreat and recross the Rappahannock, the Federal authorities made every effort to rapidly reinforce him by troops drawn from the Army of the Potomac and from Burnside's force, which had been withdrawn from North Carolina. General Lee, in order to retard the forwarding of troops and supplies to the Federal army, ordered Stuart to turn Pope's right, gain his rear, inflict as much damage as he could upon the Orange and Alexandria Railroad, and gain information of the enemy's movements. Stuart, in compliance with his instructions, crossed the Rappahannock late in the afternoon of the 21st, a few

BELOW: Black refugees flee a site devastated by battle to take refuge in Union lines.

miles above Warrenton Springs, with a brigade of cavalry, and, screening his movement by the mountain-spurs and intervening forests, he proceeded toward the village of Warrenton, passing that place after nightfall, and advanced direct upon Catlett's Station on the railroad. Arriving in the midst of a violent storm, he surprised and captured the Federal encampment at that place, which he found to contain General Pope's headquarters. He secured Pope's letter-book and papers with many other valuable articles.

On account of the heavy fall of rain the timbers of the railroad bridge at Catlett's were so saturated with water that Stuart was unable to burn it, and, being pressed for time, he failed to greatly damage the railroad. He returned, bringing with him his

valuable booty, without the loss of a man. By the capture of Pope's papers Lee gained an accurate knowledge of the situation of the Federal army. Acting on it, he ordered Jackson to advance his corps to Jeffersonton and secure the bridge over the Rappahannock at Warrenton Springs. Jackson moved up the river, leaving his train to follow under the escort of Trimble's brigade. The Federals, being tempted by the appearance of a large train in their vicinity, sent a strong detachment to intercept it. Trimble, reinforced by Hood's brigade of Longstreet's corps, met this detachment, and after a fierce combat drove it back with heavy loss. Jackson, on arriving at Jeffersonton in the afternoon of the 22nd found that the bridge on the Warrenton turnpike had been destroyed by the

ABOVE: Station on the Orange and Alexandria Railroad at Warrenton, Virginia. Here Jeb Stuart discovered Pope's plans for the disposition of Federal troops.

Federals. The river being low, he succeeded in sending Early's brigade with one of Lawton's Georgia regiments across the river on an old mill-dam to act as a corps of observation. During the night the river was made impassable by heavy rains. The next day, the Federals beginning to appear in great force, Early with great dexterity took a position in a wood adjacent to the river, so as to effectually conceal his lack of strength. The river having fallen during the day, he recrossed at night without loss. The Federals burned the railroad bridge of Rappahannock Station, and moved their left higher up the river. On the 23rd, Lee ordered Longstreet's corps to follow Jackson and mass in the vicinity of Jeffersonton. The headquarters of the army was also moved to that place.

* * *

General Longstreet made a feint on the position of Warrenton on the morning of the 24th, under cover of which Jackson's corps was withdrawn from the front to the vicinity of the road from Jeffersonton to the upper fords of the Rappahannock. Jackson was then directed to make preparation to turn the Federal position and seize their communications about Manassas Junction. Longstreet continued his cannonade at intervals throughout the day, to which the Federals replied with increasing vigor, showing that Pope was massing his army in Lee's front.

It was the object of Lee to hold Pope in his present position by deluding him with the belief that it was his intention to force a passage of the river at that point, until Jackson by a flank movement could gain his rear. Longstreet, on the morning of the 25th, resumed his cannonade with increased energy, and at the same time made a display of infantry above and below the bridge. Jackson then moved up the river to a ford eight miles above; crossing at that point and turning eastward, by a rapid march he reached the vicinity of Salem. Having made a march of twenty-five miles, he bivouacked for the night. Stuart's cavalry covered his right flank, the movement being masked by the natural features of the country. The next morning at dawn the march was resumed by the route through Thoroughfare Gap.

The cavalry, moving well to the right, passed around the west end of Bull Run Mountain and joined the infantry at the village of Gainesville, a few miles from the Orange and Alexandria Railroad. Pressing forward, still keeping the cavalry well to the right, Jackson struck the railroad at Bristoe Station late in the afternoon, where he captured two empty trains going east. After dark he sent a detachment under Stuart to secure Manassas Junction, the main dépôt of supplies of the Federal army. The cavalry moved upon the flanks of this position, while the infantry, commanded by Trimble, assaulted the works in front and carried them with in-

OPPOSITE: Two photographers lunching in the field before the Second Battle of Bull Run.

BELOW: Erecting Confederate fortifications at Manassas. The Second Bull Run campaign ran from August 9 until September 2.

237

significant loss, capturing two batteries of light artillery with their horses and a detachment of 300 men, besides an immense amount of army supplies. The next morning, after effectually destroying the railroad at Bristoe, Jackson left Ewell with his division and a part of Stuart's cavalry to retard the Federals if they should advance in that direction, and moved his main body to Manassas, where he allowed his troops a few hours to refresh themselves upon the abundant stores that had been captured. About twelve o'clock the sound of artillery in the direction of Bristoe announced the Federal advance. Not having transportation to remove the captured supplies, Jackson directed his men to take what they could carry off, and ordered the rest to be destroyed.

General Ewell, having repulsed the advance of two Federal columns, rejoined Jackson at Manassas. The destruction of the captured stores having been completed, Jackson retired with his whole force to Bull Run and took a position for the night, a part of his troops resting on the battle-field of the previous year. Pope, on hearing of the interruption of his communications, sent a force to get information of the extent of the damage that had been done to the railroad.

Upon learning that Jackson was in his rear, he immediately abandoned his position on the Rappahannock and proceeded with all despatch to intercept him before he could be reinforced by Lee. His advance having been arrested on the 27th by Ewell, he did not proceed beyond Bristoe that day. Lee on the 26th withdrew Longstreet's corps from its position in front of Warrenton Springs, covering the withdrawal by a small rear-guard and artillery, and directed it to follow Jackson by the route he had taken the day before. The trains were ordered to move by the same route and to keep closed on Longstreet's corps.

* * *

The corps bivouacked for the night in the vicinity of Salem. On the morning of the succeeding day, the 27th, a messenger appeared bringing the important and cheering news of the success of Jackson at Bristoe and Manassas. These tidings were received with enthusiasm by the soldiers, who, animated with high hopes of victory, pressed on with the greatest energy, and that evening reached the plains a few miles west of Thoroughfare Gap, in the Bull Run Mountains, through which Jackson's

BELOW: A column of the Union Army of the Potomac crossing Kettle Run, above Warrenton.

column had passed a few days previously.

Thoroughfare Gap was reached about noon of the 28th. It was quickly found to be occupied by a Federal force. Some slight attempt was made to dislodge the enemy, but without success, as their position proved too strong, and it seemed as if the movement of the Confederate army in that direction was destined to be seriously interfered with. Meanwhile, nothing further had been heard from Jackson, and there was a natural anxiety in regard to his position and possible peril. Unless the mountains could speedily be passed by Longstreet's corps the force under Jackson might be assailed by the whole of Pope's army, and very severely dealt with.

Under these critical circumstances General Lee made every effort to find some available route over the mountains, sending reconnoissances to right and left in search of a practicable pass. Some of the officers ascended the mountain during the evening, and perceived from its summit a large force which lay in front of the Gap. Meanwhile, the sound of cannonading was audible from the other side of the range, and it was evident that an engagement was taking place.

* * *

Fortunately, circumstances favored the Confederate cause. One of the reconnoitering parties found a woodchopper, who told them of an old road over the mountain to which he could guide them, and which might be practicable for infantry. Hood was at once directed to make an effort to lead his division across the mountain by this route. This he succeeded in doing, and the head of his column reached the other side of the range by morning. Another route had also been discovered by which Wilcox was enabled to turn the Gap.

In the mean time, Pope himself had been playing into the hands of his adversary. He had ordered McDowell to retire from the Gap and join him to aid in the anticipated crushing of Jackson. McDowell did so, leaving Rickett's division to hold the Gap. In evident ignorance of the vicinity of Longstreet's corps, this force was also withdrawn during the night, and on the morning of the 29th Lee found the Gap unoccupied, and at once marched through at the head of Longstreet's column. On reaching Gainesville, three miles beyond the Gap, he found Stuart, who informed him of Jackson's situation. The division was at once marched into position

on Jackson's right.

Pope had unknowingly favored the advance of the Confederate commander. His removal of McDowell from his position had been a tactical error of such magnitude that it could not well be retrieved. The object of the movement had been to surround Jackson at Manassas Junction, upon which place the several corps of the army were marching by various routes. Pope wrote in his order to McDowell, "If you will march promptly and rapidly at the earliest dawn upon Manassas Junction, we shall bag the whole crowd." The scheme was a good one, but for two unconsidered contingencies. Had Jackson awaited the enemy at Manassas Junction, he would have found himself in a trap. But he did not choose to do so. When the van of the Federal columns reached the Junction, they found that the bird had flown. And Longstreet's corps,

ABOVE: In an engraving from a field drawing by A. R. Waud, General Robert E. Lee is seen observing the skirmishing at Thoroughfare Gap.

BELOW: General McDowell's camp at Manassas. The Union force arrived too late at Manassas Junction to trap the forewarned General Jackson.

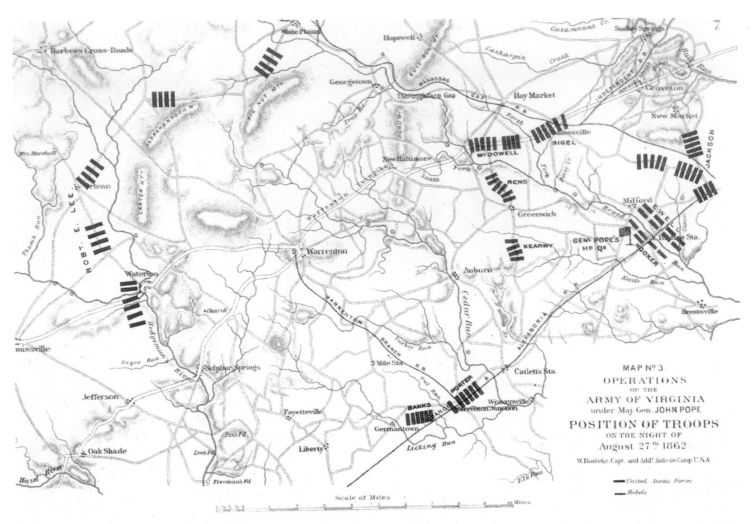

ABOVE: Map accompanying Pope's report on the battles records the positions of troops on both sides on the night of August 27.

OPPOSITE TOP: Map showing the action of August 28.

OPPOSITE BOTTOM: A Currier & Ives print attempts to show the ferocity of the fighting at Bull Run on August 29.

which might have been prevented from passing the Bull Run range, had been given free opportunity to cross to the aid of Jackson, who on the night of the 27th and morning of the 28th left the Junction and made a rapid march to the westward. The error was a fatal one to the hopes of the boasting Western general.

The cannonade at the Gap on the 28th had informed Jackson of Lee's proximity. He at once took a position north of the Warrenton turnpike, his left resting on Bull Run, near Sudley Church, and his right extending toward Gainesville. The distance of this position from the Warrenton road varied from one to two miles, the greater part of the left embracing a railroad cut, while the centre and right occupied a commanding ridge. In this position Jackson could easily unite with Lee on his passing Thoroughfare Gap, or, failing in that and being hard pressed, he could retire by the east end of Bull Run Mountain and unite with Lee on the north side of that mountain. The divisions of Ewell and Taliaferro formed the right and

centre of Jackson's line of battle, while that of A. P. Hill constituted his left. Jackson had barely completed his arrangements when a heavy column of Federal infantry (King's division of McDowell's corps) appeared on the Warrenton turnpike. In order to delay its advance several batteries were placed in position, which by a well-directed fire caused them to halt; at the same time Jackson ordered Taliaferro to deploy one brigade across the Warrenton turnpike, holding his other brigades in reserve. Ewell was directed to support him. About three o'clock the Federals bore down in heavy force upon Ewell and Taliaferro, who maintained their positions with admirable firmness, repelling attack after attack until night. The loss on both sides was considerable. Among the wounded on the side of the Confederates were Generals Taliaferro and Ewell, the latter seriously, having to lose his leg.

Jackson, with barely 20,000 men, now found himself confronted by the greater part of the Federal army. Any commander with less firmness would have sought safety in

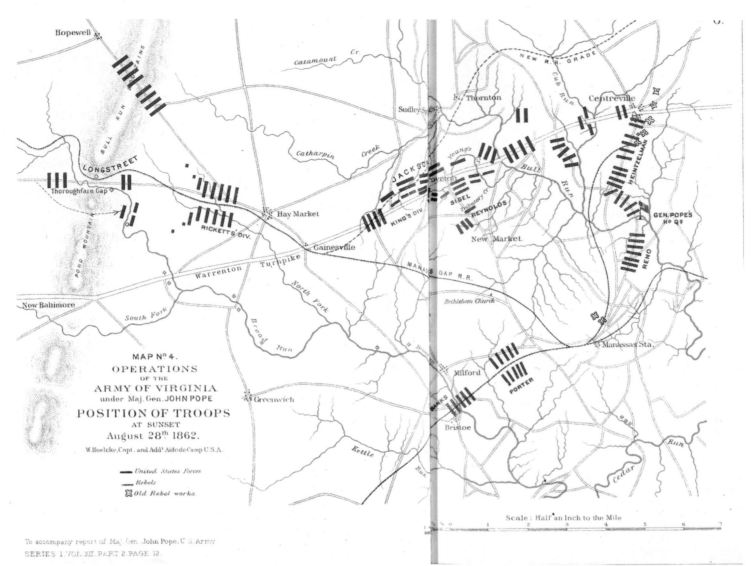

MAP Nº 4.

OPERATIONS
OF THE
ARMY OF VIRGINIA
under Maj. Gen. JOHN POPE

POSITION OF TROOPS
AT SUNSET
August 28th 1862.

W. Hoelcke, Capt. and Addl Aide-de-Camp U.S.A.

—— United States Forces
—— Rebels
✕ Old Rebel works.

Scale : Half an Inch to the Mile

To accompany report of Maj. Gen. John Pope. U.S. Army
SERIES 1. VOL. XII. PART 2. PAGE 12.

ABOVE: Ruins of Stone Bridge on the blasted battlefield at Bull Run.

retreat. But having heard the Confederate guns at Thoroughfare Gap, he knew that Lee would join him the next day. Therefore he determined to hold his position at all hazards.

By the morning of the 29th, as we have already described, Hood's division had reached the south side of the mountain, and early in the day was joined by the remainder of Longstreet's corps by way of the open Gap.

While these important movements were in progress, Pope had resumed his attack upon Jackson, and was pressing him with his whole force, hoping to crush him before he could be relieved by Lee. On the arrival of Lee, Pope discontinued his attack, and retired to the position which the year before had been the scene of the famous battle of Bull Run, or Manassas. Lee then took a position opposite, with Longstreet's corps occupying a lower range of hills extending across and at right angles to the Warrenton turn-

pike, while Jackson occupied the line of railroad before mentioned, which, slightly deviating from the general direction of Longstreet's position, formed with it an obtuse crotchet, opening toward the enemy. An elevated ridge connecting Jackson's right with Longstreet's left, forming the centre of the Confederate position, was strongly occupied with artillery to fill the interval between Longstreet and Jackson. The hills on the right, were crowned by the Washington Artillery, commanded by Colonel Walton. The remainder of the artillery was distributed at prominent points throughout the line, while Stuart's cavalry covered its flanks and observed the movements of the enemy. Since Pope's retreat from Culpeper Courthouse he had been frequently reinforced by detachments from the armies of McClellan and Burnside. The greater part of those armies having now joined him, and the remainder being in supporting-distance, his arrogance revived, and, being sure of an easy victory, he sent the most sanguine despatches to the authorities at Washington. In preparation for battle he took a position embracing a succession of low ridges, nearly parallel to, and about a mile from, the line assumed by Lee. About midway between the two armies lay a narrow valley, through which meandered a small brook, whose low murmurs seemed to invite the weary soldier to slake his thirst with its cool and limpid waters. The afternoon of the 29th was principally occupied in preparation. Longstreet's corps, on the right, was formed in two lines. Jackson, on the left, having been considerably reduced by rapid marching and hard fighting, could present only a single line with a small reserve.

On the morning of the 30th an ominous silence pervaded both armies. Each seemed to be taking the measure of its antagonist.

Lee saw threatening him the armies of Pope, McClellan, and Burnside, whose combined strength exceeded 150,000 men, while his own army was less than 60,000 strong. Notwithstanding this disparity of numbers, the presence of Lee, Jackson, and Longstreet inspired the troops with confidence far exceeding their numerical strength. About eight o'clock the Federal batteries opened a lively cannonade upon the Confederate centre, which was responded to with spirit by the battalions of Colonel Stephen D. Lee and Major Shoemaker. This practice having continued for an hour, both sides relapsed into silence. This was the prelude to the approaching contest. Between twelve and one o'clock the cannonade was resumed in earnest. The thunder of cannon shook the hills, while shot and shell, shrieking and hissing, filled the air, and the sulphurous

BELOW: Men of Company C, 41st New York Infantry at Manassas before the start of the battles. In a month, a total of 25,000 Union and Confederate soldiers who took part in the Second Bull Run campaign would be dead, wounded or missing.

smoke, settling in black clouds along the intervening valley, hung like a pall over the heavy columns of infantry which rushed into the "jaws of death." Pope, having directed his principal attack upon the Confederate left, advanced his infantry in powerful force against Jackson, whose single line behind the friendly shelter of railroad cuts and embankments received this mighty array with tremendous volleys of musketry, hurling back line after line, only to be replaced by fresh assailants. Each moment the conflict became closer and more deadly. At times the roar of musketry gave place to the clash of bayonets, and at one point, after the Confederates had exhausted their ammunition, the assailants were repelled with stones which had been thrown up from a neighboring excavation. At the critical moment when the fate of Jackson's corps was trembling in the balance, Colonel Lee dashed with his artillery into a position that enfiladed the Federal right wing and hurled upon it a storm of shot and shell. At the same moment Longstreet's infantry rushed like a tempest against Pope's left, driving everything before it. This assault was irresistible, and speedily decided the fortune of the day. Pope's left wing gave way before it at every point, and his right, being assailed in flank and threatened in rear, relaxed its efforts and began to retire.

The Confederates, seeing the enemy in re-

treat, pursued with a shout that rose above the din of battle, and pressed him with such vigor that he soon fell into disorder and broke into rapid flight toward Bull Run. The pursuit was continued until arrested by the cover of night. After the storm of battle the field presened a scene of dreadful carnage. Thirty thousand men *hors de combat*, wrecks of batteries and the mangled carcasses of horses, gave proof of the desperate character of the conflict. Pope left upon the field 15,000 killed, wounded, and prisoners, while his army was greatly reduced by stragglers, who, imbued with the sentiment, "He who fights and runs away will live to fight another day," sought refuge far beyond the range of battle. The Confederate loss was also heavy, the killed and wounded being numbered at between 7000 and 8000. Beside the heavy losses in *personnel* sustained by the Federals, a large amount of valuable property fell into the hands of the victor, the most important of which was twenty-five thousand stand of small-arms and twenty-three pieces of artillery; also a large amount of medical stores was subsequently taken at Centreville.

Pope retired to Centreville, where he was opportunely joined by Generals Sumner and Franklin with 25,000 fresh troops, upon which Pope endeavored to rally his army.

General Lee, being well aware that powerful reinforcements from McClellan's and

BELOW: The dedication of a monument to the dead of First Bull Run in Virginia. Five times as many would die in the second campaign.

Burnside's armies and from other sources had been ordered to join Pope, did not deem it advisable to immediately pursue the retreating enemy, but prudently paused to ascertain what force he had to contend with before renewing the conflict. After the close of the battle Colonel Long made a personal reconnoissance of the whole field and reported to Lee. Wishing to strike the enemy another blow before he could recover from the effects of his repulse, Lee by rapid movement turned Centreville on the 1st of September, and took a position on the Little River turnpike, between Chantilly and Ox Hill, with the view of intercepting his retreat to Washington. This movement was covered by Robertson's cavalry, while Stuart advanced to Germantown, a small village a

few miles east of Ox Hill, where he discovered the Federal army in retreat.

After a sharp attack Stuart was obliged to retire before a superior force. About dusk A. P. Hill's division encountered a large detachment of the enemy at Ox Hill. A brief but sanguinary combat ensued, . . . The combatants being separated by night and storm, Hill's division occupied the field, while the Federals resumed the retreat. In this engagement they numbered among their slain two distinguished officers (Generals Kearny and Stephens), whose loss was regretted by friends in both armies. Pope made good his retreat during the night, and we once more see the fugitives from Manassas seeking a refuge within the defences of Washington.

*   *   *

Chapter III

Antietam

With the view of shedding additional light on this period of the history of the war, we shall here introduce a scrap of personal information. On the 2d of September succeeding Pope's defeat, Colonel Long wrote from the dictation of General Lee to President Davis in substance as follows: As Virginia was free from invaders, the Federal army being within the defences of Washington, shattered and dispirited by defeat, and as the passage of the Potomac could now be effected without opposition, the present was deemed a proper moment, with His Excellency's approbation, to penetrate into Maryland. The presence of the victorious army could not fail to alarm the Federal authorities and make them draw forces from every quarter for the defence of their capital, thus relieving the Confederacy from pressure and – for a time, at least – from the exhaustion incident to invasion. The presence of a powerful army would also revive the hopes of the Marylanders, allow them a free exercise of their sympathies, and give them an opportunity of rallying to the aid of their Southern friends. Above all, the position of the army, should it again be crowned with victory, would be most favorable for seizing and making the best use of the advantages which

such an event would produce. In conclusion, a few remarks were made in regard to the condition of the army.

In anticipation of the President's concurrence, General Lee immediately began the preparation for the invasion of Maryland. On the 3d he put the army in motion, and on the 4th took a position between Leesburg and the contiguous fords of the Potomac. The inhabitants of this section of country, having been crushed by the heel of oppression, were now transported with the cheering prospect of liberty. The presence of the army whose movements they had anxiously and proudly watched filled them with unbounded joy. Their doors were thrown open and their stores were spread out in hospitable profusion to welcome their honored guest. Leesburg, being on the border, had at an early period fallen into the hands of the enemy. All of the men who were able had joined the army, and many of those who were unfit for service had retired within the Confederate lines to escape the miseries of the Northern prison; so that the women and children had been left almost alone. Now all these gladly returned to their homes, and tender greetings on every side penetrated to the deepest recesses of the heart and made them thank God that misery and woe had

BELOW: Residents of Sharpsburg, Maryland, flee the town at the approach of Confederate troops.

been replaced by happiness and joy.

The strength of the Confederate army at this time, including D. H. Hill's division, did not exceed 45,000 effective men; yet, though it had been greatly reduced in numbers during the campaign through which it had just passed, its spirit was raised by the victories it had achieved. Its numerical diminution was not so much the result of casualties in battle as that of losses incident to long and rapid marches with insufficient supplies of food and the want of shoes. It frequently happened that the only food of the soldiers was the green corn and fruit gathered from the fields and orchards adjacent to the line of march, and often the bravest men were seen with lacerated feet painfully striving to keep pace with their comrades, until, worn out with pain and fatigue, they were obliged to yield and wait to be taken up by the ambulances or wagons, to be carried where their wants could be supplied.

The invasion of Maryland being determined on, the army was stripped of all incumbrances, and, from fear that the soldiers might be induced to retaliate on the defenceless inhabitants for outrages committed by the Federal troops upon the people of the South, stringent orders were issued against straggling and plundering. These orders were strictly enforced throughout the campaign.

*   *   *

The passage of the Potomac was successfully accomplished on the 5th. The infantry, artillery, and trains crossed at White's and Cheek's fords, the cavalry having previously crossed with instructions to seize important points and cover the movements of the army. From the Potomac, General Lee advanced to Frederick, at which place he arrived on the 6th and established himself behind the Monocacy. He at the same time seized the Baltimore and Ohio Railroad, and the principal roads to Baltimore, Washington, Harper's Ferry, and the upper Potomac. From this important position radiated several lines upon which he could operate. Those toward Harper's Ferry, Baltimore, and

ABOVE: A military wagon train crosses a river on a pontoon bridge.

ABOVE: Stonewall Jackson's men wading across the Potomac at White's Ford.

Pennsylvania were unoccupied, while that in the direction of Washington was held by the Federal army.

* * *

It was not without surprise that General Lee discovered, upon reaching Frederick, that Harper's Ferry was still garrisoned. He had expected on entering Maryland that it would be at once abandoned, as it should have been had ordinary military principles been observed. Its continued occupation subjected its defenders to imminent danger of capture. Yet, through a military error, its occupation was unfavorable to the success of the Confederate movement, particularly if there was any idea entertained by General Lee of invading Pennsylvania. It would not do to leave this strongly-fortified post, on the direct line of communication of the army, in possession of the enemy; yet to reduce it needed a separation and retardation of the army that seriously interfered with the projected movements, and might have resulted adversely to the Southern cause but for the rapidity of Jackson's marches and the errors

of Colonel Miles, the commander of the garrison. This will appear when we come to describe the subsequent events.

Yet, whatever might be the effect, its reduction was absolutely necessary where any further operations of importance could be undertaken. Nor could the whole army be judiciously used for this purpose. Not only is it extremely unusual for a commander to use his whole force for a service which can be performed by a detachment, but in this case it would have necessitated a recrossing of the Potomac, with the strong probability that McClellan would take sure measures to prevent a return of the army into Maryland.

This service, had the claims of senior rank been alone considered, should have been intrusted to Longstreet; but it was given to Jackson on account of his superior qualifications for duty of this character, Longstreet making no objection. Jackson was therefore directed to move his corps on the morning of the 10th by way of Williamsport to Martinsburg, to capture or disperse the Federal force at that place, and then proceed to Harper's Ferry and take steps for its immediate reduction. At the same time, Major-general McLaws was ordered to move with his and Anderson's divisions by the most direct route upon Maryland Heights, to seize that important position and co-operate with Jackson in his attack on Harper's Ferry. Brigadier-general Walker was instructed to recross the Potomac with his division and occupy Loudoun Heights for the same purpose. The several movements were executed with wonderful celerity and precision.

Jackson on leaving Frederick marched with great rapidity by way of Middletown, Boonsboro', and Williamsport, near which latter place he forded the Potomac on the 11th and entered Virginia. Here he disposed his forces so as to prevent an escape of the garrison of Harper's Ferry in this direction and marched upon that place, the rear of which he reached on the 13th. On his approach General White evacuated Martinsburg and retired with its garrison to Harper's Ferry. On reaching Bolivar Heights, Jackson found that Walker was already the foot of Maryland Heights, the key to Harper's Ferry, since it is the loftiest of the three heights by which that place is surrounded, and is sufficiently near to reach it even by musketry. Harper's Ferry, in fact, is a mere trap for its garrison, since it lies open to cannonade

from the three heights named; so that the occupation of these renders it completely untenable.

Colonel Miles had posted a small force under Colonel Ford on Maryland Heights, retaining the bulk of his troops in Harper's

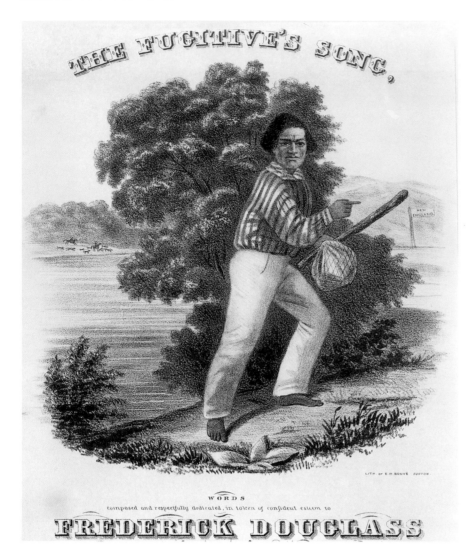

Ferry. Instead of removing his whole command to the heights, which military prudence plainly dictated, and which his subordinates strongly recommended, he insisted upon a literal obedience to General Halleck's orders to hold Harper's Ferry to the last extremity. In fact, Maryland Heights was quickly abandoned altogether, Ford but feebly resisting McLaws and retiring before his advance, first spiking his guns and hurling them down the steep declivity. This retreat left Maryland Heights open to occupation by the assailing force, and it was not long ere McLaws had succeeded in dragging some guns to the summit of the rugged ridge and placing them in position to command the garrison below. Jackson and Walker were already in position, and, by the morning of the 14th, Harper's Ferry was completely invested. During the day the summits of the other hills were crowned with artillery, which was ready to open fire by dawn . . . .

There was never a more complete trap than that into which the doomed garrison had suffered itself to fall. Escape and resistance were alike impossible. Maryland Heights might easily have been held until McClellan came up had the whole garrison defended it, but its abandonment was a fatal movement. They lay at the bottom of a funnel-shaped opening commanded by a

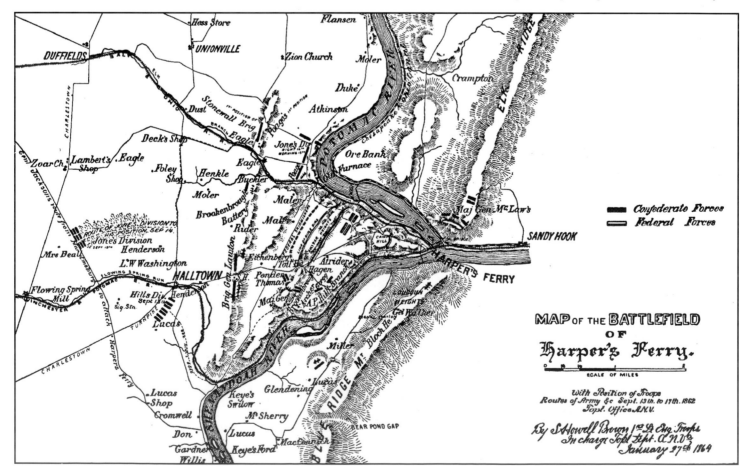

plunging fire from three directions and within reach of volleys of musketry from Maryland Heights. Two hours of cannonade sufficed to prove this, and at the end of that time Colonel Miles raised the white flag of surrender. The signal was not immediately perceived by the Confederates, who continued their fire, one of the shots killing the Federal commander. The force surrendered numbered between 11,000 and 12,000 men, while there fell into Jackson's hands 73 pieces of artillery, 13,000 stand of arms, 200 wagons, and a large quantity of military stores.

Pending the reduction of Harper's Ferry, General Lee moved by easy marches with two divisions of Longstreet's corps to the neighborhood of Hagerstown, leaving D. H. Hill with his division and a detachment of cavalry to serve as rear-guard, with instructions to hold the Boonsboro' pass of South Mountain. By taking a position between Williamsport and Hagerstown a junction could be easily effected with the troops operating against Harper's Ferry, and on the reduction of that place Lee would have a

secure line of communication through the Valley of Virginia, which would enable him to advance into Pennsylvania or to assume such other line of operation as circumstances might suggest.

Since the advance of the Confederate army into Maryland no considerable Federal force had appeared, and as yet only some unimportant cavalry affairs had occurred. After the evacuation of Virginia the Army of the Potomac had been augmented by the addition of the Army of Virginia and that of General Burnside, giving it an effective strength of about 90,000 men. This force was assigned to the command of General McClellan for active operations, and was put in motion about the 6th of September.

Although it was known in Washington that Lee had crossed the Potomac, McClellan was checked in his movements by General Halleck, who was still apprehensive that the ubiquitous Jackson or Stuart might suddenly appear before Washington.

When it became known that Lee had left Frederick and was advancing toward Hagerstown, McClellan advanced with greater

ABOVE: Union Major General Ambrose E. Burnside added his forces to McClellan's after the Federals evacuated Virginia.

OPPOSITE TOP: An abolitionist song inspired by the civil-rights activist Frederick Douglass, himself a former slave.

OPPOSITE BOTTOM: Map of troop positions and routes in the area of Harper's Ferry for the period from September 13 to 17.

confidence, and an attempt was made to relieve Harper's Ferry. Franklin was sent to force his way through Crampton's Pass, in the South Mountain range. This pass was defended by Mumford's cavalry, supported by a part of McLaws's division, under General Cobb, who had been sent back with three brigades under orders to hold Crampton's Pass until Harper's Ferry had surrendered, "even if he lost his last man in doing it." This pass is in the rear of, and but five miles from, Maryland Heights, and its occupation by the Federals would have seriously imperilled the Confederate operations. It was gallantly defended against the strong force of assailants, and, though Franklin succeeded in forcing his way through by the morning of the 15th, he was too late: Miles was already on the point of surrender. McLaws at once withdrew his force from Maryland Heights, with the exception of one regiment, and formed a line of battle across Pleasant Valley to resist the threatening corps. The surrender of the garrison immediately afterward left him a free line of retreat. He crossed the Potomac at the Ferry, and moved by way of Shepherdstown to rejoin Lee at Sharpsburg. The Confederates had in this enterprise met with the most complete and gratifying success.

The Federal army, moving with great caution and deliberation, reached Frederick on the 12th. Here occurred one of those un-

BELOW: Confederate Brigadier General Howell Cobb of Georgia successfully defended a pass to Maryland Heights until the surrender of Harper's Ferry.

toward events which have so often changed the course of wars, and which in this instance completely modified the character of the campaign. A copy of General Lee's order directing the movements of the army accidentally fell into the hands of McClellan, who, being thus accurately informed of the position of the forces of his opponent, at once determined to abandon his cautious policy and boldly assume the offensive. He therefore pressed forward with the view of forcing the South Mountain passes, held by Hill, and of intruding himself between the wings of the Confederate army, with the hope of being able to crush them in detail before they could reunite.

The order in question, addressed to D. H. Hill, was found by a soldier after the Confederate evacuation of Frederick, and was quickly in McClellan's possession. Hill has been blamed for unpardonable carelessness in losing it; yet, as the original order was still in his possession after the war, it is evident that the one found must have been a copy. The mystery is made clear by Colonel Venable, one of General Lee's staff-officers, in the following remark: "This is very easily explained. One copy was sent directly to Hill from headquarters. General Jackson sent him a copy, as he regarded Hill in his command. It is Jackson's copy, in his own handwriting, which General Hill has. The other was undoubtedly left carelessly by some one at Hill's headquarters." However that be, its possession by McClellan immediately reversed the character of his movements, which were changed from snail-like slowness to energetic rapidity. In his own words, "Upon learning the contents of this order, I at once gave orders for a vigorous pursuit."

The detachment by General Lee of a large portion of his army for the reduction of Harper's Ferry was made with the reasonable assurance that that object could be effected and a junction formed before General McClellan would be in position to press him. Though this expectation proved well based, yet it was imperilled by the unforeseen event above mentioned.

The rapid movements to which the finding of Lee's order gave rise brought the leading corps of the Federal army in front of Hill's position upon South Mountain on the afternoon of the 13th. This mountain is intersected by three passes in front of Boonsboro'. The main, or central, pass is traversed by the Frederick and Boonsboro' turnpike; the second, three-fourths of a mile south-

east of the first, is crossed by the old Sharpsburg turnpike; the third is an obscure pass behind the elevated crest, about a quarter of a mile north-west of the turnpike.

General Hill's right occupied the southeast pass, and his left held the central. The centre was posted on a narrow mountain-road connecting the right and left. The pass on the left was watched by a small cavalry force. The position of Hill was strong, as it was only assailable by the pike on the left and the road on the right and along the rugged mountain-sides.

Early on the morning of the 14th, General McClellan advanced to the attack, directing his principal efforts against the south-east pass. Hill maintained his position with his usual firmness and intrepidity, and his troops exhibited the same gallantry that had characterized them on various fields.

At this time the position of the several corps of the Confederate army was the following: Jackson was at Harper's Ferry, about fifteen miles from Sharpsburg; Longstreet, at Hagerstown, a somewhat greater distance to the north of Sharpsburg; and D. H. Hill, at Boonsboro' Gap, eastward of these positions; while McClellan's whole force, with the exception of the detachment sent toward Harper's Ferry, lay east of the Gap. Had the Gap been left undefended, as it has been recently suggested it should have been, there would have been nothing to hinder McClellan from inserting his army between the two sections of the Confederate forces and attacking them in detail. The occupation of Sharpsburg by the enemy would have placed Lee in a difficult and dangerous position. Had he retired across the Potomac, as it has been suggested was

ABOVE: General McClellan's headquarters guard, the New York 93rd Volunteers, gathers at Antietam for a photograph by Alexander Gardner, one of photographer Mathew B. Brady's staff, on September 16, 1862.

his proper course to pursue, it would have been a virtual abandonment of his trains and artillery, which were then extended along the road between Hagerstown and Sharpsburg, and could have been reached by McClellan with his cavalry in an hour or two from Boonsboro'.

The battle of Boonsboro' was therefore necessary to the security of the army; and when, on the night of the 13th, Lee received information of the rapid advance of McClellan, he at once took steps for the effective reinforcement of General Hill. Longstreet's corps was put in motion for this purpose early in the morning of the 14th, and, fortunately, arrived at the Gap in time to prevent Hill's brave men from being overwhelmed by the superior numbers of the enemy.

This timely reinforcement secured the Confederate position. McClellan, finding that his efforts against the centre and right were unavailing, at length discontinued them, with the intention of renewing the

conflict at a more assailable point. The contest during the morning had been severe and the loss on each side considerable. On the side of the Confederates, the chief loss fell on the brigade of Brigadier-general Garland. This brigade numbered among its slain its gallant commander, who fell while bravely opposing a fierce attack on South-east Pass.

When General Lee reached Boonsboro' with Longstreet's corps, he sent forward Colonel Long, Major Venable, and other members of his staff, to learn the condition of affairs in front. The pass on the left proved to be unoccupied, and a heavy Federal force was tending in that direction. In anticipation of an attack from this quarter, Hood's division was deployed across the turnpike and Rodes's was posted on the ridge overlooking the unoccupied pass, with Evans's brigade connecting his right with Hood's left. There was a small field in front of Evans and Hood, while Rodes was masked by the timber on the side of the mountain. About three

BELOW: Union scouts and guides for the Army for the Potomac photographed in October 1862 by Alexander Gardner.

o'clock the battle was renewed by McClellan, who with great energy directed his main attack against Rodes. This was successfully resisted until nightfall, when Rodes's troops gave way before the assault of a superior force. The possession of the ground that had been held by Rodes gave the Federals the command of the central pass, but they could not immediately avail themselves of their success, on account of the . . . darkness.

The Confederate position was now untenable, and its evacuation became necessary. The withdrawal of the rear-guard was assigned to General Rodes, the successful execution of the movement being in a great measure due to the sagacity and boldness of Major Green Peyton, adjutant-general of Rodes's division.

At ten o'clock the next morning the Confederate army was safely in position at Sharpsburg.

At Boonsboro', McClellan had displayed more than usual pertinacity in his attacks

LEFT: Confederate Major General James Longstreet opposed Lee's choice of Sharpsburg as the battle site. At the battle, his men formed Lee's right, anchored at Antietam Creek.

BELOW: The Boonesborough Pike crossing at Antietam Bridge in September 1862.

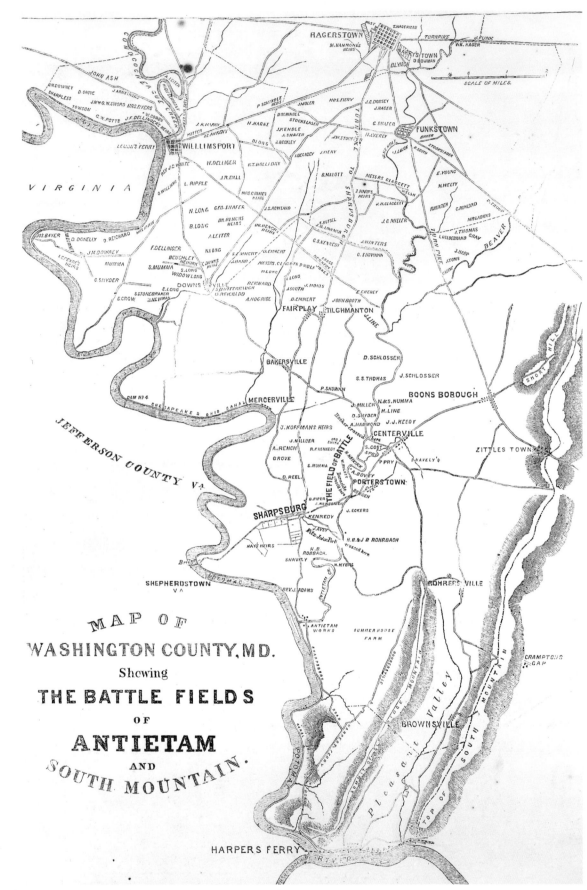

MAP OF WASHINGTON COUNTY, MD. Showing THE BATTLE FIELDS OF ANTIETAM AND SOUTH MOUNTAIN.

upon the Confederate position; yet these were met by the troops of Longstreet and Hill with a firmness worthy of the veterans of Manassas and the Chickahominy. Although Lee had been forced into an unexpected battle when his army was divided, he baffled McClellan in his designs by retarding him so as to gain time for the reduction of Harper's Ferry and to place himself where he could be easily joined by Jackson.

On the morning of the 15th, Harper's Ferry was surrendered, and about noon General

Lee received the report of its capture. Two courses now presented themselves to the general, each of which involved results of the highest importance. He might either retire across the Potomac and form a junction, in the neighborhood of Shepherdstown, with the forces that had been employed in the reduction of Harper's Ferry, or maintain his position at Sharpsburg and give battle to a superior force. By pursuing the former course the object of the campaign would be abandoned and the hope of co-operation from Maryland for ever relinquished. The latter, although hazardous, if successful would be productive of results more than commensurate with the risk attending its execution. Having a sympathy for the Marylanders, to whom he had offered his services, and a confidence in the bravery of his troops and the strength of his position, he adopted the latter course, and prepared to receive the attack of General McClellan.

Jackson's troops were hurried from Harper's Ferry and a strong defensive position was carefully selected. It embraced the heights fringing the right bank of the Antietam [the name by which the Battle of Sharpsburg is known in the North (Ed.)] east and south-east of the village of Sharpsburg and a range of hills stretching north-west to the Potomac. Lee's right and centre were protected by stone fences and ledges of rock, and his left was principally covered by a wood. The right and centre were occupied by Longstreet's corps, D. H. Hill's division, and Lee's, Walton's, and Garnett's artillery, while Jackson's corps and Stuart's cavalry occupied the left. The Federal forces having been much shattered by the battle of the 14th, McClellan did not resume his advance until late on the morning of the 15th, and did not appear before Sharpsburg until afternoon.

He employed the following day chiefly in preparations for the battle. The corps of Hooker, Mansfield, Sumner, and Franklin, constituting his right, were massed opposite the Confederate left. The hills east of the Antietam which formed the centre of the Federal position were crowned by a powerful artillery, and Burnside's corps, which occupied the left, confronted the Confederate right. Porter's corps formed the reserve, while the cavalry operated on the flanks. Late in the afternoon Mansfield and Hooker crossed the Antietam opposite Longstreet's

BELOW: Currier & Ives print of the battle at Antietam Creek, the "bloodiest day of the war."

left. Some preliminary skirmishing closed the day. Both armies now lay on their arms, conscious that the next day would be marked by the most desperate battle that had yet been witnessed in the country. The Confederates, who had never known defeat, confident in themselves, confident in the strength of their position, and confident in their glorious leader, although less in numbers than their opponents by more than one-half, never doubted that victory would again rest on their tattered banners. The Federals, on their part, burning to obliterate the marks of defeat they had lately borne, were impatient for the approaching struggle. The Federal force present on the field amounted to 90,000 men; that of the Confederates, including the division of A. P. Hill, then at Harper's Ferry in charge of prisoners and captured property, amounted to 40,000.

At dawn on the 17th the corps of Mansfield and Hooker advanced to the attack; they were met by the divisions of Anderson and Hood with their usual vigor. Being greatly outnumbered, these divisions were reinforced by Evans's brigade and the division of D. H. Hill. The contest continued close and determined for more than an hour, when the Federals began to give way. They were hotly pressed. Hooker was wounded, Mansfield was killed, and their corps were irretrievably shattered when relieved by the fresh corps of Sumner and Franklin. The

Confederates, who had advanced more than a mile, were gradually borne back to their original position. McClellan now directed his chief attack upon Lee's left, with the hope of forcing it back, so that he might penetrate between it and the river and take the Confederate position in reverse. This attack was received by Jackson's corps with intrepidity. The veterans under Early, Trimble, Lawton, and Starke gallantly held their ground against large odds. At an opportune moment the Confederate line was reinforced by the division of McLaws and Walker. The entire Confederate force, except D. R. Jones's division, on the right, was now engaged.

The roar of musketry and the thunder of artillery proclaimed the deadly conflict that raged. These deafening sounds of battle continued until about twelve o'clock, when they began to abate, and about one they ceased. The Federals had been repulsed at every point, and four corps were so much broken by loss and fatigue that they were unable to renew the contest.

After the battle had concluded on the left General Burnside prepared to assault the Confederate right with 20,000 fresh troops. He had remained inactive during the forenoon; but when the attack on the Confederate left had failed, he proceeded to force the passage of the Antietam at the bridge southeast of Sharpsburg, on the Pleasant Valley

OPPOSITE TOP: Antietam Bridge after the battles.

OPPOSITE BOTTOM: Dead bodies of Confederates from North Carolina in the "Bloody Lane," scene of heavy fighting during the Battle of Antietam.

BELOW: Photograph by Alexander Gardner at Antietam. Long believed to be the only photo of battle action made during the war, it is actually a view of reserve artillery near Union headquarters on the day after the fighting.

road, and at the ford below. These points were gallantly maintained by Toombs's brigade of Jones's division until about four o'clock, when they were carried. General Burnside then crossed the Antietam and formed his troops under the bluff.

At five o'clock he advanced, and, quickly dispersing the small division of D. R. Jones, gained the crest of the ridge south of the town. At that moment the division of A. P. Hill, 4500 strong, just arrived from Harper's Ferry, was on the road which traverses its western slope. Seeing the Federal line on its flank, the division faced to the right, and, taking advantage of the stone fence that bordered the road, delivered such destructive volleys that the Federals were forced to retire as suddenly as they had appeared. Sharply followed by Hill and raked by the artillery, Burnside was forced to recross the Antietam. Just as the sun disappeared in the west the last of Burnside's corps gained the eastern side. Thus closed the battle of Sharpsburg. The Federal troops fought well and did honor to their gallant leaders, but, being compelled to attack a strong position defended by men who had been justly characterized as the finest soldiers of the

age, they failed to obtain the mastery of the field. The casualties on both sides were heavy; the numbers have never been accurately stated. On the side of the Federals were Mansfield killed, Major-general Hooker wounded, and a number of other distinguished officers killed or wounded; on the side of the Confederates, Brigadier-general Starke was killed and Brigadiers Lawton, Ripley, and G. B. Anderson were wounded, and a number of others were put *hors de combat*. Anderson afterward died of his wound.

Among the cases of individual gallantry, one of the most conspicuous was that of General Longstreet, with Majors Fairfax and Sorrell and Captain Latrobe of his staff, who, on observing a large Federal force approaching an unoccupied portion of his line, served with such effect two pieces of artillery that had been left without cannoneers that the Federals were arrested in their advance and speedily forced to retire beyond the range of the guns.

During the night General Lee prepared for the renewal of the battle the next day. A part of his line was withdrawn to the range of hills west of the town, which gave him a very

strong and much better field than that of the previous day. He remained in his new position during the 18th, prepared for battle; but General McClellan, perceiving that his troops had been greatly disorganized by the battle of the previous day, declined resuming the attack until the arrival of 15,000 fresh troops that were hastening to his support.

Foreseeing that no important results could be achieved by a second battle with McClellan's augmented forces, and being unwilling to sacrifice unnecessarily his gallant men, Lee withdrew during the night to the south side of the Potomac, and on the 19th took a position a few miles west of Shepherdstown.

When McClellan learned, on the morning of the 19th, that the Confederate position had been evacuated, he ordered an immediate pursuit, which, however, proved unavailing, as the Confederate rear-guard was disappearing in the defile leading from the ford below Shepherdstown when the Federal advance appeared on the opposite heights. A few batteries were then put into position, and a harmless cannonade commenced, which was kept up in a desultory manner during the greater part of the day. Late in the afternoon a large detachment approached the ford, and about nightfall dislodged General Pendleton, who had been charged with its defence, and effected a

BELOW: On October 4 President Lincoln went to the Antietam battlefield to try personally to persuade General McClellan to pursue General Lee. The Union general, however, would not cross the Potomac River into Virginia until October 26.

crossing without serious opposition. This occurrence was reported about midnight to General Lee, who immediately despatched orders to Jackson to take steps to arrest the Federal advance. The division of A. P. Hill, moving with rapidity, reached the mouth of the defile leading to the river just as the Federal detachment was debouching from it, and attacked this force with such impetuosity that it was compelled to retire with heavy loss across the Potomac. McClellan made no further attempt to continue offensive operations for several weeks, this interval being passed in the neighborhood of Sharpsburg in resting and reorganizing his forces. This campaign, especially the battle of Sharpsburg, has been the subject of much discussion, in which the Northern writers generally claim for the Federal arms a complete victory; but the historian of the Army of the Potomac, with greater impartiality, acknowledges Antietam (or Sharpsburg) to have been a drawn battle. This admission is corroborated by the evidence of General McClellan in his testimony before the Congressional Committee on the Conduct of the War, since he admitted that his losses on the 17th had been so heavy, and that his forces were so greatly disorganized on the morning of the 18th, that, although General Lee still maintained a defiant attitude, he was unable to resume the attack. Swinton, however, claims for the Army of the Potomac a political victory, with apparent justice; but in reality his claim is without foundation, for Lee was politically defeated before the occurrence of a collision with McClellan by his failure to induce the Marylanders to rally in any considerable force to his standard; and even when McClellan, by accident, became aware of the disposition of his forces and his intentions, he was establishing a line of communication that would enable him to engage his opponent with no other hope of political results than such as would naturally arise from a victory, whether gained north or south of the Potomac. The severe chastisement that had been inflicted on the Army of the Potomac is evident from the long prostration it exhibited, notwithstanding the facility with which it received reinforcements and supplies.

ABOVE: Lincoln at Antietam with General McClellan. From left they are: Gen. G. W. Morell, Col. A. S. Webb, McClellan, scout Adams, Dr. J. Letterman, an unidentified officer, Lincoln, Col. H. J. Hunt, and Gen. Fitz John Porter.

Chapter IV

Fredericksburg

After remaining a few days in the neighborhood of Shepherdstown, General Lee gradually withdrew to a position between Bunker Hill and Winchester. Notwithstanding he had failed, from accidental causes, to accomplish the chief object of the invasion of Maryland, the expedition was not wholly without beneficial results, since it relieved Virginia from the presence of the enemy and gave her an opportunity to recover in a measure from the exhausting effect of war . . . .

* * *

The inactivity of General McClellan allowed General Lee several weeks of uninterrupted repose. During that interval the guardianship of the Potomac was confided to the cavalry and horse-artillery. While thus employed General Stuart made a swoop into Pennsylvania, captured a thousand horses, and after making the entire circuit of the Federal army recrossed the Potomac with only the loss of three missing . . . .

Throughout the late campaign the duty of selecting a place for headquarters usually devolved upon the writer. The general would say, "Colonel Long has a good eye for locality: let him find a place for the camp." It was not always so easy to find a desirable situation, but, as the general was easily satisfied, the difficulties of the task were greatly lightened. Only once, to my recollection, did he object to the selection made for headquarters; this was on reaching the neighborhood of Winchester. The army had preceded the general and taken possession of every desirable camping-place. After a long and fatiguing search a farm-house was discovered, surrounded by a large shady yard. The occupants of the house with great satisfaction gave permission for the establishment of General Lee not only in the yard, but insisted on his occupying a part of the house. Everything being satisfactorily settled, the wagons were ordered up, but just as their unloading began the general rode up and flatly refused to occupy either

yard or house. No one expected him to violate his custom by occupying the house, but it was thought he would not object to a temporary occupation of the yard. Being vexed at having to look for another place for headquarters, I ordered the wagons into a field almost entirely covered with massive stones. The boulders were so large and thick that it was difficult to find space for the tents. The only redeeming feature the location possessed was a small stream of good water. When the tents were pitched, the general looked around with a smile of satisfaction, and said, "This is better than the yard. We will not now disturb those good people."

While occupying this camp we were visited by several distinguished British officers – among them, Colonel Garnet Wolseley, who has since become prominent in history. Subsequently, one of the number published the following account of General Lee and his surroundings:

In visiting the headquarters of the Confederate generals, but particularly those of General Lee, any one accustomed to see

European armies in the field, cannot fail to be struck with the great absence of all the pomp and circumstance of war in and around their encampments.

Lee's headquarters consisted of about seven or eight poletents, pitched, with their backs to a stake-fence, upon a piece of ground so rocky that it was unpleasant to ride over it, its only recommendation being a little stream of good water which flowed close by the general's tent. In front of the tents were some three or four army-wagons, drawn up without any regularity, and a number of horses turned loose about the field. The servants – who were, of course, slaves – and the mounted soldiers called couriers, who always accompany each general of division in the field, were unprovided with tents, and slept in or under the wagons. Wagons, tents, and some of the horses were marked "U.S.," showing that part of that huge debt in the North has gone to furnishing even the Confederate generals with camp-equipments. No guard or sentries were to be seen in the vicinity, no crowd of aides-de-camp loitering about, making themselves agreeable to visitors and endeavoring to save their generals from receiving those who had no particular business. A large farm-house stands close by, which in any other army would have been the general's residence *pro tem.*; but, as no liberties are allowed to be taken with personal property in Lee's army, he is particular in setting a good example himself. His staff are crowded together, two or three in a

BELOW: A group of European officers who visited troops in the field near Yorktown, Va. in May 1862.

ABOVE: A Confederate camp in autumn.

RIGHT: Soldier drawing water for a hospital at Fredericksburg.

tent; none are allowed to carry more baggage than a small box each, and his own kit is but very little larger. Every one who approaches him does so with marked respect, although there is none of that bowing and flourishing of forage-caps which occurs in the presence of European generals; and, while all honor him and place implicit faith in his courage and ability, those with whom he is most intimate feel for him the affection of sons to a father. Old General Scott was correct in saying that when Lee joined the Southern cause it was worth as much as the accession of 20,000 men to the "rebels." Since then every injury that it was possible to inflict the Northerners have heaped upon him. Notwithstanding all these personal losses, however, when speaking of the Yankees he neither evinced any bitterness of feeling nor gave utterance to a single violent expression, but alluded to many of his former friends and companions among them in the kindest terms. He spoke as a man proud of the victories won by his country and confident of ultimate success

under the blessing of the Almighty, whom he glorified for past successes, and whose aid he invoked for all future operations.

Notwithstanding the ruggedness of this encampment, it proved unusually lively. Besides the foreign friends, we had numerous visitors from the army, also ladies and gentlemen from Winchester and the neighborhood, all of whom had some remark to make upon the rocky situation of our camp. This the general seemed to enjoy, as it gave him an opportunity of making a jest at the expense of Colonel Long, whom he accused of having set him down there among the rocks in revenge for his refusing to occupy the yard. Although there were no habitual drinkers on the general's staff, an occasional demijohn would find its way to headquarters. While at this place one of the officers received a present of a jug of fine old rye. Soon after its advent General J. E. B. Stuart, with Sweeney and his banjo, arrived – not on account, however, of the jug, but, as was his wont, to give us a serenade. The

ABOVE: Building a stockade at Alexandria, Virginia.

ABOVE: Night amusements around a Confederate campfire.

bright camp-fire was surrounded by a merry party, and a lively concert commenced. After a while the general came out, and, observing the jug perched on a boulder, asked with a merry smile, "Gentlemen, am I to thank General Stuart or the jug for this fine music?"

By this time the men had come to know their leader. The brilliant campaigns through which he had led them had inspired them with love and confidence, and whenever he appeared among them his approach was announced by "Here comes Mars' Robert!" and he would be immediately saluted with the well-known Confederate yell, which called forth in other quarters the exclamation, "There goes Mars' Robert – ole Jackson, or an ole hare."

*   *   *

The repose of a month had greatly improved in every way the Confederate army; it had reached a high state of efficiency, and General Lee was fully prepared to meet General McClellan whenever he might think fit to advance to attack him in his position

before Winchester. When McClellan . . . had crossed the Potomac and the direction of his advance was ascertained, Lee moved Longstreet's corps and the greater part of the cavalry to a position near Culpeper Courthouse and established his outposts along the right bank of the Rappahannock. Jackson's corps was detained in the Valley until the Federal plans should be more fully developed.

The delay that followed the battle of Sharpsburg and the deliberate manner in which McClellan resumed active operations . . . were productive of a voluminous correspondence with Mr. Lincoln and General Halleck, . . . which culminated in the removal of McClellan . . . .

*   *   *

A great diversity of opinion exists as to the military capacity of McClellan, and he has been both unduly praised and censured by his friends and foes. That his slowness and caution were elements on which the opposing general might safely count must be admitted, but that he had a high degree of

military ability cannot be denied. His skill in planning movements was certainly admirable, but their effect was in more than one instance lost by over-slowness in their execution. In this connection it will be of interest to give General Lee's own opinion concerning McClellan's ability, as related by a relative of the general, who had it from her father, an old gentleman of eighty years:

"One thing I remember hearing him say. He asked General Lee which in his opinion was the ablest of the Union generals; to which the latter answered, bringing his hand down on the table with an emphatic energy, 'McClellan, by all odds!'"

This opinion, however, could but have referred to his skill as a tactician, as it is unquestionable that Lee availed himself of McClellan's over-caution and essayed perilous movements which he could not have safely ventured in the presence of a more active opponent.

It was with surprise that the Confederate officers who knew the distinguished merit of Sumner, Sedgwick, Meade, and others learned that Burnside had been elevated above them, and General Burnside himself with diffidence accepted the high honor that had been conferred upon him. Mr. Lincoln, accompanied by General Halleck, visited the headquarters of the army near Warrenton, where a plan of operations was adopted. A rapid advance upon Richmond by the way of Fredericksburg was advised. It was supposed from the position of General Lee's forces that by gaining a march or two upon him Richmond might be reached and captured before that general could relieve it. All that prevented the immediate execution of this plan was the want of a pontoon-train, which was necessary for the passage of the Rappahannock.

Having arranged to his satisfaction with General Halleck and Mr. Lincoln in regard to a prompt compliance with his requisitions for pontoons and supplies for the army, General Burnside, about the 15th of November, put the Army of the Potomac in motion, and on the 17th, Sumner's corps reached Fredericksburg. This energetic officer would probably have immediately crossed the Rappahannock by the fords above the town, and

ABOVE: Union General Meade (fourth from right) and General Sedgwick (second from right) were both considered more able than Major General Burnside, whom Lincoln chose to elevate over them as commander of the Army of the Potomac.

ABOVE: A Federal cavalry column forms up near a pontoon bridge after crossing the Rappahannock.

RIGHT: Federal earthworks on the north bank of the North Anna River facing Confederate earthworks in the distance.

OPPOSITE TOP: Three Confederate pickets at Fredericksburg.

OPPOSITE BOTTOM: Union pontoon wagons on the way to Burnside in December.

thus have saved much delay. He was, however, restrained by Burnside, who directed him to await the arrival of the pontoons. At this time the river in the neighborhood of Fredericksburg was held simply by a small picket-force, and could have been forded without much difficulty. General Lee, having penetrated the designs of the Federal commander, prepared to oppose them. About the 18th he sent reinforcements to Fredericksburg with instructions to retard, as far as practicable, the Federal forces in the passage of the Rappahannock, and at the same time he sent orders to Jackson to join him as speedily as possible.

Upon the supposition that Burnside would cross the Rappahannock before he could form a junction of his forces, Lee proposed to take a position behind the North Anna with part of Longstreet's corps, the force then about Richmond, and such other troops as might be drawn from other points, while, with Jackson's and the remainder of Longstreet's corps united, he moved in such a manner as might enable him to fall upon the flank and rear of the Federal army when it attempted the passage of that river. But when it was ascertained that Burnside was prevented from immediately crossing the Rappahannock by a delay in the arrival of his pontoons, Lee determined to move Longstreet's corps immediately to Fredericksburg and take possession of the heights opposite those occupied by the Federal force, as these heights afforded a stronger defensive line than the North Anna.

In execution of this determination Longstreet's corps left the vicinity of Culpeper Court-house on the 24th, crossed the Rapidan at Raccoon Ford, and, proceeding by the Wilderness road, reached Fredericksburg the next day. In the mean time, Jackson was rapidly approaching from the Valley. The Army of the Potomac had been a week before Fredericksburg and the pontoons had not yet arrived, and what might have been effected a few days before without opposition could now be accomplished only by force. Even after passing the river Burnside would be obliged to remove from his path a formidable opponent before he could continue his advance upon the city of Richmond.

On arriving at Fredericksburg, General Lee caused the heights south of the river to be occupied by artillery and infantry from Banks's Ford, four miles above, to the Massaponax, five miles below the city, while the

ABOVE: General Lee fortified the heights above the city of Fredericksburg. Shown are the breastworks erected on Marye's Heights (Marye's Hill).

cavalry extended up the river beyond the United States Ford and down as far as Port Royal. The prominent points were crowned with artillery covered by epaulments, and in the intervals were constructed breastworks for the protection of infantry. The heights closely fringe the river from Banks's Ford to Falmouth; thence they recede, leaving a low ground, which gradually increases in width to about two miles; then the hills again abut upon the river a little below the mouth of the Massaponax, and, extending nearly parallel to that stream, abruptly terminate in broad, low grounds. These low grounds are traversed by the main road to Bowling Green and are intersected by several small streams. The most important of these is Deep Run, which empties into the Rappahannock a little more than a mile above the mouth of the Massaponax. That portion of the road embraced between Deep Run and the Massaponax is enclosed by embankments sufficiently high and thick to afford good covers for troops. We have here endeavored to describe some of the principal features of the Confederate position at Fred-

ericksburg, that the plan of battle may be more clearly understood.

Jackson's corps on its arrival at the end of November was posted a few miles south of the Massaponax, in the neighborhood of Guinea Station on the Richmond and Fredericksburg Railroad. From this position he could easily support Longstreet, or, in case Burnside attempted a passage of the Rappahannock between the Massaponax and Port Royal, he would be ready to intercept him. After much delay the pontoon-train reached Fredericksburg. But then the position of Lee presented a formidable obstacle to the passage of the river at that point.

General Burnside thereupon caused careful reconnoissances to be made both above and below, with the view of finding a more favorable point for crossing. But he invariably found wherever he appeared the forces of General Lee ready to oppose him. Finding no part of the river more suitable or less guarded than that about Fredericksburg, Burnside determined to effect a crossing at that place. Two points were selected – one opposite the town, and the other two miles

below, near the mouth of Deep Run – and early on the morning of the 11th of December the work was begun under cover of a dense fog. A bridge was laid at the mouth of Deep Run, and Franklin's grand division passed over without opposition. In front of Fredericksburg, however, the case was different. The gallant Barksdale with his brigade of Mississippians, to whom the defence of the town had been assigned, repelled every attempt to construct the bridges until the afternoon, when the powerful artillery of the Federal army was massed and a cannonade from one hundred and eighty guns was opened upon the devoted town, under cover of which troops crossed in boats under the direction of General Hunt, chief of artillery. Then Barksdale, fighting, retired step by step until he gained the cover of the road embankment at the foot of Marye's Heights, which he held until relieved by fresh troops. Burnside having developed his plan of attack, Lee concentrated his forces preparatory for battle. His right rested on the Massaponax, and his left on the Rappahannock at the dam in the vicinity

of Falmouth. Jackson's corps, in three lines, occupied the space between the Massaponax and Deep Run, while Longstreet's corps, with artillery, occupied the remainder of the position. The flanks were covered by Stuart's cavalry and horse artillery. It was here for the first time that the Confederate artillery was systematically massed for battle. On his arrival at Fredericksburg, General Lee assigned to Colonel Long the duty of verifying and selecting positions for the artillery, in which he was assisted by Majors Venable and Talcott and Captain Sam Johnson. On the day of battle two hundred pieces of artillery were in position, and so arranged that at least fifty pieces could be brought to bear on any threatened point, and on Fredericksburg and Deep Run, the points of attack, a hundred guns could be concentrated. The artillery on Longstreet's front was commanded by Colonels Alexander, Walton, and Cabell, and that on Jackson's by Colonels Brown and Walker. The horse artillery was commanded by Major Pelham. These officers on all occasions served with marked ability. General Pendleton, chief of

ABOVE: A sketch by war artist Arthur Lumley shows some Union troops in Fredericksburg just before the start of the main battle. Lumley was criticized in the North for depicting the soldiers engaged in looting.

artillery, exercised special control of the reserve artillery.

As Jackson's corps had been extended some distance down the Rappahannock, it was not until the night of the 11th that its concentration was completed. On the morning of the 12th of December, General Lee's entire force was in position, prepared to receive the Federal attack. The strength of the opposing armies, as on previous occasions, was disproportionate. The effective strength of the Army of Northern Virginia was about 60,000, of which about 52,000 were infantry, 4000 artillery with 250 guns, and the cavalry composed the remainder. That of the Army of the Potomac exceeded 100,000 men and 300 pieces of artillery. 90,000 men had crossed the river – 40,000 of Sumner's grand division at Fredericksburg, and Franklin's grand division of 50,000 men at Deep Run. From this disposition of forces it was ap-

parent that General Burnside designed a simultaneous attack upon the Confederate right and centre. Jackson's first line, composed of two brigades of A. P. Hill's division, held the railroad; a second line, consisting of artillery and the other brigades of Hill's division, occupied the heights immediately overlooking the railroad; and the reserves, commanded by D. H. Hill, were in convenient supporting-distance. In the centre the most conspicuous feature was Marye's Heights, behind the town of Fredericksburg and separated from it by an open space of several hundreds yards in width. The telegraph road passing between the base of the heights and a strong embankment was occupied by two brigades – Cobb's and Kershaw's of Longstreet's corps – while the crest was crowned by a powerful artillery covered by a continuous line of earthworks. A reserve of two brigades, commanded by

BELOW: Plan of the Battle of Fredericksburg, beginning on December 13, 1862. About 60,000 Confederates faced some 100,000 Federal troops.

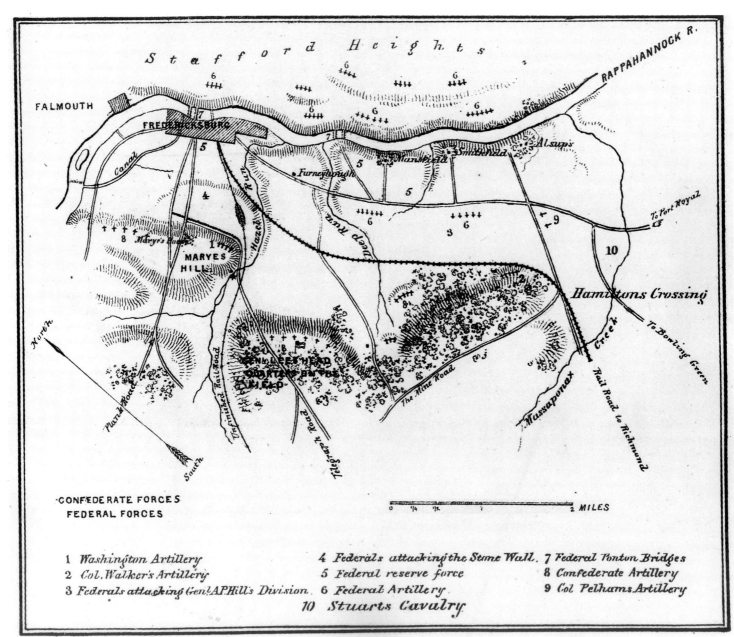

CONFEDERATE FORCES
FEDERAL FORCES

1 *Washington Artillery*
2 *Col. Walker's Artillery*
3 *Federals attacking Genl. A.P.Hill's Division*
4 *Federals attacking the Stone Wall*
5 *Federal reserve force*
6 *Federal Artillery*
7 *Federal Ponton Bridges*
8 *Confederate Artillery*
9 *Col Pelhams Artillery*
10 *Stuarts Cavalry*

Brigadier-general Ransom, occupied the reverse slope of the heights. [These troops did good service during the battle.] On the hills behind were grouped batteries so disposed that the heights in front could be raked with shot and shell in case they were carried by the Federals.

On the morning of the 13th of December, as the fog slowly lifted, a scene was unfolded which in point of grandeur has seldom been witnessed. The Stafford Heights, from Falmouth to the Massaponax, were crowned with thickly-grouped batteries of artillery, while the shores of the Rappahannock were

ABOVE: Union artillery used to soften Confederate resistance at Fredericksburg.

covered with dark masses of troops in battle array. Opposite the Confederate right the attacking force, in two lines, began to advance. Simultaneously the heights were wreathed in smoke and the thunder of artillery announced the commencement of battle. When the attacking column had become disengaged from the embankments of the river-road, Stuart's horse artillery on the right and the artillery of Jackson's corps in front opened a destructive fire, which checked it for a brief space, until its own batteries could be placed in position to occupy the opposing artillery. It then moved steadily onward, and quickly dislodged the first Confederate line from the railroad, and disappeared in the wood that concealed the greater part of the second line. A deadly conflict ensued, which, although hidden by the forest, was proclaimed by the terrific clash of musketry. Very soon the troops that had advanced so gallantly were seen to retire. At first a straggling few and then large masses came rushing out, followed by long lines of gray veterans, who dealt death at every step.

General Meade, from the want of support after his gallant achievement, was compelled to witness the present deplorable condition of his corps. Forty thousand of Franklin's grand division, remaining idly by, had beheld the defeat of their brave comrades without extending a helping hand. This apathy of Franklin was at the time regarded by the Confederates as remarkable.

During the attack on the right preparations were in progress to assail the Confederate centre. Dense masses of troops, which had been previously concentrated in and about Fredericksburg, were now formed in columns of attack to be led against Marye's Heights. About noon the attack commenced. Column after column advanced to the assault, to be hurled back with terrible slaughter. Attack after attack was hopelessly renewed until the stoutest heart quailed at the dreadful carnage that ensued. Seeing his repeated efforts unavailing, General Burnside ordered a discontinuance of the conflict. The Confederates on the next day expected the battle to be renewed with greater vigor than had been displayed on the day before, but the Federals maintained a sullen silence, and at night re-crossed the Rappahannock. The next morning the spectator could hardly believe his senses on beholding the great Federal army that had on the day previous lined the southern shore of the Rappahannock now covering the heights of Stafford, bereft of that martial spirit it had exhibited a few days before. The dispirited condition of the Federal army was not so much the consequence of losses in battle as the effect of the want of co-operation and the fruitless results of misdirected valor.

The appointment of General Burnside to the command of the Army of the Potomac had proved a mistake – more, however, from the combination of circumstances against him than from lack of conduct on his part. His successes in North Carolina had given him prominence, while his soldierly bearing and fine appearance evidently had their influence with Mr. Lincoln in the selection of him as commander-in-chief of the Army of the Potomac, while neglecting the superior claims of several others, two of whom – Generals Hooker and Franklin – could never forget their sense of superiority sufficiently to render him cordial co-operation. Bour-

rienne gives us a maxim of Bonaparte that "two great generals in the same army are sure to make a bad one." This maxim particularly applied in the present instance to the Army of the Potomac, where its truth was fully verified.

The losses sustained, as stated by General Burnside, amounted to about 10,000, among whom was General Bayard, a young officer of great merit, whose loss was sincerely felt in the army as well as by a large circle of acquaintances. The Confederate loss was numerically much less than that sustained by the enemy. The Confederates, however, numbered among their slain Brigadier-generals Gregg and Cobb, and among their mortally wounded Colonel Coleman of the artillery. The fall of these noble and gallant spirits was deeply deplored by the army.

* * *

After the battle of Fredericksburg, General Lee retained his headquarters, established previous to the battle, at a point on the road midway between Fredericksburg and Hamilton Crossing, selected on account of its accessibility. Although there was a vacant house near which he could have occupied, he preferred ... to remain in camp, thus giving an example of endurance of hardship that might prove useful to his troops

* * *

OPPOSITE: Confederate dead behind the stone wall at the foot of Marye's Heights, from behind which Longstreet's infantry poured deadly fire on the Union attackers.

BELOW: Fredericksburg viewed from the river. Rebel troops stand on what remains of the town's wrecked bridge.

Chapter V

Chancellorsville

The Army of Northern Virginia in the winter of 1862-63 began to feel seriously the want of . . . money and men. The Army of Northern Virginia was deficient in clothing, shoes, blankets, tents, provisions; in fact, everything needful was wanted except arms and ammunition . . . In order to relieve the drain upon the scanty commissariat, Longstreet was sent with two divisions to the district south of Petersburg, where provisions were still abundant, with a view of subsisting these troops, while they collected the surplus supplies to be sent to the troops in other quarters. This detachment reduced the Confederate army to barely 40,000 men, while the Federal force exceeded 100,000.

After this reduction General Lee conceived the design of adopting a position more remote from the Federal lines than the one he then occupied, . . . [but as] no position could be found which afforded greater advantages than the one he then occupied, Lee continued to hold the line of the Rappahannock, and busied himself in preparation for the ensuing campaign.

*   *   *

The appointment of Hooker to the command of the Army of the Potomac was a surprise to General Lee, who had no great respect for the military ability of his new opponent in a position of such importance. Swinton thus comments on the condition of the Army of the Potomac and the appointment of Hooker to the supreme command:

Notwithstanding the untoward fortunes the Army of the Potomac had suffered, it could hardly be said to be really demoralized, for

BELOW: By winter of 1862-63 the South began to grow short of materiel to support the war. Confederate soldiers are shown stripping clothing and boots from fallen Union soldiers.

its heart was still in the war; it never failed to respond to any demand made upon it; and it was ever ready to renew its courage at the first ray of hope. Such a day-spring came with the appointment of General Hooker to the chief command, and under his influence the tone of the army underwent a change that would appear astonishing had not its elastic vitality been so often proved. Hooker's measures of reform were judicious: he cut away the roots of many evils; stopped desertion and its causes; did away with the nuisance of the "grand-division" organization; infused vitality through the staff and administrative service; gave distinctive badges to the different corps; instituted a system of furloughs; consolidated the cavalry under able leaders, and soon enabled it not only to stand upon an equality with, but to assert its superiority over, the Virginia horsemen of Stuart. These things proved General Hooker to be an able administrative officer, but they did not prove him to be a competent commander for a great army, and whatever anticipation might be formed touching this had to be drawn from his previous career as a corps commander, in which he had won the reputation of being what is called a "dashing" officer, and carried the sobriquet of "Fighting Joe."

The new commander judiciously resolved to defer all grand military operations during the wet season, and the first three months after he assumed command were well spent in rehabilitating the army. The ranks were filled up by the return of absentees; the discipline and instruction of the troops were energetically continued; and the close of April found the Army of the Potomac in a high degree of efficiency in all arms. It numbered 120,000 men (infantry and artillery), with a body of 12,000 well-equipped cavalry and a powerful artillery force of above 400 guns. It was divided into seven corps – the First corps under General Reynolds; the Second under General Couch; the Third under General Sickles; the Fifth under General Meade; the Sixth under General Sedgwick; the Eleventh under General Howard; and the Twelfth under General Slocum.

During his period of preparation Hooker very properly resisted that spirit of impa-

ABOVE: Union General Joseph ("Fighting Joe") Hooker, who rehabilitated the Army of the Potomac in the winter 1862-63.

ABOVE: Company C of the 110th Pennsylvannia Infantry, part of Sickles's III Corps, on April 14, one week before it was cut to pieces at Chancerllorsville.

RIGHT: Hand-to-hand fighting between Union cavalry commanded by General William W. Averell and Confederates under Fitz Lee at Kelly's Ford on March 17.

tience that had characterized Mr. Lincoln in his intercourse with the previous commanders of the Army of the Potomac, and only gratified once that "up-and-be-doing" spirit that prevailed in Washington by indulging General Averill in a cavalry combat with General Fitz Lee, who guarded the upper fords of the Rappahannock. Being now fully prepared for active operations, Hooker determined to take the initiative by moving on the left of his opponent's position. By careful study of Lee's position he correctly concluded that his left was his most vulnerable point.

In order to mask his real design he sent forward a force of 10,000 cavalry under General Stoneman to operate upon Lee's lines of communication with Richmond, and sent Sedgwick with a force of 30,000 men still further to mask his movement. Stoneman crossed the Rappahannock at Kelly's Ford on the 29th, and Sedgwick appeared on the 28th on the heights below Fredericksburg. These preparatory measures having been taken, Hooker proceeded to the execution of his plan. Swinton, after a picturesque description of the passage of the Rappahannock and the Rapidan, tells us "that on the afternoon of the 30th of April four corps of the Federal army had gained the position of Chancellorsville, where Hooker at the same time established his headquarters."

Chancellorsville is situated ten miles south-west of Fredericksburg. It is not, as its name implies, a town or village, but simply a farm-house with its usual appendages, situated at the edge of a small field surrounded by a dense thicket of second growth, which sprang up after the primeval forest had been cut to furnish fuel to a neighboring furnace. This thicket extends for miles in every direction, and its wild aspect very properly suggests its name, The Wilderness. The intersection of several important roads gives it the semblance of strategic importance, while in reality a more unfavorable place for military operations could not well be found.

Hooker, however, seemed well pleased with his acquisition, for on reaching Chancellorsville on Thursday night he issued an order to the troops in which he announced that "the enemy must either ingloriously fly or come out from behind his defences and give us battle on our own ground, where certain destruction awaits him." This boast, we are told, so much in the style of Hooker, was amplified by the whole tenor of his conver-

Splendid Advance of Sykes's Regulars.

Centre of our Line of Battle.

ABOVE: Some sketches of the action at Chancellorsville by field artist A. R. Waud.

sation. "The Confederate army," said he, "is now the legitimate property of the Army of the Potomac. They may as well pack up their haversacks and make for Richmond, and I shall be after them," etc.

General Lee was fully aware of the preparations that were being made by his adversary, but calmly awaited the complete development of his plans before exerting his strength to oppose him. The presence of the enemy during the winter had made it necessary to maintain a defensive line of about twenty-five miles, the right being in the vicinity of Port Royal, while the left extended to the neighborhood of the United States Ford. This line was occupied by six divisions: Anderson's on the left, and McLaws's between Fredericksburg and the Massaponax,

RIGHT: Confederate General Fitzhugh ("Fitz") Lee led one of Stuart's two cavalry units.

OPPOSITE BOTTOM: Union pontoon bridge across the Rappahannock.

BELOW: William Henry Fitzhugh Lee, the second of Robert E. Lee's three sons, commanded the second of Stuart's two cavalry brigades.

while the four divisions of Jackson's corps occupied the space below the Massaponax. This line had been greatly attenuated by the removal of Longstreet's two divisions of 15,000 men.

Lee's whole cavalry force consisted of two brigades – Fitz Lee's and W. H. F. Lee's – under the immediate command of Stuart, and was mainly employed in guarding the fords of the upper Rappahannock. Hooker had no sooner commenced his movement than it was reported by Stuart to General Lee, and Sedgwick's appearance on the 28th came under his own observation. Perceiving that the time for action had arrived, Lee ordered Jackson to concentrate his whole corps in the immediate vicinity of Fredericksburg.

Early on the morning of the 29th, Sedgwick crossed the Rappahannock below the mouth of Deep Run, but made no other aggressive movement on that day or the day following. On the night of the 30th, Lee was informed of Hooker's arrival at Chancellorsville. He had been previously informed of Stoneman's movements against his line of operations by General Stuart, and was now satisfied that the main attack of the enemy would come from the direction of Chancellorsville. Therefore on the morning of the 1st of May he made the necessary preparations to meet it. Accompanied by his staff, he took a position on a height where one of his batteries overlooked the Rappahannock. He there observed carefully the position of Sedgwick while waiting for information from the direction of Chancellorsville. Jackson was present, while his troops occupied the telegraph road. As far as the eye could reach these men with their bright muskets and tarnished uniforms were distributed in picturesque groups, lightly chatting and laughing, and awaiting the order to march.

Very soon the sound of cannon indicated that the work had begun. At the same time couriers arrived from Stuart and Anderson informing the general that the enemy were advancing on the old turnpike, the plank road, and on the river roads, and asking for reinforcements. McLaws was immediately ordered to the support of Anderson, and shortly after Jackson was ordered to follow with three of his divisions, leaving Early with his division, Barksdale's brigade, and the reserve artillery under General Pendleton – a force of about 9000 men and 45 pieces of artillery – in observation of Sedgwick. When Jackson joined McLaws and Anderson a lively skirmish was in progress, in which he immediately participated. When General Lee arrived he found the Federals were being driven back to Chancellorsville. At the close of the afternoon they had retired within their lines.

General Lee occupied the ridge about three-quarters of a mile south-east and south of Chancellorsville. The opposing armies were hidden from each other by the intervening thicket of brushwood. By a close examination it was discovered that the Federal position was protected by two strong lines of breastworks, one fronting east and the other south. The brushwood had been cleared off for a space of a hundred yards, thus giving an unobstructed field for musketry, while the roads were commanded by artillery. Toward the north and west the position was open. It was obvious that the Federal position was too formidable to be attacked in front with any hope of success; therefore Lee proceeded to devise a plan by which the position of Hooker might be turned and a point of attack gained from

which no danger was apprehended by the Federal commander.

General Lee was informed that the Rev. Mr. Lacy, a chaplain in Jackson's corps, was familiar with the country about Chancellorsville. Mr. Lacy informed the general that he

BELOW: A prayer in Stonewall Jackson's camp. The general stands at left, with A. P. Hill seated on his right and R. S. Ewell on his left.

had been the pastor of a church near Chancellorsville, and was well acquainted with all the roads in that neighborhood, and that troops could be conducted to a designated point beyond Chancellorsville by a road sufficiently remote from the Federal position to prevent discovery. With this information Lee determined to turn the Federal position and assail it from a point where an attack was unexpected. The execution of a movement so much in accordance with his genius and inclination was assigned to General Jackson, Captain Carter acting as guide.

The above statement is made from personal knowledge of the writer, gained on the ground at the time; still, since some of Jackson's biographers have allowed their partiality for him so far to outstrip their knowledge of facts as to claim for him the origin of that movement, I will introduce, in corroboration of my statement, the following letter from General Lee published in the address of General Fitzhugh Lee before the Southern Historical Society:

LEXINGTON, VA., *October 28, 1867*
Dr. A. T. BLEDSOE, *Office Southern Review*, Baltimore, Maryland.

MY DEAR SIR: In reply to your inquiry, I must acknowledge that I have not read the article on Chancellorsville in the last number of the *Southern Review*, nor have I read any of the books published on either side since the termination of hostilities. I have as yet felt no desire to revive any recollections of those events, and have been satisfied with the knowledge I possessed of what transpired. I have, however, learned from others that the various authors of the life of Jackson award to him the credit of the success gained by the Army of Northern Virginia when he was present, and describe the movements of his corps or command as independent of the general plan of operations and undertaken at his own suggestion and upon his own responsibility. I have the greatest reluctance to do anything that might be considered detracting from his well-deserved fame, for I believe no one was more convinced of his worth or appreciated him more highly than myself; yet your knowledge of military affairs, if you have none of the events themselves, will teach you that this could not have been so. Every movement of an army must be well considered and properly ordered, and every one who knew General Jackson must know that he was too good a soldier to violate this fundamental principle. In the operations around Chancellorsville I overtook General Jackson, who had been placed in command of the advance as the skirmishers of the approaching armies met, advanced with the troops to the Federal line of defences, and

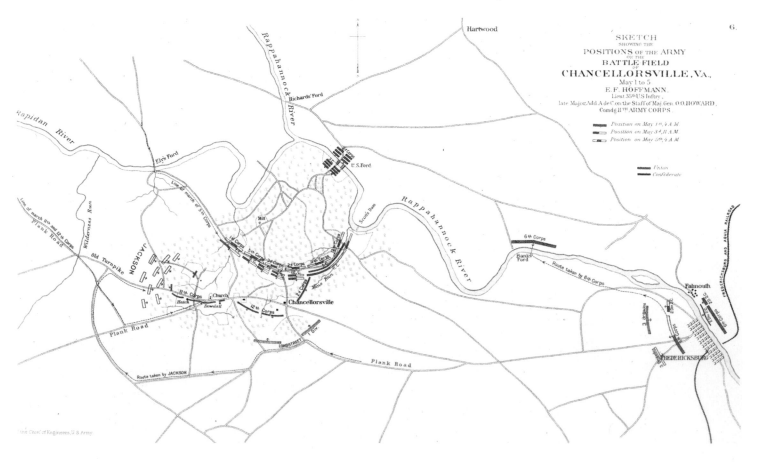

was on the field until their whole army re-crossed the Rappahannock. There is no question as to who was responsible for the operations of the Confederates, or to whom any failure would have been charged.

What I have said is for your own information. With my best wishes for the success of the *Southern Review* and for your own welfare, in both of which I take a lively interest,

I am, with great respect, your friend and servant,

R. E. LEE.

The last interview between Lee and Jackson, during which this important movement was decided upon, was an occasion of great historical interest, in regard to which the writer is fortunately able to add some information from his own knowledge of the circumstances, and that of other members of General Lee's staff. He has been favored by Major T. M. R. Talcott with certain important details of this event, conveyed in a private letter, from which the following extract is made:

My recollections of the night before the battle of Chancellorsville are briefly as follows:

About sunset General Jackson sent word to General Lee (by me) that his advance was checked and that the enemy was in force at Chancellorsville. This brought General Lee to the front, and General Jackson met him in the south-east angle of the Chancellorsville and Catharine Forge roads.

General Lee asked General Jackson whether he had ascertained the position and strength of the enemy on our left, to which General Jackson replied by stating the result of an attack made by Stuart's cavalry near Catharine Forge about dusk. The position of the enemy immediately in front was then discussed, and Captain Boswell and myself were sent to make a moonlight reconnoissance, the result of which was reported about 10 P.M., and was not favorable to an attack in front.

At this time Generals Lee and Jackson were together, and Lee, who had a map before him, asked Jackson, "How can we get at these people?" To which Jackson replied, in effect, "You know best. Show me what to do, and we will try to do it." General Lee looked thoughtfully at the map; then indicated on it and explained the movement he desired General Jackson to make, and closed by saying, "General Stuart will cover your movement with his cavalry." General Jackson listened attentively, and his face lighted up with a smile while General Lee was speaking. Then rising and touching his cap, he said, "My troops will move at four o'clock."

Having, in the manner here described, settled upon their plan of operations for the ensuing day, the two generals, accompanied by their staff officers, repaired to a neighboring pine-thicket, where an open space, well sheltered by overhanging boughs, afforded the party a good bivouac. The day having been a fatiguing one, they lost little time in preparing for the night's repose. Each selected his ground for a bed, spread his saddle-blanket, substituted his saddle for a pillow and his overcoat for covering, and was soon in a happy state of oblivion.

At dawn on the morning of the 2d, Jackson's corps, 22,000 strong, was in motion, and while it was making one of the most famous flank movements on record, General Lee, with the divisions of Anderson and McLaws, with 20 pieces of artillery, a force not exceeding 12,000 men, occupied the position he had assumed the previous evening, and General Hooker, with 90,000 men, lay behind his breastworks awaiting the Confederate attack. Having in the fore-

BELOW: Union Major General Daniel Sickles won several engagements on May 2 before the Federal defeat. (The photo was taken postwar.)

noon seen a part of Jackson's ammunition-train, Hooker believed that Lee was retreating, and sent two divisions of Sickles's corps and Pleasonton's cavalry to gain information. This movement was promptly arrested by Colonel Thompson Brown with his battalion of artillery, supported by Jackson's rear-guard. Sickles's and Pleasonton's cavalry lingered about Catharine Furnace in a state of uncertainty until recalled by Jackson's attack on the right of the Federal position.

After making a circuitous march of fifteen miles, Jackson reached a point on the Orange Court-house road three miles in the rear of Chancellorsville. Had Hooker possessed a handful of cavalry equal in spirit to the "Virginia horsemen" under W. H. F. Lee that neutralized Stoneman's ten thousand, he might have escaped the peril that now awaited him. On the arrival of Jackson on the plank road, Fitz Lee, who had covered his movement with his brigade of cavalry, conducted him to a position from which he obtained a view of the enemy, which disclosed the following scene:

Below and but a few hundred yards distant ran the Federal line of battle. There was the line of defence, with abatis in front and long lines of stacked arms in rear. Two cannons were visible in the part of the line seen. The soldiers were in groups in the rear, laughing, chatting, and smoking, probably engaged here and there in games of cards and other amusements, indulged in while feeling safe and comfortable, awaiting orders. In the rear of them were other parties driving up and butchering beeves.

ABOVE: Union General Alfred Pleasonton's artillery attacking Jackon's men at Hazel Grove on May 3.

BELOW: Woodcut of a cavalry engagement at Chancellorsville.

OPPOSITE TOP: Jackson being cheered by his troops.

OPPOSITE BOTTOM: The wounding of General Stonewall Jackson on May 2.

BELOW: Sketches by A. R. Waud show an attack by Jackson on the Union Second and Third Corps and a view of General Hooker's field headquarters.

Returning from this point of observation, Jackson proceeded to make his dispositions of attack, which by six o'clock were completed. The divisions of Rodes and Colston were formed at right angles to the old turnpike, the division of Rodes being in advance, and the division of A. P. Hill, in column on the road, formed the reserve.

Howard's corps was first assailed. This corps, being surprised, was panic-stricken and fled precipitately, and in its flight communicated the panic to the troops through which it passed. Jackson's forces followed, routing line after line, until arrested by the close of day. The rout of the Federal army was fast becoming general, and it was only saved from entire defeat by the interposition of night. When compelled to halt Jackson remarked that with one more hour of daylight he could have completed the destruction of the Federal army.

This, the most famous of all Jackson's brilliant achievements, closed his military career. After his troops had halted, and while the lines were being adjusted, he rode forward with several of his staff to reconnoitre the Federal position. It was then after nine o'clock at night. The moon faintly illuminated the scene, but floating clouds dimmed its light. The battle had ceased, and

deep silence reigned over what recently had been the scene of war's fiercest turmoil. The reconnoitering party rode several hundred yards in advance of the lines, and halted to listen for any sounds that might come from the direction of the enemy, when suddenly a volley was poured into them from the right of the road. They had been mistaken for Federal scouts by the Confederate infantry. Some of the party fell, and Jackson wheeled his horse in the wood in dread of a renewal of the fire.

This movement proved an unfortunate one. It brought him directly in front of, and not twenty paces from, a portion of his own men, who had been warned against a possible attack from the Federal cavalry. A volley saluted him, with the unfortunate effect of wounding him in three places – two bullets striking his left arm, and one his right hand. At this moment his left hand held the bridle, while his right was held erect, perhaps to protect his face from boughs, yet seemingly with the peculiar gesture which he frequently used in battle. When the bullets struck him his wounded hand dropped, but he instantly seized the bridle with his bleeding right hand, while the frightened horse wheeled and darted through the wood. As he did so the limb of a pine tree

struck Jackson in the face, hurled off his cap, and nearly flung him to the ground. Retaining his seat with difficulty, he reached the road and his own lines, where he was assisted to dismount by Captain Wilbourn, one of his staff officers, who laid him at the foot of a tree.

He was soon afterward supported to the rear by his officers, and, becoming so weak as to be unable to walk, was placed in a litter and borne from the field. His last order, as he was being carried back, was given to General Pender, who had expressed doubts of being able to hold his position. The eyes of the wounded hero flashed as he energetically replied, "You *must* hold your ground, General Pender! You *must* hold your ground, sir!"

The discharge of musketry provoked a terrible response from the Federal batteries, which swept the ground as Jackson was being borne from the field. During this movement one of the bearers stumbled and let fall his end of the litter. A groan of agony came from the wounded man, and in the moonlight his face looked deathly pale. On being asked, however, if he was much hurt, he replied, "No, my friend; don't trouble yourself about me."

There is an incident of considerable interest in relation to the wounding of General Jackson which has never yet been told, yet is worthy of being put on record as one of those remarkable coincidences which have so often happened in the lives of great men. On the morning of May 2d, Jackson was the first to rise from the bivouac above described, and, observing a staff officer (General W. N. Pendleton) without cover, he spread over him his own overcoat. The morning being chilly, he drew near a small fire that had been kindled by a courier, and the writer, who soon after sought the same place, found him seated on a cracker-box. He complained of the cold, and, as the cooks were preparing breakfast, I managed to procure him a cup of hot coffee, which by good fortune our cook was able to provide.

While we were still talking the general's sword, which was leaning against a tree, without *apparent* cause fell with a clank to the ground. I picked it up and handed it to him. He thanked me and buckled it on. It was now about dawn, the troops were on the march, and our bivouac was all astir. After a few words with General Lee he mounted his horse and rode off. This was the last meeting of Lee and Jackson.

I have spoken of the falling of Jackson's sword because it strongly impressed me at the time as an omen of evil – an indefinable superstition such as sometimes affects persons on the falling of a picture or mirror. This feeling haunted me the whole day, and when the tidings of Jackson's wound reached my ears it was without surprise that I heard this unfortunate confirmation of the superstitious fears with which I had been so oppressed.

After the fall of Jackson the command fell to General Stuart, who was co-operating with him, and was the senior officer present, General A. P. Hill having been wounded at the same time with Jackson. About midnight Lee received from Stuart the report both of Jackson's wound and his success. Instructions were sent to Stuart to continue what had been so successfully begun, and Anderson was directed to support him, while McLaws threatened Hooker's right.

Early on the morning of the 3d the attack was resumed by the Confederates with great vigor. Hooker, taking advantage of the night, had restored order in his army and strengthened his position; his troops regained courage and contested the field with great stubbornness until ten o'clock, when they yielded at every point and rapidly retreated before the impetuous assaults of Rodes, Heth, Pender, Doles, Archer, and other gallant leaders within a strong line of defences

BELOW: The death of Stonewall Jackson. Wounded by the fire of a South Carolina regiment which had mistaken his escort for Federal cavalry, Jackson died on May 10 at Guinea's Station, Virginia. He was 39.

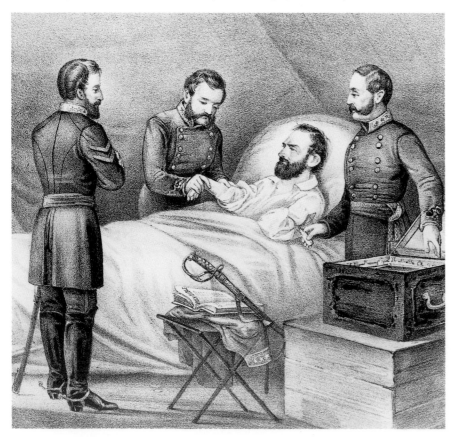

which had been previously constructed to cover the road to the United States Ford, their line of communication with the north side of the Rappahannock. When Stuart assumed the direction of affairs on the night of the 2d the command of the cavalry devolved on Fitz Lee, who operated with vigor on the flanks of the enemy during the continuance of the operations about Chancellorsville.

* * *

The troops being much fatigued and having accomplished all that could have been expected of them, Lee caused a suspension of further operations in order that they might rest and refresh themselves preparatory for the final blow. While the operations above described were in progress at Chancellorsville, General Early by skilful manoeuvring had detained Sedgwick at Fredericksburg until the 3d, when that general, by a determined advance, forced back Early, carried Marye's Heights, and proceeded toward Chancellorsville. The con-

dition of affairs was communicated to General Lee during the forenoon. Wilcox's brigade, then at Banks's Ford, was ordered to intercept Sedgwick and retard his advance, while McLaws's division was ordered to support him. Wilcox on reaching Salem Church, six miles from Chancellorsville, encountered the Federal advance, and after a sharp conflict he repulsed it with loss.

The success of Wilcox delayed Sedgwick until Anderson and McLaws could come up. The premeditated attack on Hooker being thus interrupted, Lee on the forenoon of the 4th repaired to the neighborhood of Fredericksburg. A combined attack was then directed to be made by Early on the rear, while McLaws and Anderson bore down upon the front. The battle was hotly contested during the afternoon, in which the forces of Sedgwick were defeated, and were only saved from destruction by a night-passage across the Rappahannock at Banks's Ford. On the 5th, Lee collected his forces at Chancellorsville to give the *coup de grâce* to Hooker, but that general, under cover of a

BELOW: In the aftermath of the Battle of Chancellorsville lie the remains of a Confederate caisson.

ABOVE: Removing Union dead from the battlefield.

dark and stormy night, effected his retreat beyond the Rappahannock at the United States Ford.

The losses sustained at Chancellorsville and Fredericksburg were estimated at the time at 20,000 killed and wounded, and among the wounded was General Hooker, besides a large number of prisoners. Swinton places Hooker's loss at Chancellorsville at 17,000; Sedgwick's loss at Fredericksburg must have considerably increased that number. The loss sustained by the Confederates was proportionately as great as that of the Federals. The casualties reported were about 9000. After expressing his praise and admiration for the heroic conduct of his troops, and after mentioning the names of a large number of line officers whose zeal and gallantry entitled them to special notice, General Lee thus concludes his report:

The loss of the enemy in the battle of Chancellorsville and the other engagements was severe. His dead and a large number of wounded were left on the field. About 5000 prisoners exclusive of the wounded were taken, and 13 pieces of artillery, 19,500 stands of arms, 17 colors, and a large quantity of ammunition fell into our hands. To the members of my staff I am greatly indebted for assistance in observing the movements of the enemy, posting troops, and conveying orders. On so extended and varied a field all were called into requisition and all evinced the greatest energy and zeal. The medical director of the army, Surgeon Guild, with the officers of his department, were untiring in their attention to the wounded. Lieutenant-colonel Corley, chief quartermaster, took charge of the disposition and safety of the trains of the army. Lieutenant-colonel Cole, chief commissary of subsistence, and Lieutenant-colonel Baldwin, chief of ordnance, were everywhere on the field attending to the wants of their departments; General Chilton, chief of staff, Lieutenant-colonel Murray, Major Peyton, and Captain Young, of the adjutant- and inspector-general's department, were active in seeing to the execution of orders; Lieutenant-colonel Proctor Smith and Captain Johnston of the Engineers in reconnoitering the enemy and constructing batteries; Colonel Long in posting troops and artillery; Majors Taylor, Talcott, Marshall, and Venable were engaged night and day in watching the operations, carrying orders, etc.

Respectfully submitted,
R. E. LEE, *General*.

NOTE. – Notwithstanding the unfavorable character of the country for the use of artillery, Colonels Brown, Carter, and Hardaway succeeded in placing thirty or forty guns in position to be used with effect on parts of the enemy's position, especially that in the vicinity of the Chancellor house.

On the 7th, General Lee ordered his troops to resume their former position about Fredericksburg. A few days after the sad intelligence of the death of Lieutenant-general Jackson reached the army. The estimation in which that distinguished officer was held will be best explained by the general orders of the commander-in-chief announcing his death to the army:

HEADQUARTERS ARMY OF NORTHERN VIRGINIA, MAY 11, 1863
General Orders No. 61.

With deep regret the commanding general announces to the army the death of Lieutenant-general T. J. Jackson, who ex-pired on the 10th instant at a quarter past 3 P.M. The daring, skill, and energy of this great and good soldier by the decree of an all-wise Providence are now lost us. But while we mourn his death we feel that his spirit still lives, and will inspire the whole army with his indomitable courage and unshaken confidence in God as our hope and strength. Let his name be a watchword to his corps, who have followed him to victory on so many fields. Let his officers and soldiers emulate his invincible determination to do everything in the defence of our beloved country.

R. E. LEE, *General*.

It is but just to pause at this point in our narrative, and append some remarks upon the appearance and character of this remarkable man. . . .

The writer first knew Jackson as a young man, then an officer in the First Artillery. Shortly after that time he retired from the army and became a professor in the Virginia Military Institute, which he left to join the army of the Confederacy. I next saw him in Richmond when on a brief visit to Lee to consult in regard to the projected movement against McClellan. He seemed then in much better health than before he left the United States army, but presented the same tall,

ABOVE: Cover of a song sheet dedicated to Jackson after his death.

BELOW: Burying the dead at a hospital in Fredericksburg. Casualties on both sides were great, but the Confederates once again saw the Army of the Potomac withdraw across the Rappahannock.

gaunt, awkward figure and the rusty gray dress and still rustier gray forage-cap by which he was distinguished from the spruce young officers under him. There was nothing of a very striking character in his personal appearance. He had a good face, but one that promised no unusual powers. Yet in the excitement of battle his countenance would light up and his form appear to expand, a peculiar animation seeming to infuse itself through his whole person. At the battle of Gaines's Mill, where I next saw him, he was very poorly mounted on an old sorrel horse, and in his rusty suit was anything but a striking figure. And yet as he put himself at the head of his last regiment and advanced with his face lit up with the enthusiasm of war, he looked truly heroic and appeared a man made by Nature to lead armies to victory.

I saw him frequently afterward during the progress of the war, and in the march against Harper's Ferry I wrote off the order for the movement. The conversation in regard to it between Lee and Jackson took

BELOW: Engraving of Stonewall Jackson from an original field sketch.

place in my presence, and I well remember not only his strong approval of it, but also the earnest energy with which he undertook the enterprise. He at that time seemed improved in health, and was more animated than usual in manner. It was in the camp near Winchester, however, that Jackson presented his most attractive appearance. General Stuart had made him a present of a new uniform, and a handsome horse in place of his old raw-boned sorrel. It was with some difficulty that he was induced to part with his ancient attire in favor of this new and showy dress, and it is doubtful if he was ever quite comfortable in it.

He was a very reticent man, and ordinarily seemed absorbed in his own thoughts, while he displayed some marked peculiarities of manner. One of these was a strange habit of stopping and throwing up his hands, as if in supplication to the Invisible. In religion he was a strict Presbyterian of the sternest creed, and very attentive to religious observances. He not only believed in predestination, but had a strong belief in his personal safety – a presentiment that he would never fall by the hands of the enemy that seemed singularly warranted by the result. The men under his command were to a considerable extent of his own faith. In this he presented a parallel with Cromwell, whom, indeed, he resembled in character.

Jackson was very hospitable in disposition and welcomed warmly any guest to his tent or his table. The writer has often partaken of his hospitality, and found him ever an agreeable and generous host. As for himself, he was very abstemious. He had been at one period of his life a decided dyspeptic, and was always obliged to be very careful of his diet.

*　　*　　*

After the return of the victorious army to its old quarters at Fredericksburg the remainder of May was consumed in recruiting and reorganizing. The infantry was formed into three corps of three divisions each . . . The organization of the cavalry remained unchanged, but that of the artillery demanded the special attention of the commander-in-chief . . . The plan . . . adopted was to group the artillery of the army into battalions of four batteries each. . . .

By the 1st of June the reconstruction and equipment of the army was completed, and the Army of Northern Virginia appeared the best disciplined, the most high-spirited, and enthusiastic army on the continent. It consisted of 52,000 infantry, 250 pieces of artillery, and 9000 cavalry, making an aggregate force of 65,000 men. The successful campaign which this army had recently passed through inspired it with almost invincible ardor. This splendid result had been accomplished by the almost unaided efforts of General Lee.

* * *

ABOVE: A stone marker at the spot where General Jackson fell.

LEFT: Enlistees departing near Falmouth, Virginia, after the Chancellorsville campaign.

Chapter VI

Gettysburg

By the first of June General Lee had completed his arrangements for the ensuing campaign. The army, though numerically less than it was when he commenced his operations against McClellan on the Chickahominy, had been by its recent victories imbued with a confidence that greatly increased its efficiency. Its spirit was now high, and it was anxious to grapple again its powerful foe, which still lingered on the Stafford Heights.

The object of the campaign being the defence of Richmond, General Lee could either continue on the defensive and oppose the Federal advance as he had recently done, or he might assume the offensive and by bold manoeuvring oblige the Federal army to recede from its present line of operations to protect its capital or oppose the invasion of Maryland or Pennsylvania.

The advance upon Richmond would thus be frustrated, and the attack upon that city delayed, at least for a time. The dispirited condition of the Federal army since its late defeat, and the high tone of that of the Confederates, induced the adoption of the latter plan.

This decision was reached by General Lee near the close of May and after the completion of the reorganization of the army which followed the battle of Chancellorsville. Before the movement began his plans of operation were fully matured, and with such precision that the exact locality at which a conflict with the enemy was expected to take place was indicated on his map. This locality was the town of Gettysburg, the scene of the subsequent great battle.

At the period mentioned he called the

BELOW: General Hooker's army marching past Manassas, Va. in June 1863. General Lee rejected suggestions that he engage the Army of the Potomac here.

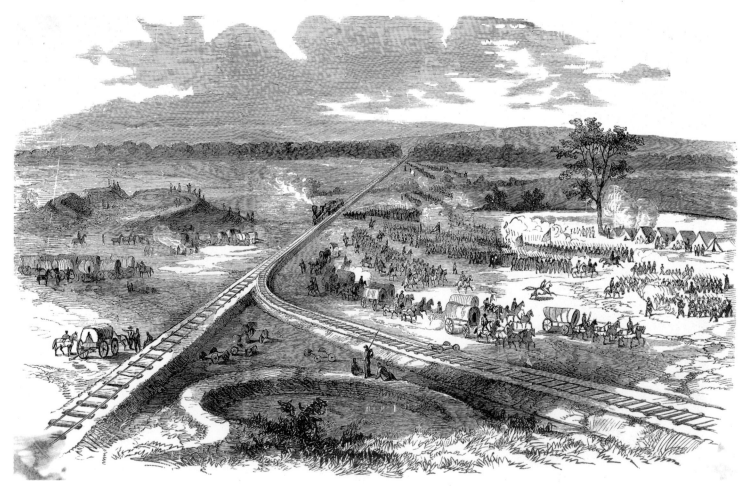

writer into his tent, headquarters being then near Fredericksburg. On entering I found that he had a map spread on the table before him, which he seemed to have been earnestly consulting. He advised me of his designed plan of operations, which we discussed together and commented upon the probable result. He traced on the map the proposed route of the army and its destination in Pennsylvania, while in his quietly effective manner he made clear to me his plans for the campaign. He first proposed, in furtherance of his design, to manoeuvre the army in such a way as to draw Hooker from the Rappahannock. At this point in the conversation I suggested that it might be advantageous to bring Hooker to an engagement somewhere in the vicinity of the old battlefield of Manassas. To this idea General Lee objected, and stated as his reason for opposing it that no results of decisive value to the Confederate States could come from a victory in that locality. The Federal army, if defeated, would fall back to the defences of Washington, as on previous occasions, where it could reorganize in safety and again take the field in full force.

In his view, the best course would be to invade Pennsylvania, penetrating this State in the direction of Chambersburg, York, or Gettysburg. He might be forced to give battle at one or the other of these places as circumstances might suggest, but, in his view, the vicinity of Gettysburg was much the best point, as it was less distant from his base on the Potomac, and was so situated that by holding the passes of the South Mountain he would be able to keep open his line of communication. York, being some twenty-five miles farther from the mountains, was a less desirable locality.

In this plan he had a decided object. There was in his mind no thought of reaching Philadelphia, as was subsequently feared in the North. Yet he was satisfied that the Federal army, if defeated in a pitched battle, would be seriously disorganized and forced to retreat across the Susquehanna – an event which would give him control of Maryland and Western Pennsylvania, and probably of West Virginia, while it would very likely cause the fall of Washington City and the flight of the Federal Government. Moreover, an important diversion would be

ABOVE: Union cavalrymen of the 3rd Pennsylvannia, commanded by Alfred Pleasonton, photographed at Gettysburg.

made in favor of the Western department, where the affairs of the Confederacy were on the decline. These highly important results, which would in all probability follow a successful battle, fully warranted, in his opinion, the hazard of an invasion of the North.

The plan which he thus indicated was already fully matured in his own mind, and the whole line of movement was laid down on the map. He alluded to the several strategic points in Maryland, but did not think it would be advisable to make any stand in that State, for the same reason as before given. This interview took place about two weeks before the movement began. The proposed scheme of operations was submitted to President Davis in a personal interview, and fully approved by him.

* * *

On the 2d of June, Ewell's corps, preceded by the cavalry, was sent forward to Culpeper Court-house. A day or two after, Longstreet, accompanied by the commander-in-chief, followed Ewell, while Hill remained at Fredericksburg to observe the movements of Hooker. By the 8th of June

the main body of the Confederate army was concentrated in the neighborhood of Culpeper and the Federal army was in motion for the upper Rappahannock. . . . On the 10th, Ewell was advanced toward the Shenandoah Valley, both for the purpose of expelling from that section a considerable Federal force, and to create an impression of

a flank movement with the view of interrupting Hooker's communications. . . . Hooker suddenly withdrew from the Rappahannock and retired to the vicinity of Manassas and Centreville, where he assumed a defensive attitude for the protection of Washington. Thus by a series of bold strategic movements General Lee removed the enemy from his path and accomplished the . . . extension of his line from Fredericksburg to Winchester in the face of an enemy of more than double his numerical strength.

*   *   *

On the 15th, Longstreet was put in motion for the Valley, and Hill was directed to follow a day later, . . . General Lee arrived with Longstreet's corps at Berryville on the 18th, . . . About the 21st he continued his advance in two columns: the one, composed of the corps of Ewell and Hill, was directed to Shepherdstown, and the other, consisting of Longstreet's corps and the supply-train, proceeded to Williamsport. Ewell crossed the Potomac on the 23d, followed by Hill on the 24th, while its passage was effected by Longstreet and the trains on the 25th at Williamsport.

As Lee's plan of operations unfolded itself, Hooker advanced to the Potomac and took possession of the fords in the neighborhood of Leesburg. When he learned that Lee had entered Maryland he immediately crossed the river and advanced to Frederick. A controversy then occurred between Halleck and himself, which resulted in his removal on the 27th and the placing of General Meade in command of the Army of the Potomac.

*   *   *

Immediately on completing the passage of the Potomac, Lee resumed his advance, directing Ewell to Carlisle, while he proceeded with Longstreet and Hill to Chambersburg. Ewell sent Early to York by way of Gettysburg, and then moved with the rest of his corps, accompanied by Jenkins's cavalry, to Carlisle. . . . Such was the disposition of the Confederate army during the latter part of June.

*   *   *

Lee first learned of the appointment of General Meade to the command of the Federal army on the 28th of June. . . . On reaching Chambersburg, General Lee . . . was

BELOW: Artillery going into action on the south bank of the Rappahannock on June 4.

ABOVE: War council of
General Meade and his
officers before the Battle of
Gettysburg.

OPPOSITE TOP: The death of
General John F. Reynolds,
Commander of the Federal I
Corps, on June 1.

OPPOSITE BOTTOM: Map of the
three-day Battle of
Gettysburg.

under the impression that the Federal army
had not yet crossed the Potomac. It was not
until the night of the 28th that he learned that
the enemy had reached Frederick. . . .

The rapid advance of General Meade was
unexpected, and exhibited a celerity that
had not hitherto been displayed by the Federal army. A speedy concentration of the
Confederate army was now necessary.
Before dawn on the morning of the 29th
orders were despatched requiring the immediate junction of the army, and on the
30th the Confederate forces were in motion
toward Gettysburg. At the same time
General Meade was pressing forward for that
place.

This movement of the Confederate army
began with the advance of A. P. Hill's corps,
which bivouacked near Greenville on the
night of the 29th, and reached Cashtown
during the next day. Orders had been sent to
Ewell to recall his advanced divisions and
concentrate in the same locality. Longstreet's corps followed on the 30th, accompanied by headquarters, and encamped that
night near the western base of South
Mountain, in the neighborhood of the
Stevens furnace. On July 1st he advanced to

Cashtown, a locality about six miles from
Gettysburg.

While Lee and his staff were ascending
South Mountain firing was heard from the
direction of Gettysburg. This caused Lee
some little uneasiness. The unfortunate
absence of the cavalry prevented him from
knowing the position and movements of the
enemy, and it was impossible to estimate
the true condition of affairs in his front. He
was at first persuaded that the firing indicated a cavalry affair of minor importance,
but by the time Cashtown was reached the
sound had become heavy and continuous,
and indicated a severe engagement.

General Lee now exhibited a degree of
anxiety and impatience, and expressed regret at the absence of the cavalry. He said
that he had been kept in the dark ever since
crossing the Potomac, and intimated that
Stuart's disappearance had materially hampered the movements and disorganized the
plans of the campaign.

In a short time, however, his suspense
was relieved by a message from A. P. Hill,
who reported that he was engaged with two
corps of the enemy, and requested reinforcements. Anderson's division, which

had just reached Cashtown, was at once pushed forward to his support, and General Lee with his staff quickly followed.

The situation in front at that time was as follows: During the forenoon of July 1st the two leading corps of the Federal army, commanded by General Reynolds, had arrived at Gettysburg; at the same time the heads of Hill's and Ewell's corps were rapidly approaching. About ten o'clock, General Heth of Hill's corps encountered a part of Buford's cavalry, which had been thrown forward on the Chambersburg road to a small stream called Willoughby Run, three miles from Gettysburg. Having driven back Buford, Heth engaged Wadsworth's division of the First corps, which was soon reinforced by other divisions of that corps, while Heth was supported by Pender's division of Hill's corps. The advance of the Eleventh corps (Howard's) and the arrival of Rodes's and Early's divisions of Ewell's corps, increased the proportions of the combat, which quickly became animated and continued with spirit until about four o'clock in the afternoon, when the Federal corps were totally defeated and driven from the field with very heavy loss. General Reynolds was killed, and his two corps were seriously reduced in numbers and greatly disorganized. The Confederate loss was much

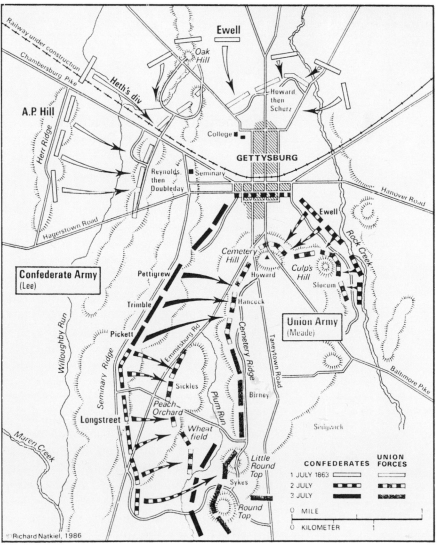

303

ABOVE: A scene of carnage at the three-day Battle of Gettysburg, July 1863.

smaller than that of the enemy; nevertheless, the fall of many gallant soldiers was to be regretted. Among the wounded was the gallant General Heth, whose command suffered severely.

Near the close of the action General Lee reached the field. Anderson's division came up soon afterward, and about the same time Longstreet arrived in advance of his corps, which was a few miles behind. As the troops were evidently very much fatigued, and somewhat disorganized by rapid marching and hard fighting, it seemed inadvisable to immediately pursue the advantage which had been gained, particularly as the retreating forces of the enemy were known to have been reinforced, and to have taken a defensive position about a mile south of the town.

This subject occupied Lee's attention upon perceiving the situation of affairs and the victory gained by his advance forces, and he entered into a conversation with Longstreet, in the presence of the writer, concerning the relative positions of the two armies and the movements it was advisable to make. Longstreet gave it as his opinion that the best plan would be to turn Meade's left flank and force him back to the neighborhood of Pipeclay Creek. To this General Lee objected, and pronounced it impracticable under the circumstances.

At the conclusion of the conversation Colonel Long was directed to make a reconnoissance of the Federal position on Cemetery Ridge, to which strong line the retreating troops had retired. This he did, and found that the ridge was occupied in considerable force. On this fact being reported to General Lee, he decided to make no farther advance that evening, but to wait till morning before attempting to follow up his advantage. This decision the worn-out condition of his men and the strength of the position held by the enemy rendered advisable. He turned to Longstreet and Hill, who were present, and said, "Gentlemen, we will attack the enemy in the morning as early as practicable." In the conversation that succeeded he directed them to make the necessary preparations and be ready for prompt action the next day. Longstreet's corps was at that time near Cashtown, but bivouacked for the night on Willoughby's Creek, about four miles from the battlefield.

I will here add that Gettysburg affords a good example of the difficulties to be encountered and the uncertainty of being able to harmonize the various elements of armies when the field of operations is extensive. This battle was precipitated by the absence of information which could only be obtained by an active cavalry force. General Lee had previously considered the possibility of engaging the enemy in the vicinity of Gettysburg, but the time and position were to have been of his own selection. This could have been easily effected had not the cavalry been severed from its proper place with the army.

At a later hour in the evening than that of the events above mentioned the writer had a further conversation with General Lee, which is of sufficient interest to be here narrated. We were then together at the bivouac, under the trees of an apple orchard.

The general, as if he had been thinking over his plans and orders, turned to me with the remark, "Colonel Long, do you think we had better attack without the cavalry? If we do so, we will not, if successful, be able to reap the fruits of victory."

"In my opinion," I replied, "it would be best not to wait for Stuart. It is uncertain where he is or when he will arrive. At present only two or three corps of the enemy's army are up, and it seems best to attack them before they can be greatly strengthened by reinforcements. The cavalry had better be left to take care of itself."

General Lee evidently agreed with me in this opinion. Much as he had been annoyed and his movements hampered by Stuart's absence, the condition of affairs was such that but one judicious course was open. An attack in force on the enemy before he could concentrate his army was very promising of success, and it was with this purpose fully determined upon in the general's mind that the events of that day ended for the Confederate army.

At this stage of the campaign the Count of Paris alludes to the tactics and strategy of

BELOW: Gettysburg and the Baltimore Pike, from Cemetery Hill.

ABOVE: Mrs. Thompson's house, General Lee's headquarters on the Chambersburg Pike.

General Lee in a tone of criticism which calls for some rejoinder on our part. He remarks:

He has four alternatives to select from: He has the choice to retire into the gaps of the South Mountain, in order to compel Meade to come after him; or to wait steadily in his present positions for the attack of the Federals; or, again, to manoeuvre in order to dislodge them from those they occupy by menacing their communications by the right or left; or, finally, to storm these positions in front, in the hope of carrying them by main force. The best plan would undoubtedly have been the first, because, by preserving the strategic offensive, Lee would thus secure all the advantages of the tactical defensive.

Could the count have seen the actual field of operation and have known the circum-

stances that governed General Lee, he would probably have taken a different view of his actions.

It must be borne in mind that in entering Pennsylvania without his cavalry General Lee was unable to accumulate supplies. In fact, the subsistence of his army mainly depended on the provisions that could be collected in the vicinity of his line of march by detachments of infantry mounted on artillery- and wagon-horses. Therefore, if Lee had adopted the count's preferred plan of operation and occupied one of the passes of South Mountain, he would have placed his army in a trap that would have, in the absence of a miracle, resulted in its destruction; for Meade with his superior forces could have enclosed him without supplies or the means of obtaining them. Lee would thus have been reduced to the alternative of laying down his arms or of cutting his way

out with great sacrifice of life and the loss of his artillery and transportation.

The above objection is also applicable to the count's second plan, with the addition that General Lee's line was too much extended to admit of a successful defence against General Meade's superior force. In answer to the count's third plan, it is only necessary to say that the proximity of the two armies and the absence of cavalry on the part of the Confederates rendered manoeuvring impracticable. The fourth is the only one that admitted of the hope of success, and was the one adopted by General Lee.

That the battle may be more clearly described it is necessary to present some of the principal topographical features of the neighborhood of Gettysburg. The town of Gettysburg, nestling in a small valley, is surrounded by numerous low ridges making

various angles with each other. The most important of them is the one situated about a mile south-west, known as Cemetery Ridge. It is terminated by two conical mounds about four miles apart. The one to the south is designated the Round Top. The one to the north is called Culp's Hill.

Immediately after the defeat of the First and Eleventh corps Cemetery Ridge was selected as the Federal position. Nearer the town is a second ridge, nearly parallel to, and about a thousand yards west of, the Cemetery Ridge. This ridge during the battle formed the Confederate centre. From its southern extremity springs obliquely a spur extending almost on a line with the Round Top. This naturally formed the Confederate right. East of the town the valley is traversed by a small stream, beyond which rises abruptly a commanding ridge which was occupied by the Confederate left. The more

ABOVE: Gatehouse to Evergreen Cemetery built at the summit of Cemetery Hill. Union troops fired at attacking Southerners from behind gravestones here.

ABOVE: General J. E. B. Stuart's cavalry was prevented from joining Lee at Gettysburg until July 2.

Maryland and Pennsylvania before he could resume his proper place with the army. This occupied him seven or eight days, and it was the 2d of July before he rejoined the army at Gettysburg in a very reduced condition, for many of his men had been dismounted, and the horses of those who remained in the saddle were much jaded by long and rapid marches. Notwithstanding the bad plight of his cavalry, Stuart, with his usual promptitude, placed it on the flanks of the army, where its presence was much needed. On the 3d it engaged the enemy's cavalry in frequent skirmishes and several fierce encounters, in one of which General Hampton was severely wounded.

The divisions of Robertson and Jones, which had been ordered up from the passes of the Blue Ridge, did not reach the army in time to take part in the battles of the 1st and 2d, and were too late to be of any service in preliminary reconnoissances. In consequence of these facts, General Lee in the whole of this campaign was deprived of the use of that portion of his force which has been truly named "the eye of the army," since without it all movements are made in the dark and the army is forced to grope its way forward.

At an early hour on the morning of the 2d the writer (Colonel Long) was directed to examine and verify the position of the Confederate artillery. He accordingly examined the whole line from right to left, and gave the necessary instructions for its effective service. As the morning advanced surprise began to be felt at the delay in commencing the attack on the right, which had been ordered to take place at an early hour. The object was to dislodge the Federal force, that had retreated after its defeat to the position known as Cemetery Ridge, before it could be reinforced to any considerable extent. By so doing Lee hoped to be able to defeat the Federal army in detail before it could be concentrated. Ewell was directed to take a position opposite the eastern termination of Cemetery Ridge, while Hill occupied the ridge parallel to it; and Longstreet, whose corps had bivouacked four miles in the rear, was to move early the next morning and assail the Federal left, while Ewell was to favor his attack by an assault upon the Federal right. Hill was to hold himself in readiness to throw his strength where it would have the greatest effect.

After completing the duties assigned him, Colonel Long returned to join General Lee,

distant view is bounded by South Mountain and its projecting spurs.

As we have said so much in regard to the absence of the cavalry and the difficulties thence arising, it is proper at this point to explain its cause. Stuart's passage of the Potomac at a point eastward of that where the Federal crossing was made was intended, as has been said, as a feint, with the view of creating a diversion in favor of General Lee by arousing fears of danger to Washington, to the vicinity of which city the cavalry advanced. However, the movement proved a highly unfortunate one, and was followed by irretrievable disaster; for Stuart had no sooner entered Maryland than his return was barred by the intrusion of a large Federal force between him and the river, and he was thus obliged to make a wide circuit through

whom he met at Ewell's headquarters about 9 A.M. As it appeared, the general had been waiting there for some time, expecting at every moment to hear of the opening of the attack on the right, and by no means satisfied with the delay. After giving General Ewell instructions as to his part in the coming engagement, he proceeded to reconnoitre Cemetery Ridge in person. He at once saw the importance of an immediate commencement of the assault, as it was evident that the enemy was gradually strengthening his position by fresh arrivals of troops, and that the advantage in numbers and readiness which the Confederate army possessed was rapidly disappearing.

Lee's impatience increased after this reconnoissance, and he proceeded in search of Longstreet, remarking, in a tone of uneasiness, "What *can* detain Longstreet? He ought to be in position now." This was about 10 A.M.

After going some distance he received a message that Longstreet was advancing. This appeared to relieve his anxiety, and he proceeded to the point where he expected the arrival of the corps. Here he waited for some time, during which interval he observed that the enemy had occupied the Peach Orchard, which formed a portion of the ground that was to have been occupied by Longstreet. This was that advance movement of Sickles's command which has given rise to so much controversy among Federal historians.

General Lee, on perceiving this, again expressed his impatience in words and renewed his search for Longstreet. It was now about 1 o'clock P.M. After going some distance to the rear, he discovered Hood's division at a halt, while McLaws was yet at some distance on the Fairfield road, having taken a wrong direction. Longstreet was present, and with General Lee exerted himself to correct the error, but before the corps could be brought into its designated position it was four o'clock. The hope that had been entertained of taking the enemy at a disadvantage and defeating him in detail no longer existed. The whole of the Federal force, except Sedgwick's corps, was strongly posted on Cemetery Ridge. Sedgwick, whose corps had made a march of thirty-five miles in twenty hours, had reached the field, though his men were too much exhausted by the length and rapidity of their march to be of immediate service. Yet the opportunity which the early morning had presented was

lost. The entire Army of the Potomac was before us!

General Longstreet has published an explanation of the causes of this unfortunate, if not fatal, delay in the arrival of his troops, yet it cannot be said that the reason which he gives is entirely satisfactory. He says that on the 1st of July the march of his corps had been greatly delayed by the occupation of the road by a division of the Second corps and its wagon-trains. Yet his whole force, except Law's brigade, had reached a position within four miles of Gettysburg by midnight. On the next day, "Fearing that my force was too weak to venture to make an attack, I delayed until General Law's brigade joined its division. As soon after his arrival as we could make our preparations the movement began. Engineers sent out by the command-

ABOVE: On July 2, Lieutenant General James ("Old Pete") Longstreet's divisions were late in arriving at their designated positions but were nevertheless able to attack within the hour.

ing general and myself guided us by a road which would have completely disclosed the move. Some delay ensued in seeking a more concealed route. McLaws's division got into position opposite the enemy's left about 4 P.M. Hood's division was moved on farther to our right, and got into position, partially enveloping the enemy's left."

This explanation, as we have said, is not satisfactory. Longstreet, as he admits, had received instructions from Lee to move *with that portion of his command which was up*, to gain the Emmettsburg road. These orders he took the responsibility of postponing on account of the absence of one brigade of his command, so that, instead of being in readiness to attack in the early morning, it was four o'clock in the afternoon when his troops reached the field.

BELOW: In the afternoon of July 2, Major General John Bell Hood's division made the first assault, against a Union corps under Sickles, in a dash for Little Round Top.

He now found the position which had been laid out for him occupied by Sickles's corps of the Federal army, which had pushed forward considerably in advance of the line of Cemetery Ridge and taken position on the lower ridge along which ran the Emmettsburg road. Cemetery Ridge at this portion of its extent is ill defined, and the movement of Sickles to occupy the advanced position was not without tactical warrant. Yet it was faulty, from the fact that his line, to gain a defensive position for its left flank, had to be bent at a considerable angle at the advanced point known as the "Peach Orchard." General Humphreys's division occupied the road, while Birney's division held the salient point at the Peach Orchard, and was stretched back through low ground of woods and wheatfields toward Round Top, near which the left flank rested in a rocky ravine.

The weak point in this line was the salient at the Peach Orchard, which formed the key of Sickles's position; and on this, when the columns of Longstreet's corps moved to the attack at 4.30 P.M., the greatest vigor of the assault felt. The first assault, however, was made by Hood's division, which attacked the left wing of Sickles's corps, extending from the Peach Orchard to the vicinity of the two elevations known as Round Top and Little Round Top.

Through an interval which lay between Sickles's left and the foot of Round Top, Hood's extreme right thrust itself unperceived by the Federals, and made a dash for Little Round Top, which, through some strange oversight, was at this moment quite unoccupied by any portion of Meade's army. The elevation known by this name is a bold spur of the loftier height called Round Top. It is very rough and rugged, covered with massive boulders, and rendered difficult of ascent by its steepness and its outcropping granite ledges. Yet it was the keypoint of that whole section of the battlefield, and had Hood dreamed of its being unoccupied, pushed a powerful force in that direction, and seized the commanding summit, the victory would have been in his grasp, since the possession of this point would not only have placed Sickles's corps in a highly perilous position, but have enabled him to take the entire line in reverse.

It was at this critical moment that the Federals discovered their error and hastened to amend it. The prompt energy of a single officer, General Warren, chief engineer of

BELOW: A youthful Confederate graduate of the Virginia Military Academy.

the army, rescued Meade's army from imminent peril. He had reached Little Round Top at the point of time in which Hood's men penetrated the undefended space between Sickles's left and Round Top, and just as the signal-officers who occupied the summit were folding up their flags preparatory to leaving the dangerous situation. Directing them to continue waving their flags, Warren hastened away in search of some available force to hold the hill, and, meeting a division of Sykes's corps which was marching to the support of Sickles's command, he detached from it Vincent's brigade, which he hurried to the threatened summit. A battery also, with great difficulty, was dragged and lifted to the top of the rugged hill.

It was a desperate rush from both sides for the possession of the important point, and the Federal brigade reached the crest just as the gallant Texans of Hood's division were swarming up the rocky slope with shouts of triumph. There ensued a desperate struggle for the contested summit. A severe volley from the Federals met Hood's men full in the face as they climbed the steep acclivity. The fight quickly became a hand-to-hand conflict, in which levelled bayonet and clubbed musket did their share in the work of death. For half an hour the contest continued. But the advantage of the Federals in their possession of the summit was not to be overcome, and, though the brave Texans stubbornly held the rocky glen at the foot of the

ABOVE: Atop Cemetery Ridge, Federal troops and artillery repulse a charge by Longstreet's exhausted troops.

hill, and worked their way up the ravine between the two elevations, they were eventually forced back by the Federals, though not without causing heavy loss to the latter. The error which had been made by the Federals was immediately retrieved by the reinforcement of Vincent's brigade, while Round Top was occupied at a later hour in the evening.

While this desperate struggle was in progress the assault on Sickles's corps was vigorously pressed by McLaws's division, particularly at the salient in the Peach Orchard, which was evidently the weak point of the line. The Federal resistance was stubborn, and reinforcements were hurried up to the imperilled point; yet the Confederate onslaught proved irresistible, pushing the line back to a wheatfield in the rear of the Peach Orchard, and eventually breaking it and hurling the enemy in disordered flight toward the high grounds in the rear.

This success rendered the Federal position untenable. The flanks of the broken line were exposed right and left, and, though reinforcements were in rapid succession hurried to the front, the whole line was gradually forced back toward Cemetery Ridge, leaving the hotly-contested field stewn with thousands of dead and wounded. Thus, after

a severe conflict for several hours, Longstreet had gained the position which he could have occupied earlier in the day without opposition. His advantage had not been gained without heavy loss, and, though the Confederates had gained the base of Cemetery Ridge, its crest was crowned with troops and artillery too strongly placed to be driven out by Longstreet's men in their exhausted condition.

A desperate effort to carry the ridge was made, but it proved unsuccessful, and the battle on that part of the line ended without a decisive result. It had been contested with great determination, and the loss on both sides had been heavy, but the Confederate success had consisted in driving the Federals out of an intrinsically weak position, while the strong defensive line of Cemetery Ridge remained intact in their hands. Whether the result would have been different had the original assault been made on this line is a question which it is impossible now to answer, and the advantage or disadvantage of Sickles's advance movement cannot be determined except from the standpoint of military strategy.

During Longstreet's assault on the right Hill's corps had made strong demonstrations against the Federal centre, but Ewell's demonstration on the left, which was ordered to be made at the same time, was delayed, and the corps only got fairly to work about sunset. The assault was maintained with great spirit by the divisions of Early and Edward Johnson until after dark. Early carried Cemetery Ridge, but was forced to relinquish it by superior numbers. The left of Ewell's corps penetrated the breastworks on the extreme right of the Federal line, and this position was held during the night. The ill-success of Early's movement was due to lack of support, the columns on his right failing to reach the contested point until after he had been forced to relinquish the position he had gained on the crest and retire to his original ground.

In the words of Colonel Taylor, "The whole affair was disjointed. There was an utter absence of accord in the movements of the several commands, and no decisive results attended the operations of the second day." This discordance was one of the unfortunate contingencies to which every battle is subject, and is in no sense chargeable to General Lee, whose plan had been skilfully laid, and had it been carried out in strict accordance with his instructions would probably have led to a very different result. On both sides the disregard by corps commanders of the express intentions of their superiors had changed the conditions of the battle. Sickles's advance beyond the position designed to be held by General Meade had exposed his corps to repulse and heavy loss, which possibly might have been avoided had he held the line of Cemetery Ridge, while Longstreet's assumption of the responsibility of delaying the assault ordered certainly had a most important influence on the result of the battle.

The dawn of the 3d of July found the two armies in the position in which the battle of the preceding day had ended. Though Cemetery Ridge remained intact in the hands of the Federals, yet the engagement had resulted at every point in an advantage to the Confederates. Longstreet had cleared his front of the enemy, and occupied the ground from which they had been driven. Ewell's left held the breastworks on Culp's Hill on the extreme right of the Federal line. Meade's army was known to have sustained heavy losses. There was, in consequence, good reason to believe that a renewed

BELOW: Field sketch made on July 2 of an officer assisting his men in repositioning a gun during the battle.

ABOVE: Confederates
renewing their attack on
Culp's Hill on the morning of
the third day.

assault might prove successful. Ewell's position of advantage, if held, would enable him to take the Federal line in reverse, while an advance in force from Longstreet's position offered excellent promise of success. General Lee therefore determined to renew the assault.

Longstreet, in accordance with this decision, was reinforced, and ordered to assail the heights in his front on the morning of the 3d, while Ewell was directed to make a simultaneous assault on the enemy's right. Longstreet's dispositions, however, were not completed as early as those of Ewell, and the battle opened on the left before the columns on the right were ready to move. Johnson, whose men held the captured breastworks, had been considerably reinforced during the night, and was on the point of resuming the attack when the Federals opened on him at four o'clock with a heavy fire of artillery which had been placed in position under cover of the darkness. An infantry assault in force followed, and, though Ewell's men held their ground with their usual stubbornness, and maintained

their position for four hours, they were finally forced to yield the captured breastworks and retire before the superior force of the enemy.

This change in the condition of affairs rendered necessary a reconsideration of the military problem, and induced General Lee, after making a reconnoissance of the enemy's position, to change his plan of assault. Cemetery Ridge, from Round Top to Culp's Hill, was at every point strongly occupied by Federal infantry and artillery, and was evidently a very formidable position. There was, however, a weak point upon which an attack could be made with a reasonable prospect of success. This was where the ridge, sloping westward, formed the depression through which the Emmettsburg road passes. Perceiving that by forcing the Federal lines at that point and turning toward Cemetery Hill the right would be taken in flank and the remainder would be neutralized, as its fire would be as destructive to friend as foe, and considering that the losses of the Federal army in the two preceding days must weaken its cohesion and

ABOVE: The wreckage of a
Union battery following the
massive bombardment
preceding Pickett's Charge.

consequently diminish its power of resistance, General Lee determined to attack at that point, and the execution of it was assigned to Longstreet, while instructions were given to Hill and Ewell to support him, and a hundred and forty-five guns were massed to cover the advance of the attacking column.

The decision here indicated was reached at a conference held during the morning on the field in front of and within cannon-range of Round Top, there being present Generals Lee, Longstreet, A. P. Hill, and H. Heth, Colonel A. L. Long, and Major C. S. Venable. The plan of attack was discussed, and it was decided that General Pickett should lead the assaulting column, to be supported by the divisions of McLaws and Hood and such other force as A. P. Hill could spare from his command. The only objection offered was by General Longstreet, who remarked that the guns on Round Top might be brought to bear on his right. This objection was answered by Colonel Long, who said that the guns on Round Top could be suppressed by our batteries. This point being

settled, the attack was ordered, and General Longstreet was directed to carry it out.

Pickett's division was fresh, having taken no part in the previous day's fight, and to these veterans was given the post of honor in the coming affray, which promised to be a desperate and terrible one.

About twelve o'clock the preparations for the attack were completed and the signal for battle was given, which was immediately followed by the concentrated fire of all the Confederate artillery on Cemetery Hill, which was promptly responded to by the powerful Federal batteries. Then ensued one of the most tremendous artillery engagements ever witnessed on an open field: the hills shook and quivered beneath the thunder of two hundred and twenty-five guns as if they were about to be torn and rent by some powerful convulsion. In the words of General Hancock in reference to the performance of the opposing batteries, "Their artillery fire was the most terrific cannonade I ever witnessed, and the most prolonged – . . . one possibly hardly ever paralleled."

For more than an hour this fierce artillery

conflict continued, when the Federal guns began to slacken their fire under the heavy blows of the Confederate batteries, and ere long sank into silence – an example which was quickly followed by the Confederates.

A deathlike stillness then reigned over the field, and each army remained in breathless expectation of something yet to come still more dreadful. In a few moments the attacking column, consisting of Pickett's division, supported on the left by that of Heth commanded by Pettigrew, and on the right by Wilcox's brigade of Anderson's division, appeared from behind a ridge, and, sweeping over its crest, descended into the depression that separated the two armies. The enemy for a moment seemed lost in admiration of this gallant array as it advanced with the steadiness and precision of a review. Their batteries then opened upon it a spasmodic fire, as if recovering from a stunning blow. The force that moved to the attack numbered about 15,000 men. It had a terrible duty to perform. The distance which it was obliged to traverse was more than half a mile in width, and this an open plain in full front of the enemy, who thickly crowded the

crest of the ridge, and within easy range of their artillery.

But the tempest of fire which burst upon the devoted column quickly reduced its strength. The troops of Heth's division, decimated by the storm of deadly hail which tore through their ranks, faltered and fell back in disorder before the withering volleys of the Federal musketry. This compelled Pender's division, which had marched out to support the movement, to fall back, while Wilcox, on perceiving that the attack had failed, fell back, after severe loss, leaving Pickett's men to continue the charge alone. The other supports, Hood's and McLaws's divisions, which had been expected to advance in support of the charging column, did not move, and were too remote to offer any assistance. The consequence was that Pickett was left entirely unsupported.

Yet the gallant Virginians marched steadily forward, through the storm of shot and shell that burst upon their devoted ranks, with a gallantry that has never been surpassed. As they approached the ridge their lines were torn by incessant volleys of musketry as by a deadly hail. Yet with un-

ABOVE: Assault and repulse of George Pickett's Virginians on Cemetery Hill.

OPPOSITE TOP: Scenes of Federal troops in the field, from the opening engagement, at upper left, to withdrawal on July 5, at lower right.

OPPOSITE BOTTOM: The artillery engagement at noon on the third day of battle.

faltering courage the brave fellows broke into the double-quick, and with an irresistible charge burst into the Federal lines and drove everything before them toward the crest of Cemetery Hill, leaping the breastworks and planting their standards on the captured guns with shouts of victory.

The success which General Lee had hoped and expected was gained, but it was a dearly-bought and short-lived one. His plan had gone astray through the failure of the supporting columns. Now was the time that they should have come to the aid of their victorious comrades; but, alas! Heth's division, which had behaved with the greatest gallantry two days before, had not been able to face the terrible fire of the Federal lines, while the other supports were too remote to afford timely relief. The victory which seemed within the grasp of the Confederate army was lost as soon as won. On every side the enemy closed in on Pickett's brigades, concentrating on them the fire of every gun in that part of their lines. It was impossible to long withstand this terrific fusillade. The band of heroes broke and fell back, leaving the greater part of their number dead or wounded upon the field or captive in the hands of their foes.

In justice to Heth's division it must be remembered that on the 1st it was the first to

attack the enemy, and maintain an unequal contest until it was reinforced by General Pender with his gallant North Carolinians, and a little later by two divisions of Ewell's corps, and that it continued to oppose the enemy with great gallantry to the close of the action, and suffered heavily both in officers and men, which greatly impaired on the 3d its usual firmness. The brigades of Pender's division had been heavily engaged both on the 1st and 2d, and on the 3d the brigades of Lane and Scales behaved with distinguished gallantry under General Trimble. Wilcox's brigade had gallantly supported Longstreet's attack on the afternoon of the 2nd, and on the 3rd was prevented by difficulties of the ground from keeping pace with the attacking column; and when it was seen that Pickett's attack had failed, it fell back in good order after having sustained heavy loss. All must admit that the troops from the different States were equally distinguished for valor and patriotism.

The Confederates lost in this attack about 4000 men, the most of whom were in Pickett's division. No troops could have behaved better than those of the Army of Northern Virginia on witnessing Pickett's repulse. The officers of every grade on that part of the field exerted themselves with the utmost coolness in preserving order and in endeavoring to re-form the broken ranks, and the men so promptly obeyed the call to rally that their thin ranks were soon restored to order and the whole line was again established. The army was not discouraged or dispirited, and its sole wish was for an opportunity to efface the mortification of its first serious repulse. The desire was general that Meade should assume the offensive and in his turn make an attack, and no doubt was felt of the ability to give him a yet hotter reception than that which Pickett had received. But Meade found his army so much shattered and discouraged by his recent losses that he deemed it inadvisable to attempt to follow up his success.

That this view is correct is proved by the following passage from Mr. William Swinton's *History of the Army of the Potomac*. Mr. Swinton says:

I have become convinced from the testimony of General Longstreet himself that attack would have resulted disastrously. "I had," said that officer to the writer, "Hood and McLaws, who had not been engaged; I had a heavy force of artillery; I should have liked nothing better than to have been attacked, and have no doubt that I should have given those who tried as bad a reception as Pickett received."

OPPOSITE TOP: General Pickett receiving his orders to charge from General Longstreet.

OPPOSITE BOTTOM: At a point in the Union defenses known as the "Angle," General Lewis Armistead, his hat on his sword, destroys a Union battery before being cut down.

BELOW: Amputation at a Federal surgery at Gettysburg. In the fighting, the North suffered some 23,000 casualties and the South about 28,000, taking some 4000 casualties alone during Pickett's attack.

Mr. Swinton further informs us that besides the heavy loss it had sustained by Pickett's attack, the Army of the Potomac was thrown into much confusion by the intermingling of the troops of different divisions and corps. Among the wounded were Major-generals Hancock and Gibbon, two of its most prominent officers. The same writer also informs us that the aggregate loss of the Army of the Potomac during the three days' battle was 23,000 men. Among the officers killed was Major-general J. F. Reynolds, whose gentlemanly bearing and soldierly qualities were unsurpassed in any other officer of either army. In view of this heavy loss, while admitting that General Lee was defeated, it must be acknowledged that Generel Meade was so much crippled that he could not reap any advantage of victory.

The attack of Pickett's division on the 3d has been more criticised, and is still less understood, than any other act of the Gettysburg drama. General Longstreet did not enter into the spirit of it, and consequently did not support it with his wonted vigor. It has been characterized as rash and object-less, on the order of the "charge of the Light Brigade." Nevertheless, it was not ordered without mature consideration and on grounds that presented fair prospects of success. By extending his left wing west of the Emmettsburg road, Meade weakened his position by presenting a weak centre, which being penetrated, his wings would be isolated and paralyzed, so far as regarded supporting each other. A glance at a correct sketch of the Federal position on the 3d will sufficiently corroborate this remark, and had Pickett's division been promptly supported when it burst through Meade's centre, a more positive proof would have been given, for his right wing would have been over-whelmed before the left could have disengaged itself from woods and mountains and come to its relief.

Pickett's charge has been made the subject of so much discussion, and General Lee's intentions in ordering it have been so misunderstood, that it is deemed proper to here offer, in corroboration of what has been said above, the testimony of one who was thoroughly conversant with all the facts.

BELOW: Confederate prisoners, taken at Gettysburg, before being marched to captivity.

Colonel Walter H. Taylor, adjutant-general on the staff of General Lee, in *Southern Historical Society Papers*, vol. iv. p. 83, states as follows:

Later, General Lee rode over to General Ewell's front and conferred as to future movements. He wanted to follow up the success gained – thought that with Johnson's division, then up, that General Ewell could go forward at dawn next day. Ewell, Early, and Rodes thought it best to await Longstreet's arrival and make the main attack on the enemy's left. This was determined on. Longstreet was then about four miles off, with two of his divisions. He was expected early on the morning of the 2d. Orders were sent him to move up to gain the Emmettsburg road. He did not reach the field early, and his dispositions were not completed for attack until four o'clock in the afternoon. In his report General Longstreet says he received orders to move with the portion of his command that was then up, to gain the Emmettsburg road on the enemy's left, but, fearing that he was too weak to attack, he delayed until one of his brigades (Law's) joined its division, and that he began the movement as soon after its arrival as his preparations would admit. It seemed impossible to get the co-operation of the commanders along the line. When Longstreet did attack, he did it in handsome style – drove the enemy and captured prisoners, artillery, and other trophies. So far, we had succeeded in every encounter with the enemy. It was thought that a continuance of the attack as made by Longstreet offered promise of success. He was ordered to renew the fight early on the 3d; Ewell, who was to co-operate, ordered Johnson to attack at an early hour, anticipating that Longstreet would do the same. Longstreet delayed. He found that a force of the enemy occupying high ground on their left would take his troops in reverse as they advanced. Longstreet was then visited by General Lee, and they conferred as to the mode of attack. It was determined to adhere to the plan proposed, and to strengthen him for the movement he was to be reinforced by Heth's division and two brigades of Pender's of Hill's

BELOW: Union soldiers killed in the first days' fighting lie near the Chambersburg Pike.

ABOVE: A young Confederate sniper lies dead in the Devil's Den, a sharpshooters nest at the foot of The Round Top.

corps. With his three divisions which were to attack Longstreet made his dispositions, and General Lee went to the centre to observe movements. The attack was not made as designed: Pickett's division, Heth's division, and two brigades of Pender's division advanced. Hood and McLaws were not moved forward. There were nine divisions in the army; seven were quiet, while two assailed the fortified line of the enemy. A. P. Hill had orders to be prepared to assist Longstreet further if necessary. Anderson, who commanded one of Hill's divisions and was in readiness to respond to Longstreet's call, made his dispositions to advance, but General Longstreet told him it was of no use – the attack had failed. Had Hood and McLaws followed or supported Pickett, and Pettigrew and Anderson been advanced, the design of the commanding general would have been carried out: the world would not

be so at a loss to understand what was designed by throwing forward, unsupported, against the enemy's stronghold so small a portion of our army. Had General Lee known what was to happen, doubtless he would have manoeuvred to force General Meade away from his strong position by threatening his communications with the East, as suggested by –; but he felt strong enough to carry the enemy's lines, and I believe success would have crowned his plan had it been faithfully carried out.

* * *

But one course remained open for General Lee. Retreat was necessary. . . . He had still an army of 50,000 men, unbroken in spirit and quite ready to sustain any attack which might be made upon them. But it was quickly evident that Meade had no intention of making an aggressive movement, and a renewed assault on the part of the Confederates would have been madness. . . .

Under these circumstances General Lee determined upon a retreat, but not such an immediate or hasty one as would present the appearance of flight. That he had deeply felt the failure of his effort is unquestionable, yet he preserved much of his ordinary calmness of demeanor, and not one word came from his lips to show that he laid blame on any subordinate . . . .

* * *

During the interval between the repulse of Pickett's charge and the night of July 4th . . . General Lee . . . caused the dead to be buried and the severely wounded to be carefully provided for. . . . When it became dark the withdrawal of the army began. First the trains, under protection of Hill's corps, moved out on the Fairfield road; Longstreet followed Hill; then came Ewell, bringing up the rear. The movement was so much impeded by soft roads, darkness, and rains that the rear-guard could not be withdrawn until daylight on the morning of the 5th. General Meade did not attempt to harass the retreating columns of Lee until the rear-guard had reached the neighborhood of Fairfield; then a pursuing column appeared on the neighboring heights, which Early promptly prepared to meet by throwing the rear-guard across its path. After exchanging a few shots the enemy retired, and the retreat was continued . . . .

* * *

BELOW: To cover Lee's retreat from Pennsylvannia, railroad tracks were destroyed.

RIGHT: General Meade's August encampment at Culpeper Court-house, Virginia.

The army bivouacked on the night of the 5th in South Mountain Pass, and on the morning of the 6th entered the rich and beautiful Cumberland Valley. . . . Reaching Williamsport on the 7th, and finding his pontoon bridge destroyed and the Potomac swollen far above the fording-point, General Lee occupied a strong position, covering Williamsport and Falling Waters, the point where he had left his bridge on advancing into Pennsylvania. As day after day passed without the appearance of the enemy, General Lee was able to complete his defences, so that when Meade arrived in force on the 12th the Army of Northern Virginia was eager to encounter its old antagonist, though double its numerical strength.

* * *

Notwithstanding the Army of the Potomac after its departure from Gettysburg was reinforced to its former numerical strength, General Meade did not attack, but employed the 12th and 13th in fortifying his position. On the other hand, General Lee, now that his bridge was finished and that the river had fallen so as to be fordable for cavalry and empty and lightly-loaded wagons, being unwilling to engage in a battle that could not promise important results, withdrew from his position on the night of the 13th, and retired across the Potomac. The movement was completed during the forenoon of the 14th without interruption, and the broad Potomac rolled between the hostile armies. . . . General Lee continued to retire slowly toward Winchester, and shortly after Meade moved down the river to the neighborhood of Harper's Ferry, and late in July entered Virginia east of the Blue Ridge, whereupon Lee withdrew from the Valley and took a position behind the Rapidan about the 1st of August, while General Meade occupied the neighborhood of Culpeper Court-house.

The losses of the army in killed, wounded, and prisoners were heavy, reaching nearly 16,000 men . . . Having placed the army in position on the Rapidan, and fearing the failure of his campaign in Pennsylvania might have caused the Confederate authorities to lose confidence in him, and feeling unwilling by retaining command of the army to embarrass them in their future plan of operations, General Lee sent his resignation to the President; which was, however, returned by Mr. Davis with every assurance of confidence.

* * *

Chapter VII

Wilderness, Spottsylvania, and Cold Harbor

For several weeks both armies remained inactive in the positions they had assumed – Lee on the Rapidan, and Meade in the vicinity of Culpeper Court-house. During that time so many convalescents and other absentees were restored to the ranks that the Army of Northern Virginia, with a small accession from other sources, was raised to a strength of nearly 60,000 men. . . . Within the same period two corps had been detached from the Federal army, . . . This reduction brought the opposing forces more nearly to a numerical equality than had previously been the case, and the change of conditions in his favor induced Lee to make an effort to force Meade to an engagement while his army was reduced in numbers.

* * *

In pursuance of his plan of operations, on the 9th of October Lee crossed the Rapidan. . . . Being much retarded by difficult roads, he did not reach his objective point near Culpeper Court-house until the afternoon of the 11th, too late to assail the Federal position that day. Meanwhile, Meade had become aware of the movement of the Confederate army. . . . On the approach of Lee his alert opponent had hastily retired, yet with such

BELOW: Army ambulances leaving for the front. The treatment of wounds had progressed little since the eighteenth century. Nevertheless, many convalescents returned to the ranks.

skill that nothing of value was left behind. Lee's purpose of bringing the enemy to battle south of the Rappahannock had been foiled by this rapid retreat. ... There is reason to believe that Meade was as willing to accept battle as Lee was to offer it, but neither general had any desire to fight at a disadvantage, and a brisk series of manoeuvres for the advantage of position began.

*   *   *

On the morning of the 13th the Federal army was again concentrated on the north of the Rappahannock.

*   *   *

Meade had made the best use of the several unavoidable delays of the Confederate army, and though Hill, who was seeking to intercept the Federal retreat at Bristoe Station, made all haste in his march, he arrived there only in time to meet the rearguard of Meade's army. He made a prompt attack on the Federal column, which was hastening to pass Broad Run, which the remainder of the army had already crossed. The assault proved unfortunate. ... General

Cooke, who led the charging brigade, was severely wounded, and his command repulsed ... By the next morning the Federal army had crossed Bull Run, behind which they were erecting fortifications. Meade was safe from any further pursuit, with the intrenchments around Washington and Alexandria to fall back upon in the event of a repulse or to retire to if he wished to avoid a battle. Lee felt it expedient to withdraw, and after destroying the railroad from Cub Run to the Rappahannock, he retired on the 18th to the line of that river, leaving the cavalry in the enemy's front.

*   *   *

Lee remained on the Rappahannock until the railroad track was broken up and the rails removed for a distance extending from Catlett's Station to Culpeper Court-house. Meanwhile, the Federal army had again advanced, rapidly repairing the railroad as they moved forward, and on November 7th reached the Rappahannock. Lee's army was now encamped at Culpeper, with advanced forces near the river. ... Meade threw his whole army across the river and advanced on Culpeper, Lee retiring to his former posi-

BELOW: Northern soldiers and civilians on November 19 wait for a train to carry them to the dedication of the military cemetery at Gettysburg.

tion on the Rapidan. . . . The summer campaign having been one of unusual activity, and the late operations having entailed severe hardships, it was thought advisable to go into winter quarters, . . .

Yet Meade was not of this opinion. . . . Having failed to satisfy the expectations of the Washington authorities, Meade determined to strike a blow that might accomplish some desirable result. Therefore, about the last of November he advanced his entire force to Germanna Ford, hoping to cross the Rapidan at that point and surprise Lee in his extended winter quarters. . . . Meade began his march upon the Rapidan on November 26th. . . . Yet his advance had but fairly begun when the watchful Stuart discovered the movement, and hastened to report it to the Southern commander, who at once instituted measures for the rapid concentration of his army. . . .

Ewell's corps, which was at hand, was concentrated quickly, while Hill, who had from fifteen to twenty miles to march, was but a few hours later in taking his position. . . . Meanwhile, Meade's army was advancing in the lightest marching order. . . . Yet there were unforeseen causes of delay . . . so that by the time the river was crossed twenty-four hours had elapsed.

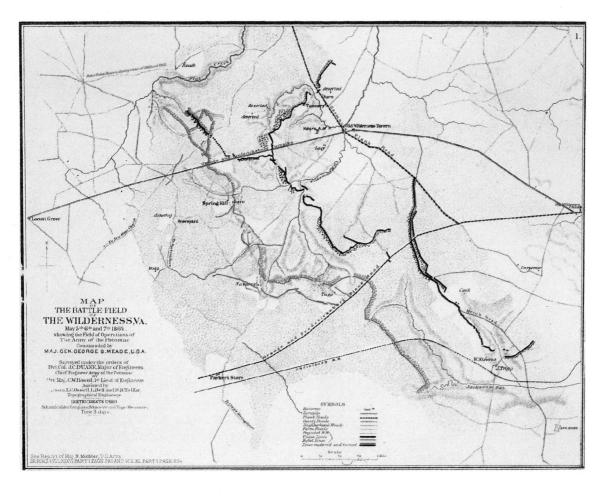

LEFT: Map of the Wilderness battlefield, an area familiar to Lee but unknown ground to General Grant.

This delay gave Lee all the time he needed. . . . In a remarkably short space of time an extended line of works was erected, composed of double walls of logs filled in with earth and with a strong abatis in front. The position had . . . become formidable.

* * *

It was a bitter disappointment to General Meade to find that his well-laid plans had been utterly foiled by the skill and alertness of his antagonist. The next two days were spent in reconnoitering movements, in hope of finding a favorable point of attack. On the 29th, Warren reported favorable conditions for assault on the Confederate right, while Sedgwick discovered what seemed a weak point on its left. Orders for an assault at both points on the next morning were accordingly given, and at the appointed time the artillery of the right and centre opened briskly on the Confederate lines.

But not a sound came from Warren on the left. A new conclusion had been reached in that quarter – a verdict of the men themselves. . . . As the hour for the assault arrived it was found that each man had pinned to his blue blouse a scrap of paper with his name written thereon, that he might be recognized by his friends in case of death. This signifi-

cant indication of the verdict of men whom long experience had made as expert military critics as their officers, was not to be disregarded. Warren, and after him Meade, made a new reconnoissance of the works before them, and the designed assault was pronounced hopeless. . . .

* * *

Finding that the enemy was not inclined to attack, Lee decided to give them a surprise, and to assail their lines on the morning of December 2nd. . . . But with the dawning of the next day it was discovered that . . . Meade's army was in full retreat toward the Rapidan. Pursuit was immediately made. But it was in vain. The light marching equipment of General Meade enabled him to far outstrip his pursuers. . . . The season was now so far advanced that neither general contemplated the prosecution of further operations during the winter; therefore preparations were commenced for going into winter quarters.

* * *

The hostile armies having remained opposed to each other for more than six months were aware that the ensuing campaign would be one of the most formidable

OPPOSITE TOP: Abraham Lincoln delivering his "little speech," the Gettysburg Address, before a crowd of 15,000.

OPPOSITE BOTTOM: Army winter quarters in Virginia.

ABOVE: Union General Benjamin Butler was supposed to support Grant's campaign against Lee by mounting a diversionary attack on Richmond from the Virginia peninsula. Like many other Butler operations, this one was mismanaged and failed to produce any useful result.

character. Therefore, each side made full use of its resources in preparation for the coming struggle. . . . In March, 1864, General Ulysses S. Grant was appointed lieutenant-general and assigned to the command of all the Federal armies. These were formed into two grand divisions. That of the West was assigned to the command of General Sherman, while that of the East was commanded by General Grant in person. Having established his headquarters with the Army of the Potomac, he applied himself to the study of the military situation in Virginia and . . . caused the Army of the Potomac to be raised to the imposing strength of 140,000 men, . . . General Lee . . . could only raise an effective force of 64,000 men. . . . In addition to the difference in numbers there was as marked

a difference in condition. The Army of the Potomac was well clothed and amply supplied. The Army of Northern Virginia was in ragged clothing and but half fed. . . . But, as on previous occasions of the kind, the soldiers were ready to fight. . . .

* * *

The new Federal general . . . determined on [a] southward movement through Virginia with his main army, while sending General Butler with 30,000 men to operate against Richmond from the James, and Sigel with a considerable force to advance through West Virginia and up the Shenandoah Valley.

Yet as the position of General Lee behind the Rappahannock was too strong to warrant a direct attack, . . . Grant [decided to cross] the Rapidan below Lee's right, and to endeavor to turn that flank of the Confederate army. This line, besides being shorter, possessed the advantage of preserving intact the communication with Washington, while it threatened to sever Lee's connection with Richmond.

The line being decided on and the necessary preparations being completed, General Meade on the 4th of May, under the eye of General Grant, put the Army of the Potomac in motion. The corps of Sedgwick and Warren moved forward on the road to Germanna Ford, while Hancock's corps proceeded to Ely's Ford, each column being preceded by a large force of cavalry. The passage of the river was effected without opposition.

This easy passage of the Rapidan does not seem to have been anticipated by General Grant. In his report he says: "This I regarded as a great success, and it removed from my mind the most serious apprehension I had entertained, that of crossing the river in the face of an active, large, well-appointed, and ably-commanded army." Lee had made no movement to dispute the passage of the stream. He could, had he chosen, have rendered its passage extremely difficult. But perceiving that Grant was making the mistake that had proved so disastrous to Hooker, by plunging with his army into that dense and sombre thicket well named "The Wilderness," he took care to do nothing to obstruct so desirable a result.

On reaching the southern side of the stream, Grant established himself at the intersection of the Germanna and old plank roads and at Chancellorsville. The position embraced the upper part of what is known as the Wilderness of Spottsylvania.

Lee simultaneously ordered the concentration of his forces on Mine Run, a position about four miles north-west of that occupied by Grant. The corps of Ewell and Hill and the artillery of Long and Walker gained their positions on Mine Run during the evening and night of the 4th; Longstreet's corps, which since its arrival from Tennessee had been posted at Gordonsville, distant twenty miles from the point of concentration, was necessarily delayed in reaching the scene of the coming struggle.

There seemed no good reason to believe that General Lee would risk the hazard of a battle in open field, and expose his small force to the danger of being overwhelmed by Grant's enormous army. That he would offer battle somewhere on the road to Richmond was unquestionable, but Grant naturally expected his adversary to select some point strong alike by nature and art, and which must be forced by sheer strength ere the march to Richmond could be resumed. He did not dream that Lee would himself make the attack and force a battle with no other intrenchments than the unyielding ranks of his veteran troops.

Yet Lee had already tried the woods of the Wilderness as a battlefield, and knew its advantages. Its intricacies, which were familliar to him and his generals, were unknown ground to Grant. In them he had already vanquished a large army with half its force. The natural hope of success in baffling his new opponent which this gave him he did not fail to avail himself of, and Grant found himself on his southward march unexpectedly arrested by the presence of the Confederate army in the wilds in which, just a year before, Hooker's confident army had been hurled back in defeat.

The writer spent the night of the 4th at Lee's headquarters, and breakfasted with him the next morning. The general displayed the cheerfulness which he usually exhibited at meals, and indulged in a few pleasant jests at the expense of his staff officers, as was his custom on such occasions. In the course of the conversation that attended the meal he expressed himself surprised that his new adversary had placed himself in the same predicament as "Fighting Joe" had done the previous spring. He hoped the result would be even more disastrous to Grant than that which Hooker had experienced. He was, indeed, in the best of spirits, and expressed much confidence in the result – a confidence which was well founded, for there was much reason to believe that his antagonist would be at his mercy while entangled in these pathless and entangled thickets, in whose intricacies disparity of numbers lost much of its importance.

On the morning of the 5th, Lee's army advanced in two columns, Ewell taking the Orange Court-house and Fredericksburg turnpike, while Hill moved on the plank road. After advancing about three miles, Ewell encountered the enemy's outposts. Jones's brigade and a battery of artillery were then placed in position to cover the further deployment of Ewell's corps. Rodes's division formed in line to the right and at right angles to the road. The divisions of Early and Edward Johnson executed a similar deployment to the left.

Before this movement was finished Jones's brigade was ordered to change its position, and while in the execution of this was suddenly attacked by a heavy Federal force which had advanced unobserved under cover of a dense thicket. Before it could be extricated General Jones, its gallant leader, was killed, with the loss of several hundred of his men, either killed, wounded, or taken prisoner. This was the

BELOW: A view of the edge of the tangled area known as the Wilderness, in May 1864.

prelude to a succession of battles.

About four o'clock in the afternoon a collision occurred between the Federal right and the Confederate left. The hostile forces were concealed from view by a wilderness of tangled brushwood until they were within musket-range of each other. Then the Confederates, being in position, were prepared to deliver a staggering volley the moment their antagonists appeared, which was followed up so persistently that the Federals were driven back with heavy loss for nearly a mile. This affair closed the operations on the left.

On the right Hill met the enemy on the plank road and engaged in a heavy conflict. Hancock, who was opposed to him, made desperate efforts to drive him from his position, but in vain. "The assaults," as General Lee wrote, "were heavy and desperate, but every one was repulsed." Night fell, leaving both parties in the postiion which they held at the beginning of the fight. Neither had advanced or retired, but Hill had held his post and established his connection with Ewell.

The two armies had now assumed a most singular attitude. They had enveloped themselves in a jungle of tangled brushwood so dense that they were invisible to each other at half musket-range, and along the lines of a battle in many places objects were not discernible half the length of a battalion. A Northern writer aptly described this region as a "terra incognita." It formerly had been an extensive mining district, from which the timber had been cut to supply fuel for feeding the smelting-furnaces, and since then the young growth had sprung up ten times thicker than the primeval forest. The roads traversing it and the small brooks meandering through it, with a few diminutive clearings, were the only openings in this dismal wilderness.

As soon as General Grant had crossed the Rapidan and enveloped himself in the Wilderness of Spottsylvania, General Lee determined, as above said, to bring his adversary to an engagement in a position whose difficulties neutralized the vastly superior force against him. "Neither General Grant nor General Meade believed that aught but a small force was in front of Warren to mask the Confederate retreat, as it was not deemed possible that Lee, after his defensive line had been turned, could have acted with such boldness as to launch forward his army in an offensive sally. It was therefore at once resolved to brush away or capture this force, but as this determination was formed under a very erroneous apprehension of the actual situation, the means employed were inadequate to the task" (Swinton).

In corroboration of this statement may be quoted a remark ascribed to General Meade in conversation with Warren, Sedgwick, and others on the morning of the 5th: "They have left a division to fool us here, while they concentrate and prepare a position toward the North Anna; and what I want is to prevent those fellows from getting back to Mine Run."

Before nightfall of that day it was discovered that "those fellows" had other objects in view, and were not to be brushed away with a wave of the hand. Grant had become convinced that Lee was advancing upon him in force, and hastened to put his whole army in battle array. His line, crossing the plank road and old turnpike nearly at right angles, extended from Todd's Tavern on Brock road to within a short distance of Germanna Ford, presenting a front of about five miles.

General Lee had accompanied the advance of Hill on the plank road, and wit-

BELOW: Elements of the Army of the Potomac moving across the Rapidan and into the Wilderness.

nessed the noble firmness with which the divisions of Heth and Wilcox maintained the conflict against greatly superior odds until relieved by the coming of night. Perceiving that these troops had sustained considerable loss and were greatly fatigued by the exertions of the day, he wished to relieve them by Longstreet's corps, which had bivouacked during the evening about five miles from the field of battle. He therefore sent a message to General Longstreet to hurry him forward.

Notwithstanding the severe conflicts during the day, the troops of both Ewell and Hill maintained their unshaken courage, and lay upon their arms during the night in anticipation of a renewal of the attack.

Early on the following morning Hill's division was assailed with increased vigor, so heavy a pressure being brought to bear upon Heth and Wilcox that they were driven back, and, owing to the difficulties of the country, were thrown into confusion. The failure of Longstreet to appear came near causing a serious disaster to the army. But as this critical moment he arrived and attacked with such vigor that the enemy was driven back and the position regained.

Colonel C. S. Venable of General Lee's staff, in his address before the Southern Historical Society, thus describes this event:

The assertion, made by several writers, that Hill's troops were driven back a mile and a half is a most serious mistake. The right of his line was thrown back several hundred yards, but a portion of his troops still maintained their position. The danger, however, was great, and General Lee sent his trusted adjutant, Colonel W. H. Taylor, back to Parker's Store to get the trains ready for a movement to the rear. He sent an aide also to hasten the march of Longstreet's divisions. These came the last mile and a half at a double-quick, in parallel columns, along the plank road.

General Longstreet rode forward with that imperturbable coolness which always characterized him in times of perilous action, and began to put them in position on the right and left of the road. His men came to the front of the disordered battle with a steadiness unexampled even among veterans, and with an *élan* that presaged restoration of our position and certain victory. When they arrived the bullets of the enemy on our right flank had begun to sweep the field in the rear of the artillery-pits on the left

of the road, where General Lee was giving directions and assisting General Hill in rallying and re-forming his troops.

It was here that the incident of Lee's charge with Gregg's Texas brigade occurred. The Texans cheered lustily as their line of battle, coming up in splendid style, passed by Wilcox's disordered columns and swept across our artillery-pit and its adjacent breastwork. Much moved by the greeting of these brave men and their magnificent behavior, General Lee spurred his horse through an opening in the

ABOVE: A line of Confederates awaiting a Union advance in the Wilderness.

BELOW: Confederate General James Longstreet, whom Lee called "my old warhorse."

ABOVE: Troops of the 14th New York Infantry camped between a double line of breastworks on the night of May 6.

trenches and followed close on their line as it moved rapidly forward. The men did not perceive that he was going with them until they had advanced some distance in the charge. When they did recognize him, there came from the entire line as it rushed on the cry, "Go back, General Lee! go back!" Some historians like to put this in less homely words, but the brave Texans did not pick their phrases: "We won't go on unless you go back. . . ."

Just then I turned his attention to General Longstreet, whom he had been seeking, and who sat on his horse on a knoll to the right of the Texans directing the attack of his divisions. He yielded with evident reluctance to the entreaties of his men, and rode up to Longstreet's position. With the first opportunity I informed General Longstreet of what had just happened, and he with affectionate bluntness urged General Lee to go farther back. I need not say the Texans went forward in their charge and did well their duty. They were eight hundred strong, and lost half their number killed and wounded on that bloody day. The battle was soon restored and the enemy driven to his position of the night before.

Wilcox's and Heth's divisions, to whom Longstreet's arrival and General Lee's presence had done much to restore confi-

dence, were placed in line a short distance to the left of the plank road. Shortly afterward Anderson's division arrived from Orange Court-house. Longstreet now advanced from his own and Anderson's divisions three brigades to operate on the right flank of the enemy, while himself advancing on their front.

Attacked with great vigor by these fresh troops and his right flank rolled up at the same time that a heavy onslaught fell upon his front, Hancock's force was completely defeated, and sent reeling back toward the Brock road, the important highway to the seizure of which Lee's efforts were directed. That this purpose would be achieved seemed highly probable when an unfortunate accident put a stop to the Confederate advance. General Longstreet, who afterward declared that he "thought that he had another Bull Run on them," had ridden forward with his staff in front of his advancing line, when he was fired upon by a portion of his own flanking column, who mistook the party for Federal cavalry. He was struck by a musket-ball, and fell from his horse severely wounded.

This accident – which, as will be seen, bears a striking resemblance to that in which Lee's other great lieutenant, Jackson, was disabled in a previous battle in that same region – threw the lines into disorder and put a stop to the advance. General Lee, as soon as he learned of the accident, hastened to the spot to take command of the corps. But a considerable time elapsed before the divisions were ready for a renewal of the assault, and in the mean time the enemy had recovered from his confusion and had been strongly reinforced.

The battle was renewed about four o'clock in the afternoon, the columns of Longstreet and Hill, now commanded by Lee in person, making a most vigorous assault upon Hancock's men, who now lay intrenched behind a strongly-built breastwork of logs. The battle raged with great fury. The incessant volleys set fire to the woods, as at Chancellorsville, and flames and smoke soon filled the valley in which the contest was raging. The flames ere long caught to the breastworks of the enemy, which were soon a mass of seething fire. The battle went on through smoke and flame, and a portion of the breastworks were carried, though they were not long held. The few who had entered them were quickly driven out by a forward rush of a Federal brigade. With this charge ended the main action of the day.

In this engagement the attack of General Meade was conducted with such vigor by Hancock, Warren, and Burnside that under ordinary circumstances, with his great superiority of force, it would have been successful; but here the difficulties of the country prevented his making systematic combinations, and failure was the consequence.

While the battle was in progress on our right a spirited combat ensued between a part of Ewell's and Sedgwick's corps which terminated without important results. General Grant, being satisfied that any further attempt to dislodge Lee would be fruitless, determined to draw him out by a change of position. Therefore on the 7th he made his preparations to withdraw by night toward Spottsylvania Court-house.

* * *

The casualties of both armies during the 5th and 6th were heavy. The Confederates, besides the loss of 7000 men killed and wounded, had to lament the severe wound of General Longstreet, which disabled him during the remainder of the campaign. . . . The Federal loss was much greater.

* * *

Grant . . . designed by a rapid flank movement to seize the important position of Spottsylvania Court-house, fifteen miles south-east of the Wilderness battlefield. But [having] been informed by Stuart on the afternoon of the 7th that the wagon-trains of the Federal army were moving southward, Lee at once divined Grant's intention, and . . . placed his army, which was supposed to be fifteen miles in the rear, squarely across Grant's line of advance to Richmond. . . .

* * *

On the morning of the 10th, General Grant formed a powerful combination of the corps of Warren, Burnside, and Hancock with the design of attacking Lee's left centre near the point of junction of the corps of Longstreet and Ewell. . . . At five o'clock the main assault was made. Hancock's and Warren's men advanced with great intrepidity against the strong Confederate works, but were repulsed with terrible slaughter. . . . In the afternoon, . . . the Sixth corps made a heavy attack on Ewell's left. . . .

* * *

During the hottest portion of this engagement, when the Federals were pouring through the broken Confederate lines . . . Genereal Lee rode forward and took his position at the head of General Gordon's column, then preparing to charge. . . .

"No! no! General Lee to the rear! General Lee to the rear!" cried the men. "We will drive them back if General Lee will only go to the rear."

BELOW: Union corps commander John Sedgwick is brought down by a Confederate sharpshooter on May 9 during a battle around Spottsylvania Court-house.

ABOVE: The fight with Stuart's cavalry at Yellow Tavern. Here Jeb Stuart was mortally wounded. Of him, General Lee wrote, "A more zealous, ardent, brave, and devoted soldier than Stuart the Confederacy cannot have."

As Lee retired Gordon put himself at the head of his division and cried out in his ringing voice, "Forward! charge! and remember your promise to General Lee!"

The charge that followed was fierce and telling. . . . The works were retaken, the Confederate line again established, and an impending disaster converted into a brilliant victory.

During the 11th, General Grant was employed in shifting the positions of his corps preparatory to a new assault upon the Confederate lines. Before daylight on the morning of the 12th his army . . . was able to advance unobserved, to break through Johnson's line, and to capture his whole division. . . .

This success inaugurated one of the most desperate conflicts that occurred during the war. The long breach made by the capture of Johnson's division admitted the Federals in heavy masses. . . . From four o'clock in the morning until night the battle continued, marked by terrible slaughter. . . . At last the persistent attacks of the enemy were obliged

to yield to constant repulse and the Federals discontinued the contest.

*   *   *

The succession of bloody combats which had marked the career of Grant in the Wilderness had by this time so greatly reduced his army that he was obliged to pause and await reinforcements.

*   *   *

During the operations about Spottsylvania Court-house, Sheridan conceived the idea of capturing Richmond by a *coup de main*, and on the 9th proceeded to its execution. Of this movement General Stuart quickly became aware, and with his usual promptitude threw himself in Sheridan's path, and encountered him on the 10th at the Yellow Tavern, a few miles north of Richmond. A severe conflict ensued, in which Stuart fell mortally wounded, and his troops were compelled to retire before the superior numbers of the foe.

*   *   *

Sheridan had been so much delayed by Stuart's assault that the small force which had been left for the defence of Richmond had time to reach the works, which were very feebly garrisoned on Sheridan's first approach. He carried the first line, but recoiled from the second, and retired toward the Chickahominy.

*   *   *

No further effort was made by Grant on the desperately-fought field of Spottsylvania. Having been reinforced by 40,000 reserves, on the 20th of May he disappeared from the front of Lee's army. As in the Wilderness, he began a movement to turn the impregnable position of Spottsylvania by a flank march.

General Lee, however, with his usual alertness, had his men on the march the instant the movement of his adversary was discovered, and he advanced with such rapidity as to reach Hanover Junction, at the intersection of the Fredericksburg and Richmond and the Central railroads, in advance of Grant. This objective point of the Federal army was occupied by Lee on the 22nd. He at once took up a strong position, and when Grant arrived on the 23rd it was to find himself again intercepted by his active opponent.

*   *   *

General Grant on this occasion did not exhibit his usual pertinacity, but seemed satis-

BELOW: A Timothy O'Sullivan photograph of engineers building a road at Jericho Mill, on the North Anna River, in 1864.

fied by observation alone that the Confederate position could not be carried by main strength. He therefore proceeded down the North Anna to the Pamunkey, which he crossed on the 28th. . . .

*　　*　　*

Proceeding on his march from the Pamunkey, Grant found his advance upon Richmond again arrested by Lee, . . . Grant did not at this point attempt to force his opponent from his path, but moved slowly by his left flank toward the Chickahominy, while Lee, by a similar movement to his right, kept pace with him and constantly confronted him at every stage.

*　　*　　*

[By the first of June, the] old battlefield of Cold Harbor was again occupied by the contending forces, though in an inverse order.

The Confederate right now occupied the position that had been previously held by the Federals, and the Federal left held that which had been occupied by the Confederates. This field was about to become the theatre of a second conflict more desperate than the first.

Apparently with the intention of blotting out the memory of the defeat of the Federal arms on the former occasion, General Grant massed the flower of his army for battle. A portion of the Confederate line occupied the edge of a swamp of several hundred yards in length and breadth, enclosed by a low semi-circular ridge covered with brushwood. On the previous night the troops assigned to this part of the line, finding the ground wet and miry, withdrew to the encircling ridge, leaving the breastworks to be held by their picket-line. The attacking column quickly carried this part of the line, and advanced

BELOW: Union cavalry crossing Chesterfield Bridge over the North Anna River, moving toward the battlefield at Cold Harbor.

through the mud and water until arrested by the deliberate fire of the Confederates.

The battle that succeeded was one of the most desperately contested and murderous engagements of the war. Along the whole Federal line a simultaneous assault was made on the Confederate works, and at every point with the same disastrous result. Rank after rank was swept away until the column of assault was almost annihilated. Attack after attack was made, and men fell in myriads before the murderous fire from the Confederate line. While Hill, Breckenridge, Anderson, and Pickett repulsed Grant's desperate assaults upon the right, Early with Rodes, Gordon, and Ramseur on the left successfully opposed Burnside and Warren. In the brief space of one hour the bloody battle of the 3rd of June was over, and 13,000 dead and wounded Federals lay in front of the lines behind which little more than 1000 of the Confederate force had fallen.

A few hours afterward orders were sent to the corps commanders to renew the assault, and transmitted by them through the intermediate channels to the men. Then an event occurred which has seldom been witnessed on a battlefield, yet which testified most emphatically to the silent judgment of the men on the useless slaughter to which they had been subjected. Though the orders to advance were given, not a man stirred. The troops stood silent, but immovable, presenting in this unmistakable protest the verdict of the rank and file against the murderous work decided on by their commanders.

Thus ended Grant's overland campaign, in which his losses aggregated the enormous total of 60,000 men – a greater number than the whole of Lee's army at the beginning of the campaign. Lee's losses, on the contrary, were not more than 20,000. As to the *morale* of the two armies, that of Lee's continued excellent. Their successful defence against their powerful opponent had raised the spirits of the men and their confidence in their general to the highest pitch. On the contrary, the dreadful slaughter to which Grant's army had been subjected produced an inevitable sense of depression in the ranks, and a feeling that they were destined to destruction before the terrible blows of their able antagonist.

It is an error to suppose that in this campaign Lee was afraid to meet his adversary in open field, as had been asserted by Northern writers. He was always ready for action, whether offensive or defensive, under favorable circumstances. "I happen to know," says General Early, "that General Lee had always the greatest anxiety to strike at Grant in the open field." It was the practice of both armies, whenever encamping, to build intrenchments, and it would have been utter folly for Lee to leave his when he found his antagonist willing to attack him behind his breastworks, thus giving him that advantage of a defensive position which the smallness of his army imperatively demanded. Had he advanced against Grant, it would only have been to find the latter behind his works, and the comparative size of the two armies did

ABOVE: A. R. Waud's sketch of an artillery duel on June 2 at Cold Harbor.

not warrant this reversal of the conditions of the contest.

At the beginning of the campaign, perceiving that General Grant's *rôle* was fighting and not manoeuvring, General Lee restrained his desire for the bold and adventurous offensive and strictly confined himself to the defensive, hoping in the course of events to reduce his opponent sufficiently near a physical equality to warrant his attacking him openly with reasonable hope of success. Believing that object had been accomplished after the battle of Cold Harbor, General Lee was anxious to assume the offensive and attack Grant before his army could recover from the stunning effect of its defeat on that occasion; but being obliged to send a large detachment from his army to oppose Sigel and Hunter in the Valley, he was compelled to continue on the defensive.

Grant, on his part, had been taught a costly lesson by his many bloody repulses, and after the battle of Cold Harbor changed his whole plan of operations, deciding to endeavor to accomplish by patient siege what he had failed to achieve by the reckless application of force. With this decision began a new chapter in the history of the war, and one of the most remarkable sieges known to history was inaugurated – that in which the Confederate commander behind the breastworks of Petersburg for a full year baffled every effort of his powerful foe.

*   *   *

OPPOSITE TOP: Engraving of a cavalry charge at Cold Harbor on June 1.

OPPOSITE BOTTOM: A fruitless assault by New York artillery on the Confederate position on June 3.

BELOW: Collecting remains for reburial long after the battle at Cold Harbor. In the last day's fighting, Grant lost some 13,000 killed and wounded, Lee about 1000.

Chapter VIII

The Siege of Petersburg

The war in Virginia [in 1864] had now been reduced to the attack and defence of Richmond – in other words, to a siege whose termination was only a question of time.

*   *   *

The battle of Cold Harbor had taught Grant the inutility and peril of direct assaults upon the Confederate intrenchments. He therefore determined upon siege operations, and about the middle of June he threw a large portion of his army south of the James and extended his line of investment so as to embrace the city of Petersburg. This caused Lee to make a counter-movement in order to cover that place and protect the rail-roads leading to it. The capture of Petersburg was of primary importance to the Federals, as it would enable them to cut of two lines of communication very necessary for the support of Richmond, and at the same time to greatly contract their line of circumvallation. Therefore its possession was much desired.

*   *   *

General Grant, having failed in his various attempts to force the Confederate lines, acquiesced in a proposal to supplement the musket and the sabre with the spade and the pick. About the last of June it was proposed to mine and blow up a Confederate salient that was opposite to Burnside's position. At

BELOW: From mid-June 1864, the city of Petersburg, a rail center about 25 miles south of Richmond, was the focus of a Federal siege.

ABOVE: A railroad station near Petersburg. The city defied the Union siege for almost 10 months, until April 3, 1865.

that point the two lines were sufficiently near to warrant such an attempt. The conduct of this mining operation was assigned to the person by whom it had been originally proposed, Lieutenant-colonel Henry Pleasants of the Forty-eighth Pennsylvania, a skilful mining engineer. Pleasants found a suitable point to commence operations about five hundred feet distant from the salient to be blown up. His working-parties were drawn from his own regiment, which contained a number of experienced miners. The work was pushed forward so expeditiously that by the 23rd of July the mine was completed, and was charged with 8000 pounds of powder. The tamping was completed and the mine was pronounced ready for explosion by the 28th. It was decided that the mine should be sprung early on the morning of the 30th, and to that end the necessary preparations were made.

General Grant, in order to mask his real design, on the 26th sent Hancock and Sheridan with the Second corps and two divisions of cavalry to the north side of the James River, with instructions to threaten Lee's right, and thus to create the impression that a real attack was to be made in that quarter, while he perfected his arrangements for making the assault on Petersburg upon the explosion of the mine. At this time the Confederate force about Petersburg did not exceed 13,000 men, whilst opposed to this Grant had over 65,000. On the 29th were made the final dispositions for attack.

Hancock was directed on the night of the 29th to return from the north of the James with all secrecy and despatch, and to take part in the assault, while Sheridan was to pass in rear of the army and with his whole cavalry corps operate toward Petersburg from the south and west. On the evening of the 29th, Meade issued his orders of battle. As soon as it was dusk Burnside was to mass

his troops in front of the point to be attacked, and form there in columns of assault, taking care to remove the abatis, so that the troops could debouch rapidly, and to have his pioneers equipped for opening passages for the artillery. He was to spring the mine at 3.30 A.M., move rapidly through the breach, and seize the crest of Cemetery Hill, a ridge four hundred yards in rear of the Confederate lines.

Ord was to mass the Eighteenth corps in rear of the Ninth, immediately follow Burnside, and support him on the right. Warren was to reduce the number of men holding his front to the minimum, concentrate heavily on the right of his corps, and support Burnside on the left. Hancock was to mass the Second corps in rear of the trenches at that time held by Ord, and be prepared to support the assault as events might dictate.

Engineer officers were detailed to accompany each corps, and the chief engineer was directed to park his pontoon-train at a convenient point, ready to move at a moment's warning.

Meade having assured himself that the Confederates had no second line on Cemetery Hill, as he had formerly supposed and as Duane had positively reported, was now sanguine of success. He made these preparations to meet the contingency of the meagre Confederate force retiring beyond the Appomattox and burning the bridges; in which event he proposed to push immediately across that river to Swift Creek and open up communication with Butler at Bermuda Hundred, before Lee could send any reinforcements from his five divisions north of the James.

The commanders of the white divisions of Burnside's corps decided by lot which division should have the honor of making the assault, the chance favoring Ledlie's division, though, as the sequel shows, it had but little heart for . . . it.

On the morning of the 30th, shortly before the hour appointed for springing the mine, all the columns were in position ready for action. Half-past three arrived, but the silence of the morning was unbroken; minute after minute went by, while a painful suspense pervaded the expectant columns. Time passed on, yet silence continued to reign. The suspense became almost unbearable. The delay could not be understood, and various conjectures flew rapidly among the troops. At last it was discovered that the fuse had gone out within fifty yards of the mine.

All this time the Confederates lay in

OPPOSITE TOP: Men of the 48th Pennsylvania carrying powder to the mine.

OPPOSITE BOTTOM: Soldiers from Colonel Pleasants's regiment digging the tunnel toward the Confederate salient.

BELOW: Union soldiers in the trenches before Petersburg.

peaceful slumber, unconscious of the terrible storm that was about to burst upon them. The fuse was relighted, and at about half-past four the flame reached the powder in the mine.

A tremendous explosion instantly followed, and there was hurled into the air an immense column of smoke and earth, which, after rising to a great height, burst into fragments of timber, stone, broken gun-carriages, muskets, and black and mutilated corpses, which quickly returned in a heavy shower upon the earth. Two hundred men were killed by the explosion, and a rent was torn in the Confederate lines 135 feet long, 90 feet wide, and 30 feet deep.

The whole Confederate line was aroused by the explosion. The men in the immediate vicinity of the line were for some minutes paralyzed by the shock, while those on the more distant portions of the lines remained a while in a state of ignorance and wonder as to what had occurred.

But the troops stationed near the mine soon became conscious of the catastrophe, and, alive to the importance of immediate action, Lieutenant-colonel John Haskell, who commanded the artillery at that point, turned his guns upon the approaches to the breach, and poured such a destructive fire of canister and shell upon them as to render the advance of the enemy extremely diffi-

BELOW: The explosion of the mine under Confederate defenses on July 30. General Grant lost 5000 men in the ensuing disaster.

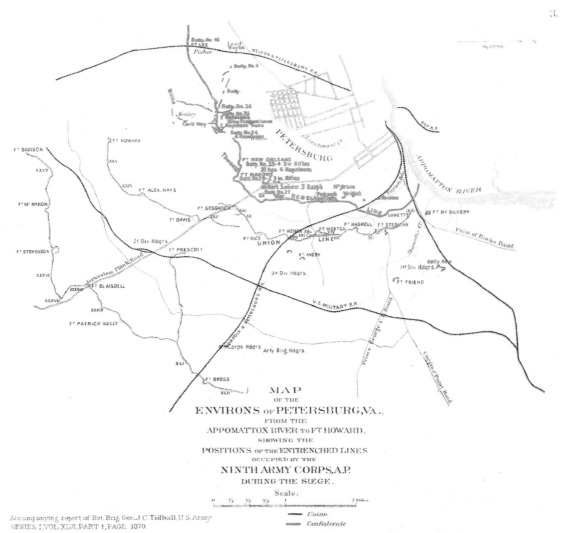

MAP
OF THE
ENVIRONS OF PETERSBURG, VA.,
FROM THE
APPOMATTOX RIVER TO FT HOWARD,
SHOWING THE
POSITIONS OF THE ENTRENCHED LINES
OCCUPIED BY THE
NINTH ARMY CORPS, A.P.
DURING THE SIEGE.

Scale:

Accompanying report of Bvt.Brig.Gen.J.C.Tidball, U.S.Army
SERIES I, VOL. XLVI, PART 1, PAGE 1070.

— Union
— Confederate

LEFT: Map showing the siege lines at Petersburg, less than a mile apart.

cult. Some time elapsed before the assaulting column could be got in motion, and when it cleared the breastwork it was met by such a storm of shot and shell that it was thrown into confusion, and the men were so demoralized that they hastily sought shelter. Great numbers rushed into the crater of the mine; others hid themselves behind traverses; some even crouched close beneath the Confederate breastworks, and no efforts of their officers could induce them to advance. The delay thus occasioned enabled the Confederates to collect a force sufficient to defend the breach.

General Lee, who had been early apprised of the disaster, sent Colonel Venable of his staff to hasten forward troops from other parts of the line. This energetic officer first found General Mahone, whose division was already under arms, and instructed him to proceed to the threatened point. Mahone rapidly advanced, and on reaching the crater promptly formed a cordon of bayonets and took decisive steps to expel the Federal forces that had effected a lodgment upon the Confederate works. Mahone's

forces were rapidly reinforced by other troops, and the fighting now became desperate. The Federals, who had for some time been delayed, pushed forward with great resolution and with the determination to counteract the effects of the blunder that had been made in the first assault. But all their efforts were unavailing, and by ten o'clock they were driven back within their own lines.

The mine, instead of opening the gate to victory, had proved a sepulchre. General Grant lost 5000 men in his attempt to pass the breach. Although the distance between the hostile breastworks was barely a hundred yards, only a few of the Federals succeeded in establishing on the Confederate works. The only advantage to the Federals was in the blowing up of 200 Confederates and the killing and wounding of a few hundreds more. The men thus lost by the Confederates could never be replaced, and to this extent General Grant saw himself a step nearer the end.

Generals Lee and Beauregard were eyewitnesses of the gallant defence of the

ABOVE: Confederate General P. G. T. Beauregard commanded the 50,000 defenders of Petersburg until Lee's arrival on June 18.

RIGHT: Colonel David Weisiger led the brigade that repelled the attackers from the crater.

breach and the signal repulse of the enemy. Colonel Weisiger, whose brigade encircled the crater, repelled the enemy with great determination, and his gallantry won for him the grade of brigadier-general. Captain Girardey, for his gallant conduct, received a similar promotion, while the names of Lieutenant-colonels John Haskell, Pegram, and many others of the artillery obtained prominence in the roll of honor.

Critical remarks in reference to the strategic bearings of this mining operation are perhaps uncalled for. The mine itself proved useless and became a death-trap to its excavators; yet, if we accept the Federal statements, this was a result of bad management after the explosion, and has no necessary bearing on the question of the military value of the undertaking itself. To mine fortified works which cannot be breached or scaled has long been a common expedient in siege operations, but to attack an earthwork by such a method had never before been attempted, and its ill-success on this occasion will probably prevent its being quickly again essayed.

Federal historians and military authorities ascribe the non-success of the enterprise to an unwise withdrawal, at the last moment, of the black troops, who had been carefully drilled for this special service, and their replacement by a brigade of whites, who were very badly led and held back from charging until the Confederates in the vicinity had recovered from their temporary panic and had hastened to the defence of their imperilled lines. Yet this censure of General Ledlie seems hardly just in view of all the circumstances of the case. The crater into which its division plunged was very difficult to pass – much more so than an ordinary earthwork. And the lack of previous training of his men, or of any full comprehension on his part of the character of the work before him, operated as a serious disadvantage. Had men trained to the work been given the advance in the charge, the result might possibly have been very different. It cannot be denied that the Confederate position was for a short time in serious jeopardy, and that had the Federals taken instant and decided advantage of their opportunity they might have gained an important victory. There has seldom been a case in which the old adage, "Delay is dangerous," more fully applied, yet it was one of those cases in which delay is almost unavoidable, and it becomes a question, therefore, whether there was suffi-

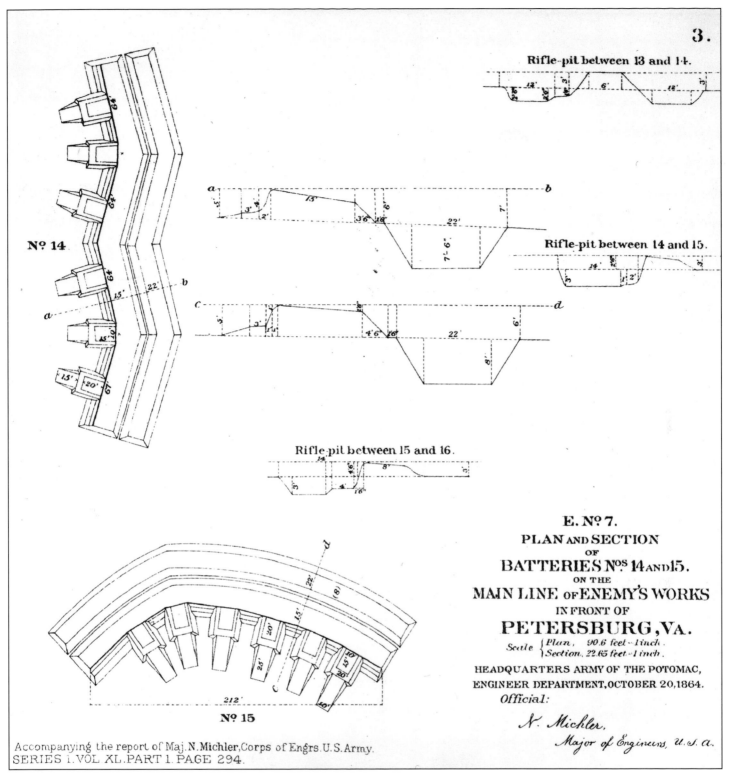

3.

Rifle-pit between 13 and 14.

No 14

a
b

Rifle-pit between 14 and 15.

c
d

Rifle-pit between 15 and 16.

No 15

E. No 7.
PLAN AND SECTION
OF
BATTERIES Nos 14 AND 15.
ON THE
MAIN LINE OF ENEMY'S WORKS
IN FRONT OF
PETERSBURG, VA.
Scale { Plan, 90.6 feet - 1 inch.
{ Section, 22.65 feet - 1 inch.
HEADQUARTERS ARMY OF THE POTOMAC,
ENGINEER DEPARTMENT, OCTOBER 20, 1864.
Official:

N. Michler.
Major of Engineers, U. S. a.

Accompanying the report of Maj. N. Michler, Corps of Engrs. U. S. Army.
SERIES 1. VOL. XL. PART 1. PAGE 294.

cient probability of success to warrant such a dangerous enterprise.

* * *

After the failure of the mining enterprise direct assaults flagged, and during the remainder of the summer and the autumn the spade took the place of the musket, and both armies employed themselves in constructing new and strengthening old works.

* * *

Large detachments which had been with-

drawn from Grant's army, first to oppose Early, and subsequently for [an] expedition against Wilmington, had so reduced his force as to prevent very vigorous operations against Richmond and Petersburg. [He spent the winter of 1864-1865 in rebuilding his army for a final assault on Lee's defenses. (Ed)]

In the mean time, Lee, finding himself too weak to hazard a serious blow, did all he could to preserve his army from the constant attrition that was wearing it away. . . .

* * *

ABOVE: Army of the Potomac engineers drew these plans of Confederate batteries and rifle pits in front of Petersburg.

During this period, on February 6, 1865, [General Lee was appointed] commander-in-chief of all the Confederate armies. Had this appointment been made two years earlier, it is probable that a different state of affairs would have existed. . . . But as the spring opened it became daily more apparent that human power and endurance could do no more, and that a forced evacuation of the beleaguered cities was near at hand.

*   *   *

Grant had begun the concentration of his forces in order to complete his interior cordon or line of investment. . . . While his adversary was thus active, Lee was not idle. He had formed a plan to surprise the enemy's centre by a night-attack, which if successful would have given him possession of a commanding position in the enemy's rear and control of the military railroad to City Point – a very important part of Grant's communications.

*   *   *

Now was the time for the supporting column to advance. . . . For some reason which has never been made very clear this advance was not made. . . . Gordon with his small force was left to bear the whole brunt of the Federal assault which quickly fell upon him. . . .

This unsuccessful effort was quickly followed by a vigorous advance on the part of Grant, who concentrated his principal force south and west of Petersburg with the view of assailing the Confederate right. Early on the morning of March 29th the corps of Warren and Humphreys broke camp and moved toward Lee's intrenchments on the extreme right, while Sheridan, with the cavalry, made a wider sweep and occupied Dinwiddie Court-house, six miles south-west of the point reached by the infantry.

Yet, swiftly and secretly as this movement was made, it did not escape Lee's vigilant eye. He quickly divined where the blow was to fall, and, leaving the works north of the James under Longstreet and those at Petersburg under Gordon but weakly garrisoned, he removed the remainder of his army, con-

ABOVE: This Confederate soldier died on April 2, 1865, the day General Lee finally evacuated his position and led his troops out of Petersburg.

OPPOSITE TOP: A battery of the 3rd New York Artillery in the trenches before Petersburg.

OPPOSITE BOTTOM: A section of the trenches, which would be occupied by soldiers for almost 10 months.

RIGHT: Union troops of the 5th Corps bivouaced in their rifle pits near Petersburg, Va., in August 1864, from a sketch by A.R. Waud.

BELOW: The harbor at City Point is filled with ships from the industrial North unloading supplies for Grant's army in Virginia.

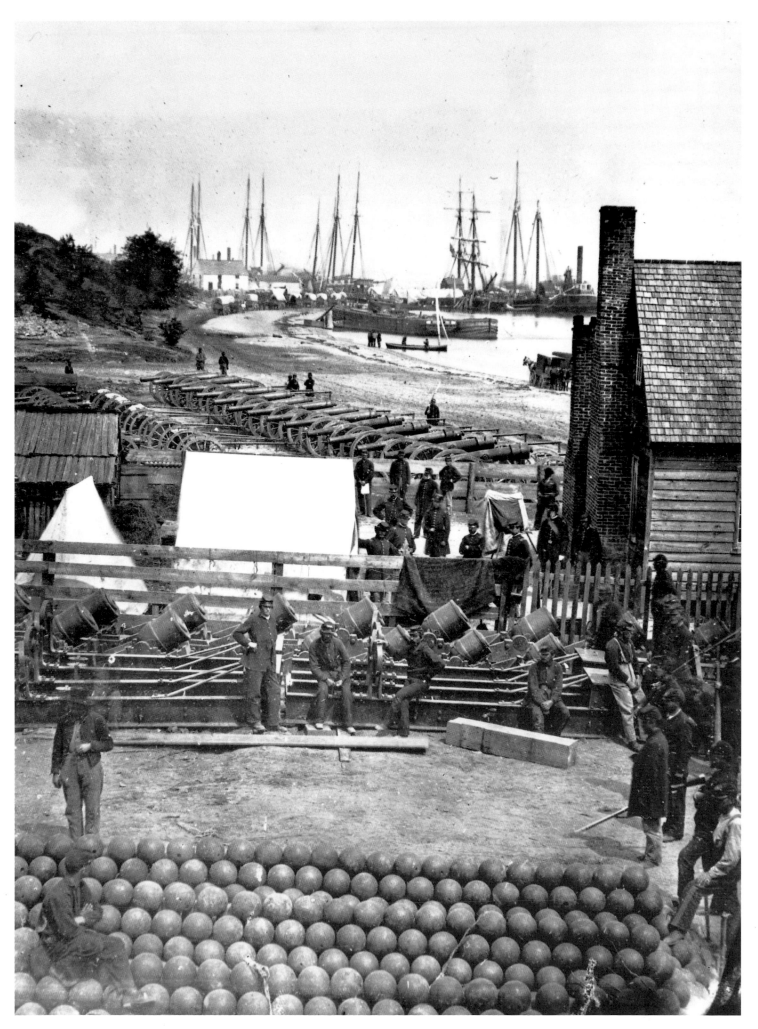

sisting of about 15,000 infantry and 2000 cavalry, into the works along the White Oak road.

Here, on the morning of the 31st, Lee made the flank attack which he had so often attempted with success against the Federal columns. Not waiting for the assault, he boldly took the initiative, and fell upon their exposed flank while they were entangled in the intricacies of a swampy forest. So sudden and heavy was the blow that the divisions encountered hastily gave way. But upon meeting the main body of the Federal troops he found it so thickly massed and well posted as to render an assault hopeless. He therefore fell back to his works.

On the same day Sheridan advanced toward Five Forks. Before reaching that point, however, he was encountered by the Confederate cavalry under the chief command of General Fitz Lee, supported by the infantry under Pickett. A severe combat ensued, in which Sheridan was driven back to Dinwiddie Court-house. . . .

On the 1st of April, Sheridan was reinforced by two corps of infantry, and with this powerful aid he renewed his attack upon Five Forks, which place was carried late in the evening and the Confederates driven back.

General Lee, perceiving that his forces were too weak to combat successfully with the enemy, ordered Longstreet on the afternoon of the 1st to bring his corps with all speed from before Richmond to Petersburg, with the object of supporting his right wing.

Early on the morning of the 2nd the Federals renewed the attack, breaking the lines of the Confederates and forcing them from their position. The Federals then took possession of the Southside Railroad with little opposition, while the Confederates fell back toward Petersburg, followed by the victorious enemy. The pursuit was continued until it was arrested by the guns from two redoubts, Forts Alexander and Gregg, which with great gallantry held the enemy in check until Longstreet came up and interposed his corps, effectually arresting the further advance of the Federal columns.

In the conflict here described fell many gallant warriors, chief among them Lieutenant-general A. P. Hill, who was slain while endeavoring to reach Heth's division, which had been ordered to support Pickett on the right. No man had been more distinguished throughout the war for chivalric bearing than this brave soldier. On every field where appeared the Army of Northern Virginia he had borne a conspicuous part, and now in the last battle of that noble army he found a hero's grave.

BELOW: View of the Appomattox River in April 1865, showing a bridge, railroad cars, and workshops which were burned by the Confederates on evacuating Petersburg.

ABOVE: A Confederate soldier lies dead at Fort Mahone after the evacuation of Petersburg.

LEFT: The occupation of the Petersburg defenses by Union troops on April 2, 1865.

Chapter IX

Appomattox

The success of the Federal army in breaking the lines of Petersburg had rendered the retreat of the Confederate force imperative.... But by abandoning his works and concentrating his army, which still amounted to about 30,000 men, General Lee might retire to some natural stronghold in the interior, where the defensible features of the country would enable him to oppose Grant's formidable host until he could rally strength to strike an effective blow.

*   *   *

Along the north bank of the Appomattox moved the long lines of artillery and dark columns of infantry through the ... night [of April 2nd], over the roads leading to Amelia Court-house. By midnight the evacuation was completed....

*   *   *

The retreat of Lee's army did not long remain unknown to the Federals ... and they lost no time in taking possession of the abandoned works and entering the defenceless cities. On the morning of the 3rd of April the mayor of Richmond surrendered the city to the Federal commander in its vicinity....

As soon as Grant became aware of Lee's line of retreat he pushed forward his whole available force ... in order to intercept him on the line of the Richmond and Danville Railroad.... Lee pressed on as rapidly as possible to Amelia Court-house, where he had ordered supplies to be deposited for the use of his troops on their arrival.... Through an unfortunate error ... not a single ration was found to be provided for the hungry troops.... The only chance remaining to the Army of Northern Virginia was to reach the hill-country without delay.... By the morning of the 5th the whole army had

BELOW: Federal columns moving on Richmond. On April 2 whole sections of the Confederate capital were burned by troops preparing to abandon it to the approaching Federals.

ABOVE: The evacuation of Richmond. Nearly one thousand buildings were destroyed in the fires, and many were damaged.

LEFT: Federal troops entered Richmond on April 3, and raised the Stars and Stripes over the Southern Capitol that morning. Mrs. Robert E. Lee remained in the city under protective guard.

RIGHT: Union soldiers survey
the ruins of occupied
Richmond.

reached the place of general rendezvous. Bitter was its disappointment to learn that no food was to be had. . . .

*   *   *

Sheridan's cavalry was already upon the flank of the Confederate army, and the infantry was following with all speed. On [the afternoon of the 6th]. . . . Ewell's, the rearmost corps in the army, closed upon those in front at a position on Sailor's Creek, a small tributary of the Appomattox River . . . [but] his corps was surrounded by the pursuing columns and captured with but little opposition. About the same time the divisions of Anderson, Pickett, and Bushrod Johnson were almost broken up, about 10,000 men in all being captured. The remainder of the army continued its retreat during the night of the 6th, and reached Farmville early on the morning of the 7th, where the troops obtained two days' rations. . . .

*   *   *

The heads of the Federal columns beginning to appear about eleven o'clock, the Confederates resumed their retreat. The teams of the wagons and artillery were weak, being travel worn and suffering from lack of forage. Their progress, therefore, was necessarily slow, and as the troops were obliged to move in conformity with the artillery and trains, the Federal cavalry closed upon the retreating army. . . .

*   *   *

Desperate as the situation had become, and irretrievable as it seemed hourly growing, General Lee could not forego the hope of breaking through the net that was rapidly enclosing him and of forming a junction with Johnston. In the event of success in this he felt confident of being able to manoeuvre with Grant at least until favorable terms of peace could be obtained. . . .

On the 8th the retreat, being uninterrupted, progressed more expeditiously than on the previous day. Yet, though the Federals did not press the Confederate flank and rear as on the day before, a heavy column of cavalry advanced upon Appomattox Station, where the supplies for the Confederate army had been deposited. . . . When Lee in the afternoon reached the neighborhood of Appomattox Court-house, he was met by the intelligence of the capture of the stores placed for his army. . . .

RIGHT: Jubilant Union soldiers
pose for a photo at
Appomattox Court-house.

On the evening of that day the last council of the leaders of the Army of Northern Virginia was held around a bivouac-fire in the woods, there being present Generals Lee, Longstreet, Gordon, and Fitz Lee. This conference ended in a determination to make a renewed effort on the following morning to break through the impediments in front. . . . At three o'clock on the morning of the 9th of April the Confederates moved silently forward.

*   *   *

Colonel C. S. Venable of General Lee's staff graphically tells what took place at headquarters on that eventful morning. His story is of great interest, as showing how reluctantly yet how nobly the heroic commander submitted to the inevitable after having till the last minute, like a lion at bay, faced the overwhelming force of his opponent:

At three o'clock on the morning of that fatal day General Lee rode forward, still hoping that we might break through the countless hordes of the enemy who hemmed us in. Halting a short distance in rear of our vanguard, he sent me on to General Gordon to ask him if he could break through the enemy. I found General Gordon and General

BELOW: A wounded Zouave and his campanion are the sole occupants of a deserted camp as the war draws to an end.

ABOVE: Ulysses S. Grant and two of his staff. Grant's surrender terms were simple and generous.

Fitz Lee on their front line in the dim light of the morning arranging an attack. Gordon's reply to the message (I give the expressive phrase of the gallant Georgian) was this: "Tell General Lee I have fought my corps to a frazzle, and I fear I can do nothing unless I am heavily supported by Longstreet's corps."

When I bore this message back to General Lee he said, "Then there is nothing left me but to go and see General Grant, and I would rather die a thousand deaths."

Convulsed with passionate grief, many were the wild words which we spoke as we stood around him. Said one, "Oh, general, what will history say of the surrender of the army in the field?"

He replied, "Yes, I know they will say hard things of us: they will not understand how we were overwhelmed by numbers. But that is not the question, colonel: the question is, Is it right to surrender this army? If it is right, then *I* will take *all* the responsibility."

The artillery had been withdrawn from the heights, as above stated, and parked in the small valley east of the village, while the infantry, who were formed on the left, stacked arms and silently waited the result of the interview between the opposing commanders.

The flag of truce was sent out from General Gordon's lines. Grant had not yet come up, and while waiting for his arrival General Lee seated himself upon some rails which Colonel Talcott of the Engineers had

BELOW: General Lee's signed acceptance of Grant's terms of surrender.

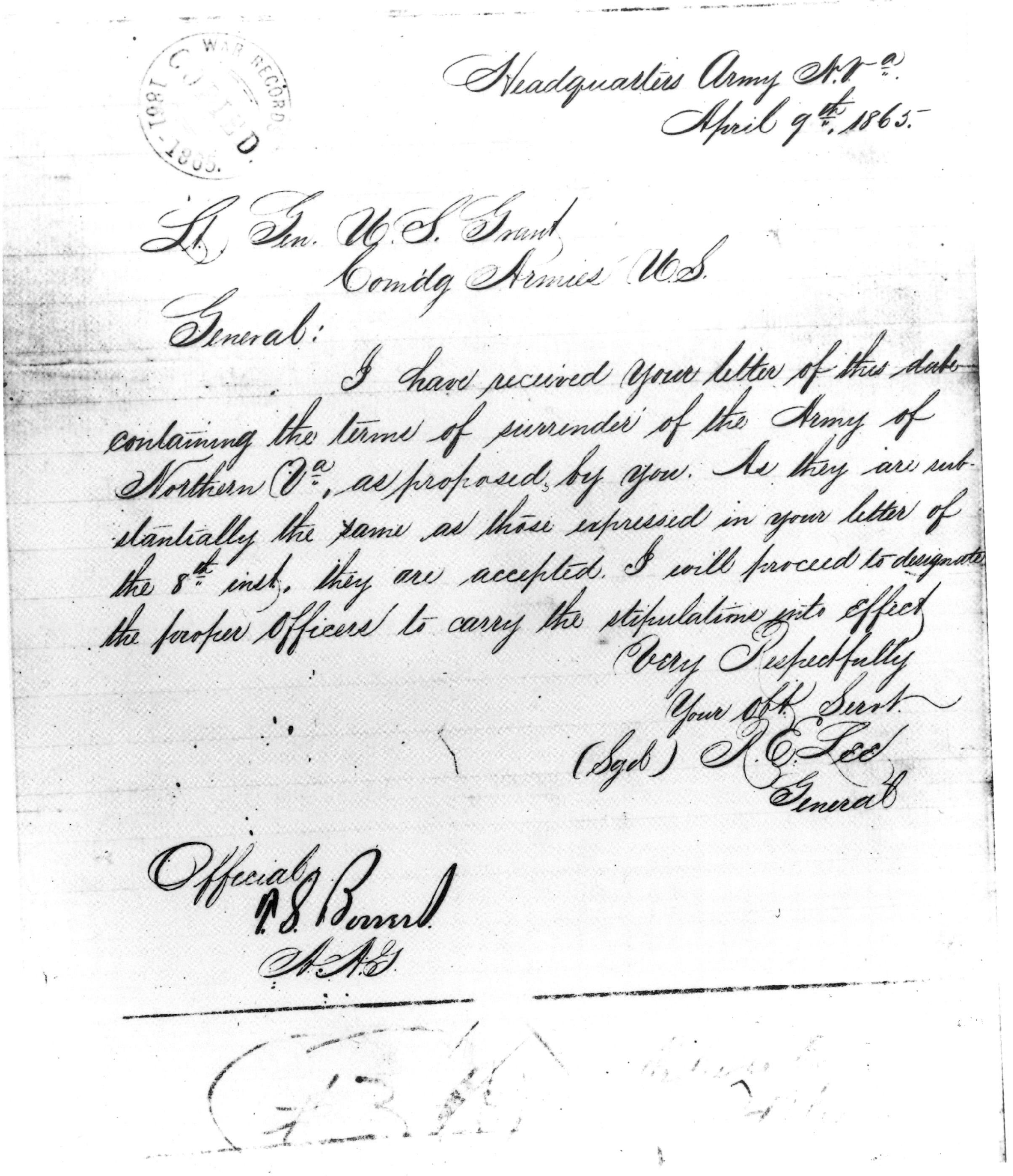

1861 WAR RECORDS 1865 COPIED.

Headquarters Army N. Va.
April 9th, 1865.

Lt. Gen. U. S. Grant
Comdg Armies U.S.

General:

I have received your letter of this date containing the terms of surrender of the Army of Northern Va., as proposed by you. As they are substantially the same as those expressed in your letter of the 8th inst., they are accepted. I will proceed to designate the proper Officers to carry the stipulations into effect.

Very Respectfully
Your Obt. Servt.
(Sgd) R. E. Lee
General

Official
T. S. Bowers
A.A.G.

LEFT: Confederate General Fitzhugh Lee, a nephew of Robert E. Lee, who led a cavalry brigade under J.E.B. Stuart in several campaigns and commanded his uncle's cavalry on the retreat to Appomattox.

BELOW: Inscribed with part of a quotation from Lee, "Peace, the Sole object of All," and with the words, "Truce –then Peace," Thomas Nast's evocative, bold sketch of the defeated commander captures Lee's solid nobility.

fixed at the foot of an apple tree for his convenience. This tree was half a mile distant from the point where the meeting of Lee and Grant took place, yet widespread currency has been given to the story that the surrender took place under its shade, and "appletree" jewelry has been profusely distributed from the orchard in which it grew.

About 11 o'clock General Lee, accompanied only by Colonel Marshall of his staff, proceeded to the village to meet General Grant, who had now arrived. The meeting between the two renowned generals took place at the house of a Mr. McLean at Appomattox Court-house, to which mansion, after exchanging courteous salutations, they repaired to settle the terms on which the surrender of the Army of Northern Virginia should be concluded.

A conversation here took place which General Grant, as he himself tells us, led to various subjects divergent from the immediate purpose of the meeting, talking of old army matters and comparing recollections with General Lee. As he says, the conversation grew so pleasant that he almost forgot the object of the meeting.

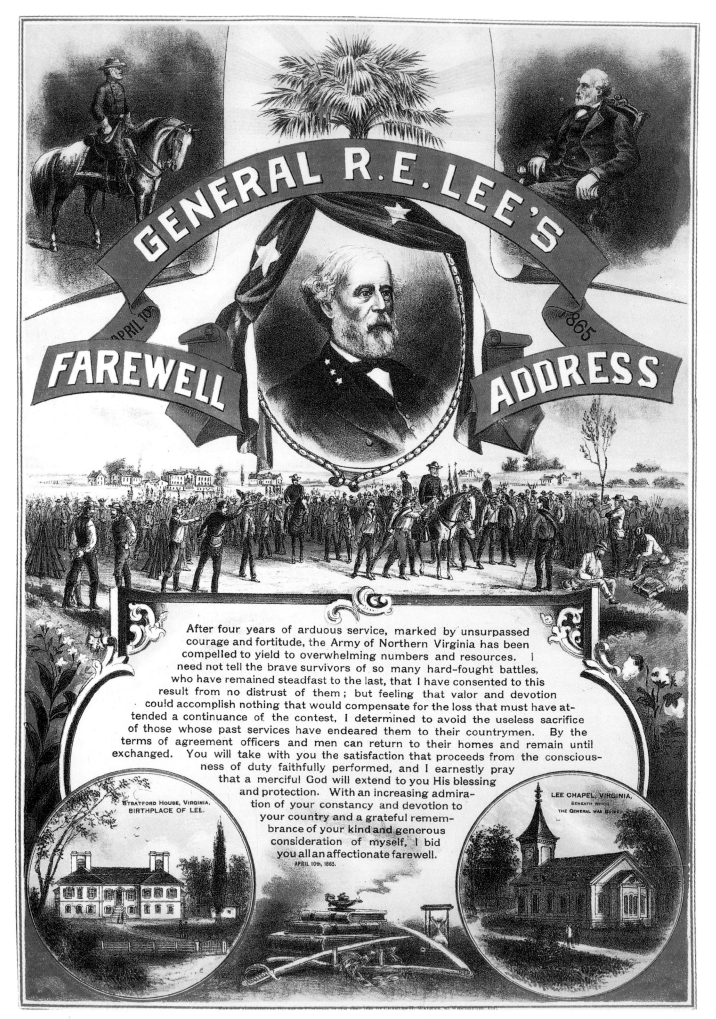

GENERAL R. E. LEE'S FAREWELL ADDRESS

After four years of arduous service, marked by unsurpassed courage and fortitude, the Army of Northern Virginia has been compelled to yield to overwhelming numbers and resources. I need not tell the brave survivors of so many hard-fought battles, who have remained steadfast to the last, that I have consented to this result from no distrust of them; but feeling that valor and devotion could accomplish nothing that would compensate for the loss that must have attended a continuance of the contest, I determined to avoid the useless sacrifice of those whose past services have endeared them to their countrymen. By the terms of agreement officers and men can return to their homes and remain until exchanged. You will take with you the satisfaction that proceeds from the consciousness of duty faithfully performed, and I earnestly pray that a merciful God will extend to you His blessing and protection. With an increasing admiration of your constancy and devotion to your country and a grateful remembrance of your kind and generous consideration of myself, I bid you all an affectionate farewell.

APRIL 10th, 1865.

STRATFORD HOUSE, VIRGINIA, BIRTHPLACE OF LEE.

LEE CHAPEL, VIRGINIA, BENEATH WHICH THE GENERAL WAS BURIED.

General Lee was obliged more than once to remind him of this object, and it was some time before the terms of the surrender were written out. The written instrument of surrender covered the following points: Duplicate rolls of all the officers and men were to be made, and the officers to sign paroles for themselves and their men, all agreeing not to bear arms against the United States unless regularly exchanged. The arms, artillery, and public property were to be turned over to an officer appointed to receive them, the officers retaining their side-arms and private horses and baggage. In addition to this, General Grant permitted every man of the Confederate army who claimed to own a horse or mule to retain it for farming purposes, General Lee remarking that this would have a happy effect. As for the surrender by General Lee of his sword, a report of what has been widely circulated, General Grant disposes of it in the following words: "The much-talked of surrendering of Lee's sword and my handing it back, this and much more that has been said about it is the purest romance."

After completion of these measures General Lee remarked that his men were badly in need of food, that they had been living for several days on parched corn exclusively, and requested rations and forage for 25,000 men. These rations were granted out of the car-loads of Confederate provisions which had been stopped by the Federal cavalry. As for forage, Grant remarked that he was himself depending upon the country for that. The negotiations completed, General Lee left the house, mounted his horse, and rode back to headquarters.

It is impossible to describe the anguish of the troops when it was known that the surrender of the army was inevitable. Of all their trials, this was the greatest and hardest to endure. There was no consciousness of shame; each heart could boast with honest pride that its duty had been done to the end, and that still unsullied remained its honor. When, after his interview with Grant, General Lee again appeared, a shout of welcome instinctively ran through the army. But instantly recollecting the sad occasion that brought him before them, their shouts sank into silence, every hat was raised, and the bronzed faces of the thousands of grim warriors were bathed with tears.

As he rode slowly along the lines hundreds of his devoted veterans pressed around the noble chief, trying to take his hand, touch his person, or even lay a hand upon his horse, thus exhibiting for him their great affection. The general then, with head bare and tears flowing freely down his manly cheeks, bade adieu to the army. In a few words he told the brave men who had been so true in arms to return to their homes and become worthy citizens.

Thus closed the career of the noble Army of Northern Virginia.

OPPOSITE: General Robert E. Lee's April 10 farewell to the men of the Army of Northern Virginia.

LEFT: General Lee, mounted on his famous horse Traveller, returning to his veterans after the surrender to General Grant. The sketch is probably by the artist A. R. Waud.

BELOW: General Lee's farewell to his soldiers.

Chapter X

General Lee as a Soldier

With the surrender of the Army of Northern Virginia, General Lee's military career ended. My intimate relations with him continued to the close of his life.

I frequently visited him at his home in Lexington, Va., and saw him in the discharge of his duties as a college president, but before laying aside my pen it is proper that I should attempt some estimate of him as a soldier and a man.

General Lee was both by nature and by education a great soldier. By diligent study under the most favorable conditions, and by long and varied experience, he became a master of the science of war in all its branches. In early life he was especially distinguished as an engineer. All the important points from the coast of Georgia to New York bear witness to his engineering skill, and his name will be identified with the Rip Raps, Fort Carroll, and the defences of New York

BELOW: The famous postwar photo of General Robert E. Lee and his horse Traveller, taken in September 1866.

Gen's R. E. LEE and J. E. JOHNSTON.

D. J. Ryan, Savannah, Ga.

BELOW: General Lee with General Joseph E. Johnston in a photo taken about 1870, the year of Lee's death.

harbor until those granite structures crumble into dust.

Perhaps even more important than his work on the Atlantic coast was that on the Mississippi and Des Moines rapids, of which General Meigs, U. S. A., has kindly furnished for this volume a highly interesting account.

The Mexican War opened to him a wider field, and the quick eye of General Scott discovered in the young captain of Engineers "a man of all kinds of merit."

On assuming command in Virginia in April, 1861, General Lee once showed his talents for administration and organization. He found the country almost destitute of the essentials of war, and, as if by magic, he created and equipped an army. His very ability as an organizer made many doubt whether he could be great in other directions, and it was only after successful trial that they were willing to recognize his wonderful versatility.

It was with surprise that they saw him showing himself equal to all the demands made upon him as the commander of a great army in the field. As they looked on, their surprise changed to admiration; the glory of the engineer and organizer was first dimmed, and then eclipsed, by that of the strategist and tactician.

The great soldier is something more than a fighter of battles. He must have a breadth of view sufficient to take in widely-separated movements and to form great and far-reaching combinations. That General Lee had this breadth of view, this subtle intuition, which constitutes the very flower of military genius, is shown by the whole history of the war. The reader will recall how, when he was contemplating an attack on McClellan on the Chickahominy, he sent Jackson to make a vigorous movement in the Valley. He nicely calculated the moral effect of that movement. He intended it to alarm the authorities at Washington – to hold McDowell in position near the Federal capital, and thus prevent his joining in the coming battle.

The Pennsylvania campaign had a wider outlook: it was charged with great possibilities. The defeat of Meade's army in Pennsylvania might be expected to be much more than the simple defeat of that one army. Its effect would be felt on the Mississippi; Grant's army would be needed in the East; the siege of Vicksburg would be raised, and Pemberton's army released for active service. What else might follow it was easy to conjecture. Lee fought, and knew that he

OPPOSITE: General Winfield Scott with his staff. The U.S. Army commander early recognized Lee's military talents.

ABOVE: A Confederate soldier of Company A, 18th Virginia Infantry, in dress uniform.

Ridge for a while seemed successful, then the Muse of History took up her pen to record the birth of a new nation.

Breadth of plan is often neutralized by neglect of details. General Lee did not make that mistake. Before a battle he neglected nothing that might be needful either for attack or defence; in the battle he was quick to see and prompt to meet emergencies. He knew his men, rank and file – what they could do, and how far he might trust them. He was careful to know the ground on which he was to operate, and also to seize and use every advantage of position: he made a league with rivers and mountains and mountain-passes. He studied his adversary, knew his peculiarities, and adapted himself to them. His own methods no one could foresee; he varied them with every change in the commanders opposed to him. He had one method with McClellan, another with Pope, another with Hooker, and yet another with Grant. But for a knowledge of his own resources, of the field, and of his adversary some of his movements might have been rash. As it was, they were wisely bold. Because he was so attentive to details, and guarded so rigidly against the accidents of battle, he was sometimes supposed to be over-cautious; because he sometimes supposed to be over-cautious; because he sometimes attacked greatly superior numbers or divided his forces, he was often thought over-bold. The truth is, that there was in him that harmonious blending of caution and boldness without which a general must often either rashly expose himself to defeat or lose an opportunity for victory.

Whatever other qualities a man may have, he cannot be a great soldier unless he has the power to win the confidence and inspire the enthusiasm of his men. General Lee had this power; few men have had it in a higher degree. No privation or suffering or disaster could shake the confidence of his men in him. In the darkest hour the sight of his form or the mention of his name stirred the hearts of his veterans. They spoke of him with an affection and pride that have not been dimmed by the lapse of years.

It is sometimes said that while General Lee was without a peer in defence, he was not so great in attack. That he was great in defence is witnessed by the series of combats from the Wilderness to Cold Harbor. Hardly anything in the history of warfare, ancient or modern, equals the skill and

fought, for a great stake. That he did not succeed and that the movement came too late, even if it had been successful, to affect the result at Vicksburg, detracts nothing from the brilliancy of the conception. The one pertinent thing is that the Confederate general saw that by a single bold and successful stroke it might be possible virtually to end the war and secure the independence of the Southern Confederacy. That success was possible is shown by the narrow chance by which it failed. It has been well said that when the Confederate charge at Cemetery

Great Seal of the
Confederate States of
America.

LEFT: An engraving of notable
Confederate generals. At
center, Stonewall Jackson;
clockwise from top, Jeb
Stuart, Leonidas Polk, John
B. Magruder, A. P. Hill, James
Longstreet, R. S. Ewell, John
Pemberton, and Sterling
Price.

RIGHT: Confederate President
Jefferson Davis surrounded
by his senior officers.
Clockwise from top, P. T. G.
Beauregard, Robert E. Lee,
Braxton Bragg, G. N. Hollins,
Simon B. Buckner, A. S.
Johnston, and Joseph E.
Johnston.

adroitness with which he met and repulsed Grant's obstinate and persevering assaults. But, on the other hand, in the second battle of Manassas and at Chancellorsville he was the aggressor; he went to seek the enemy. And even in those cases in which he was resisting the enemy's advance he often struck a blow in preference to waiting to receive one.

But perhaps the readiest way to fix Lee's position and to realize his greatness would be to compare him with others. It is significant that in attempting to do this no one ever thinks of comparing him with any but men of the first rank. Among the distinguished soldiers on the Confederate side his position was peculiar. He came from the old army with a brilliant reputation, and during the war he occupied the most prominent and responsible position. It is no injustice either to

the living or the dead to say that by common consent he holds the first place among Southern soldiers.

Among the dead heroes of the war Albert Sidney Johnston challenges admiring attention. He had great qualities; anything that skill, courage, and a lofty, unselfish character might accomplish seemed possible to him; but he died at Shiloh. Jackson was Lee's most trusted lieutenant, and deserved all the confidence that his commander reposed in him. In the sphere of his operations he had no superior, nor can it be known that he would not have shown himself equal to a greater sphere. All honor to that brave, true soldier! but it would not be proper to compare him with his chief. There was no rivalry between them living; let there be none now that they are dead. There was A. P. Hill, a modest man, always ready; one of the finest

soldiers in the army: he had the best division when he had a division, and one of the best corps when he had a corps. Lee and Jackson agreed in their admiration of Hill, and both mentioned him in the delirium of death; but no one thinks of comparing him with Lee.

There is a sort of infallibility in an undivided popular judgment, and the whole South looked to Lee as its greatest man. So impressed was Grant with the devotion of

ABOVE LEFT: Engraving of General Stonewall Jackson.

ABOVE: Photographic portrait of General Jackson.

the Southern people to Lee that after the surrender at Appomattox he sought his influence, being convinced that if he should advise the surrender of all the Southern armies, the advice would be followed with alacrity. And in his report of the operations of the Army of the Potomac in 1864-65 he attributes it to General Lee's example that, as he says, "the armies lately under his leadership are at their homes, desiring peace and quiet, and their arms are in the hands of our ordnance officers."

Nothing is more characteristic of General Lee, or reveals more clearly his simple moral grandeur, than the fact that when no more could be accomplished by arms he used his influence to promote peace and good feeling toward the people against whom he had been waging war.

Of the great soldiers opposed to General Lee, some may have equalled him in single qualities, none in the combination of qualities. They were great in some directions; he in many. Let it not be forgotten that his was a long and varied career, and that he was distinguished in every part of it. He was called on to do many things, and he did them all in a masterly way.

In judging him account must be taken not only of what he did in the war between the States, but also of what he did before the Mexican War, in the Mexican War, and after the Mexican War, and in the last years of his life. When all these things are considered, and when we take into the account his perfect acquaintance with his art, his organizing power, his skill in combining, his wisdom in planning, his boldness and vigor in execution, his power to awaken enthusiasm and to lead men, we must place him first among the great soldiers of both armies. The time has not yet come to compare him with soldiers of the past and of other lands. They show great in the haze of time and distance, but the time will come when by the suffrages of all he will take his place among the greatest of those who have marshalled armies to battle.

OPPOSITE: Sketch by A. R. Waud of the railroad bridge over the Rappannock at Fredericksburg. Burned before the Union attack, it became a place where men of both sides came to exchange jibes.

BELOW: Men of the Union VI Corps fighting in the woods at the Battle of the Wilderness.

OPPOSITE: Ruins of the city of Richmond in April 1865.

We turn now from Lee as a soldier to Lee as a man; and here it is difficult to find suitable words in which to speak of him. In a private conversation a gentleman once said to an officer who had been intimately associated with him, "Most men have their weak point. What was General Lee's?" After a thoughtful pause, the answer was, "I really do not know." This answer may be taken for that of the great majority of those who knew him personally or who have studied his character. He was singularly free from the faults which so often mar the character of great men. He was without envy, jealousy, or suspicion, self-seeking, or covetousness; there was nothing about him to diminish or chill the respect which all men felt for him. General Grant speaks of him as "a large, austere man, difficult of approach to his subordinates." "Austere" is not the word to use in speaking of him. I should rather say that he was clothed with a natural dignity which could either repel or invite as occasion might require. He could pass with perfect ease from familiar, cheerful conversation to earnest conference, and from earnest conference to authoritative command. He had a pleasant humor, could see the ludicrous side of things, and could enjoy an anecdote or a joke. But even in his lightest moods he was still the cultivated gentleman, having that just degree of reserve that suited his high and responsible position.

His character was perfectly simple; there were in it no folds or sinuosities. It was simple because guided by a single principle. It is common to say that this principle was duty. This is not the whole truth. Duty is faithfulness to obligation, and is measured by obligation. That which moulded General

BELOW: Confederate soldiers withdraw after the Battle of Gettysburg.

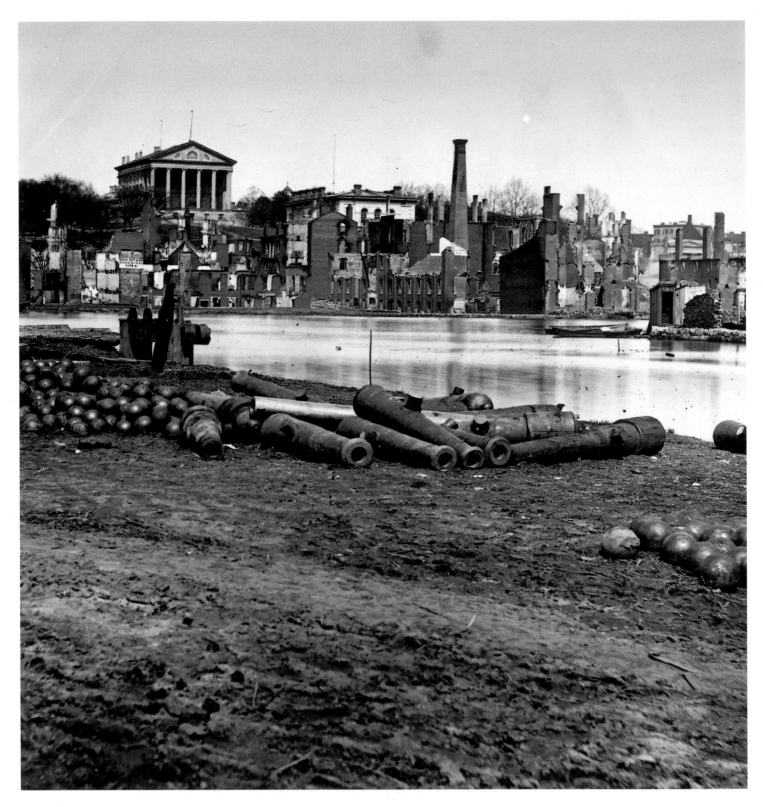

ABOVE: The state house at Richmond rises above the ruins of the business district.

Lee's life was something more than duty. It was a fine soldierly instinct that made him feel that it was his business to devote his life and powers to the accomplishment of high impersonal ends. Duty is the highest conception of Roman stoicism; it was the ambition of the Christian soldier to serve. General Grant interpreted him correctly when he said, "I knew there was no use to urge him to anything against his ideas of right."

If there are any who blame him for resigning his position in the United States army and taking part with the South, they must at the same time acknowledge that he was influenced by no unworthy motive. What he did involved sacrifice of feeling, or position, and of interest: he might have had the highest place in the old army; he had but to consent to take it. A man of smaller mould might have been dazzled and attracted by the prospect of leading a successful revolution and establishing a new nation, but in all my association with him I saw no indication that any feeling of personal ambition was present with him. If he had such feeling it was checked by a consciousness of the great interests confided to him.

As he appeared to me, so he appeared to others. When the Confederate capital was transferred from Montgomery to Richmond, the Virginia forces, of which he was commander-in-chief, were incorporated in the Confederate army. He then lost his independent command. While the transfer was yet in contemplation the Confederate authorities were anxious to know whether an apparent lowering of his rank would offend to make him less zealous in the service of the Confederacy. When Mr. Stephens, the Confederate Vice-President, mentioned the matter to him, he promptly said, "Mr. Stephens, I am willing to serve anywhere where I can be useful."

It was in perfect accord with his character that he was no stickler for rank or position. In the early part of the war the positions held by him were not such as to attract public attention; the duties assigned to him, while very important, were not of a showy kind. Others were winning distinction in the field and rising into prominence, while he was in the background. No great laurels could be won in the mountains of West Virginia or in strengthening the coast defences of South Carolina and Georgia. In the estimation of the general public his reputation was suffering; it was said that his former distinction had been too easily won. During this time he uttered no word of complaint, and gave no intimation that he felt himself in any way wronged or overlooked. One might wonder whether this sweetness of spirit, this calmness, this cheerful content, did not spring from a consciousness of power and assured belief that he had only to bide his time; but a close acquaintance with the workings of his mind convinced me that it was rather from a single-hearted desire to be useful, and the conviction that the best way to be useful was to work contentedly and to the best of his ability in the place assigned him.

It was his constant feeling that he was living and working to an end that constituted the source of General Lee's magnanimity and put him far above any petty jealousy. He looked at everything as unrelated to himself,

BELOW: Confederate soldiers of Company B, 9th Mississippi Infantry, camped at Warrington Navy Yard, Pensacola, Florida.

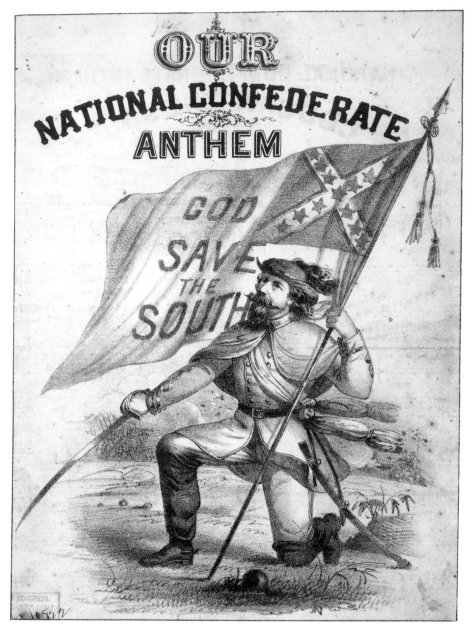

ABOVE: Music cover for the Confederate anthem "God Save the South."

RIGHT: Union soldiers at the west end of Arlington House, Lee's former residence. The grounds of the house became Arlington National Cemetery.

and only as it affected the cause he was serving. This is shown in his treatment of his subordinates. He had no favorites, no unworthy partialities. On one occasion he spoke highly of an officer and remarked that he ought to be promoted. Some surprise was expressed at this, and it was said that that particular officer had sometimes spoken disparagingly of him. "I cannot help that," said the general; "he is a good soldier, and would be useful in a higher position." As he judged of the work of others, so he judged of his own. A victory gave him pleasure only as it contributed to the end he had in view, an honorable peace and the happiness of his country. It was for this cause that even his greatest victories produced in him no exaltation of spirits: he saw the end yet far off. He even thought more of what might have been done than of what was actually accomplished. In the same way a reverse gave him

LEFT: Townsfolk and students gather at Washington College chapel in Lexington to mourn the death of Robert E. Lee.

OPPOSITE: Robert E. Lee posed for Mathew Brady after the war at his home in Richmond. He is seated between his son, George Washington Custis Lee, and his adjutant general of four years, Colonel Walter H. Taylor.

pain, not as a private but as a public calamity. He was the ruling spirit of his army. His campaigns and battles were his own.

He frequently consulted others that his own judgment might be informed, not that he might lean on their judgment or advice. It was because he felt himself so completely the commander of his army that he sometimes assumed the responsibility of the failure of movements which a less strong and generous spirit would have made his subordinates bear.

There was no hesitation or vacillation about him. When he had once formed a plan the orders for its execution were positive, decisive, and final. The army which he so long commanded is a witness for him. He imbued it with his own spirit; it reflected his energy and devotion. Such an army, so responsive to orders, so rapid in movement, so sturdy and prompt in action, so often victorious, sometimes checked but never

defeated, so patient in the endurance of hardships, yielding at last rather to the friction of battle and the pressure of hunger than to the power of the enemy, gives indication that its commander was gifted with that imperial quality . . . command.

As I recall the past, and the four years of the war come back and move in silent procession before me, I can easily forget that more than twenty years have passed away since I selected for General Lee the spot at Appomattox where his tent was pitched for the last time. His image stands out clearly before me, but it is unnecessary to describe his personal appearance. The majesty of his form will endure in marble and bronze, while his memory will pass down the ages as representing all that is greatest in military art, as well as what is truest, bravest, and noblest in human life – a soldier who never failed in duty, a man who feared and trusted God and served his generation.

BELOW: A gathering on the portico of the Lee family home, Arlington House, in Virginia.

CHRONOLOGY

January 19, 1807 Robert Edward Lee was born at his family's mansion, Stratford Hall, near Montross, Virginia, the son of Ann Hill Carter and Henry ("Light-Horse Harry") Lee.

January 1, 1808 As required by the U.S. Constitution, the importation of slaves from abroad is ended. But the buying and selling of slaves in the U.S. continues, as does the illegal importation. (The families of both the future wives of Lee and Grant are slave owners.)

1811 Because of his heavy debts, Lee's father moves the family to Alexandria, Virginia. Lee is educated with the intention of enrolling him in West Point.

1812 Lee's father is injured in a Baltimore riot; to aid his recovery he goes (1813) to the Caribbean island of Barbados.

March 25, 1818 On his way home to Virginia, Lee's father dies at the home of his old Revolutionary War comrade, Nathanael Greene, in Cumberland, Georgia.

March 3, 1820 The so-called Missouri Compromise comes into effect with the admission of Missouri as a slave state to balance the admission of Maine as a free state. Also, slavery is forbidden in any of the territory of the Louisiana Purchase above 36° 30'.

April 27, 1822 Hiram Ulysses Grant is born in Point Pleasant, Ohio, to Hannah Simpson and Jesse Root Grant. (When he enters West Point, through an error he is registered as Ulysses Simpson Grant, and he will end up adopting that as his name.)

March 17, 1825 Lee enters West Point.

1828–1835 Grant attends subscription schools in Georgetown, Ohio. He works on the family farm and becomes an expert horseman.

1829 Lee graduates from West Point, 2nd in class of 46 and with no demerits for his four years. He is given the rank of 2nd Lieutenant in the Corps of Engineers and assigned to duty near Savannah, Georgia, where he was to assist in constructing Fort Pulaski. His mother dies within a month after he graduates.

1831 Lee is transferred to Fort Monroe, Virginia, from where he is able to court Mary Anne Randolph Custis. She is the great-granddaughter of Martha Custis Washington by Martha's first marriage, but her father had been adopted by George Washington.

June 30, 1831 Lee marries Mary Custis. They live at her family's home, Arlington, on a hill overlooking Washington, D.C. They will have seven children.

November 1832–March 1833 Certain people in South Carolina have been threatening to nullify the federal tariff acts that they see as favoring northern manufacturing states. They even seem to be threatening to secede on the grounds that states can "nullify" their joining the United States. In December President Andrew Jackson issues a proclamation warning the people of South Carolina that nullification will not be tolerated. In the weeks that follow, Henry Clay and others work to effect a compromise and Jackson signs on to this on March 2nd.

1834–40 Lee serves as Assistant to Chief Engineer of the Army. At first he is assigned to the Office of Engineers in Washington, D.C., but during the following years he sees service on a commission to mark the boundary line between Ohio and Michigan and, on assignment in St. Louis, he participates in a survey and plans for improving navigation of the Mississippi River. He is promoted to 1st Lieutenant in 1836 and to Captain in 1838.

April 1836 North Americans in Texas have revolted against the Mexican government and set up their own republic; their constitution allows for slavery, so these Texans' request to join the United States will be rejected for some years.

June 1839 Grant enters West Point.

1840 Lee returns to the Washington headquarters of the Corps of Engineers.

1841 Lee is placed in charge of improving Fort Hamilton, Fort Lafayette, and other defenses in New York Harbor.

July 1, 1843 Grant graduates from West Point, ranked 21st out of class of 39. He is commissioned a brevet 2nd Lieutenant and assigned to the Fourth Infantry Regiment at the Jefferson Barracks in St. Louis, Missouri.

February 1844 Grant meets Julia Dent, sister of his West Point roommate, Frederick Dent.

May 1844 Grant's regiment is ordered to the Louisiana border of Texas. After a leave during which he proposes marriage to Julia Dent, he joins his regiment there in June.

June 1844 Lee is briefly assigned to West Point on its Board of Visitors.

March 1845 The U.S. Congress has passed a joint resolution accepting Texas as a state.

May 1845 Recently inaugurated President James Polk, determined to make Texas a state, orders Gen. Zachary Taylor with a detachment of the U.S. Army to guard the border of southeastern Texas against an "invasion" by Mexico.

September 1845 Grant's unit moves on to Corpus Christi, Texas, where it becomes part of the army being assembled by Gen. Taylor.

December 1845 Texas is admitted as a state. Grant is promoted to full 2nd Lieutenant.

March–May 1846 Under orders from President Polk, Gen. Taylor leads his troops over to the left bank of the Rio Grande, always recognized as Mexican Territory. Grant's regiment goes with this force. Taylor proceeds to build fortifications near Matamoros. When Mexican forces attack this so-called Fort Texas, Taylor's forces engage the Mexicans in two battles—Palo Alto (May 8) and Reseca de la Palma (May 9). Grant first experiences combat at Palo Alto and briefly leads his company in Battle of Resaca de la Palma.

May 13, 1846 President Polk signs the War Bill (passed by Congress on May 11–12) declaring that "a state of war exists" with Mexico.

August 19–September 24, 1846 With his 4th Infantry Regiment, Grant sets off with Gen. Taylor on his pursuit of the Mexican army to Monterrey, which the US forces capture on September 24.

August 1846–January 1847 Lee joins the staff of Gen. John E. Wool in San Antonio, Texas. He accompanies Wool's force as it moves toward Chihuahua in northern Mexico. Lee's duties are those of an engineer—bridge-building and road repair—but he also engages in some reconnoitering.

December 1846 Grant's unit is assigned to the mouth of the Rio Grande, where Gen. Winfield Scott is assembling an invasion force that will eventually march on Mexico City.

February 1847 Lee is transferred to Brazos, Mexico, where he joins the staff of Gen. Winfield Scott, now preparing for the landing at Vera Cruz and the march to Mexico City.

March 9–28, 1847 Scott's forces make an amphibious invasion of the coast surrounding Vera Cruz. Lee is responsible for setting up the artillery batteries that lead to the city's surrender. Grant also participates in the siege that ends with the city's surrender on March 28th.

April 8, 1847 Scott sends his first units out on the 260-mile march to Mexico City. Both Grant and Lee are part of this force. Grant is now the quartermaster of his regiment. but will always try to get into the thick of the action during engagements with the enemy. Lee distinguishes himself by his bold reconnaissance.

April 17–18, 1847 The first US units have moved about 50 miles inland to Cerro Gordo ("big hill"), where they meet heavy resistance from the Mexicans. Lee makes the reconnaissances and in three days' time places batteries in positions that Gen. Santa Anna had judged inaccessible, enabling Scott to carry the heights and rout the enemy. Grant also participates in this battle.

May 15, 1847 After subduing relatively light resistance from the Mexican forces, the American army takes Puebla, a large city on the road to Mexico City. Grant participates in this action; Lee enters the city two weeks later with Gen. Scott and his staff.

August 7, 1847 US forces depart Puebla for Mexico City. Grant is part of the advance force. Lee will follow several days later with staff of Gen. Scott. All along the way to Mexico City, Lee will perform valuable advance reconnaissances.

August 17–19, 1847 US forces take the well-fortified villages of San Augustin and San Antonio. Lee has scouted ahead for the best routes and then participates in the action. Grant also takes part in this action.

August 20, 1847 US forces engage in fierce battles at Contreras and Churubusco. Both Grant and Lee participate. Gen. Scott will later single out Lee for "the greatest feat of physical and moral courage performed by any individual in my knowledge." Lee himself, reporting on the brave actions of the various officers in these battles, referred to "Lieutenant Grant, regimental quartermaster, who was usefully employed in his appropriate duties."

September 8, 1847 Both Grant and Lee participate in the battle at Molino del Rey. Lee is promoted to brevet Lieutenant-Colonel.

September 12–13, 1847 Grant and Lee participate in the Battle for Chapultepec, the last major fortress guarding Mexico City. In the storming of Chapultepec, Lee is slightly wounded, and due to total exhaustion, faints; after Chapultepec Lee was recommended for the rank of colonel. During the battle, as the American forces approached the gate of San Cosme at the outskirts of Mexico City, they were stopped by Mexican artillery. Grant leads his unit around to one side and has a howitzer carried up into a church belfry, from which point he is able to fire down on the Mexicans. He will be cited by Gen. Scott for this action. That night the first American troops begin to enter Mexico City

September 14, 1847 Gen. Scott leads the American forces into the main plaza of Mexico City for a surrender ceremony. Lee is at his side. Grant is among the troops who move through the city.

September 16, 1847 Grant is promoted to 1st Lieutenant. He will be stationed on the edge of Mexico City as part of the occupation forces. Lee is stationed in Mexico City at the headquarters of the occupation forces.

February 1848 The United States signs the Treaty of Guadalupe Hidalgo with Mexico, ending the war and taking over vast territory that will eventually become the states of California, Nevada, Utah, most of New Mexico and Arizona, and parts of Colorado and Wyoming. Texas is also conceded to belong to the United States. This new land will lead to disputes between pro- and anti-slavery forces.

June 1848 Lee returns to the United States and is assigned to the headquarters of the Corps of Engineers in Washington.

July 23, 1848 Grant arrives back in the United States and goes on extended leave.

August 22, 1848 Grant marries Julia Dent of St. Louis, Missouri. They will have four children.

November 17, 1848–52 Following his honeymoon, Grant reports to duty at Detroit, Michigan, and from there is assigned to Sackets Harbor, New York, on the eastern shore of Lake Ontario. In April 1849 he returns to regimental headquarters in Detroit. Grant is reassigned to Sackets Harbor in June 1851.

During this same time, Lee is assigned to the Corps of Engineers at Fort Carroll in Baltimore Harbor and is charged with constructing defense works to supplement those at Fort McHenry.

September 9–12, 1850 After months of negotiation, Congress adopts—and President Millard Fillmore signs—the five bills that come to be known as the Missouri Compromise. They allow for the admission of California as a no-slavery state but recognize the rights of other territories to allow slavery. Although the slave trade in the District of Columbia will be abolished, another act strengthens the federal enforcement of the Fugitive Slave Act.

June 1851 *Uncle Tom's Cabin*, by Harriet Beecher Stowe, begins to appear as a serial novel in the *National Era*, an anti-slavery paper.

1852–54 In May 1852, Grant is assigned to San Francisco. Arriving there in August, he is assigned to remote posts, first at Fort Vancouver on the Columbia River, and then (1853) to Humboldt Bay, California. The combination of the isolation, separation from his family, and a dislike for his commanding officer leads Grant to decide to resign from the army. He submits his resignation on April 11, 1854, the same day he is notified of promotion to Captain.

1852–55 Lee—at first reluctantly—serves as the ninth Superintendent of West Point Academy. Although he never totally enjoys the position, his tenure proves to be successful and respected.

1854–58 In August 1854, Grant returns to Missouri and joins Julia and his children. He moves to a 60-acre farm near St. Louis that belongs to Julia but depends on selling cut firewood for supporting his family.

1855–61 Lee is appointed Lieutenant Colonel of the Second Cavalry and serves in Texas in wars against the Kiowa and Comanche Indians there. At various times he returns home to Virginia to take care of family matters.

1858–59 Having failed at farming, Grant works at selling real estate with a cousin of Julia's, but this, too, proves unsuccessful.

October 17–18, 1859 On one of his visits home from Texas, Lee is assigned to lead a U.S. Marine detachment to Harpers Ferry, Virginia, where he puts down the insurrection led by John Brown.

May 1860 Grant moves to Galena, Illinois, to work as a clerk in his father's leather store.

1860–61 Lee is assigned to command of the Department of Texas.

November 6, 1860 Abraham Lincoln is elected president.

December 20, 1860 South Carolina is the first state to secede from the Union. In the ensuing weeks, ten more states will also secede and form the Confederacy.

January 23, 1861 Following the events unfolding in the South from Texas, Lee writes his son Custis, "The South, in my opinion, has been aggrieved by the acts of the North." But at this same time he writes to another son, Rooney: "As an American citizen I prize the Union very highly and know of no personal sacrifice that I would not make to preserve it, save that of honour."

March 16, 1861 Texas having seceded from the Union (Feb. 1), Lee has returned to Arlington, Virginia. He is appointed colonel of First Cavalry.

April 12–13, 1861 After 32 hours of bombardment from Confederate batteries, Fort Sumter in the harbor of Charleston, South Carolina, surrenders.

April 18, 1861 Through Lincoln's emissaries, Lee is offered the command of United States Armies. Lee refuses the offer by stating: "I cannot raise my hand against my birthplace, my home, my children…."

April 20, 1861 Lee resigns commission in United States Army.

April 23. 1861 Lee accepts rank of Brigadier General and is placed in command of all of Virginia's military and naval forces as Virginia secedes and joins the Confederacy.

April 29, 1861 Grant becomes military aide to Illinois governor Richard Yates

May–July, 1861 Lee organizes troops and advises President Jefferson Davis in Richmond.

June 15–28, 1861 Grant is appointed commander of the militia infantry regiment; on the 17th he is appointed its colonel; on the 28th, the regiment is taken into the U.S. Army's service as the 21st Illinois Volunteers.

July 1861 After training his regiment, Grant leads them into Missouri to perform guard duties.

August 5, 1861 Grant is appointed Brigadier General.

August–October, 1861. Lee is in charge of abortive campaign in the western counties of Virginia. His lack of success there—most especially at Cheat Mountain—temporarily damages his reputation as a field commander.

September 1, 1861 Grant is appointed commander of the District of Southeast Missouri and establishes his headquarters at Cairo, Illinois.

November 1861 Lee is placed in charge of coast defenses in South Carolina, Georgia, and Florida.

November 7, 1861 In his first combat engagement as a general, Grant leads a raid on the Confederate camp at Belmont, Missouri; his troops stop to loot the camp and the Confederates regroup, so Grant has to withdraw.

February 6–16, 1862 In the first Union victory of strategic importance, Grant takes Fort Henry and Fort Donelson, both in Tennessee. His message to the besieged Confederate forces in Fort Donelson—"No terms except immediate and unconditional surrender can be accepted"—soon makes him nationally famous as "Unconditional Surrender" Grant.

March 1862 Lee is recalled to Richmond by Jefferson Davis and becomes the president's military advisor. Lee will soon find himself organizing the defenses of Richmond, and as Gen. George McClellan's Federal forces start their campaign on the Peninsula, Lee plans the diversionary campaign of Gen. Thomas "Stonewall" Jackson in the Shenandoah Valley.

April 6–7, 1862 Grant meets the Confederate forces at the Battle of Shiloh (so named after a church in the battlefield). In two days of extremely bloody fighting, the Union troops suffer higher casualties but force the Confederates to start retreating from Tennessee.

June 1, 1862 In McClellan's Peninsular Campaign, Confederate General J.E. Johnston is severely wounded at the battle of Seven Pines (Fair Oaks). Lee assumes command of the Army of Northern Virginia.

June 25–July 2, 1862 Lee commands the Confederate forces in the Seven Days' Battles that force McClellan away from Richmond and back down the Peninsula. But Lee is unable to destroy the Union forces.

July–November 1862 Grant has been given command of all Union troops between the Mississippi and Tennessee and moves his headquarters to Corinth, Mississippi. For the next four months, he will be occupied largely in command duties. Not until November 2 does Grant move out into the field again in what is the beginning of a long campaign to capture Vicksburg, Mississippi.

August 30, 1862 Lee defeats Union forces under Gen. John Pope at Second Manassas (Second Bull Run).

September 5–16, 1862 Lee crosses the Potomac and begins to advance into Maryland. He and his forces fight a series of battles along the way.

September 17, 1862 Along Antietam Creek, near Sharpsburg, Maryland, Lee's forces confront the Federals commanded by Gen. McClellan. At the end of what is known as "the bloodiest single day of the war" (and probably in American history), the battle ends in a draw. On the 18th, however, Lee is persuaded to withdraw, and in so doing the Confederate cause takes a major turn for the worse.

December 13. 1862 At Fredericksburg, Virginia, Lee commands a masterful defeat of the Federal forces under Gen. Ambrose Burnside.

December 1862 Lee moves his forces into winter quarters until March.

February–April 1863 Grant commands a series of unsuccessful attempts to take Vicksburg, Mississippi.

May 2–3, 1863 At Chancellorsville, Virginia, Lee again commands a decisive victory over the Union forces under Gen. Joseph Hooker, but Lee's strongest general, "Stonewall" Jackson, is wounded and dies on May 10th.

May 12–22, 1863 As part of his strategy to take Vicksburg, Grant moves his forces between two Confederate armies and ends up defeating them both in battles at Jackson, Champion Hill, and Big Black River. His final assaults on the city (May 19th–22nd) fail, and he settles down for a long siege.

June 3–30, 1863 Lee initiates his plan to invade the North and moves north from Fredericksburg, Virginia, into southern Pennsylvania.

July 1–3, 1863 At Gettysburg, in three days of aggressive fighting, although the Confederates are conceded to have won the first two days' battles, they are defeated on the third day and brought to a halt with "Pickett's Charge."

July 4, 1863 Grant accepts the Confederate forces' surrender of Vicksburg. The Confederacy is now virtually cut in half at the Mississippi, and large Federal forces under Grant and others are freed for other campaigns.

July 4–13, 1863 The inaction of the Federals at Gettysburg, commanded by Gen George Meade, allows Lee to retreat and get back across the Potomac with all his forces.

August 1863 Following a fall from a horse in New Orleans, Grant spends the summer with his family in a house near Vicksburg. His leg is so badly swollen that he is bedridden for weeks and uses crutches until October.

August 8, 1863 Because of the criticism following the defeat at Gettysburg, Lee hands in his resignation to President Davis, who refuses to accept it.

October 23–November 25, 1863 After the defeat of the Union forces at Chickamauga, Union Gen. William Rosecrans retreats to Chattanooga, Tennessee, where he is soon besieged. Grant is now ordered to relieve the siege and arrives outside Chattanooga on October 23rd. After a series of major battles, culminating in the one at Missionary Ridge, Grant drives the Confederates from the field.

October 9–November 9, 1863 Lee conducts the Bristoe Campaign; during several engagements, Lee forces the vastly superior Union forces of Gen. Meade to retreat.

November 26–December 1, 1863 Gen. Meade launches an offensive against Lee, but fails to dislodge the Confederates along the Mine Run. Following this, both armies go into winter quarters.

March 3–12, 1864 Grant is ordered to report to Washington D.C. (on the 3rd) where he has been confirmed as a Lieutenant General, the highest rank at that time. On the 9th, he is given his commission by President Lincoln himself and on March 12, he is appointed General-in-Chief of all U.S. armies.

May 5–7, 1864 Grant has taken to the field to direct the Federal Army of the Potomac in what is hoped will be a quick campaign to take Richmond, the Confederate capital. During the Battle of the Wilderness, Grant and Lee face each other for the first time as commanders. The battle itself is something of a draw, but although the Union forces lose twice as many men as the Confederates, the North can better afford to make up its losses.

May 7–20, 1864 In the Spotsylvania campaign, Grant is once again thwarted by Lee, and the results of the battle are inconclusive. On May 11, Grant writes another of his famous dispatches: "I propose to fight it out on this line if it takes all summer."

May 21–June 1, 1864 Lee conducts operations on interior lines.

May 31–June 3, 1864 The Battle of Cold Harbor. In the main frontal assault on June 3, Grant loses 7000 men in an hour. Lee loses 1500. Grant will admit that this was one of his greatest blunders as a general. Again, although the Federal casualties greatly exceed those of the Confederate—50,000 vs 32,000— the North can more readily provide replacements.

June 15–July 30, 1864 Grant has decided to try a new approach to taking Richmond: he wants to capture Petersburg, the major rail junction south of Richmond and so cut it off. In order to exercise close command, he relocates his headquarters to City Point, Virginia, along the James River, 10 miles from Petersburg. The first direct assaults fail (June 15th–18th). Lee himself arrives in Petersburg on the 18th. The Union forces decide to resort to a siege instead of assaults, but they do attempt the ill-fated explosion of the subterranean mine they have dug; the explosion occurs on July 30 and creates a giant crater, but the Union forces who then attempt to advance are repulsed at great cost of lives. Although Lee was not on the scene that day, he did approve the operation. Lee himself directs this defense.

August 1864–April 1865 In the months following the disastrous mine assault, a whole series of battles are fought around Petersburg and Richmond.

February 9, 1865 Newly appointed commander-in-chief of all Confederate forces, Lee issues his first general order.

April 2–3, 1865 In the final Union assault on Petersburg, the Confederates have to abandon the city during the night of April 2–3. Grant enters the city on the 3rd. During the day of the 2nd, Lee also has to leave Richmond and it is occupied by Union forces on the 3rd.

April 3–9, 1865 Lee heads southwest, hoping to elude the Federals and join up with the Confederate forces operating in North Carolina. Grant leads the pursuit and soon has Lee's army in disarray and then trapped. On the 7th, Grant writes to Lee and asks that he surrender his forces.

April 9, 1865 At Appomattox Court House in Virginia, in the home of Wilmer McClean, Lee surrenders his Army of Northern Virginia to Grant. Although hostilities continue elsewhere for some time, this effectively marks the end of the Civil War.

April 10, 1865 Lee issues his Farewell Address to the Army of Northern Virginia.

May 1865–May 1868 Grant retains his post as head of the U.S. Army (Congress promotes him to full General in 1866), but he carries on a series of visits to various cities throughout the nation that amount to a virtual triumphal tour—and clearly mark him as presidential material. At first he supports President Andrew Johnson's policies with the former Confederate states, but gradually he begins to separate himself from Johnson.

June 13, 1865 Lee applies for pardon. His home in Arlington, Virginia, is confiscated by the Union Army (and is now part of Arlington National Cemetery). Although there is some call in the North for trying Lee as a traitor, it never comes to pass, but his civil rights are suspended and his United States citizenship is withdrawn. (Grant signed the oath of allegiance to the United States that was required before a pardon could be granted, but it was misplaced and did not surface until 1970. Lee's full citizenship was restored by Congress and President Gerald Ford in 1975.)

August 4, 1865 Lee is elected President of Washington College, Lexington, Virginia. (After his death it will be renamed Washington and Lee University.)

February 4, 1867 Lee declines to be a candidate for the governorship of Virginia.

May 21, 1868 Grant is nominated as a candidate for president by the Republican National Convention in Chicago. During the summer, Grant hardly strays from his home in Galena, Illinois, and does little active campaigning.

November 3, 1868 Grant is elected president by a landslide.

March 4, 1869 Grant is inaugurated President of the United States. During his first four years in office, although he does work for reconciliation between the North and South and to protect the rights of the newly freed African Americans, Grant seems powerless as corruption spreads through all levels of the government. Part of it is due to the "spoils system," under which the party in power gets to appoint its supporters, friends, and relatives to government jobs. Grant himself does not profit from any of this, but when it is revealed that his brother-in-law has promised financial speculators that he can get Grant to hold off selling gold, Grant is tainted even thought the plot fails.

March–April, 1870 In failing health, Lee visits Georgia in search of convalesence.

October 12, 1870 Lee dies at his home in Lexington, Virginia. He is buried in the chapel on the campus of Washington and Lee University.

November 5, 1872 Grant is elected by an even larger majority. Again, his term is marred by a financial panic (1873) and a series of financial scandals. Grant again remains largely untouched by the corruption, although he is revealed to have accepted some personal gifts. He remains so popular, though, that the Republicans urge him to run for a third term, but he declines.

May 1877–September 1879 Grant takes his family on a trip around the world. Everywhere he goes, he is greeted by crowds.

June 2–8, 1880 Grant is unsuccessful in securing the Republican nomination for President. It is generally conceded that he was really not desirous of holding office again.

December 24, 1883 Grant suffers a serious injury to his hip; he will walk with crutches or a cane for the rest of his life.

May 1884 The brokerage firm of Grant and Ward fails on Wall Street, and Grant will lose his entire fortune. He had been a silent partner in the firm with his son and Ferdinand Ward, who robbed the company and was eventually jailed. Days before the bankruptcy, Ward begs Grant for a loan of $150,000 to save the Marine Bank. Grant raises the money through a personal loan from multimillionaire William Vanderbilt; he eventually repaid Vanderbilt with his war trophies and uniforms (some of which are on display in the Smithsonian). The Grant and Ward failure plunges Grant into a prolonged depression.

September 1884 Grant is diagnosed as having cancer of the throat. Realizing that he will not have long to live, and wanting to leave his wife some money to live on, he soon begins work on his memoirs.

January–March, 1885 The cancer has spread and Grant is now in great pain, barely able to eat liquid food. He continues to write.

June 16, 1885 Grant moves with his family to Mt. McGregor, near Saratoga Springs, New York, because of the cooler climate. He is down to 120 pounds weight and is extremely weak.

July 10, 1885 Grant finishes his memoirs. All this time he has also been reading page proofs of as fast as the printers have been sending them to him.

July 23, 1885 At 8:00 AM, Grant dies, surrounded by his family and physicians. Eventually (1897) his body will be interred in the monumental tomb above the Hudson River on upper Manhattan Island, New York City. The tomb was paid for by private subscriptions.

Autumn 1885 The first of the two volumes of *Personal Memoirs of U.S. Grant* is published. It quickly becomes a best seller, and in Julia's remaining lifetime over 300,000 copies are sold, earning his widow an estimated $450,000 (the equivalent of at least 10 times that in terms of buying power today).

Memoirs of Robert E. Lee, by Armistead Long, is published. Although it is well received, it never attains the status of Grant's memoirs.

RECOMMENDED READING

It is a well-known bit of trivia that the Civil War allegedly has inspired more books than any other subject under the sun (at least in American history). Thus there can be no pretense that a list such as this does anything more than scratch the surface. But the criteria have been two: relevance to the topics of this book, and available editions. It does not claim to be a scholar's bibliography. It is for individuals who would like to pursue some of the topics at greater length.

BIOGRAPHICAL

Anderson, Nancy Scott and Dwight Anderson. *The Generals–Ulysses S. Grant and Robert E. Lee.* New York: Knopf, 1988.

Bowman, John S., ed. *Who Was Who in the Civil War.* North Dighton, Mass.: World Publications, 2002.

Brooks, William E. *Grant of Appomattox: A Study of the Man.* Westport, Conn.: Greenwood Press, 1971.

Grant, Ulysses S. *Personal Memoirs of U.S. Grant.* New York: Library of America, 1990.

Brown, Robert R. *And One Was a Soldier: The Spiritual Pilgrimage of Robert E. Lee.* Shippingsport, Penn.: White Mane Pub., 1998.

Fellman, Michael. *The Making of Robert E. Lee.* New York: Random House, 2000.

Freeman, Douglas Southall. *Lee.* (Abridgement of 4-volume biography.) New York: Scribner's, 1961.

——— *Lee's Lieutenants: A Study in Command.* (Abridgement of 3-volume work.) New York: Scribner's, 1998.

Fuller, J.F.C. *Grant and Lee, A Study in Personality and Leadership.* Bloomington, Ind.: Indiana University Press, 1957.

Gragg, Ron, ed. *A Commitment to Valor: A Unique Portrait of Robert E. Lee in His Own Words.* Nashville, Tenn.: Rutledge Hill Press, 2001.

Golay, Michael. *To Gettysburg and Beyond: The Parallel Lives of Joshua Lawrence Chamberlain and Edward Porter Alexander.* New York: Crown, 1994.

Kaltman, Al. *The Genius of Robert E. Lee.* New York: Prentice Hall, 2001.

Long, Gen. Armistead L. *Memoirs of Robert E. Lee.* New York and Philadelphia: Stodddart & Co., 1887.

Lyman, Theodore. *With Grant and Meade from the Wilderness to Appomattox.* Lincoln: Univ. of Nebraska Press, 1994.

Marshall-Cornwall, James Hardyside. *Grant as Military Commander.* New York: Van Nostrand-Reinhold, 1970.

McCartney, Clarence. *Grant and His Generals.* New York: McBride, 1957.

McFeely, William S. *Grant: A Biography.* New York: Norton, 1981.

Nolan, Alan. *Lee Considered: General Robert E. Lee and Civil War History.* Chapel Hill: Univ. of North Carolina Press, 1991.

Sherman, William T. *Memoirs of General W.T. Sherman.* New York: The Library of America, 1990.

Simpson, Brooks D. *Ulysses S. Grant: Triumph Over Adversity, 1822–1865.* Boston: Houghton Mifflin, 2000.

——— *Let Us Have Peace: Ulysses S. Grant and the Politics of War and Reconstruction, 1861–1868.* Chapel Hill: Univ. of North Carolina Press, 1991.

Smith, Gene. *Lee and Grant: A Dual Biography.* New York: McGraw-Hill, 1984.

Smith, Jean Edward. *Grant.* New York: Simon & Schuster, 2001.

Thomas, Emory M. *Robert E. Lee: A Biography.* New York: Norton, 1995.

MEXICAN WAR

Chidsey, Donald Barr. *The War With Mexico.* New York: Crown, 1968.

Eisenhower, John S.D. *So Far From God: The United States War With Mexico.* New York: Random House, 1989.

Lewis, Lloyd. *Captain Sam Grant.* Boston: Little Brown, 1950.

McCaffrey, James. *Army of Manifest Destiny: The American Soldier in the Mexican War, 1846–1848.* New York: New York Univ. Press, 1992.

Connor, Seymour V., and Odie B. Faulk. *North America Divided: The Mexican War, 1846–1848.* New York: Oxford Univ. Press, 1971.

Singletary, Otis. *The Mexican War.* Chicago: Univ. of Chicago Press, 1960.

CIVIL WAR: MILITARY HISTORY

Arnold, James. *Grant Wins the War: Decision at Vicksburg.* New York: John Wiley, 1997.

Boothe, F. Norton. *Great Generals of the American Civil War and Their Battles.* New York: Gallery Books, 1986.

Boritt, Gabor S. *The Gettysburg Nobody Knows.* New York: Oxford Univ. Press, 1997.

Bowden, Scott, and Bill Ward. *Last Chance for Victory: Robert E. Lee and the Gettysburg Campaign.* New York: Da Capo Press, 2001.

Burne, Alfred H. *Lee, Grant and Sherman: A Study in Leadership in the 1864–65 Campaign.* New York: Scribner's, 1939.

Bryant, Samuel H. *Grant Moves South.* Boston: Little Brown, 1960.

Carter, Samuel III. *The Final Fortress: The Campaign for Vicksburg, 1862–1863.* New York: St. Martin's Press, 1980.

Chamberlain, Joshua L. *Through Blood and Fire…Selected Civil War Papers.* Mechanicsville, Penn.: Stackpole Books, 1996.

Coddington, Edward. *The Gettysburg Campaign: A Study in Command.* New York: Scribner's, 1987.

Daniel, Larry J. *Shiloh: The Battle that Changed the Civil War.* New York: Simon & Schuster, 1997.

Dowdey, Clifford. *The Seven Days' Campaign: The Emergence of Lee.* Boston: Little Brown, 1964.

Eicher, David J. *The Longest Night: A Military History of the Civil War.* New York: Simon & Schuster, 2001.

Foote, Shelby. *The Civil War: A Narrative.* 3 Volumes. New York: Random House, 1990 edition.

Griffith, Paddy. *Battle Tactics of the Civil War.* New Haven: Yale Univ. Press, 1989.

Johnson, Swafford. *Great Battles of the Civil War.* New York: Crescent Books, 1992.

Linderman, Gerald. *Embattled Courage: The Experience of Combat in the Civil War.* New York: The Free Press, 1987.

McDonough, James L. *Chattanooga: A Death Grip on the Confederacy.* Knoxville: Univ. of Tennessee Press, 1984.

Miers, Earl Schenck. *The Last Campaign: Grant Saves the Union.* Philadelphia: Lippincott, 1972.

Pitkin, Thomas. *The Captain Departs: Ulysses S. Grant's Last Campaign.* Carbondale: Southern Illinois Univ. Press, 1973.

Sears, Stephen W. *Chancellorsville.* Boston: Houghton Mifflin, 1996.

——— *Landscape Turned Red: The Battle of Antietam.* New Haven: Ticknor & Fields, 1983.

——— *To The Gates of Richmond: The Peninsular Campaign.* New York: Ticknor & Fields, 1992.

GENERAL HISTORY

Bowman, John S., ed. *The Civil War, Day by Day.* Greenwich, Conn.: Dorset Press, 1991.

Hagerman, Edward. *The American Civil War and the Origins of Modern Warfare: Ideas, Organization, and Field Command.* Bloomington: Indiana Univ. Press, 1982.

McPherson, James. *Battle Cry for Freedom: The Civil War Era.* New York: Ballantine, 1989.

——— *For Cause and Comrades: Why Men Fought in the Civil War.* New York: Oxford Univ. Press, 1977.

Meltzer, Milton, ed. *Voices from the Civil War: A Documentary History of the Great American Conflict.* New York: Crowell, 1989.

Golay, Michael. *A Ruined Land: The End of the Civil War.* New York: John Wiley, 1999.

Potter, David M. *The Impending Crisis, 1848–1861.* New York: HarperCollins, 1977.

Royster, Charles. *The Destructive War.* New York: Knopf, 1991.

Sears, Stephen, ed. *The American Heritage Century Collection of Civil War Art.* New York: McGraw-Hill, 1974.

Simpson, Brooks D. *Let Us Have Peace: Ulysses S. Grant and the Politics of War and Reconstruction.* Chapel Hill: Univ. of North Carolina Press, 1991.

Sneden, Private Robert Knox. *Eye of the Storm: A Civil War Odyssey.* New York: The Free Press, 2000.

Stampp, Kenneth, ed. *The Causes of the Civil War.* 3rd edition, rev. New York: Simon & Schuster, 1991.

Thomas, William G., and Alice E. Carter. *The Civil War on the Web: A Guide to the Very Best Sites.* Wilmington, Del.: Scholarly Resources, 2000.

Ward, Geoffrey C., with Ric and Ken Burns. *The Civil War: An Illustrated History.* New York: Knopf, 1990.

Wills, Garry. *Lincoln at Gettysburg: The Words That Remade America.* New York: Simon & Schuster, 1992.

Wyatt-Brown, Bertram. *Southern Honor: Ethics and Behavior in the Old South.* New York: Oxford Univ. Press, 1983.

GUIDES

Cromie, Alice. *A Tour Guide to the Civil War.* 4th edition. Nashville, Tenn.: Rutledge Hill Press, 1992.

Eicher, David J. *Civil War Battlefields: A Touring Guide.* Dallas, Texas: Taylor Publ., 1995.

Fullenkamp, Leonard, Stephen Bowman and Jay Luvass, eds. *Guide to the Vicksburg Campaign.* Lawrence, Kansas: Univ. Press of Kansas, 1998.

Greene, A. Wilson. *National Geographic Guide to the Civil War National Battlefield Parks.* Washington, D.C.: National Geographic Society, 1993.

Kennedy, Frances H., ed. *The Civil War Battlefield Guide.* 2nd edition. New York: The Conservation Fund/Houghton Mifflin, 1998.

Large, George R. *Battle for Gettysburg: The Official History by the Gettysburg Battlefield Board.* Shippensburg, Penn.: Burd Street Pr./White Mane Publ., 1993.

Luvaas, Jay, and Harold W. Nelson, eds. *Guide to the Battle of Antietam: The Maryland Campaign of 1862.* Lawrence, Kansas: Univ. Press of Kansas, 1996.

———— *Guide to the Battles of Chancellorsville and Fredericksburg.* Lawrence, Kansas: Univ. Press of Kansas, 1995.

———— *Guide to the Battle of Gettysburg.* Lawrence, Kansas: Univ. Press of Kansas, 1994.

Luvaas, Jay, Stephen Bowman and Leonard Fullenkamp, eds. *Guide to the Battle of Shiloh.* Lawrence, Kansas: Univ. Press of Kansas, 1996.

Siegel, Charles G. *No Backward Step: A Guide to Grant's Campaign in Virginia.* Shippensburg, Penn.: White Mane Publ., 2000.

Vandiver, Frank E., and Michael Golay, eds. *Civil War Battlefields and Landmarks: A Guide to the National Park Sites, With Official National Park Service Maps for Each Site.* New York: Random House, 1996.

FICTION

Bahr, Howard. *The Black Flower: A Novel of the Civil War.* New York: St. Martin's Press, 2000.

Banks, Russsell. *Cloudsplitter.* New York: HarperCollins, 1998.

Bierce, Ambrose. *In the Midst of Life.* Secaucus NJ: Citadel Press, 1993.

Byrd, Max. *Grant: A Novel.* New York: Bantam, 2000.

Crane, Stephen. *The Red Badge of Courage* (1895). New York: Norton, 1976.

Frazier, Charles. *Cold Mountain.* New York: Atlantic Monthly Press, 1997.

Johnston, Mary. *Cease Firing* (1912). Baltimore: Johns Hopkins Univ. Press, 1996.

———— *The Long Roll* (1911). Baltimore: Johns Hopkins Univ. Press, 1996.

Mitchell, Margaret. *Gone With the Wind* (1936). New York: Warner Books, 1994.

Shaara, Michael. *The Killer Angels.* New York: Ballantine, 1993.

Stowe, Harriet Beecher. *Uncle Tom's Cabin.* New York: The Library of America, 1982.

PERIODICALS

These are the major periodicals that are either entirely devoted to the Civil War or that frequently carry articles on the subject. Many state and regional magazines also carry such articles.

American Heritage. 8 issues per year. 60 Fifth Avenue, New York, NY. www.americanheritage.com

American History. Bimonthly. 6405 Flank Drive, Harrisburg, PA 17112. www.thehistorynet.com

America's Civil War. Bimonthly. Primemedia History Group, 741 Miller Drive SE, Leesburg, VA, 20175. www.thehistorynet.com

Blue & Gray. Bimonthly. 522 Norton Road, Columbus, Ohio 43228. www.blueandgraymagazine.com

Civil War Book Review. Quarterly. U.S. Civil War Center, Louisiana State University, Baton Rouge LA 70803. www.civilwarbookreview.com

Civil War History. Quarterly. Dept. of History, Kent State University, Kent OH 44242. www.kent.edu

Civil War Times Illustrated. Bimonthly. Primemedia History Group, 741 Miller Drive SE, Leesburg, VA, 20175. www.thehistorynet.com

Columbiad. A Quarterly Review of the War Between the States. 6405 Flank Drive, Harrisburg, PA 17112. www.thehistorynet.com

Mail Call Journal: Where the Spirit of the Civil War Soldier Lives. Bimonthly. P.O. Box 5031, South Hackensack NJ 07606 www.historyonline.net

MHQ: The Quarterly Journal of Military History. Primemedia History Group, 741 Miller Drive SE, Leesburg, VA, 20175. www.thehistorynet.com

Military Heritage. Bimonthly. 1121 Jean Park Road, Manotick, Ontario K4M 1E4, Canada. www.militaryheritage.com

Military History. Primemedia History Group, 741 Miller Drive SE, Leesburg, VA, 20175. www.thehistorynet.com

Military Images: Photographic History of the U.S. RR 1, Box 99-A, Henryville PA 18332. www.civilwar-photos.com

Smithsonian. Monthly. 900 Jefferson Drive, Washington, D.C. 20560 www.smithsonianmag.si.edu

ACKNOWLEDGMENTS

Anne S. K. Brown Military Collection, Brown University Library, 41, 51 (top), 52 (top), 53, 68, 83, 109, 112, 124, 134, 139, 206, 233, 246, 259 (bottom), 268, 271 (bottom), 275 (bottom), 283, 285 (top), 287, 290, 291 (top), 316 (both), 317, 338

Brompton Photo Library, 59 (top), 65, 67, 68–69, 90, 99 (top), 106, 110 (bottom), 116 (bottom), 125 (top), 135 (both), 151 (both), 172, 180 (bottom), 187 (right), 198

Chicago Historical Society, 50 (left), 66, 120 (top), 278–279, 320, 321

John Haye Library, Brown University, 204

Library of Congress, 45, 45 (both), 46, 47, 48, 49, 50 (both), 50 (top right), 51 (both), 51 (bottom), 52 (both), 53 (bottom), 54, 54 (both), 55, 56, 57, 57 (left), 58, 59, 59 (bottom), 60, 60 (bottom), 61, 62, 63, 63 (bottom), 64, 65, 66, 67 (top), 68, 70, 71, 76, 77, 78, 79, 81, 82, 84, 85, 87, 89, 91, 94, 95, 100, 101, 102, 103, 104, 105, 106, 107 (bottom), 112, 113 (bottom), 114, 115, 117, 118, 122, 123, 124, 125 (top), 130, 132, 133 (bottom), 134, 135, 136, 137, 138, 139, 141, 142, 143, 144, 145, 147, 148, 150, 155, 157, 158, 162, 163, 165, 166, 169, 170, 171, 173, 174, 175, 176, 177, 178, 180 (bottom), 182, 183, 184, 185, 188, 189, 190, 191, 192, 193, 194, 195, 196, 197, 198, 199, 200, 202, 203, 204, 205, 206, 207 (bottom), 208, 209, 210, 211, 212, 213, 214, 215, 218, 222 (both), 224, 225, 226, 227 (both), 229 (both), 230, 232 (top right), 234, 239 (both), 241 (bottom), 243, 244, 247, 250 (top), 251, 255 (top), 256, 258, 259 (top), 260, 262–263 (both), 266, 267, 269, 270 (bottom), 273, 277, 280, 281, 282 (bottom), 284 (both), 285 (bottom), 289 (bottom), 290 (bottom), 292, 293, 295 (both), 296, 297 (bottom), 299, 323, 326, 328 (both), 330, 331, 332, 333 (bottom), 334, 335, 336–337, 339, 340, 342 (bottom), 343, 344, 345, 346 (top), 347, 350 (both), 352 (both), 355, 356, 358, 359 (top), 362–363, 364–365, 369 (both), 370, 371 (top), 372, 379 (right), 380, 384, 385, 391

National Archives, 46–47, 56–57 (left), 60, 62, 64 (top), 82, 85 (right), 95, 98, 101, 114, 118 (top), 119 (both), 122, 123 (both), 125 (bottom), 126 (top), 142, 145, 146 (top), 147, 152–153 (right), 154–155 (left), 157 (top), 177 (both), 178–179, 182 (bottom), 185, 187 (left), 190, 194 (top), 205, 207, 212–213, 228, 235, 236, 237, 242, 249 (both), 270 (top), 271 (top), 279, 282 (top), 288, 294, 311 (bottom), 319, 354 (both), 360–361, 366

National Portrait Gallery, 102

Naval Academy Museum, Courtest of Beverly R. Robinson Collection, 94 (top)

New York Public Library, 75 (top)

Norfolk Southern Corporation, 136–137

Old Courthouse Museum Collection, Vicksburg, MS, 88, 108 (bottom)

Richard Natkiel, 303 (bottom)

Rutherford B. Hayes Presidential Center, 81 (top and right), 333 (top), 379 (left)

The Bettman Archive, 220 (both), 231, 232 (bottom left), 238, 245, 248, 252, 254, 255 (bottom), 257, 261 (top), 264, 265, 275 (top), 276, 289, 297 (top), 298, 300 (top), 302, 303 (top), 307, 312, 314, 318 (both), 327, 341, 342 (top), 346 (bottom), 348, 353, 357 (both), 359 (bottom), 367, 368, 371 (both), 373, 374–375, 376, 377 (both), 378, 381, 382–383 (both), 386–387 (both), 388–389

The Museum of the Confederacy, 272, 274, 324–325

The Western Reserve Historical Society, Cleveland, Ohio, 28

US Army Military History Institute, Carlisle, PA, 100, 133 (top), 186, 221, 253

US Army Photograph, 223

US Military Academy Archives, 171 (top and right), 175

US Naval Historical Center, 166 (bottom)

US Naval Historical Photograph, 261 (bottom)

V. M. I Museum, 304

Valentine Museum, Cook Collection, 70 (bottom)

Virginia State Library, 159 (top)

INDEX